Cambridge Monographs and Texts in Applied Psycholinguistics

Exceptional language development in Down syndrome

Cambridge Monographs and Texts in Applied Psycholinguistics
General Editor: Sheldon Rosenberg

The present volume, by J. A. Rondal, is part of the series entitled Cambridge Monographs and Texts in Applied Psycholinguistics. The general aim of this series is to bring together work from all of the subfields of applied psycholinguistics by authors who approach applied problems from the vantage point of basic research and theory in psycholinguisitics and related areas of cognitive psychology. Because of this orientation, the volumes in the series, including the present one, make important contributions to our understanding of both applied and basic problems in psycholinguistics.

Books in the series

Ann M. Peters *The units of language acquisition*

Sheldon Rosenberg, Editor *Advances in applied psycholinguistics, Volume I: Disorders of first-language development*

Sheldon Rosenberg, Editor *Advances in applied psycholinguistics, Volume II: Reading, writing, and language learning*

Nicola Yule and Jane Oakhill *Children's problems in text comprehension*

Jean A. Rondal *Exceptional language development in Down syndrome: Implications for the cognition-language relationship*

Exceptional language development in Down syndrome

Implications for the cognition-language relationship

JEAN A. RONDAL
University of Liège

 CAMBRIDGE
UNIVERSITY PRESS

Published by the Press Syndicate of the University of Cambridge
The Pitt Building, Trumpington Street, Cambridge CB2 1RP
40 West 20th Street, New York, NY 10011-4211, USA
10 Stamford Road, Oakleigh, Melbourne 3166, Australia

First published 1995

Printed in the United States of America

Library of Congress Cataloging-in-Publication Data
Rondal, Jean A.
Exceptional language development in Down syndrome : implications
for the cognition-language relationship / Jean A. Rondal.

p.   cm. – (Cambridge monographs and texts in applied
psycholinguistics)

Includes bibliographical references and index.

ISBN 0-521-36167-2 (hardback). – ISBN 0-521-36966-5 (pbk.)

1. Mentally handicapped – Language – Case studies.   2. Mentally
handicapped – Language.   3. Language acquisition.   4. Modularity
(Psychology).   I. Title.   II. Series.
RC570.2.R64   1994
616.85'88–dc20   94-6090
                                                              CIP

A catalog record for this book is available from the British Library.

ISBN 0-521-36167-2 hardback
ISBN 0-521-36966-5 paperback

A la mémoire du Professeur Henri Breny, décédé avant d'avoir vu ce livre qu'il aurait beaucoup aimé lire; et à Stéphane, David, Amélie, et Alexandra, my precious loved ones.

Contents

Foreword

This intriguing study of a Down syndrome subject by Professor Rondal has a well-grounded basis in the very early studies of thought and language and their interconnections by the two outstanding psychologists Piaget (1923) and Vygotsky (1929/1962) who both addressed the problem of the relationship between language and thought. At that time, the interaction of the two was seen in simple developmental terms in such a manner that, for example, thought could at first occur in the absence of language and subsequently speech or language could develop in the child in such a way that at a certain stage "thought could become speech and speech thought," as Vygotsky expressed verbal development in children. However, two aspects to these kinds of studies distinguish them from more recent studies of the interaction of speech and thought. They do not reflect the complexity of current psycholinguistics, on the one hand, and they do not study abnormalities of language development, on the other. An exception to the latter point are the studies of Luria (1961), in which linguistic deficiencies in the control of behaviour are referred to, and in some instances Luria suggests that weakness in the control of motor behaviour in some oligophrenic children can be compensated for and brought under better control through the supplementary use of speech. In this kind of study, Luria makes use of Pavlov's differentiation of the primary (conditioning) and secondary (speech) signalling systems. The major difference between the two systems is, of course, the additive but slow action of conditioning as compared with the immediacy and generality of the secondary (speech) system. O'Connor and Hermelin (1963) report a series of experiments concerned with speech and thought in severely mentally handicapped children in which they show that logic in linguistic structure in this group does not necessarily imply equally good logic in the relationship between speech and events.

What in effect is shown in this work is not only that logic in linguistic structures does not necessarily imply logic in other operations, but also, for example, that the absence of verbal concepts does not mean that the handicapped person cannot use nonverbal logic correctly. This statement which summarises this early work from one point of view is in direct sympathy with the thorough and detailed demonstration of the behaviour of the Down syndrome subject Françoise, the subject of Professor Rondal's careful study. Whereas, of course, the early work of Luria and O'Connor and Hermelin and others clarifies a simple and basic theme, Rondal, taking advantage of the complexities of modern psycholinguistics, has illuminated the possibility that in verbal development in Down syndrome, it is not simply the case that grammatical and semantic development are both retarded forms of normal speech and language growth. Such observations go along with the presentation of language as at least to some degree modular.

The presentation of this fascinating study which uses Halliday's (1985) functional grammar to demonstrate the paradox of Françoise who despite a relatively low level (65) of 'intelligence' manages to offer conversational replies which are both pertinent and to a degree semantically and grammatically adequate. A number of these verbal skills are also present in lexical and scriptory form. Clearly Professor Rondal has brought the study of this type of phenomenon to a level which equals that of Cromer's study of the spina bifida woman (1991) who, although having an inspection time within the mentally handicapped range, had a linguistic competence that appeared to be governed by separate modular abilities of a different level, one much nearer normality.

This leads us to consider another very interesting aspect of Rondal's study of the Down syndrome woman, namely, the degree to which her relative verbal ability represents an independent modular ability similar to that shown by idiot savants like those first noted by Down when he discussed the case of the renowned painter Gottfried Mind in the last century (1887).

Some aspects of the performance of some idiot savants can involve unusual memory – for example, for music, as Sloboda, Hermelin and O'Connor (1985) showed. Professor Rondal is careful to indicate the levels of competence shown by Françoise, not only in her verbal development but in relevant skills such as expressive and symbolic gesturing, short-term memory, and some aspects of semantic memory. Her appreciation of order in auditory memory is shown to be superior, for example, to her awareness of the order of visual items. In drawing attention to competence differences of this kind, Rondal delineates differing features of modularity, suggesting that an oversimplified Fodorian modularity would not provide an adequate account of Françoise's conversational success.

In a general overall analysis of such exceptional mentally retarded children or adults as Françoise, Rondal notes that the productive and receptive language function was normal or nearly so in its phonology and grammar, but more retarded in its lexical, semantic, and pragmatic features. This finding is in accordance with the Chomskyan (1981) view that the former operations are autonomous and independent of cognitive abilities, whereas the latter are not. This approach to exploring cognitively related and cognitively independent functions in examining savantlike abilities in persons with mental retardation throws up a revealing technique for comparing the basic notion of mental handicap and the idea of independent modular talents.

This is an important study which brings a new level of linguistic analysis to the understanding of the functioning of savants, and, in this case of a Down syndrome subject, which might be extended to other groups of malfunctioning subjects. It is of great interest that Rondal has demonstrated the possibility of savant qualities not in autism, where it occurs commonly, or in cases of spina bifida, where it is known to occur, but in a mentally handicapped subject of known genetic defect. Professor Rondal deserves considerable praise for the thoroughness and ingenuity with which he has advanced this area of psycholinguistic study.

Neil O'Connor

Former Director
Medical Research Council,
Developmental Psychology Unit
and University of London

References

Chomsky, N. (1981). *Lectures on government and binding*. Dordrecht: Foris.

Cromer, R. (1991). *Language and thought in normal and handicapped children*. London: Blackwell.

Down, J. L. (1887). *On some of the mental affections of childhood and youth*. London: Churchill.

Halliday, M. (1985). *An introduction to functional grammar*. London: Arnold.

Luria, A. R. (1961). *The role of speech in the regulation of normal and abnormal behaviour*. London: Pergamon.

O'Connor, N., & Hermelin, B. (1963). *Speech and thought in severe subnormality*. London: Macmillan.

Piaget, J. (1923). *Le langage et la pensée chez l'enfant*. Neuchâtel: Delachaux & Niestlé.

Sloboda, J., Hermelin, B., & O'Connor, N. (1985). An exceptional music memory. *Music Perception, 3*, 155–170.

Vygotsky, L. S. (1962). *Thought and language*. Cambridge, MA: MIT Press. (First publication in Russian, 1929)

Acknowledgments

The present work is a tribute to the exceptional level of expressive and receptive language attained by Françoise, my Down syndrome subject. Her language performance and the mental organization supporting it raise most intriguing questions given that Françoise's general cognitive functioning is average for standard trisomy 21. These questions and others are addressed in the course of this book.

The work herein has benefitted from many collaborations that I gratefully acknowledge. Jean-Jacques Deltour and Jean-Paul Broonen (Service de Psychométrie, Service d'Orientation Universitaire, respectively) tested Françoise's intellectual abilities. Jean-François Bachelet (Laboratoire de Psycholinguistique) spent several hours interacting with Françoise in free conversation, resulting in the corpus of speech to be analyzed. He also made the first transcription of the corpus with the assistance of Anne Grosjean (advanced student in speech pathology at the time). Annette Lafontaine and Fabienne Hagelstein (Laboratoire de Psycholinguistique) helped with the linguistic analysis of the corpus. Annick Comblain (Laboratoire de Psycholinguistique) prepared and tested Françoise on a long series of tasks to assess her working memory, metalinguistic judgment and awareness, semantic-lexical organization, and her (intellectual) operational level in the sense of Piaget. I am most grateful to Annick for her efficient, always good-humored, and almost daily elegant assistance in documentation as well as in manuscript preparation. Michèle Fayasse (Laboratoire de Psycholinguistique) also helped with data collection, in particular administering the measures on spontaneous speech rhythm to Françoise, as well as a small control group of Down syndrome and nonretarded adults. Myriam Monseur (at the time, a member of the Laboratoire de Psycholinguistique) collected the necessary data for assessing Françoise's written language capability and administered several lexical and grammatical tests. Some data on Françoise's memory functioning as well as corresponding control data on normal adults and adults with Down syndrome are quoted from Sabine Gilon's excellent thesis on memory problems and their clinical assessment (Gilon, 1988), which I am happy to acknowledge. Joëlle Marnette (Laboratoire de Psycholinguistique) helped with the assessment of cerebral specialization with Françoise as well as with a group of other Down syndrome adults attending La Fermette, an occupational center located in the vicinity of Liège. I wish to thank my good friend Mr. Richard Bonjean, La Fermette's director and distinguished general secretary of the European Down's Syndrome Association, for authorizing this and other parts of the research to be conducted in his center and for helping in many ways. Mr. Marc Lambrecht, La Fermette's psychologist at the time, Mrs. Françoise Goffart, Annie Bastyns, Isabelle Montulet, and Hélène Fonsny, respectively the speech pathologist, the psychologist, the psychopedagogist, and the physiotherapist of the APEM (Association de Parents d'Enfants Mongoliens) – the major Belgian association devoted to Down's syndrome – as well as Mrs. Annie Krins, friend, admirable founder, and tireless director of the APEM since its inception in 1977, were also helpful in supplying control data on a number of adults, adolescents, and children with Down syndrome.

I am grateful to Jean-Marc Grailet and to Marianne Van Der Kaa (Service de Neuropsychologie) for supplying information concerning Francoise's developmental and medical antecedents, to Dr. Martine Timsit-Berthier for her information regarding Françoise's more recent medical dossier, to my colleague Professor Lucien Koulischer (Service de Génétique) for several indications concerning Françoise's karyotype, and to Denis Javaux (Service de Psychologie du Travail et d'Ergonomie) for writing the computer program necessary for conducting the dual tasks in the assessment of cerebral dominance. I am indebted to my colleague and friend Professor Martial Van der Linden (Service de Neuropsychologie), who kindly loaned us portions of his material to assess Françoise's working memory capacity, for several important exchanges on the proper interpretation of Françoise's memory performance and capacity, as well as for critically reading portions of the manuscript.

The study, of course, owes much to Françoise, to her good will and good temper, and to her willingness to interact with people in a friendly manner. I thank her very much and wish her the best in her life. I am also much indebted to Françoise's father for allowing us to contact her, test her abilities, record her speech, and talk to her as many times as we wished and as was necessary to conduct the study. He also kindly supplied us with invaluable information on Françoise's education, schooling, and language training.

Chapter 2 "Language development in Down syndrome" is based in part on a text that I wrote as a chapter for a book entitled *Language development in exceptional circumstances*, edited by Dorothy Bishop and Kay Mogford, originally published by Churchill Livingstone (1988) and republished by Erlbaum (1993). It is used and updated here with permission of the publishers, whom I should like to thank. One part of Chapter 5, Section 5.4.1.2.1 explaining the major analytical concepts of Michael Halliday's (1985) *Functional grammar*, is closely related to the original work (London: Arnold, Chapters 3–9). I obtained permission to use this material here from Edward Arnold Publishers, and I should like to acknowledge their professional courtesy. A summary and discussion of several exceptional cases of language development in mental retardation (Rondal, 1993a), based on the present work, appeared in the *Proceedings of the Trinity College Anniversary Conference on Speech and Language Pathology* (Leahy & Kallen, 1993). Finally, a partial summary of Françoise's case appeared as a part of a chapter in Helen Tager-Flusberg's edited book *Constraints on language acquisition* (Rondal, 1993b).

I also wish to express my gratitude to the Belgian National Board for Scientific Research (F.N.R.S.) for its continuing support of my research activities and for financially facilitating many of my professional trips over the past 20 years. A number of colleagues have offered me bibliographical suggestions, various information, remarks, and constructive criticism regarding specific points of the analysis and the theoretical treatment. Locally, this is the case for Serge Brédart (Service de Neuropsychologie), who, in addition, was kind enough to read a version of the manuscript and point out a number of shortcomings; for my good friend Jean-Paul Broonen (Service d'Orientation Universitaire); for Ezio Tirelli (Service de Psychologie Biologique) for a number of specifications regarding particular aspects of the central nervous system, and many exciting discussions; and, overall, for Jean-Pierre Thibaut, first assistant in the Laboratoire de Psycholinguistique, with whom I interacted almost daily during the writing phase of this monograph, discussing many aspects of the case, relevant points in the specialized literature, venturing hypotheses, and so on. I am happy to report that he survived this potentially intoxicating treatment and even could find the mental resources to read and criticize constructively the prefinal version of the manuscript. I am grateful to all of these people for their encouragement and sympathy. I am thankful to my friends Eric Esperet, Jean and Josiane Caron, Catherine and Gilles Tourrette, and Daniel Gaonac'h from the Laboratoire de Psychologie du Langage of Poitiers University, France, where I spent several months in the course of 1991, and to Frédéric François from the Linguistics Department of René Descartes University in Paris (Sorbonne) for lively discussions and exchanges on the theme of this book and related topics. Several of the ideas developed herein found support with Yvan Lebrun, head of the Neurolinguistic Department of Vrij Universiteit Brussels, who kindly supplied me with reprints of his own research on a case of hyperlexia favoring a modular interpretation, and with John Van Borsel (same department and also Ghent University), who kindly reported to me on an interesting Down syndrome case that he is currently studying. I am also grateful to my longtime friend Ernst Moerk of the University of California at Fresno, for discussions and exchanges on the proper interpretation to give to Françoise's particular language development, although Ernst would probably disagree with some aspects of the final interpretation made and would certainly disagree with my assessment of the learning literature on language acquisition herein. My good friends Michael Beveridge, University of Bristol, and James Hogg, University of Dundee, formerly senior researchers under Peter Mittler in the Hadrian Hester Research Center, Victoria University of Manchester, had me invited to the prestigious Forum on Mental Retardation organized in London at the Royal Society of Medicine in May 1991. There I had the opportunity to present a summary of the Françoise case and to benefit from theirs and other experts' remarks and suggestions. I am pleased to acknowledge it. I have also benefitted from exchanges with Noam Chomsky, Massachusetts Institute of Technology, and Derek Bickerton, Linguistic Department, University of Hawaii at Honolulu, whose encouragement and support I gratefully mention. I am also much indebted to Neil O'Connor, formerly head of the Developmental Psychology Unit of the Medical Research Council in London, for personal discussions, exchange of letters, and for supplying me with a whole series of reprints from his very fine studies of "idiot savants," as he calls these cases after Langdon Down and Binet. Neil was one of the very first researchers to study such cases systematically, having understood, well before the "modularity wave" in the eighties, the particular significance of dissociation cases for cognitive theory. He took time but to read the prefinal version of the manuscript and to write a foreword to the present opus.

Last but not least, it is my pleasure to acknowledge the friendly support of Sheldon Rosenberg, series editor. Sheldon helped organize and kindly corrected early drafts of the manuscript. I am also much indebted to Susan Curtiss who did her best to improve the quality of the monograph and made a large number of fine remarks and ingenious suggestions. Of course, the remaining obscurities, infelicities, and possible errors of interpretation are fully mine. I am most grateful to Julia Hough, editor, Psychology and Cognitive Science, Cambridge University Press, Karen Atkins, senior editorial assistant, Edith Feinstein, production editor, and Robert Racine, copy editor, for their cordial and efficient editorial guidance. Finally, Agnula Castias and Anastasia Piat-Di Nicolantonio were extremely effective in typing and in processing the text of several versions of the manuscript. I am indebted to them for their patience and the high quality of their work.

Jean A. Rondal

1   Introduction

I met Françoise, my Down syndrome (henceforth DS) subject, a few years ago, at La Fermette, an occupational center for DS adults managed by APEM (Association de Parents d'Enfants Mongoliens), to which I am a consultant. La Fermette is located 30 km from Liège, in the eastern part of Belgium. Upon conversational contacts in the center, Françoise's productive language as well as her apparent excellent comprehension struck me as unusually close to normal for a DS person. In searching the specialized literature, I found that the case appeared unique enough to justify undertaking a full-scale study.

Françoise was recorded during 2 hours of free conversation with one member of my research team. She was also given a very large number of tests, verbal and non-verbal intelligence, perceptual, mnemonic, and so forth. Retrospective information was obtained on her development, education, and life since birth. This book is the product of this compilation and of the analysis and interpretations made of the data. It addresses several central questions.

First, is normal or quasi-normal language development and functioning possible in spite of severe central cognitive limitations, particularly conceptual ones? The answer, as it would appear, is partially a positive one. Normal phonological and grammatical functioning are indeed possible in such cases.

Second, how can this be the case? One possible answer, and the one that is favored in what follows, is that phonology and grammar may be acquired and function relatively independently from other central processes. Current indications in the specialized literature suggest the hypothesis of a loose tie between general cognition and particular components of the language system, such as phonology and syntax. Convincing evidence comes from studies of other "exceptional," mentally handicapped persons.[1] If proven correct, such an interpretation would have important implications for theories of language development and functioning, as well as for theoretical conceptions of mental handicap.

The book is organized in the following way. Chapter 2 summarizes major aspects of the literature on speech and language problems in DS individuals, including the controversial issue of their cerebral hemispheric specialization for speech and language functions. Chapter 3 reviews the available data regarding the published cases of hyperlinguistic development in mentally retarded (MR) subjects. The state of the

1

cognition hypothesis in first-language acquisition is analyzed in Chapter 4. The more traditional Piagetian hypothesis is examined together with recent modularity perspectives on the cognition-language issue. Chapter 5 supplies the information on the Françoise case including the results of the many tests and analyses performed on her productive and receptive language abilities (oral and written), metalinguistic ability, nonlinguistic abilities (general intelligence and operational development, computational capacity, spatial abilities, memory functioning, etc.), and cerebral hemispheric specialization. An expanded theoretical discussion follows in Chapter 6. Several possible explanations of the observed facts are considered. Simple teaching-learning and global developmental cognitive explanations are rejected on the grounds of implausibility. The possible role of information treatment mechanisms, such as working memory, is examined. It is argued that language-exceptional subjects, such as Françoise, operate on the basis of an implicit grammatical knowledge that they cannot have developed via learning or conceptual growth given their cognitive limitations. Chapter 7 summarizes the major data and the arguments of the preceding chapters. A complete reference list follows. Nine appendixes are supplied that display the speech excerpts used in the analyses of Françoise's speech (including their English translations), the lists of sentences and paragraphs employed in the receptive language assessment, a written text and dictation taken by Françoise, as well as some reading and visuographic testing material.

Note

1. By *exceptional language development* (sometimes, *hyperlinguistic development*, which ought to be, actually, *relative hyperlinguistic development*), in this context, I mean an abnormal condition characterized by an ability to comprehend and to use language that far exceeds the other cognitive attainments of the individual and that would not have been predicted on the basis of his relatively low level of general intellectual attainment. In other words, the exceptionality in language development denotes the surprising level of mastery that an individual with mental deficiency and restricted psychological functions (among other limitations and problems) has in understanding and/or in producing language. (In this book, contrary to the growing practice in U.S. scientific literature, I use the masculine pronoun generically in deference to a simple writing habit.)

2   Language development in Down syndrome

Detailed reviews of the literature on the development of speech, language, and communication skills in persons with DS and other mental handicaps are readily available (e.g., Gunn, 1985; Rondal, 1985a, 1988a, 1988b; J. Miller, 1987; C. B. Mervis, 1988; Dodd & Leahy, 1989; Barrett & Diniz, 1989). The following presentation, therefore, will only summarize major data. (For an update on the general problems of DS envisaged in a developmental-organizational perspective, see the contributions gathered by Cicchetti & Beeghly, 1990, including their own review chapter.)

A general indication in the specialized literature has sometimes been for DS to be more detrimental to language development than are other syndromes leading to mental retardation (e.g., Zisk & Bialer, 1967; Gibson, 1981). Exact reasons and detailed supporting analyses for this claim have never been provided, however, and there are opposing views (e.g., Evans & Hampson, 1968).[1] Nevertheless, a number of observations may be recalled (also J. Miller, 1987) in relation to the important speech and language deficits in DS persons. None of them are pathognomonic of DS, but their accumulation in this syndrome is remarkable.

2.1 Language-related deficiencies in Down syndrome

Two series of problems may be envisaged: first, organic malformations and difficulties affecting speech; second, central processes of a cognitive nature.

2.1.1 Mechanical problems in speech

Benda (1949) and Buddenhagen (1971) have detailed peripheral pathological factors associated with defective speech in DS. These factors include a buccal cavity too small for the tongue and a protruding tongue, a larynx located too high in the neck with thickening of fibrotic mucosa, vocal fold edema, myxedema of the pharynx, an edematous tongue that does not groove properly for the distinction between sounds like [ʃ] and [s] and is impaired in its motility, hypotonia of the speech muscles – tongue, lips, soft palate, breathing muscles. Also to be mentioned are broad lips with irregularities in the shape including lateral inversions of the lower lip (Oster, 1953), limited lip motility, palate anomalies (Spitzer, Rabinowitch, & Wybar, 1961), fis-

3

sured tongue (Blanchard, 1964), excessive salivation, flabbiness of tongue and too small a jaw (Strazzula, 1953), defective teeth and irregular tooth implantation (Kraus, Clark, & Oka, 1968), flattened nose, underdevelopment of sinuses and nasal passages (Spitzer et al., 1961), enlarged tonsils and adenoids, common respiratory infection, frequent inflammation of the pharynx, laryngitis, and bronchitis producing coughing, hoarseness, and reduced breathing capacity.

Voice quality deviations have been noted (Montague & Hollien, 1973, 1974). They include breathiness and roughness. There is still disagreement among experts as to voice fundamental frequency in DS subjects. Some (e.g., Weinberg & Zlatin, 1970) report a higher fundamental frequency in DS children. Others indicate that differences vanish when proper control is exercised for factors like karyotype, verbal task (spontaneous vs. elicited speech), degree of closeness in matching DS and nonretarded (NR) subjects or MR subjects of other etiologies than DS (see Montague & Hollien, 1974).

Other mechanical factors influencing communication through speech include auditory and visual defects. Hearing loss is more frequent in DS subjects (children as well as adults) than in NR subjects and other mental retardation categories at comparable mental levels (Fulton & Lloyd, 1968; Keiser, Montague, Wold, Maune, & Pattison, 1981). In Rigrodsky, Prunty, and Glovsky's report (1961), hearing impairment was indicated to affect 60% of the DS sample. The loss was mainly in the lightly to moderately impaired range (i.e., mean decibel range 25–55 bilaterally over the frequencies 500, 1,000, and 2,000 hertz) with the loss being half conductive and half sensorineural and "mixed" impairment. Other reports signal lower figures of hearing loss in DS subjects and prevalent rates of conductive loss over sensorineural and mixed ones (e.g., Clausen, 1968). Recent work with brainstem auditory evoked responses (BAEPs) in children with DS (Gigli, Ferri, Musumeci, Tomassetti, & Bergonzi, 1984; Ferri et al., 1986) confirms the existence of conductive loss in a large proportion of the subjects studied. Moreover, numerous DS subjects show BAEP abnormalities indicating a brainstem conduction dysfunction that appears to be positively correlated with their degree of mental retardation. Evenhuis, van Zanten, Brocaar, and Roerdinkholder (1992), in one rare study of middle-aged (institutionalized) persons with DS, indicate a possible influence of age on hearing loss (with losses of 20 to over 90 decibels) beyond 35 years (up to 62 years in this study).

Ocular defects in DS include strabismus and other refractive problems, myopia, nystagmus, and lens opacities. All impede sustained visual focus (MacGillivray, 1968). Watering eyes, conjunctivitis, and respiratory infections may also appreciably reduce visual efficiency (Pueschel, 1988).

Finally, the deficits in motor coordination, timing, and the generalized hypotonia characteristic of DS subjects particularly during the first years (see McIntire & Dutch, 1964; Cowie, 1970) adversely affect the speech production system (O'Connor & Hermelin, 1963; Rosin, Swift, & Bless, 1987). Frith and Frith (1974) have hypothesized that DS subjects show a deficit in developing and utilizing pre-programmed motor sequences. This hypothesis has received independent empirical support in an experimental work (finger-tapping task) by Seyfort and Spreen (1979). Such problems may be at least partially responsible for the relatively high proportion of stuttering or stutteringlike phenomena observed in these subjects, from 33 to 59%, depending on the particular study (e.g., Gottsleben, 1955; Zisk & Bialer, 1967; Preus, 1972); although it could also be that stutterers with DS have a somewhat different speech motor organization than do more fluent speakers with DS (see Devenny, Silverman, Balgley, Well, & Sidtis, 1990).

2.1.2 Perceptual and cognitive problems

Goddard (1916) claimed that the mental capacity of DS subjects was almost always approximately that of 4- or 5-year-old normal children. Benda's classical curve of mental growth for DS individuals (Benda, 1949) culminates around 40 months mental age (MA) reached between 10 and 15 years chronological age (CA). Modal intelligence quotient (IQ) in standard trisomy 21 (see later in this chapter) seems to be between 45 and 50 points (Moor, 1967; Gibson, 1981). The literature on psychological development sees mental evolution in DS in three "stages" (Gibson, 1981). Mental growth is steady during the first 18 months MA, developed over 4 or 5 years CA. This phase witnesses the DS child's evolution through the stages of Piaget's sensorimotor intellectual subcategories. The beginning of conceptual-symbolic development is also evident. The second and third periods of mental growth occur between 5 and approximately 15 years CA. They cover the MA range from 2 to 5 years. Five years MA seems to be the realistic upper limit of mental growth for most DS subjects, which they reach between 12 and 15 years CA. It is known, however, that mental development may continue beyond this level into the third decade of life for a number of DS persons, albeit more slowly (Ross, 1961; Berry, Groeneweg, Gibson, & Brown, 1984).

Among the most often cited cognitive problems of DS individuals, matched for CA or MA with NR individuals, are limited efficiency in information processing, limited attentional capacity, slower reaction time, deficit of auditory-vocal processing, limitation of short-term memory, slower retrieval of learned information from long-term memory, reduced perceptual discrimination and generalization capability, deficit of symbolization capacity (particularly with reference to nonconcrete entities), and inability with respect to the abstract attitude (see Owens, 1989, for a comprehensive review).

The list is extensive. One can wonder how language can develop at all in such adverse conditions. The fact that it does to some extent in most DS individuals may certainly be taken to indicate the robustness of basic language organization in humans.

2.2 Language development in Down syndrome

In what follows, data collected over the past 25 years are summarized according to five categories: speech sounds, lexicon, semantic structures, morpho-syntax and pragmatics. The data on which the summary is based are fully explained in the following sources: Barrett and Diniz (1989); Bilovsky and Share (1965); Coggins (1979); Dale (1977); Dodd (1972, 1976); Dodd and Leahy (1989); Fishler, Share, and Koch (1964); Lambert and Rondal (1980); Layton and Sharifi (1979); Michaelis (1977); Rondal (1975a, 1985a, 1988a, 1988b); Rondal, Lambert, and Chipman (1981); Ryan (1975); Share (1975); and Smith and Oller (1981).

2.2.1 Speech sounds

Those types of sounds in babbling that can be considered to belong to the input language are relatively similar in DS and NR infants. Similar developmental sequences and timing hold for the two groups. Front and central vowels like [i], [ɛ], and [ʌ] appear first, then back vowels like [u] and [a] (Smith & Oller, 1981). For stoplike sounds, up to approximately six months, velars like [k] and [g] tend to dominate. They then decrease in frequency and alveolar stops [t] and [d], and nasal [n] become dominant. Labial stops [p] and [b], and nasal [m] remain intermediate in frequency throughout the first 12 months. Reduplicated babbling begins around 8 months (range 6 to 10 months) in normally developing as well as in DS infants (Smith & Oller, 1981).

By contrast, articulatory development (i.e., the setting up of phonological contrasts in production) is slow and difficult in many DS children for a number of reasons, including the delays and uncertainties of lexical development, but the overall progression appears to parallel development in NR children (e.g., Smith & Oller, 1981; Stoel-Gammon, 1980, 1981; Menn, 1983). Vowels, semivowels, and nasal and stop consonants are produced and mastered first. The fricatives [f], [θ], [s], [ʃ], [v], [z], [δ], and [z] are more delicate to articulate. They take longer to be mastered (when they are). Intelligibility of speech remains low in most DS subjects (Ryan, 1975; Rondal, 1978a). The articulatory simplifications are of the same type, albeit more inconsistent and more variable from trial to trial in the same subjects and from subject to subject even at comparable IQ and MA levels, as those observed in the speech of NR children (mainly feature changes, cluster reductions, and assimilations) (Dodd, 1976; Rosin, Swift, Bless, & Vetter, 1988; Dodd & Leahy, 1989; Van Borsel, 1993). Most DS adolescents and adults exhibit a pattern of phonological performance similar to that of older DS children (Jarvis, 1980; Rondal & Lambert, 1983; Van Borsel, 1988).

2.2.2 Lexicon

The onset of meaningful speech (one-word utterance) is delayed in DS children (first recognizable words are often recorded between 24 and 30 months of age; see Cunningham, 1979; Lambert & Rondal, 1980). At this time, however, the proportion of meaningful words in the vocal productions of most DS children is still lower than 5% (Smith, 1977). This figure slowly increases with age up to around 4 years CA when more numerous meaningful vocalizations are produced. DS and NR children exhibit a similar pattern of early vocabulary development, with both groups acquiring social words and a few object names at first and later acquiring relational words and more object names (Gopnik, 1987; also Gilham, 1979). The object name vocabularies acquired by young DS children have contents similar to those acquired by NR children (Cunningham & Sloper, 1984). Receptively, DS children first comprehend object names at approximately the same MA (around 14 months) as do NR children. The former have similar-sized vocabularies in comprehension as do MA-matched NR children (between 13 and 21 months) (Cardoso-Martins, Mervis, & Mervis, 1985). Later, at corresponding MAs, DS and NR children are also able to define, understand, and use about as many words. Similarly, word association tasks yield corresponding results for DS and MA-matched NR children (see Rondal, 1975a, 1985a, for reviews of this literature). DS and MR subjects of other etiologies do not differ noticeably in their receptive and productive lexical developments (Lyle, 1960, 1961; Mein, 1961; Ryan, 1975, 1977; see Barrett & Diniz, 1989, for a review).

As it seems, MA is a satisfactory predictive variable of receptive and productive lexical development in MR children. This is true for NR children, too, as the high correlation between the Peabody Picture Vocabulary Test (PPVT; Dunn & Dunn, 1965) and the Wechsler or Stanford-Binet Intelligence Tests indicate (Dunn & Dunn, 1982).[2] Early conceptual development does not appear to be qualitatively different in DS and NR children (see C. B. Mervis, 1990). As conceptual development, very likely, sustains lexical development, MA measures reflecting, at least partially, the former correctly predict the latter.

2.2.3 Semantic structures

When they begin to combine two and three words within the same utterance (usually not before 4 to 5 years CA, sometimes later), DS children appear to express the same range of relational meanings or thematic roles and relations as reported by the students of early combinatorial language in the NR child (e.g., Brown, 1973) and pertaining to the semantic structure[3] of the natural languages (see Fillmore's, 1967, basic propositional cases or Chafe's, 1970, componential meaning analysis). Examples of early semantic relations expressed by DS, as well as by NR, children are *notice* or *existence, denial, disappearance, recurrence, attribution, possession, location, agent, action, patient, instrument, source, agent-action, action-patient,* and *agent-action-patient* (Rondal, 1978a; Coggins, 1979; Layton & Sharifi, 1979). DS children also appear to correctly understand the same set of structural meanings when they are realized in the speech of others (Duchan & Erickson, 1976). There is no indication that the elementary semantic-structural basis of language, as it is put to

Table 2–1. *Mean length of utterance (MLU) and standard deviations (SD) in DS subjects*

Study	Chronological age[a]		MLU[b]	
	Group mean	SD[c]	Group mean	SD
Rondal (1978a)[d]				
Group 1	4.01	0.09	1.26	0.23
Group 2	6.06	2.01	1.94	0.19
Group 3	9.09	1.09	2.87	0.14
Rondal, Lambert, & Sohier (1980a)[e]	11.06	1.08	3.40	0.95
Rondal & Lambert (1983)[d]	26.00	1.07	5.98	2.62

[a] In years and months.
[b] Computed in number of words plus grammatical morphemes, after Brown's rules (1973).
[c] Standard deviation.
[d] Study conducted with American-English-speaking subjects.
[e] Study conducted with Belgian French-speaking subjects.

use in early language production and reception, is markedly different in DS and NR children at corresponding levels of language development.

2.2.4 Morpho-syntax

Grammatical development is never complete in DS subjects. Some progress is obvious, however, with increased CA (Lenneberg, Nichols, & Rosenberger, 1964). It is reflected in the progressive lengthening of the utterances as captured by MLU (mean length of utterance; Brown, 1973). Table 2–1 summarizes MLU data obtained by Rondal (1978a), Rondal and Lambert (1983), and Rondal, Lambert, and Sohier (1980a) through spontaneous speech analyses in free-play and free-conversation conditions.

Several remarks are in order regarding the data supplied in Table 2–1. First, they are cross-sectional data used in a longitudinal problem and are therefore subject to the usual criticisms. Second, Rondal's study (1978a) was conducted with American-English-speaking DS children; Rondal, Lambert, and Sohier's study (1980a) and Rondal and Lambert's study (1983) had Belgian French-speaking DS subjects. No metric exists for relating MLU computed on different languages (even for as lexically and grammatically close languages as English and French). Third, the MLU data from the American-speaking children were obtained through free-play interactive sessions at home with the mothers. The MLU data in the two French studies were recorded in dyadic free-conversation situations between the retarded adolescents or young adults and a familiar NR adult, either at school (for the DS adolescents) or in an occupational facility (for the DS adults). Fourth, as indicated in Table 2–1, the adult MLU data exhibit a larger interindividual variability to the extent that the mean reported may be partially misleading as a summary index for this group of subjects. It is possible that the differences in MLU data in the three studies reflect only these dissimilarities between the studies and the variability problem. However, the hypothesis of a moderate MLU growth between adolescence and early adulthood, at least in some DS individuals, cannot be ruled out on the basis of this data. Longitudinal MLU data gathered by Fowler (1988) with a group of 11 DS subjects aged 4 to 13 years at the beginning of the study supports this hypothesis. She reports a modest MLU growth beyond puberty (until 19 years, reaching MLU 4 to 6 in some subjects).

Whether MLU growth with increased CA is fully warranted or not, the spontaneous combinatorial language of DS individuals remains largely telegraphic (in the sense of R. Brown, 1973). It is characterized by a reduced use of function words (articles, prepositions, auxiliaries, copulas, pronouns, conjunctions). The lack of appropriate feature marking on pronouns and anaphors may render the referring expression opaque to the nonfamiliar interlocutor. Word ordering, however, is usually correct. It would seem that reproducing standard word order in short and simple utterances is within the early capacity of DS as well as other moderately and severely MR subjects. Such a state of affairs largely persists into the adult years as indicated by an analysis of conversational data gathered by Rondal and Lambert (1983) with DS adults living in the community (see Table 2–2). Less than half of the utterances recorded in that study were grammatical sentences. When the verb was expressed, it was properly inflected only approximately half of the time. The tense most often used was the present indicative, even in narrative contexts clearly referring to completed past events. There was less than one article per utterance and slightly over one inflection marking gender or number on the noun phrase in two utterances.

2.2.5 Understanding active and passive sentences

Little systematic information is available on the treatment of advanced linguistic material by DS persons. This is not to say, of course, that no substantial work was ever conducted on advanced aspects of language acquisition in MR children (see, e.g., Carrow, 1968, who reports serious difficulties with reversible passives in moderately and severely MR subjects; also see Rosenberg & Abbeduto, 1986, for additional data, and Rondal, 1975a, 1985a, for analytic reviews of this literature). But it was often the case at the time that DS subjects' performance was not singled out in the data from other MR subjects (see Semmel & Dolley, 1970, however, for one exception, as well as the more recent study by Rosenberg & Abbeduto, 1986).

One specific study was conducted by Rondal, Cession, and Vincent (1988) on the comprehension of declarative monopropositional sentences varying according to

Table 2–2. *Mean scores (group) and standard deviations (SD) for DS adults*

Indices	DS adults	
	Mean	SD
Lexical aspect		
1. TTR (type-token ratio)	0.575	0.075
Morphosyntactic parameters		
2. MLU (mean length of utterance)	5.980	2.620
3. Proportion of grammatical sentences	0.412	0.311
4. Sentence complexity	0.217	0.173
5. Number and gender on noun phrase	0.563	0.235
6. Proportion of articles	0.381	0.212
7. Verbal inflections	0.547	0.365
8. Proportion of pronouns	0.624	0.504
Informative aspect		
9. Proportion of information	0.972	0.040
10. Proportion of new information	0.692	0.121
11. Conversational continuity	0.833	0.077

Note: TTR was computed by dividing the number of different words (types) – all grammatical categories – by the number of words sampled (tokens), after Siegel and Harkins's rules (1963). MLU was computed after R. Brown's rules (1973). *Proportion of grammatical sentences* is the ratio of the number of sentences that were grammatical – i.e., not lacking any obligatory constituent – to the total number of utterances. *Sentence complexity* is the ratio of the number of compound verbs (e.g., i*s going, have made*) plus subordinate clauses to the total number of utterances. *Number and gender* is the ratio of the number of morphological markers for plurality and for gender on the noun phrase to the total number of utterances. *Proportion of articles* is the ratio of the number of articles produced to the total number of utterances. *Verbal inflections* is the ratio of the number of times a verb used was properly inflected to the total number of utterances. *Proportion of pronouns* is the ratio of the number of personal and other pronouns to the total number of utterances. *Proportion of information* is the ratio of the quantity of information supplied verbally to the total number of utterances. By *information* is meant a complete relational meaning [i.e., a predicate with its obligatory argument(s) in the sense of Chafe, 1970], an elliptical statement, or a question referring back to an immediately preceding utterance. Echoic and onomatopoeic productions were not counted as instances of informative utterances. *Proportion of new information* is the ratio of the quantity of information not previously stated in the conversation to the total quantity of information given verbally. *Conversational continuity* is the ratio of the number of times the MR subject correctly followed on the topic introduced or developed by the conversational partner.
Source: After Rondal and Lambert, 1983.

voice and semantic transitivity features (see Hopper & Thompson, 1980). As the report of this study is not currently available in print, I shall summarize the research below and stress the major conclusions.

A group of 17 young adults with DS (mean CA: 27 years and 5 months) were individually tested for comprehension of a set of plausible and (thematic or event) reversible active and passive declarative sentences. Kinesis (i.e., degree of "actionness") of verbs (see Hopper & Thompson, 1980) was systematically varied. Subjects were requested to choose between two pictures. One correctly represented the thematic relations encoded in the sentence heard (e.g., girl pushing boy, for the sentence *The girl pushes the boy*); the other picture corresponded to a reversal of the same thematic functions (e.g., boy pushing girl, for the same sentence).

As it is known, passive sentences do not differ from active ones in the thematic relations expressed but only in the overt realization of these relations. Passive sentences have their underlying logical subject (ULS) realized in the surface form of an oblique object most often introduced by the preposition *by* (e.g., *the boy* in the sentence *The girl was pushed by the boy*) and their underlying logical object (ULO) realized in the form of the surface subject (*the girl* in the same sentence). NR children understand active as well as passive sentences earlier and better when the sentences are constructed around action verbs (e.g., *push, carry*), that is, verbs taking agent as subjects, as opposed to so-called mental verbs (e.g., *imagine, like, see*) (Maratsos Fox, Becker, & Chalkley, 1985; Sudhalter & Braine, 1985; Rondal, Thibaut, & Cession, 1990). In line with the work of Kosslyn (1980) and Paivio (1971, 1986), Rondal, Thibaut, and Cession (1990) have speculated that the action verb effect could be due to a particular supporting role of mental image to the computations involved in sentence processing especially when the analytic task is more complex or with certain types of formal structures – the construction of a mental image being favored in the case of concrete and action verbs (e.g., Paivio, 1986). This hypothesis has been corroborated in a study by Thibaut, Rondal, and Kaens (in press); see also Kaens (1988) on the role of mental imagery in children's sentence comprehension. The experimental results obtained by Rondal, Cession, and Vincent (1988) indicate that the same facilitating effect of kinesis is true of the DS adults studied as it is of NR children except that with the former the effect is limited to active sentences. DS adults with relatively higher IQs (40 to 60) correctly interpreted 83% of the action verb actives versus 73% of the nonaction ones. DS adults with relatively lower IQs (20 to 39) obtained 75 and 50% correct interpretation, respectively. These differences are statistically significant at the conventional $p < .05$ level. For the nonaction verb passives, the profiles of responses also diverged according to IQ level: The higher IQ group interpreted the passive sentences proposed as if they were corresponding actives in 60% of the cases versus 70% for the lower IQ group (significant at the $p < .05$ level). The action verb passives were interpreted at chance level in the two groups (50 and 47% for the higher and the lower IQ groups, respectively). This research shows, first, that in a large majority of the cases, DS adults do not correctly understand the morphosyntactic and semantic aspects associated with the passive voice, and second, that the reversible declarative active sentences are correctly understood in a good proportion of the cases, particularly when action verbs are used and at the higher IQ levels. For active sentences, therefore, the same facilitating effect of semantic kinesis can be shown in DS adults as in NR children. It may be supposed that the structural complexity of the passive not only makes problems of comprehension for DS subjects, but also blocks potentially facilitating semantic actionality effects.[4]

2.2.6 Pragmatics

Although formally reduced, the language of DS individuals is not devoid of communicative value as further indicated by Rondal and Lambert's study (1983) – see Table 2–2. Conversational topics are dealt with in such a way as to allow for the necessary continuity in the exchange between interlocutors. Language content is informative and new information is exchanged (Bolognini, Guidollet, Plancherel, & Bettschart, 1988). Major illocutionary types of sentences are used. Other research (e.g., Veit, Allen, & Chinsky, 1976; Bedrosian & Prutting, 1978; Berry, Pountney, & Powell, 1978; Owings & McManus, 1980) demonstrates the capacity of moderately and severely MR adults (including DS individuals) to take part efficiently in conversation with other MR persons or with NR people at least in simplified contexts (i.e., dyadic or triadic ordinary conversation in familiar settings) – another indication that pragmatic skills cannot be analyzed and described without reference to context (Bates, 1976). In experimental settings, young adults with mild to moderate mental retardation have proved able to judge topic maintenance correctly (Oetting & Rice, 1991). MR adults exhibit similar types of conversational controls as do NR adults. Rosenberg and colleagues (Abbeduto & Rosenberg, 1980; also see Rosenberg & Abbeduto, 1986) have examined the communicative competence of moderately to mildly MR adults engaged in triadic conversation with retarded peers. The conversational turn-taking organization functions well in these subjects. They are also quite able to recognize those illocutionary acts requiring a response on the interlocutor's part from those that do not. The exchange of information is active and correctly controlled. It can be concluded that MR subjects seem to function not unlike NR people for some pragmatic aspects of language. There are limitations, however. I have already mentioned one concerning feature marking on pronouns and anaphors. Additionally, MR subjects seem to express few indirect speech acts in their conversational behaviors (Abbeduto & Rosenberg, 1980). Also they express little clarification request in uninformative extralinguistic contexts in comparison with MA-matched NR subjects (e.g., Abbeduto, Davies, Solesby, & Furman, 1991).

Younger DS subjects already make use of a variety of illocutionary devices in relating verbally to the interlocutor, as shown in the data gathered by Rondal (1978a) – see Table 2–3. Those data were obtained in free-play interactions at home with the mothers. In such situations, mothers (of MR as well as of NR children) are known to lead the interaction in asking questions and giving orders more often than the children. Similarly, studies by Leifer and Lewis (1984) and Scherer and Owings (1984) demonstrate nontrivial conversational capacities and an ability to respond correctly to simple verbal requests in DS children around 5 years CA.

Table 2–3. *Frequency (in mean percentage) of various structural types of sentences and utterances in DS children at three MLU levels*

	Children					
	DS MLU levels[a]			Normal MLU levels[a]		
Indices	1	2	3	1	2	3
1. Utterances without verb	0.87	0.76	0.58	0.90	0.74	0.55
2. Modifiers per utterance[b]	0.21	0.29	0.43	0.19	0.35	0.41
3. Declaratives	0.02	0.14	0.31	0.04	0.18	0.28
4. Imperatives	0.02	0.03	0.05	0.02	0.04	0.07
5. YES/NO questions with inversion[c]	0.00	0.00	0.00	0.00	0.00	0.01
6. YES/NO questions based on intonation	0.00	0.00	0.01	0.01	0.01	0.02
7. WH-questions	0.05	0.05	0.04	0.00	0.02	0.05
8. Total questions	0.05	0.05	0.05	0.01	0.03	0.08

[a] MLU level 1: 1.00–1.50. MLU level 2: 1.75–2.25. MLU level 3: 2.50–3.00. MLU was computed after R. Brown's rule (1973).
[b] Modifier was defined as adjective and/or adverb.
[c] Of the auxiliary verb with the subject noun phrase.
Source: After Rondal, 1978a.

2.3 Karyotype and behavioral variability

Trisomy 21 cases are usually subdivided according to three etiological subcategories: (1) standard trisomy, (2) translocation, and (3) mosaicism (Berg, 1975). In 97% of the cases (standard trisomy 21), the genetic error takes place in the ovula or the spermatozoid before syngamy or during the first cell division. All the living cells of the embryo receive three chromosome 21s. In 1% of the cases (Hamerton, Giannelli, & Polani, 1965; 2%, according to Richards, 1969), the genetic error takes place during the second or the third cell division. In those cases, the embryo develops with a mosaic of normal cells containing the regular number of 46 chromosomes and cells with three chromosome 21s. In the remaining 2% (1%?) of the cases, the additional chromosomic material is not a triplicate of chromosome 21 but a part or the totality of another chromosome (often chromosome 14 or 22). In about 66% of the translocation cases, the genetic error takes place during the formation of the ovula or the spermatozoid, or during the first division of the embryo cell. In 34% of the cases, one of the parents, although phenotypically normal in all respects, carries the translocation in his genotype.

A natural question is Does the difference in karyotype make a difference through its variations in the psychological outcomes of Down syndrome? The question was first raised by Clarke, Edwards, and Smallpiece (1961), who described a case of trisomy mosaicism in a normally intelligent girl presenting some features of the syndrome. Other reports since have explored frequency of aberrant cells and level of intelligence. Overall findings (see Gibson, 1981, for a review of the literature) suggest (1) that mosaic DS subjects are less severely retarded than translocation or standard trisomy DS subjects and (2) that translocation DS subjects display less intellectual deficit than standard trisomy DS subjects. But the extent of agreement between the studies is far from perfect.

Few specific data exist on the same problem regarding language capacities. Fishler and Koch (1991) have reported a mean IQ difference of 12 points (on Wechsler's scales) between a group of 30 persons with standard trisomy 21 (mean IQ 52, SD 14.6) and a group of mosaic DS subjects (mean IQ 64, SD 13.8). The two groups were matched for CA (between 2 and 18 years), sex, and parental socioeconomic background. As indicated by the authors, many subjects with mosaicism (but none of the regular DS subjects) showed better verbal abilities (actually receptive lexical ability, as assessed by the PPVT), and some demonstrated normal or normal like visuoperceptual skills in paper-and-pencil tasks.

2.4 Cerebral specialization

Recent research in which investigators examined cerebral specialization in individuals with DS has yielded intriguing results. Dichotic-listening studies seem to indicate that individuals with DS are more likely than those without DS to display a left-ear/right-hemisphere advantage for speech sounds. However, evidence from other experimental paradigms makes a simple model of reversed cerebral dominance in those individuals untenable (Elliott, Weeks, & Elliott, 1987). Let us consider the relevant data.

2.4.1 Reversed cerebral specialization

Over the past decade, several studies designed to examine cerebral specialization in DS individuals have been conducted using dichotic listening (e.g., Reinhart, 1976; Sommers & Starkey, 1977; Anderson, 1978; Zekulin-Hartley, 1978, 1981, 1982; Hartley, 1981; Pipe, 1983; Tannock, Kershner, & Oliver, 1984; for a detailed review of these studies, see Elliott et al., 1987). In such tasks, syllables, speech sounds, digits, or rhymed pairs of words (e.g., *goat – coat*) are presented at exactly the same time to the ears of subjects through earphones. A simple pointing response may be used to circumvent possible expressive language problems (pointing to pictures depicting the stimulus words presented along with decoys). The neural pathways from ear to brain include both ipsilateral and contralateral pathways. Consequently, the stimulus is normally "projected" to both cerebral hemispheres. However, in the competitive dichotic presentation situation, contralateral pathways prevail. In such a situation, therefore, one can attempt to investigate lateralized apprehension and processing of acoustic material. In NR people, starting around 3 years of age or even before, a right-ear advantage is usually observed, which is taken to be indicative of a left-hemispheric dominance for speech functions.[5] It would seem that this dominance is statistically more marked in males than in females (Lake & Bryden, 1976; Witelson, 1977; Bryden, 1982; Hiscock & Decter, 1988; for a full neurological analysis and biological theory of cerebral lateralization, see the review of Geschwind & Galaburda, 1985, as well as their 1984 collection of essays; for an analysis of sex differences in the brain, see the reviews by Devries, Debruin, Uylings, & Corner, 1984, and by Kimura, 1992).

Most studies with DS individuals have reported a marked tendency for a left-ear/right-hemisphere advantage for speech sound reception. In opposition, control groups of NR children and MR subjects of other etiologies than DS but comparable MAs have been shown to exhibit the expected right-ear/left-hemisphere superiority. The reversed dominance of (many) DS subjects, therefore, may not be a function of mental retardation per se but rather of the specific genetic syndrome. Two studies, however (Sommers & Starkey, 1977; Tannock et al., 1984), failed to find any clear ear asymmetry in groups of DS children and adolescents. However, upon closer examination of the data from individual subjects in the Tannock et al. study, it was revealed that the low-laterality index for the DS group on the verbal tests resulted from a clear right-ear advantage for some subjects and a clear left-ear advantage for others. Sommers and Starkey's negative data, however, remain unaccounted for.

This line of evidence is not easy to interpret as methodological objections may be raised. For example, failures to find ear asymmetries in DS subjects may be due to performance variables unrelated to cerebral specialization such as stimulus bias, that is, a tendency to report one stimulus over another, unintentional priming, and/or other listening strategies (see, e.g., Hiscock & Kinsbourne, 1980). If, for some reason, those phenomena were more prevalent among DS persons than among other individuals, then perhaps studies that fail to find ear asymmetries should be carefully scrutinized from a methodological perspective.

Although the argument continues as to whether DS individuals have a reversed hemispheric cerebral localization for speech sounds or not, it would seem sufficiently clear from the literature that contrary to other MR subjects, at least some of them and probably many do not exhibit typical right-ear/left-hemisphere dominance for speech sounds and related verbal material in tests of dichotic listening. Hartley (1982) has suggested that this situation is responsible for the performance dissociation between serial and parallel cognitive processing in DS subjects. It is known indeed that DS individuals as a group perform more poorly than other MR persons of similar MAs on tasks of vocal imitation (Mahoney, Glover, & Finger, 1981), verbal imitation (strings and sentences) (Rondal, 1980a; Rondal, Lambert, & Sohier, 1981), and auditory sequential memory (Marcell & Armstrong, 1982; see Rondal, 1977a, for other data along the same line coming from a review of studies using the Illinois Test of Psycholinguistic Abilities – ITPA – but see also Hulme & Mackenzie, 1992, for no-difference data between DS and non-DS MR subjects in auditory short-term memory – STM). Conversely, DS persons exhibit comparable or better performance than MA-matched MR subjects of other etiologies on tasks of motor imitation (Rondal, Lambert, & Sohier, 1981), visual pattern discrimination, and visuomotor tasks (Silverstein, Legutki, Friedman, & Takayama, 1982). However, Hartley's equating of serial processing with language tasks and parallel processing with non-language tasks is questionable. Linguistic processing may be as much parallel as serial and the processing of nonlinguistic information may involve similar or different but equally complex processing parameters. Regardless of the possible interest of Hartley's hypothesis, it must be kept in mind that dichotic listening is only an index of cerebral dominance for speech *receptive processing*. Other types of tasks must be considered when it comes to speech production.

2.4.2 A left-right hemisphere dissociation hypothesis

Dual-task studies supply relevant data for analyzing cerebral dominance for speech *production*. The basic premise is that when right-handed individuals are required to speak while performing a unimanual task, such as rapid finger tapping, the concurrent speech is expected to interfere more with right-hand movements than with left-hand movements (see Kinsbourne & Hiscock, 1983, for a review of corroborating studies on NR individuals). According to Kinsbourne and Hicks (1978), this is due to interference between brain centers controlling the verbal and the manual tasks: Right-hand movements are more interfered with than left-hand movements because the former are controlled by the left hemisphere, which is also in control of speech production. However, not all experts agree that evidence coming from dual-task performance is that transparent to interpret. It could also be the case that the observed interference emerges because of peripheral response competition or because of serial scheduling conflicts either central or peripheral (see Howe & Rabinowitz, 1989, for a discussion).

Harris and Gibson (1986), quoted by Elliott, Weeks, & Elliott (1987), and Elliott, Edwards, Weeks, Lindley, & Carnahan (1987) had DS and NR subjects (no detail is supplied on the matching procedure employed) perform a rapid unimanual finger-tapping task alone and while sound shadowing high-frequency words. Expectedly, NR subjects outperformed those with DS in all conditions. For both groups, however, the concurrent speech disrupted right-hand but not left-hand performance (actually, in the Elliott et al.'s study, the disruptive effect was only observed in the male subjects, suggesting the possibility that NR and DS females are less lateralized for speech production than are males).

Synthesizing the current literature, Elliott, Weeks, and Elliott (1987) tentatively proposed that most DS individuals perceive speech with their right cerebral hemisphere but depend on their left hemisphere for speech production. The same authors speculate that the language problems of DS persons may be related to a dissociation between cerebral areas responsible for speech perception and production. Such a dissociation may cause difficulties or delays of communication between functional systems that normally overlap. It could be added that if, as is currently held, the left cerebral hemisphere is primarily a sequential analyzer and if the cortical mechanisms for speech reception are located within the right hemisphere in (most or many) DS persons, certain types of function in these people are remote from the neural mechanisms best equipped to handle these functions.

Notes

1.. The differential point of view (not to be confounded with the delay-difference controversy in language development of MR children in general – see Chapter 3) was echoed again in recent papers by Fowler (1990) and Kernan (1990). I have reviewed the sources mentioned by Fowler and by Kernan, as well as a number of other sources, and could not identify clear empirical indications supporting the hypothesis of a language deficit specific to DS. It is correct to note that in many cases the phonetic (articulatory) aspects of the DS subjects' speech leave more to be desired than the speech of other MR subjects of comparative developmental levels. These differences are most probably due to a higher incidence of organic problems related to speech in DS (see later this chapter). It would perhaps also be worth checking DS subjects' ability to allocate attentional resources to phonological encoding, particularly with continuous speech and in social situations (i.e., the cognitive capacity constraint alluded to by Shriberg & Widder, 1990, in their study of the speech and prosody characteristics of MR adults). The existence of truly deviant articulatory patterns in DS, however, seems highly implausible to me. Similarly, some *quantitative* variation may exist as to other language aspects (e.g., lexicon, syntax) between DS and other MR subjects depending on the particular studies, but to the best of my knowledge, no consistent *qualitative* differential pattern has emerged. This should not be taken to suggest that there is nothing language-wise deserving peculiar attention in DS or in other syndromes conducive to mental retardation (see Rondal in press). The combination of delicate voice and articulatory problems with lexical, semantic, syntactic, and pragmatic difficulties is typical of DS. These problems *considered together* (as they have to be from a clinical point of view) may be said to be specific to DS (a sort of "systemic specificity"), but I do not see any solid basis for claiming that language is markedly more affected in DS than in other mental retardation syndromes.
2. For older NR children and older and/or mildly MR children, the relationship between lexical knowledge and MA may depend more largely on the nature of the vocabulary test. For such subjects, MA is more strongly related to knowledge of abstract relational terms (as assessed, e.g., by the Boehm Test of Basic Concepts; Boehm, 1971) than to the more simple comprehension of object and event labels (as assessed, by the PPVT) (see Miller, Chapman, & Mackenzie, 1981, and, particularly, Byrd Fazio, Johnston, & Brandl, 1992, for a discussion).
3. In this monograph, I take the expressions semantic structure(s), relational or structural meanings, and thematic relations to be equivalent. I therefore am not adopting Pinker's (1989a), Grimshaw's (1990), and Gropen, Pinker, Hollander, and Goldberg's (1991) distinctions between primitive thematic roles (as developed by Fillmore and others and discussed later in this volume) and the more recent so-called semantic structure theories envisaging verbs' meanings as multidimensional structures in which various events (e.g., notions, changes) are represented in separate but connected substructures.

4. Using the same picture-designating technique as Rondal, Cession, and Vincent (1988), Comblain (1989) confirms that DS adults, as a group, interpret reversible passive sentences with action or nonaction verbs at chance level or below. However, one aspect of Comblain's work deserves additional consideration. She presented her subjects with series of monopropositional active and passive sentences randomly mixing plausible (e.g., *Le garçon frappe la fille – The boy hits the girl*) and implausible statements (e.g., *Le vélo est détesté par le livre – The bike is hated by the book*). Treating such series of sentences, the DS adults – but not the NR adults constituting the control group – also interpreted the actives at or near chance level. This shows how relatively fragile and semanticopragmatically dependent even the linguistic treatment of simple active declarative sentences remains in DS subjects. Corresponding indications are supplied by Kernan (1990) on the basis of his experimental research on the comprehension of syntactically indicated temporal sequences (using *then*, *before*, *after*) in DS adults.

5. The left hemisphere seems to control speech in 96% of right-handed individuals. The same is true of 70% of left-handed people, while in 15% of these individuals speech is controlled by the right hemisphere, and in the remaining 15% control is bilateral. Current estimates suggest that approximately 10% of the population is left-handed (Bresson, 1991). It is better to speak of *speech* in the preceding and not of *language* (i.e., linguistic organization per se) because the verbal performances involved in dichotic-listening and dual-task studies (see later) imply no or only very little semantic, pragmatic, and or syntactic patterning. Current neuropsychological work as to hemispheric specialization for language functions points toward a heavy involvement of the left hemisphere in the processing of speech sounds and the assembly of phonemes into words, speech rhythms, the selection of word forms, and the treatment of word morphological structures, grammatical morphology, and syntax, as well as to an important participation of the right hemisphere in semantic and pragmatic processing (e.g., Eisele, 1991; Koenig, Wetzel, & Caramazza, 1992). It would also seem that the superiority of the left hemisphere is clear for maternal language in general, regardless of type of language (tone vs. nontone) (see Ke, 1992) and regardless of modality (manual vs. oral) (see Poizner, Klima, & Bellugi, 1987). In second-language learning, however, there could be more right-hemisphere processing (e.g., Genesee, Hamers, Lambert, Mononen, Seitz, & Starck, 1978).

3   Exceptional language development in mentally handicapped individuals

The preceding review of studies on language development in DS may have left the impression of a relative uniformity in the patterns of development. Indeed, research on language development in DS children has most often been conducted from an implicit theoretical stance assuming basic uniformity. Few data bear on the question of variation in language acquisition and functioning in DS subjects (see J. Miller, 1988, for a significant exception). In so doing, this subfield of psycholinguistics, as it applies to DS, mirrors the general tendencies that can be observed in developmental psycholinguistics at large. Much research on language in the NR children has been concerned with the supposedly invariable course of development, not only for particular languages, but also at a more abstract level and between languages (e.g., Slobin, 1985). A so-far limited number of studies have shown, however, that there is considerable inter- and intraindividual variation in rate or quantitative aspects of language acquisition as well as noticeable differences in patterns and/or styles of acquisition (see Peters, 1983; Goldfield & Snow, 1985; Bates, Bretherton, & Snyder, 1988; Bates & MacWhinney, 1987, for reviews and discussions). Observing and explaining variations in patterns of development is important because it may indicate the extent to which language acquisition may be constrained by a number of factors, such as the characteristics of the target language, the physical and the verbal environment in which development takes place, and of course, the child.

Due to its intrinsic robustness as a species-specific trait, language develops in a number of unfortunate cases that constitute as many natural experiments (in the sense of Bronfenbrenner, 1979) for testing hypotheses about the course of language development (see the contributions gathered by Bishop & Mogford, 1988, and by Tager-Flusberg, 1993). These hypotheses otherwise would seldom be amenable to experimental manipulation because they are unethical under normally planned conditions. Of course, one must beware of oversimplistic conclusions in interpreting natural experiments, for there are many possible – and sometimes subtle – ways in which the relevant factors, whether environmental or organic, may interact. For example, the educational experiences of the MR child may differ in several important respects from those of the NR child, beyond the intellectual limitations of the for-

19

mer. It cannot simply be assumed that the only or always major cause of abnormal development in mental retardation is the mental handicap per se.

Exceptional circumstances may provide evidence with respect to a large number of issues in language development. For example, what quality and quantity of a given language does a child need to hear to be able to develop competence in this language? Is there a critical period for first-language acquisition? Relevant here are studies of children whose verbal environment is restricted or nil. Cases where children develop language in peculiar, or despite adverse, circumstances provide interesting information relevant to the quality-quantity issue. Other possible questions are: Can language be learned by passive observation alone, or is it the child's own activity that crucially determines the course of language acquisition? What of the role of visual information in language learning? Of course, researchers have already undertaken the investigation of such and related topics (see, e.g., Landau & Gleitman, 1985; Curtiss, 1988; Mills, 1993; Mogford, 1993; and Skuse, 1993; see also later in this book).

A central question, in my view, is To what extent does language development depend on cognitive development? Such a question, to stand a chance of being answered properly, demands that the two phrases "language development" and "cognitive development" be further defined. For language development and functioning, it is necessary to distinguish, at least minimally, between several components of the linguistic system: phonetics, phonology, lexicon, semantics, pragmatics, morphology, and syntax. Additionally, there is the need to consider the possibility that language expression and language comprehension involve separate computational procedures or, minimally, are constituted along non-(completely) overlapping domains. For cognitive development and functioning, one must introduce a basic distinction between the cognitive structures together with the particular processes and mechanisms relating to them, and the contents or concepts produced by these structures.

In normal language development, aspects of phonetics, phonology, lexicon, semantics, pragmatics, morphology, and syntax are mastered over relatively short periods of time. This gives the impression that they are intimately related or that they depend on each other. In the same way, the cognitive and the linguistic structures may appear to be closely related to each other. These patterns render the distinct contributions of the various functions and subsystems more difficult to identify and assess. Exceptional (e.g., pathological) conditions bring about interesting dissociations between these functions and subsystems, and they supply a vantage point from which it is possible to understand better the functional "architecture" of the entities under study. Mental retardation is particularly interesting in this respect as it reveals, beyond the commonly observed delays in development, the existence of important dissociations between language components and some aspects of nonlinguistic cognitive functioning. Even more interesting, in the same respect, is the small series of cases of exceptional language development in MR subjects attested to in the specialized literature, to which the case of Françoise, fully described in this book, is to be added.

Assuming that pathological dissociations are indeed revealing as to the functional (and at times, the physical) organization of the language system qua language system, as is done in this book (as well as in current neuropsychological work; see, e.g., Shallice, 1988; Schwartz & Chawluck, 1990), an interesting possibility is that careful studies of individual differences in NR children (as well as adults, possibly) could demonstrate dissociable language mechanisms akin to the ones revealed by the effect of pathological factors.[1] This may be at least partially the case judging from data gathered in a number of differential studies. Basic language components can be observed to develop at different rates in different children. Comprehension-production splits exist within the domains of lexicon and grammar. However, Bates et al. (1988) claim that individual differences largely cut across assumed boundaries between grammatical and lexical components.[2] It could perhaps be argued, therefore, that pathology does not actually (only) reveal dissociations but largely creates them and, consequently, that the dissociations documented in pathological cases are of limited relevance for theories about nonpathological language. This would seem to be the interpretation favored by Bates et al. (1988) when they suggest that their and others' differential observations are supportive of a "unified approach" to language development. I, on the contrary, would maintain that normal language has the general effect (or may largely be defined as the effect) of "holding tight" the several language components with the consequence that they appear more united than they are in reality. In other words, these components interact in normal functioning, but they are not unified. Examining the normal differential data in language development supplied by Bates et al. and others (e.g., Nelson's, 1973, seminal contribution in this respect), I have the impression that these data could easily be summarized according to a (admittedly, somewhat schematic) binary distinction between the analytic and the non- (or less-) analytic. Roughly put, one seems to have – from the beginning or very early in development – on the one side, more analysis-oriented children presenting a so-called referential style (i.e., vocabularies with a high proportion of common object names, more use of adjectives later on, greater variety and flexibility within lexical categories, and a lesser propensity toward imitation) and on the other side, less analysis-oriented children exhibiting an "expressive" style (i.e., more heterogeneous vocabulary, a greater propensity toward imitation leading to the inclusion of more formulaic expressions in their productions). Regarding phonology, the referential-style children appear to focus more than the expressive-style children on speech segmentation, breaking out the lexical units into syllabic and phonemic units, and building them up gradually into lexical forms. The expressive-style children seem to concentrate more on prosody and intonation both at the word and at the utterance levels. Syntactically, the referential children (or formerly so) tend to exhibit a particular early grammatical style, labeled nominal style (Bloom, Lightbown, & Hood, 1975), consisting in forming multiword constructions composed primarily of nouns and other major category words. This gives their productions a sort of "telegraphic" character (R. Brown, 1973). In contrast, the expressive children (or formerly so) tend to demonstrate a so-called pronominal style, that is, multiword constructions in which the meaning is realized with nonspecific pronominal forms. Eventually (between 2 and 3 years), however, and happily for them, all the children develop the whole language system, therefore paying more attention later on to those aspects that they had tended to neglect or to use less earlier in development.

A number of language dimensions appear to be sensitive to variables such as cognitive style (see Wardell & Royce, 1978; and Huteau, 1987, on cognitive styles; see Tourrette, 1991, for an extensive analysis of the relationships between language and cognitive style). A cognitive style favoring a more analytic approach of reality versus a more relational one (a parameter entering in the composition of the field dependency factor according to Wardell & Royce's and Huteau's theoretical analyses) could be expected to lead to a referential-nominal approach in early language acquisition. A more relational approach (as part of a cognitive style characterized by a greater field dependency) would induce an expressive-pronominal strategic approach in early language acquisition (and, most likely, not the reverse, i.e., a type of language approach ulteriorly inducing general field dependency/independency, as – in my view, erroneously – suggested by Reuchlin & Bacher, 1989, p. 64). By definition, the effects of the cognitive styles may be expected to cut across the boundaries to the language components (as a cognitive style qua cognitive style must express itself across various sectors of personality and mental functions), yielding the picture interpreted by Bates et al. (1988) as supporting a unified approach to language development. My view is that Bates et al. mistakenly confound two sets of different indications: the effects of cognitive style on language development (and, possibly, language functioning if, as suggested by differentialists such as Tourrette, 1991, and Reuchlin & Bacher, 1989, stable individual differences in language were to be demonstrated as holding beyond the developmental period) and the functional architecture of the language system. Nontrivial qualitative individual differences in language development and in language functioning may probably be expected also in pathological cases "over and above" the dissociations between language components brought to light by pathological processes. Or, more exactly, individual differences can probably be demonstrated in MR and other pathological cases within the various components of the language system (as already said, this has been little undertaken so far, but most people in these fields would expect it to be true, I believe), and, yet, these components may prove to be significantly dissociated from each other, revealing the basic functional architecture of the language system. What I am suggesting is that individual differences and (pathological) dissociations may not be at the same level. The components of the language system may be relatively autonomous. That does not prevent them from being the object of noticeable individual differences (inter- as well, possibly, as intraindividual). The pathological dissociative observations relate to the former point, and they, probably genuinely, contribute to revealing the functional organization of the system. Cognitive styles, likely to induce differential approaches to language acquisition and perhaps to overall language functioning, relate to the latter point.

The proper way of conceiving of these two aspects of the problem may be according to a set-subset relationship. The stylistic variations reported so far in the differential studies on language acquisition therefore may not be entirely relevant to the specification of the functional organization of the language system. More relevant in this respect perhaps might be studies more concerned with finely assessing individual quantitative and rate variations (developmental and/or otherwise) within different components and functions of language in normal people. Such studies could reveal moderate but significant functional dissociations and developmental dyssynchronies interpretable along the same lines as the pathological dissociations.

In the rest of the chapter, I will summarize the available information on several exceptional cases of language development in MR subjects (the full analysis of Françoise's case is presented in Chapter 5) and present some preliminary conclusions. I will also show, in reviewing the relevant literature, that dissociative tendencies corresponding to the dissociations exemplified in the language of the exceptional MR subjects exist in the language development and functioning of language-wise nonexceptional MR subjects.[3]

3.1 Exceptional written language development in Down syndrome

Seagoe (1965) has documented higher than average written verbal development in a DS person (Paul), IQ about 60. Paul kept a diary from age 11 to 43. Seagoe does not report the etiological subcategory of DS. The diagnosis was reached by the family physician during the first year of life. Paul made no attempt to walk until he was more than 2 years of age and to speak until after he was 6. He had all the physical signs of DS and Paul was kept in the community (he lived with his family) until he was 43, at which time residential placement was made. He died at the age of 47. At the request of the parents, private tutors taught the boy to speak, write, and read. Seagoe's report is primarily about Paul's written language capacity. She does not supply any detailed information on the child's oral language capacity except that his level could be compared with that of a normally developing 5-year-old, admittedly an above-average achievement for a DS person. Nevertheless, a careful examination of the written material produced by Paul supplies interesting information on his grammatical abilities. The boy's reading instruction began at 6 years 9 months, first with teaching him to speak understandably, then to read and write by the kinesthetic method developed by Fernald and Keller (1936), basically an analytic method associating specific motor expressive movements with the various phoneme–grapheme links. By the age of 8, Paul was beginning to read, recognizing over 200 words. At

Table 3–1. *Statistical analysis of 10 diary entries per year*

Analytical categories	Subject's CA									
	13	15	17	19	21	24	26	33	37	41
1. Total words per entry	14.9	33.7	36.8	35.5	66.4	68.1	72.9	42.1	40.8	27.7
2. Different words per entry	8.9	16.0	17.5	17.4	35.2	24.0	30.9	21.0	21.9	16.1
3. Verbs per entry	2.7	5.2	5.0	4.8	7.5	9.7	10.5	6.2	2.3	0.6
4. Verb/adjective ratio	0.73	1.13	0.66	0.61	0.61	0.88	1.01	1.24	1.15	0.29
5. First-person pronoun per entry	1.8	5.0	4.0	4.0	1.1	7.7	1.9	1.2	.00	.00
6. Average words per sentence	6.25	7.14	8.33	7.14	12.50	6.25	6.25	7.62	4.17	4.76
7. Flesch Readability Index	95.9	84.8	87.0	89.1	55.5	93.4	99.3	98.8	57.2	30.3

Source: Modified after Seagoe, 1965.

14, reading achievement was above 3rd-grade level. On residential placement, when he was beginning to show mental deterioration, his grade placement on the Wide Range Achievement Test in word reading was still 7.8. In arithmetic, at the same testing, his grade placement was only 1.2. (Unfortunately no comparative indications are supplied by Seagoe.)

Paul's educational environment was truly exceptional (especially for the time). He was fully accepted as a functioning part of all the activities of his family, including frequent travels. A tutor was available to him on a 24-hour basis. Speaking, as well as reading and writing instruction, was always built around his abilities and rewarded. By the age of 11, he was keeping a record of his travels and continued to do so until he was 43. Seagoe's report contains 10 randomly selected entries of the diary from age 13 to 41. Table 3–1 summarizes the data supplied by Seagoe for the written material analyzed.

The records for ages 13 to 41 show the rise to the age of maturity (circa 25 years) and the decrease later in life with the sharp decline at age 41. The increase and decrease in verbal output, diversity of vocabulary, use of verbs and adjectives, and words per sentence (except for the peak at 21 years for this latter indication) all reflect this process. Seagoe (1965) also computed a text readability index, labeled Flesch Readability Index (apparently varying from at least 30 to 100; she does not supply any information or reference on this index). The index is particularly high when Paul was 13 years old and later between 24 and 33 years.

Seagoe's article contains several excerpts of Paul's diary. I have reproduced one such excerpt here. It was written at age 21.

Last night we took the sleeper for Polish frontier. The countryside from Moscow to Polish frontier enroute to Warsaw is like a neglected cemetery. The houses are tumbling down and little agricultural activity. This cold morning it was not uncommon sight to see peasants and their children bare-footed and with overcoats on. Women wait on and cook food in railroad depots. The general employment of women in manual work is to let men enter the enormous Russian military services.

Just before we reached the frontier we saw a large military stockhouse. Pop removed his Russian diary notes from my book to avoid trouble at the border, which was lucky as diary was inspected entering Poland. The Polish officers confiscated Pop's Soviet paper translated in English. Passing from Russia to Poland the countryside is at once changed to a beautifully cultivated farmland. The trains are far superior and the train crews consisting of men is a striking contrast. We crossed the large river Vistula into Warsaw.

The text sounds rather "normal." Seagoe does not report whether Paul's writing, as it appears in the article, was corrected for spelling and/or edited in any other way. I am not particularly concerned with Paul's orthographic capacity. Rather I am examining his text to find testimony of his alleged well-developed linguistic capability. This excerpt is conventionally segmentated into 12 sentences. The MLU (computed according to R. Brown's rules) varies from 9 to 30 with a mean of 16.75, which by all standards is quite remarkable even knowing that written speech tends to be longer than oral speech (assuming, of course, that one possesses the necessary skills to make it longer). Several sentences are composed of coordinated or subordinated clauses. Few syntactic errors are committed (e.g., in the 3rd sentence, the second clause is clearly incomplete). The lexicon displayed is also remarkable with the correct use of words that are not commonplace in English (e.g., *to confiscate, contrast*). From this excerpt and others of the same linguistic caliber supplied by Seagoe, it may be suggested that Paul's linguistic capability was well developed and close to normal, regardless of whatever expressive speech problems he might have had. The linguistic level reached is truly exceptional for a DS person. The only explanation for this achievement provided by Seagoe is the highly stimulating familial environment. We do not know unfortunately how Paul's linguistic skills developed after he started to speak (i.e., later than 6 years). Was his development relatively rapid within a period of 2 or 3 years or did he demonstrate gradual progress between 6 and 13 years (the time at which we have the diary data demonstrating an already well-organized language). No answer is available to these questions.

3.2 Hyperlinguistic mentally retarded adolescents with Williams syndrome

Bellugi, Marks, Bihrle, and Sabo (1988) have documented the cases of three adolescents with Williams syndrome (two girls, Van and Crystal; one boy, Ben) exhibiting unusual linguistic capabilities for their level of mental retardation. They were aged 11, 15, and 16 years, respectively, at the time of the study. People with Williams syndrome suffer from supravalvular aortic stenosis (a narrowing of the aorta) in association with mental retardation and a peculiar facial appearance (starlike pattern in the iris, medial eyebrow flare, depressed nasal bridge with anteverted nares). The unusual command of language combined with an open, gentle manner had already been noted by Von Armin and Engel (1964). It was confirmed in a report by Meyerson and Frank (1987). Bellugi and her team extensively analyzed the linguistic, metalinguistic, and cognitive abilities of three Williams syndrome subjects. The subjects' full-scale IQ scores Wechsler Intelligence Scale for Children (WISC) varied between 49 and 54. On a number of tasks assumed to measure cognitive growth, as viewed within a Piagetian framework (e.g., seriation, classification, conservation), they clearly demonstrated preoperational functioning. On tasks of drawing, spatial orientation, spatial transformation, and spatial arrangements, the subjects' scores were uniformly depressed, at the level of normal 5-year-olds or below (with strikingly preserved subabilities, however, such as copying geometric figures, and recognizing and discriminating unfamiliar faces presented in different orientations). On the language side, the three Williams syndrome adolescents demonstrated impressive abilities, receptive as well as productive, although not quite at CA levels. Their MLUs (computed according to R. Brown's rules, 1973) varied from 8.6 to 13.1. Their language productions included full passives, embedded relative clauses, a range of conditionals, and multiple embeddings. The syntax was correct although there were occasional errors of overgeneralization of morphology and pronoun usage. One peculiar facet of the Williams syndrome children's language ability seems to be the use of unusual vocabulary items. Bellugi et al. (1988) noted the appropriate use of low-frequency words such as *surrender*, *sauté*, *nontoxic*, *commentator* (p. 182). These lexical and morphosyntactic observations made through the analysis of the free conversational speech of the three subjects were corroborated by the results of the application of several tests of receptive language (PPVT-Revised, Clinical Evaluation of Language Functions, Test for Reception of Grammar; no reference supplied for the last two tests). The subjects demonstrated comprehension of full reversible passives, affirmative and negative comparative and equative relational expressions, and other complex linguistic structures. Receptive vocabulary was evaluated at the 9- to 12-year level, depending on the particular subject. On the productive side, a sentence completion test (adapted from Bellugi, 1968) was used. On this test, subjects are given a set of incomplete sentences that they are to complete appropriately when provided with a picture stimulus. The majority of errors were at the phrasal level and included absence or incorrect use of grammatical markers (e.g., omitted possessive marker, incorrect tense marking) or incorrect choice of lexical items (predominantly incorrect pronoun usage).

The subjects were also asked to detect and correct linguistic anomalies requiring (at least) an implicit knowledge of the constraints determining semantic appropriateness and syntactic well-formedness (so-called grammaticality judgments). A test adapted from Linebarger, Schwartz, and Saffran (1983b) was used. The sentences proposed were ungrammatical due to violations of subcategorization features, phrase structure rules, and errors in reflexive pronoun usage (e.g., violations of coreferential agreement in number, gender, and/or person). The three Williams syndrome adolescents proved perfectly able not only to detect but also to correct the ungrammatical sentences, confirming quite a sophisticated grammatical capacity.

3.3 Hydrocephalic mentally retarded subjects with exceptional language capabilities

Other interesting data and analyses confirm the indication that grammar can be acquired in spite of severely impaired general cognitive development. Cromer (1987) quotes from an older study by Hadenius, Hagberg, Hyttnas-Bensch, and Sjogren (1962), reporting on six hydrocephalic children in whom mental retardation was observed associated with "a good ability to learn words, articulate, talk, and not knowing much what they are talking about." These authors coined the expression "cocktail-party syndrome" for describing this condition. Other studies have supplied additional information on this so-called syndrome also named "chatter-box syndrome." Swisher and Pinsker (1971) studied 11 children, ranging in age from 3 years 2 months to 7 years 10 months, with spina bifida and history of hydrocephalus. Their language was compared with that of a group of children matched for age, physical handicap (congenital), and time spent in hospitals. The hydrocephalic children used more words and initiated more speech than did the control group. Anderson and Spain (1977) report a study of 145 spina bifida children at 6 years of age. Among these, 40% showed the hyperverbal characteristics mentioned in previous studies, although only half of them exhibited it to an important degree. These subjects were typically female, had lower IQs, and presented considerably higher verbal than performance skills. They used complex syntax but often semantically inaccurately. They also produced a much higher rate of ready-made or "cliché" phrases than a group of NR children matched for verbal IQ on the Wechsler Preschool and Primary Scale of Intelligence (WPPSI) test. Tew (1979) compared a group of spina bifida children exhibiting the cocktail-party syndrome with other spina bifida children who did not. The children judged to be hyperverbal also had lower IQs than the other spina bifida childen. They exhibited fluent speech coupled with poor understanding.

Cromer (1988) mentions several other studies on MR hydrocephalic children and adolescents, a number of whom also evidence the feature of possessing quite complex productive language and fluent speech coupled with limited understanding. Cromer (1991) reports his personal study of D.H., a spina bifida adolescent girl with arrested hydrocephalus, exhibiting chatterbox syndrome.[4] D.H. performs at the severely retarded level on standardized tests of intellectual ability (i.e., performance IQ below 35). She has been unable to learn to read and write, and she cannot handle money properly. In contrast, her speech is correctly articulated and fluent. Her language is meaningful with extensive vocabulary, and it incorporates the normal use of pragmatic devices. D.H.'s language contains complex syntactic forms, such as elaborated noun phrases and verb phrases, conditionals, complex subordinate, and embedded clauses. Judging from the limited excerpt of conversational speech supplied by Cromer (1991), D.H.'s use of grammatical morphology would appear to be correct. Also, she gave current evidence of understanding the contents of conversation and was quite able to monitor and follow its course in dyadic situations. This would seem to indicate that contrary to previous reports on other hydrocephalic MR subjects, D.H. understood what she was talking about as well as what was conveyed to her by others in regular conversations. Unfortunately, Cromer does not supply the outcome of any formal test of language comprehension conducted with D.H. to substantiate the impression from conversation.

A somewhat different but also exceptional case of hydrocephalus with mild to moderate mental retardation is reported by O'Connor and Hermelin (1991). The subject, Christopher, a man of 29 years, had a performance IQ of 67 and a verbal IQ of 102 on the Wechsler Adult Intelligence Scale (WAIS). This discrepancy between the two partial IQs was due, in part, to his very poor block design and object assembly subscores, signaling important problems in spatial cognition. Christopher exhibited a good level of ability to translate into English, from three languages, French, German, and Spanish, and to express himself in these languages (although to a different degree depending on the particular language). His comprehension of the lexicon and the morphosyntactic structures of the three languages also appeared to be quite satisfactory. For example, Christopher's "lexical IQs" obtained on the PPVT in English, and on German, French, and Spanish translations of the PPVT, were 121, 114, 110, and 89, respectively.

3.4 Hyperlinguistic mentally retarded subjects from other etiologies

Curtiss and associates (Curtiss, Fromkin, & Yamada, 1979; Curtiss, 1981, 1982, 1988, 1989; Curtiss, Kempler, & Yamada, 1981; Curtiss & Yamada, 1981; Yamada, 1981, 1983, 1990) have reported on the study of three language-exceptional MR subjects [a boy child named Antony and two adolescents: one girl, Marta (real name Laura, as she is referred to in Yamada's book, 1990; in what follows, following Yamada, I will call her Laura), and one boy, Rick]. Rick suffered severe anoxia at birth. In the other two cases, mental retardation is of unknown etiology.

Antony was 6 to 7 years at the time of the study. His IQ was estimated to be about 50. At CA 5 years 6 months, his estimated MA was 2 years 9 months. His logical sequencing (ordering pictures representing familiar events) was at the 2-year-old level. His hierarchical construction (constructive praxis), as well as his classification skills, were below the 2-year-old level. His logical conservation level could not be assessed. The parents reported onset of speech at 1 year and full sentences at 3 years in spite of many developmental delays in other areas. Antony's language is described by Curtiss as "well formed phonologically and syntactically and [was] structurally rich . . . fully elaborated with inflectional and derivational bound morphology and 'free' grammatical morphemes, and it included syntactic structures involving movement, embedding, and complementation" (Curtiss, 1988, p. 374). In contrast to this remarkable morphosyntactic ability, Antony's language was semantically deficient. He tended to use words incorrectly and, when requested to define them, incompletely and sometimes inaccurately. This, at times, resulted in miscommunications with others. It is to be noted, as specified by Curtiss (1988), that

notably, none of Antony's lexical errors involved violations of syntactic class, subcategorization features, grammatical case, or word order. Almost all of his errors were in semantic feature specification. Errors with lexical substantives involved confusions or inadequate definitional differentiation between words within a particular semantic area (e.g., 'birthday' for 'cake', 'cutting' for 'pasting'). Errors with prepositions were in marking direction, location or semantic case, or function (e.g., 'to' for 'from', 'in' for 'with'). Pronoun errors concerned in gender or animacy (e.g., 'who' for 'what', 'that' for 'he'). At times, Antony exploited his grammatical knowledge to compensate for his deficient lexicon, creating a different kind of error. These errors involved creating nouns from verbs in his vocabulary for words that already have a derivationally simple noun form (e.g., 'sweeper' for 'broom', 'sewing' for 'spool'). These latter errors reveal a productive knowledge of derivational morphology and the syntactic class such morphology creates. (p. 374)

Antony's language was also deficient in terms of content. He is reported as frequently failing to grasp the full meaning of his own and others' utterances. On the pragmatic and discursive sides, Curtiss (1981, 1982, 1988) reports that Antony had mastered a wide range of basic pragmatic functions and communicative intentions (e.g., turn taking, requesting, commenting, responding to requests and questions), using the proper language means to these effects. However, he had poorly developed topic maintenance skills, was only moderately sensitive to the interest of his interlocutors, and was apparently only little concerned with the need to be relevant or informative in conversation (see Grice's maxims; Grice, 1975).

Rick was a 15-year-old at the time of the study (IQ not reported). His language was quite parallel to that of Antony. He had well-developed phonological, morphological, and syntactic abilities, alongside poorly developed lexical and semantic abilities. Rick was extremely social and he made appropriate use of social routines and other conventionalized conversational forms. However, his semantic deficiencies much reduced the efficiency of his propositional communications, since he often had difficulties in correctly understanding the meaning of the utterances addressed to him and often made mistakes in the meaning aspects of his lexical and propositional realizations. Rick's nonlanguage performance profile also was similar to that of Antony. His classification abilities were those of children aged 2 to 3 years. His seriation skills also were clearly preoperational. His drawing and copying abilities were prerepresentational, corresponding to an early preschool level.

Laura's case is documented in several publications by Curtiss (e.g., 1988), and it is the topic of a monograph by Yamada (1990). She was studied for several years from the time she was 16 years old. In addition, her parents supplied written documentation on Laura's early development. At 14 years 9 months, her full-scale IQ estimate was 41, her performance IQ 32, and her verbal IQ 52. Laura was developmentally delayed from birth on, including speech and language. From the age of 4 to 5 years, however, language could easily be identified as her area of greatest strength. Overall Laura's linguistic profile is similar to those of Antony and Rick, with the proviso that her lexicon was richer, in particular containing more quantifiers and adverbs. Laura's level on the PPVT was estimated to be 6 years 1 month. But despite her larger vocabulary, Laura presented semantic deficiencies akin to those of Antony and Rick. The same was basically true for her pragmatic and discursive organizations. However, her language was phonologically correct, fully elaborated morphologically, and contained complex and well-formed syntactic structures. For example, she used truncated and full passives, sentences with coordinated and subordinated clauses, including WH-relatives, multiple embeddings, infinitival complements, and complements containing participial forms. Laura was also perfectly able to use elliptical utterances, confirming her sophisticated productive grammatical abilities.

Receptively, however, the picture was different. In addition to her previously mentioned semantic deficiencies, Laura seemed to demonstrate genuine grammatical difficulties in comprehension. She was given the Curtiss-Yamada Comprehensive Language Evaluation (CYCLE, 1992). Her receptive performance on the CYCLE battery of syntax was poor. She performed at or below the 2-year-old level on most subtests, including the object manipulation version of various tests (e.g., active voice word order, passive voice word order, WH-questioning of grammatical subject and object, relativization tests). In her spontaneous speech, Laura produced many of the structures that she failed to understand on the comprehension tests. In some cases, Laura proved able to understand syntactic structures in conversational context but did poorly on the corresponding formal receptive tests. Of course, in current conversation, the availability of semantic and extralinguistic cues probably considerably helped her. Yamada (1990) reports that she tried to reduce the conceptual and the nonlinguistic demands of the test tasks in several ways, but that Laura still performed poorly. Yamada (1990) concludes, "It seemed clear that her production exceeded her comprehension, accounting in part for the non-sensical quality of many of her utterances" (p. 144, N. 2). Laura was also given the Token Test (De Renzi & Vignolo, 1962). This test evaluates the ability to understand sentences of varying syntactic complexity. She also performed poorly on this test, scoring 17 out of a total of 39, which is below the mean score of normal children aged 3 years 6 months (i.e., 19.55).

Laura's comprehension of grammatical morphemes likewise was reduced. On the CYCLE battery of morphology, she demonstrated mastery over only two grammatical morphemes (i.e., tense/aspect marker -*ing* and comparative -*er*). Her results indicated that her receptive knowledge of the grammatical forms was reduced. Again, it is remarkable that she spontaneously and correctly used some of the same forms in her speech. Moreover she could detect and correct surface syntactic and morphological errors in imitation tasks, therefore demonstrating at least minimal capacity for

grammatically judging forms that she could be proved not to (completely) understand. For example, when given an ungrammatical sentence such as *She wear his
shirt*, Laura would readily amend it into its correct form. However, she would score
only 20% correct comprehension on the part of the CYCLE morphological comprehension subtest concerned with third-person singular marking on main verbs.

On a dichotic-listening task, Laura exhibited a great deal of difficulty, but her performance was consistent in demonstrating a slight right-ear advantage, which, as
indicated in the preceding chapter, suggests left-hemisphere dominance for receptive
language processing.

As with Antony and Rick, Laura's nonlinguistic performance showed marked dissociations between her grammatical performance and domains of general knowledge. She lacked the concept of number and could not even correctly apply basic
counting principles to concrete objects. Her drawing and copying were at the preschool level. Her reasoning (assessed in Piagetian seriation, classification, and conservation tasks) was clearly at the preoperational level. She proved unable to order
pictures into logical sequences. Finally, her hierarchical construction capacity
(praxis) was estimated to be at the 2-year-old level.

3.5 Dissociative tendencies in the language of typical mentally retarded subjects

A large number of data also exist that show delays in some aspects of language
development in typical moderately and severely MR children that are greater than
those that would be predicted on the basis of MA. This has been referred to, in the
specialized literature, as the MA lag, and it pertains to the so-called delay-difference
question in discussions of language development in MR children (adapting from the
general theoretical framework set by Zigler, 1966, and N. Ellis, 1963, in mental
retardation; see Rondal, 1980b, for a discussion; also see Hodapp & Zigler, 1990, for
an updating). I have reviewed and discussed these (language) studies in much detail
elsewhere (Rondal, 1984, 1985a, 1988a; for other reviews and discussions much
along the same line as mine, see Cromer, 1988, 1991). It will be sufficient for the
present argument to reproduce an up-to-date tabular summary of my reviews (Table
3–2) and to comment on the major outcomes of the studies from the present point of
view. The interested reader can consult the original sources for additional information.

As the data in Table 3–2 indicate, basic lexical, semantic-structural, and pragmatic
developments in MR children seem to follow with increasing MA or MLU. One of
the very few discrepancies reported in the studies between MA-matched MR and NR
children concerns word definition (a metalinguistic activity). In Papania's study
(1954), MR children of varied etiology were observed to produce fewer abstract and
more concrete word definitions than did MA-matched NR children.[5] However, the
MR subjects present delays and deficiencies in the phonological, grammatical-mor-

Table 3–2. *Data on the delay-difference issue in moderately and severely mentally retarded children*

Item	Linguistic aspect	Study	Matching variable	Subjects' CA in years (unless otherwise indicated)	Expression (E) or comprehension (C)	Etiology of retardation	Major result
Babbling and phonological development							
1.	Characteristic sounds of babbling; phonetic patterns and sequences of development	Dodd (1972)	CA	1	E	V	—
		Smith & Oller (1981)	CA	0–2	E	V	—
2.	Phonological aspects of (meaningful) speech (phoneme substitutions and approximations in the articulation of k,f, and Θ)	Smith & Oller (1981)	CA	2–5	E	DS	—
3.	Frequency of phonological errors made in picture naming and in elicited imitation	Dodd (1976)	MA	6–15	E	V	NR>MR
4.	Acoustical clarity and intelligibility of speech	Ryan (1975)	MLU	5–19	E	V	NR>MR
		Rondal (1978a)	MLU	3–12	E	DS	NR>DS
Lexical development							
5.	Producing and understanding common object and action words	Lyle (1961)	MA	6–13	E; C	V	—
6.	Understanding spatial words (e.g., *big, long, in, on, under*)	Cook (1977)	MA	3–6	C	DS	—
7.	Understanding lexical items on the Carrow Auditory Test of Language Comprehension (Carrow, 1973)	Bartel, Bryen, & Keehn (1973)	MA	9–13	C	V	—

32

#	Skill	Study		Age			Result
8.	Basic Vocabulary	Mein & O'Connor (1960)	MA	10–30	E	V	—
		Beier, Starkweather, & Lambert (1969)	MA	11–24	E	V	—
		Lozar, Wepman, & Hass (1972)	MA	5–15	E	V	—
9.	Word definition	Papania (1954)	MA	9–16	E	V	NR>MR
10.	Responses on word association and word generalization tasks	Sersen, Astrup, Floistad, & Wortis (1970)	MA	2–14	E	V	—
		O'Connor & Hermelin (1959)	MA	9–16	E	V	—
		O'Connor & Hermelin (1963)	MA	10–20	E	V	—
11.	Type-token ratio (index of lexical diversity of speech)	Rondal (1978a)	MLU	3–12	E	DS	DS>NR
		Harris (1983)	MLU	2–6	E	DS	DS>NR
		Miller, Chapman, & Mackensie (1981)	MA	1–7	E	V	MR>NR
12.	Diversity of noun vocabulary	Ryan (1975)	MLU	5–9	E	V	MR>NR
13.	Beginning of word comprehension (familiar words of nursery rhymes)	Glenn & Cunningham (1982)	MA	9–15 months	C	DS	—

continued

33

Table 3–2. (cont.)

Item	Linguistic aspect	Study	Matching variable	Subjects' CA in years (unless otherwise indicated)	Expression (E) or comprehension (C)	Etiology of retardation	Major result
14.	Object name vocabularies	Cardoso-Martins, Mervis, & Mervis (1985)	MA	17–37 months	E; C	DS	—
15.	Vocabulary size	Dooley (1976)	MLU	3–5	E	DS	—
Semantic-structural development							
16.	Frequency and type of basic semantic relations	Buium, Rynders, & Turnure (1974)	MLU	4	E	DS	—
		Rondal (1978a)	MLU	3–12	E	DS	—
		Coggins (1979)	MLU	1–6	E	DS	—
		Dooley (1976)	MLU	2–5	E	DS	—
		Layton & Sharifi (1979)	MLU	7–2	E	DS	—
17.	Comprehension of basic semantic relations	Duchan & Erickson (1976)	MLU	4–8	C	V	—
Grammatical-morphological development							
18.	Use of familiar English inflections as assessed by the subtest Auditory-Vocal Automatic or Grammatical Closure of the Illinois Test of Psycholinguistic Abilities	Mueller & Weaver (1964)	MA	10–16	E	V	NR>MR
		Bateman & Whetherell (1965)	MA	6–12	E	V	NR>MR
		Bilovsky & Share (1965)	MA	9–16	E	DS	NR>DS

34

continued

No.	Description	Reference	Measure	Age	Type	Comparison	Result
19.	Omission, substitution, and incorrect generalization of grammatical inflections in free conversational speech	Ryan (1975)	MLU	5–10	E	V	—

Syntactic development

No.	Description	Reference	Measure	Age	Type	Comparison	Result
20.	Change in relative proportions of types of words produced at early stages of language development	Mein (1961)	CA	3–7	E	V	—
21.	Progression through various stages of early language development (mostly babble, mostly words, primitive phrases, and sentences) with increasing CA	Lenneberg, Nichols, & Rosenberger (1964)	CA	3–22	E; C	DS	—
22.	Progressive use of imperative, affirmative and negative active declarative, and interrogative sentences with increasing MA	Lackner (1968)	MA	2–9	E	V	—
		Gordon & Panagos (1976)	MA	3–5	E	DS	—
23.	Rank ordering of syntactic difficulties in a sentence comprehension task	Mittler (1970)	MA	8–12	C	V	—
		Wheldall (1976)	EPPVT	9–15	C	V	—
24.	Comprehension of grammatical words, gender and number agreement, and double object construction	Semmel & Dolley (1970)	CA	6–14	C	DS	NR>DS
		Bartel, Bryen, & Keehn (1973)	MA	9–13	C	V	NR>MR

35

Table 3–2. (cont.)

Item	Linguistic aspect	Study	Matching variable	Subjects' CA in years (unless otherwise indicated)	Expression (E) or comprehension (C)	Etiology of retardation	Major result
25.	Comprehension of affirmative active declarative sentences	Semmel & Dolley (1970)	CA	6–14	C	DS	—
26.	Comprehension of passive declarative sentences	Semmel & Dolley (1970)	CA	6–14	C	DS	NR>DS
27.	Comprehension of affirmative active declarative sentences including *ing* forms and possessive constructions	Dewart (1979)	CA	7–18	C	O	—
		Chipman (1979)	CA	8–15	C	O	—
		Berry (1972)	EPPVT	10–16	C	V	—
28.	Comprehension of temporal clauses and temporal relationships between clauses	Barblan & Chipman (1978)	MA	6–10	C	V	NR>MR
29.	Upper bound (i.e., longest utterance in a corpus of speech)	Rondal (1978a)	MLU	3–12	E	DS	—
30.	Number of modifiers per utterance	Rondal (1978a)	MLU	3–12	E	DS	—
31.	Incidence of utterances without verb	Rondal (1978a)	MLU	3–12	E	DS	—
32.	Productivity (number of words and utterances produced in a corpus of speech obtained in a given period of time)	Rondal (1978a)	MLU	3–12	E	DS	—
33.	Proportions of imperative, declarative, wh-interrogative, and yes-no interrogative sentences in a corpus of speech	Rondal (1978c)	MLU	3–12	E	DS	—

34.	Proportion of complete and incomplete sentences	Ryan (1975)	MLU	5–9	E	V	—
35.	Proportion of so-called *cliché* and *readymade* utterances	Ryan (1975)	MLU	5–9	E	V	—
36.	Range and variety verb transformations	Ryan (1975)	MLU	5–9	E	V	—
37.	Word order	Ryan (1975)	MLU	5–9	E	V	—
38.	Word order in early combinatorial speech	Dale (1977)	MLU	4–6	E	DS	—
39.	Strategies used to identify agents and objects in basic strings received (chance performance first, semantic-lexical strategies second, and responses based on word order third)	Dale (1977)	MLU	4–6	C	DS	—
40.	Reversal of order of subject and copula or auxiliary verb *be* in interrogative sentences (Lee's Developmental Sentence Scoring Procedure, 1975)	Rondal (1978b)	MLU	5–12	E	DS	NR>DS
41.	Frequency of use of elementary main verbs (i.e., uninflected verbs like *I see you*, copula like *it's red*, *is* + verb + *ing* like *He is coming*, *can*, *will*, *may* + verb like *I can go*) (Developmental Sentence Scoring Procedure)	Rondal (1978b)	MLU	5–12	E	DS	DS>NR

continued

Table 3–2. *(cont.)*

Item	Linguistic aspect	Study	Matching variable	Subjects' CA in years (unless otherwise indicated)	Expression (E) or comprehension (C)	Etiology of retardation	Major result
42.	Frequency of use of secondary verbs (i.e., complementing infinitives like *I wanna see, I'm gonna see*, noncomplementing infinitives like *I stopped to play*, complementing present and past participles like *I see a boy running, I found the toy broken*) (Developmental Sentence Scoring Procedure)	Rondal (1978b)	MLU	5–12	E	DS	NR>DS
43.	Proportion of sentences that are grammatically correct in every respect (Developmental Sentence Scoring Procedure)	Rondal (1978b)	MLU	5–12	E	DS	DS>NR
44.	Frequency and type of indefinite pronouns (Developmental Sentence Scoring Procedure)	Rondal (1978b)	MLU	5–12	E	DS	NR>DS
45.	Developmental level of personal pronouns used (Developmental Sentence Scoring Procedure)	Dale (1977)	MLU	4–6	E	DS	NR>DS
46.	Proportion of erroneous but progressive forms (e.g., *I want go*)	Dale (1977)	MLU	4–6	E	DS	NR>DS

Pragmatic development

47.	Illocutionary devices	Rondal (1978a)	MLU	3–12	E	DS	—
48.	Conversational skills	Leifer & Lewis (1984)	CA	18–23 months		DS	NR>DS
			MLU	3–5		DS	DS>NR
			– double matching procedure –				
49.	Nonverbal response to action requests	Scherer & Owings (1984)	MLU	5–7		DS	—
50.	Production of clarification requests in uninformative extralinguistic contexts	Abbeduto, Davies, Solesby, & Furman (1991)	MA	9–10	E	O	NR>MR

Note: CA, chronological age; MA, mental age; MLU, mean length of utterances (in number of words plus grammatical morphemes); EPPVT, English Peabody Picture Vocabulary Test; V, mentally retarded subjects of various etiologies including Down syndrome; DS, Down syndrome subjects; O, mentally retarded subjects of other etiology(ies) than Down syndrome; — indicates no significant difference between MR and NR subjects; $x > y$ indicates significant difference in favor of x, where x and y are NR, MR, or DS subjects; the asterisk (e.g., item 46) indicates that the utterance is ungrammatical.

Source: Modified and updated after Rondal, 1984.

phological, and syntactic organization of language that go beyond what can be predicted on an MA or MLU basis. They lag behind MA- or MLU-matched NR children in aspects of phonological development and as to the correct use of grammatical morphemes (although, in this latter respect, free speech can mask deficiencies demonstrated on the formal tests, as Ryan's observations suggest; Ryan, 1975). In (early) syntactic development, the general sequences (e.g., progression through various substages of language development, rank ordering of syntactic difficulties) seem to be similar in MR and in NR children (if one disregards, of course, the marked delays of the former). No or little difference appears in the simplest aspects of sentence comprehension and expression (see items 20, 25, 27, 29, 30, 31, 32, 37, 38, and 39, in Table 3–2). However, at corresponding MA or MLU levels, MR subjects present significant differences in more sophisticated aspects of the syntactic treatment and the syntactic patterning of language (e.g., comprehension of function words, gender and number agreement, double-object construction, passive comprehension, comprehension of temporal clauses and temporal relationship between clauses, reversal of order of subject and copula or auxiliary *be* in interrogative sentences, frequency and developmental level of personal and indefinite pronouns produced; see items 24, 26, 28, and 40–6, in Table 3–2).[6]

From the preceding data, it can be concluded that if the general language problems of MR subjects reflect their cognitive limitations, general cognitive level per se (as captured in the MA measures) is no satisfactory explanation for language development and functioning in these subjects when it comes to "advanced" phonological, grammatical-morphological, and syntactic aspects of language. It is my opinion that these discrepancies in the typical MR subjects between components of the language system, and between general cognitive level and the phonological and the grammatical aspects of language, reveal the same basic dissociative trends as those neatly exemplified in the exceptional cases of language development in MR subjects reviewed in the preceding sections. (The only and quite interesting difference between the two sets of observations is that with respect to the relationship between language and general cognition the dissociations go in opposite directions for the typical and the exceptional MR subjects: The former have lower phonological and grammatical levels from what can be expected on an MA or MLU basis; the converse is true for the latter.)

A part of these indications begs the question of the exact relationship (particularly development-wise) between MA (CA) and MLU in MR (as well as in NR) subjects. Miller and Chapman (1981; see also J. Miller, 1981) have studied the relationship between children's CA and MLU in a sample of 123 NR middle- to upper-middle-class children aged 1 year and 5 months to 4 years and 11 months (MLU range 1 to 5). A significant correlation ($r = .88$) was found between CA and MLU. CA accounted for 77% of the variance in MLU. It was observed that MLU increased at an average rate of 1.2 morphemes per year, with variability also increasing in MLU with age. De Villiers and De Villiers (1973) have reported a Pearson product-moment correlation of .78 (significant at the .001 level) between CA and MLU in a sample of 21 NR children aged 16 to 40 months (MLU range 1 to 4). Rondal, Ghiotto, Brédart, and Bachelet (1987) also computed a Pearson product-moment correlation to measure the degree of linear relationship between the child's CA and MLU in a sample of 21 American-English-speaking NR children (8 girls; 13 boys) ranging in age from 1 year and 8 months to 2 years and 8 months (MLU range 1 to 3). The correlation coefficient reached .75 and was statistically significant. Since, by definition, in NR children, MA is equal to or close to CA, it follows that the evolution in MA is closely associated with the gradual increase in utterance length in young children. The same was found to be true for 21 DS subjects aged 3 to 12 years CA with MLUs between 1 and 3.50 words plus grammatical morphemes (Pearson product-moment correlation between CA and MLU was .87, significant at the .001 level; see Rondal, Ghiotto, Brédart, and Bachelet, 1988). These correlations justify the use of studies having employed MA and MLU matching procedures (see Table 3–2) in the preceding discussion on the dissociative trends in the language development and functioning of regular MR subjects. However, interpretation of these correlations needs two major caveats in considering the relationships between MA-CA and MLU in more general terms and in specifying further the significance of MLU measures for language development.

First, the correlation coefficients just reported relate to relatively large MLU ranges covering extended periods of development and therefore necessarily involving somewhat developmentally heterogeneous subjects. This favors obtaining larger correlation coefficients, for statistical reasons, as is known. If one restricts age and MLU range, the group becomes less heterogeneous, the variance decreases, and consequently, the magnitude of the resulting correlation may decrease. For this reason, and to ascertain more precisely the statistical association between age and MLU, Rondal et al. (1987) computed Pearson product-moment correlations for subsamples of the group of NR children previously referred to. A tendency for the coefficients of correlation to decrease as a result of restricting MLU range was indeed observed. For MLUs between 1 and 2 (12 subjects; age range 20 to 28 months), the r (age/MLU) was .62 (significant at the $p < .05$ level). For MLUs between 1.50 and 2.50 (10 subjects; age range 20 to 29 months), the r (age/MLU) was .78 ($p < .001$). And for MLUs between 2 and 3 (9 subjects; age range 26 to 32 months), the r (age/MLU) was .37 (nonsignificant). Klee and Fitzgerald (1985) have also reported a Pearson product-moment correlation for NR children between MLU 2.50 and 4 (18 subjects; age range 25 to 47 months) amounting to .26 (nonsignificant). Corresponding observations were made by Rondal et al. (1988) with subsamples of DS children. Between MLU 1 and 2 (12 subjects; CA range 36 to 120 months), the r (CA/MLU) was .81 ($p < .001$). Between MLU 1.50 and 2.50 (8 subjects; CA range 46 to 124 months), the r (CA/MLU) was .78 ($p < .02$). And between MLU 2 and 3.50 (9 subjects; CA range 78 to 144 months), the r (CA/MLU) was .004 (nonsignificant). These subsample correlational data indicate that age and MLU are significantly related up to MLU 2.00, approximately, in NR as well as in MR children. In the latter subjects, MA, by definition, is a fraction of CA (at IQ 50, or so, this fraction is often considered to be approximately one-half in younger MR children, changing to one-third, one-fourth, and less with increasing CA, which reflects the progressively growing discrepancy between MA and CA along the time dimension) (Zeaman & House, 1962, once proposed that MA is proportional to logarithm CA in DS subjects; the equation MA = 18 × logCA works reasonably well from CA 6 years on). MA as a reflection of general mental level of development (albeit a rough and imperfect one, since there are many different psychometric ways to obtain the same MA given that it is a composite measure; see Baumeister, 1967, for a discussion) is only related to early combinatorial language development, likely indicating that the child has matured up to a level where he can form sequential associations, use language formulas (see Peters, 1983) that he has heard many times, and express elementary predicate-argument structures in simple terms. There is no contradiction between the MA-MLU relationship, as observed and as just discussed, and the autonomy of (advanced) grammatical development and functioning from general cognitive development and functioning, attested in the language-exceptional cases reported in preceding sections (nor in the corresponding dissociative trends observed in regular mental retardation).[7]

Second, MLU is a reliable and valid measure of morphosyntactic development only within narrow developmental boundaries. Putting together Klee and Fitzgerald's (1985) and Rondal et al.'s (1987) data, it may be suggested that utterance length is a valid predictor of morphosyntactic complexity [estimated with reference to the Language Assessment, Remediation and Screening Procedure (LARSP) analytical technique developed by Crystal, 1979, in these two studies] up to approximately MLU 3.00. Beyond that stage (and already noted by R. Brown, 1973), prediction of grammatical development and syntactic complexity from utterance length is limited since the children are increasingly able to make constructions of a greater variety that are not always or not directly reflected in an increase in utterance length. MLU remains valid, as an index, only for those few aspects of grammatical development that are most directly tied to utterance lengthening, like the use of bound morphemes and clausal connectives. As to (intrasample) MLU variability, it is relatively small between MLU 1 and 2. It grows moderately between MLU 2 and 3. Beyond MLU 3 and particularly 3.50, the variability is larger and may be considered to be less acceptable from a measurement point of view (Klee & Fitzgerald, 1985; Rondal et al., 1987). Similar conclusions were reached by Rondal, Ghiotto, Brédart, and Bachelet (1988) regarding the measure of MR (DS) children's language development in terms of utterance length.

Briefly touching on the so-called delay-difference question in the language development of MR children (see Mittler, 1972; Yoder & Miller, 1972; Rosenberg, 1982; Rondal, 1984, 1987, for analyses and discussions bearing on this general problem), that is, roughly stated, the question of whether language development in MR subjects is "simply" delayed and quantitatively different or whether it is qualitatively different from language development in NR children, the resulting picture, as may be expected from what precedes, is complex. A strict delay position captures only the most trivial aspects of the developmental language problem of MR, including DS, children. Language development in the retarded is not a slow motion picture of the same development in NR children, even if it is correct to say that lexical, semantic, and pragmatic developments regularly follow with the evolution in MA and that the sequences in the acquisition of elementary aspects of phonological, morphological, and syntactic structures seem to be the same as in NR children. However, differences exist in several aspects of language, particularly in grammar, with the gradual unfolding of the acquisition process in MR and NR children. These differences seem to deepen with time and with the various developmental plateaus affecting the course of language development in MR children (see Fowler, 1988, 1990) until this development, yet incomplete in many respects, comes to a stop. In view of this and as argued in more detail in Rondal (1988a), it may be suggested that the delay-difference framework is not appropriate for characterizing language development in the retarded (for a corresponding point of view, see Kamhi & Masterson, 1989). A strict delay-difference dichotomy may even be largely misleading. There are indications in the literature (e.g., Wishart & Duffy, 1990) that the same conclusion applies to cognitive development in the mentally retarded as well.

3.6 Conclusions

The data summarized in this chapter are illustrative of the existence of interesting dissociations in language organization and between language and nonlanguage cognition. A first dissociation to consider is the one between so-called *computational*[8] (i.e., phonological and grammatical) aspects of language and general cognition and cognitive development, whereas so-called *conceptual* (i.e., lexical, semantic-structural, and pragmatic) aspects of language are much more in line with cognitive development and functioning. The existence of a dissociation between computational aspects of language and nonlinguistic cognitive functioning is well demonstrated in the exceptional cases of language development reported in MR subjects. It is also exemplified, in my opinion, in the discrepancies documented in regular MR subjects between MA or MLU levels and levels of phonological and overall grammatical functioning (in the reverse direction from the one in language-exceptional mental retardation, since regular MR subjects tend to exhibit grammatical regulations that are significantly lower than what can be expected on an MA or MLU basis). A corresponding dissociation between computational aspects of language and cognitive functioning is also obvious in another category of children, not studied here, but analyzed in the specialized literature, that is, children with specific language impairment (SLI), sometimes labeled developmental dysphasia. For careful and extensive studies of the phonological and grammatical problems of SLI children particularly with respect to English and Italian, see the work of Leonard and associates (Leonard & Brown, 1984; Leonard, 1985, 1989, 1992; Leonard, Schwartz, Swanson, & Frome Loeb, 1987; Leonard, Sabbadini, Volterra, & Leonard, 1988; Leonard, Bortolini, Caselli, McGregor, & Sabbadini, 1992; Leonard, Bortolini, Caselli, & Sabbadini, 1992). For German, and with particular respect to morphological and syntactic problems, see the analysis of Clahsen (1989). For French, see Gerard's synthesis (1991). The SLI children, by definition, have normal or normallike nonverbal intellectual capacities. There is no reason, therefore, to believe that their grammatical impairment is secondary to conceptual deficit (Gopnik, 1990; Marshall, 1990). In the next chapter, I will return to the cognition-language issue and analyze it more extensively.

A second type of dissociation, particularly clearly observed in the Curtiss-Yamada cases, as well as in a number of the hydrocephalic MR subjects with exceptional language capabilities (but not all; e.g., apparently not with Cromer's D.H. or with O'Connor & Hermelin's Christopher), is between expressive and receptive aspects of language. Antony and Rick, two of the language-exceptional subjects studied by Curtiss and associates, presented comprehension difficulties due to their lexical and semantic problems (as well as attentional and other cognitive limitations). Laura, the language-exceptional subject studied by Curtiss and by Yamada, presented the clearer dissociation between language expression and language comprehension capabilities. In addition to semantic (but not lexical) difficulties of the same basic type as those of Antony and Rick, Laura exhibited what seemed to be true receptive grammatical problems, finding herself in the curious situation of failing to completely understand grammatical-morphological and syntactic structures that she could correctly express and about which she could detect and correct surface errors in an imitation task. Cases such as these, particularly Laura's, are indicative of the depth of the dissociation that may exist between components of the language system in their expressive and receptive aspects. Some time ago, Chomsky (1966), paraphrasing a passage from von Humboldt (1836/1960), asserted that language perception requires that the same generative system be put in action as in language expression (language expression and language reception are but modulated expressions of the same "linguistic dynamism" – in von Humboldt's terms adapted for English). I am not aware that he (Chomsky) has changed his mind in any basic way on the problem since the sixties. However, cases such as Laura make one appreciate the differences existing, besides likely common factors, in language expression and comprehension. From there, it would not be too farfetched to seriously consider a hypothesis stating that there may exist more duplication of subsystems and procedural knowledge across expressive and receptive language functions than has been contemplated most often.[9]

A third type or subtype of dissociation is between particular components of the language system. Regrouping language components in two series or aspects (i.e., computational and conceptual),[10] as previously suggested, is a descriptive maneuver simply intended to do justice to the empirical fact that different components of the language system relate in different ways to nonlanguage cognition (the conceptual system). It does not purport to mean that the computational components, on the one side, and the conceptual components, on the other side, have compulsory intricate relationships in and between themselves. Indeed, numerous observations go against such an indication. For example, casual observation of NR children and adults show that motor phonetic and grammatical abilities are independent of each other. It is well known that some persons, although exhibiting excellent grammatical competence, have functional or organic articulation difficulties. Stuttering or stammering may coexist with intact linguistic function. Anarthria, in its pure form, seemingly may occur without any other language pathology in people with particular cerebral lesions (Hecaen & Albert, 1978). Conversely, aphasias witness important comprehension and production difficulties involving grammatical problems, without (major) articulatory problems (including in children; Van Hout, 1991).

The relationship between grammar and semantics is complex and calls for additional specification. Roeper (1987a, 1987b; Finer & Roeper, 1989) (based on Chomsky, 1981, 1982, 1986a) argues that the definition of semantic categories (e.g., agent) must originally be linked to two different parts of the mind: an inference (i.e., cognitive) system and a syntactic system. He claims that the cognitive definition "covers too much territory" (1987a, p. 324) and must be restricted linguistically. According to Roeper's proposal, there are "duplicate" formal notions of the cognitive categories, and they constitute the semantic basis of language. For agency, for example, there is a cognitive agent and a linguistic agent. The latter has three main features (a cognitive agent, a verb, and an affix – *er*, like, e.g., in *robber*). Such a view implies that the simple cognition of, say, agency, in the world of experience, is not sufficient for establishing the role of agent in a grammar. One has to assume the presence of a universal grammar (UG, see Chapter 4) containing the features necessary for defining linguistic-semantic roles. Equipped with such a set of instructions, the child has to search for a cue – for example, the presence of an affix indicating that linguistic-thematic roles are present. As indicated before, regular MR subjects develop basic semantic relational structures in proportion with their MLU evolution and in the absence of obvious difficulties in this respect, in spite of the fact that their grammatical development is very slow and quite restricted. It should be questioned, however, whether they have mastered the thematic roles in a true linguistic sense (i.e., including their reflection in morphology and syntax). No clear data exist on this question in the literature to the best of my knowledge. It might be important, therefore, with these subjects especially, to distinguish the semantic (propositional) status of the thematic roles from their *theta* status (see Chapter 4).

In my opinion, semantic propositional knowledge is best considered as being constructed on the basis of a common world experience (cognitive categories), an utterance context, and the meaning of individual words (see Slobin, 1977; Pinker, 1987). In other words, there exist cognitive categories and "purely" semantic categories. The latter are reworked through the operations of the grammatical system referring to them in ways that may be those indicated by Roeper and Chomsky. But semantic categories exist in themselves and may probably sustain some elementary combinatorial language production and reception. They may be affected separately from the grammatical processes in pathological cases. Semantic categories also are distinct from corresponding cognitive categories from which they develop, as neuropsychological data demonstrate. For example, Caplan and Hildebrandt (1988) report cases of aphasic patients demonstrating severe problems in the encoding and the decoding of thematic roles (notions of agent, instrument, goal, etc.) and no evidence for dissolution of the underlying conceptual relations themselves.[11]

The existence of dissociations between grammatical and pragmatic competence is attested to in the cases of Antony, Rick, and Laura. Such dissociations are not unheard of in the domain of specific language impairment either (see McTear & Conti-Ramsden, 1992). John, a possible case of "minimal cerebral dysfunction" reported by Blank, Gessner, and Esposito (1978), illustrates the further possibility of a dissociation between semantics and pragmatics. This subject demonstrated age-appropriate language functioning in terms of grammar and semantics (he was 3 years and 3 months old at the time of study). But he was little able to use these systems in interpersonal communication. He could not answer questions with relevant statements or follow on the interlocutor's discourse in regular conversations. His attempts at initiating verbal exchanges were bizarre and mostly devoid of the usual pragmatic conventions. Corresponding dissociations between grammatical and semantic/pragmatic abilities have often been reported of young schizophrenic and autistic children. Features of "noncommunicative language" in these subjects were already signaled by Kanner (1943). Such children (when they do develop combinatorial language beyond rudimentary stages, which is not the case for the majority of them; see Leblanc & Page, 1989) are characterized as using a mixture of grammatical utterances, jargon with neologisms, nongrammatical fragments, and verbatim imitations or echolalia (e.g., Despert, 1968; Shapiro, Roberts, & Fish, 1970; Fay, 1993). Their difficulties with the appropriate use of personal pronouns and, more generally, with deictics have often been noted (e.g., Fay & Schuler, 1980; Rosenbaum & Sonne, 1986). It seems generally accepted that autism involves a primary deficit in pragmatics (Tager-Flusberg, 1981, 1985), which may be related to a corresponding deficiency in nonverbal communication (Fay & Schuler, 1980). However, the difficulties of these subjects with relational meanings should not be underestimated (see Menyuk & Quill, 1985). Moreover, it might be the case that for those autistic children who develop expressive language to a certain extent, the expressive ability is comparatively better than the comprehension one, for reasons that may not be truly linguistic but may have to do particularly with the poor processing capacity of these children when it comes to rapidly presented multilevel information (Lord, 1985).

The theoretical status of the language dissociations mentioned and documented in the preceding pages has not been fully established yet. Assuming that the language faculty corresponds to a modular or a "modular-like type of organization," what type of modularity theory should one contemplate? A beginning toward an answer to this difficult question is available in the next chapter, where Fodor's explicit theory of modules (Fodor, 1983) is presented together with additional theoretical considerations, and in Chapter 6, where the neuropathological literature on language modularity is reviewed and alternative theoretical presentations to that of Fodor are considered. But first, it is necessary to have a look at some major theoretical points of view on the relationship between cognition and language, and on language development.

Notes

1. Such a possibility is rejected by Fodor (1983), who argues that modules or "vertical faculties of the mind [see my Chapter 4] are to be inferred from the discovery of competences that are relatively invariant across subject populations" (p. 20). Differences between individuals are not likely to reveal interesting things about the organization of mental abilities, *unless those individuals have suffered some kind of brain damage*. It is correct to specify, however, that Fodor does not reject the possibility that developmental asynchronies between aspects of language acquisition in NR children can provide evidence regarding dissociable language mechanisms. He does claim that individual differences of the sort described by Bates, Nelson, and others would not provide evidence for dissociations.

2. Bates et al. (1988) find no evidence for a neat division between grammar and lexicon at the earliest stages of language development, up through 2½ years of age (the upper limit in their study). But, as this will be documented later in this chapter and later in the book, the major dissociations between grammar and lexical semantics (expectedly) become more visible at more advanced stages of grammatical patterning.

3. Throughout the book, I will refer to these subjects as (language-wise) nonexceptional, with regular or standard mental retardation.

4. The report, unfortunately, is only a short summary of the case published after Richard Cromer's untimely death in June 1990. Another paper (Cromer, 1993) does not contain more specific information on this case.

5. As also indicated in Table 3–2, MR children – including DS children – use a more diversified set of vocabulary terms (e.g., as measured by the TTR index) or a more diversified noun vocabulary than MLU- or MA-matched NR children. One possible explanation (already suggested in Rondal, 1978a), adapted from Kohlberg (1968) to language development, is that "general life" experience plays an important role in lexical use. This would appear to be consistent with current work on the nature of lexical knowledge and word meaning in NR children (e.g., Carey, 1985; Keil, 1989). MR children may be more advanced in some aspects of lexical development than their MLU- or MA-matched NR peers, because they have lived longer and experienced more even if with limited cognitive means. The same type of tentative explanation can be advanced for Leifer and Lewis's observation (1984) that DS children have more advanced conversational skills (early in development) than their MLU-matched NR peers. [See McTear & Conti-Ramsden, 1992, for a corresponding suggestion to explain observations – e.g., Meline, 1986, – showing pragmatic skills such as encoding new information or referential communication being superior in SLI (specific language impairment) children to those of language-matched normal peers.] Sometimes, it is even possible to observe MR children and adolescents exhibiting better lexical abilities than MA-matched (necessarily younger) NR children. See, e.g., a recent study by Facon and Bollengier (1991) with French-speaking MA-matched NR and MR subjects (MA: 5 years; CA: 10 and 15 years, for two groups of MR subjects, respectively) demonstrating significantly higher scores on the Receptive Vocabulary Test of Legé and Dague (1974) – the French equivalent of the PPVT – in MR subjects (and, additionally, significantly higher scores in the older MR group than in the younger MR one), but not on Raven's Progressive Matrices (Raven, 1981). Life experience and the like presumably may compensate, or sometimes more than compensate, for intellectual limitations in MR subjects when it comes to tasks that are particularly sensitive to the influence of environmental factors, such as referential lexical activity, but not to more remote ones, such as reasoning on abstract spatial stimuli.

6. The results reported under items 41 and 43, which may appear to be in contradiction with the interpretation offered, actually are in line with the argument. DS children matched for MLU with younger NR children use significantly more elementary main verbs (according to the definition of the Developmental Sentence Scoring – DSS – Procedure of Lee, 1975) but significantly less secondary verbs (DSS; item 42 in Table 3–2). In the same way, the former children spontaneously produce significantly larger proportions of sentences that "are grammatically correct in every respect" (DSS); correspondingly, they produce significantly smaller proportions of "erroneous but progressive forms" (as reported by Dale (1977) – item 46 in Table 3–2. Summing up these observations, it can be suggested that MR (DS) subjects are taking fewer "syntactic risks" than NR children at corresponding levels of productive language development and that they tend to rely more on simpler formulaic expressions.

7. There is no contradiction between the suggested autonomy of grammatical development and the sometimes observed relationship between IQ (a global, composite, and rough index of mental capacity) and (global aspects of) combinatorial language development. It is well known that the subjects' language capacity decreases with a corresponding decrease in IQ (from psychometric normality to mild, moderate/severe, and profound mental retardation). Not surprisingly Lenneberg et al. (1964) and Fowler (1988), for example, report that MR subjects with higher IQs seem to develop slightly better language-wise [in terms of MLU values, in Fowler's study; in terms of localization in a global characterization of types of utterances produced (e.g., mostly words, primitive phrases) in Lenneberg et al.'s study]. Both studies suggest an IQ cutoff of 50 or so to explain differences of language levels achieved by DS subjects. Such indications solely attest to the global influence of the general level of mental efficiency on language development. This influence most likely is mediated through the semantic component of language, but it can be blocked by the existence of grammatical deficiencies (as illustrated in Rondal, Cession, & Vincent's experiment, 1988, with actional and nonactional active and passive sentences in DS adult subjects; see Chapter 2). Also, quite clearly, the limited influence of the IQ variable on grammar is illustrated by the exceptional cases of grammatical development in MR subjects presented earlier in this chapter, as well as by the corresponding case of Françoise to come.

8. I am using Chomsky's distinction (1980) between "interacting but distinct" (p. 54) computational and conceptual aspects of the language system. Chomsky (1980) writes: "We might discover that the computational aspect of language and the conceptual system are quite differently represented in the mind and brain, and perhaps that the latter should not strictly speaking be assigned to the language faculty at all but rather considered as part of some other faculty that provides 'common sense understanding' of the world in which we live . . . . The two systems interact. Thus certain expressions of the linguistic system are linked to elements of the conceptual system and perhaps rules of the linguistic system refer to thematic relations. But it nevertheless might be correct, in a fuller theory of the mind, to distinguish these systems much as we distinguish the visual and circulatory system, though of course they interact. The conceptual system, for example, might have a central role in all sorts of mental acts and processes in which language plays no significant part, might have a different physical basis and different evolutionary history and so on" (p. 55). Actually, as this quotation illustrates, Chomsky speaks of the conceptual system and not of conceptual aspects of language. It is probably permissible to speak of conceptual aspects of language in a Chomskyan line. The expression may have two "topological" senses. Either the conceptual aspects of language are located at the intersection of two distinguishable sets, the linguistic system and the conceptual system, or the linguistic system is to be considered as split between two subsystems, the computational and the conceptual ones. The first solution is unlikely as it would amount to confounding semantics with cognition and, therefore, to undermining the notion of "language faculty," which Chomsky continues to use [e.g., Chomsky, 1988; although, at times, with some reservations, e.g., Chomsky, 1979, 1984); these reservations have mostly to do with the notion of "language," which Chomsky finds very vague indeed. He probably has more in mind a notion such as "grammar (in the strict sense) faculty" when he writes, for example, "Languages are not characteristics of people, grammars are" (1984, p. 29)]. Also, Chomsky (1980) does not explicitly list the pragmatic organization among the conceptual aspects of language as I have done (see also Bickerton, 1984, p. 187). It is questionable (but this is an empirical question) whether pragmatic competence should best be considered a part of the conceptual system (since it very likely contains sets of constitutive rules) or whether it is a truly distinct language component underlying the ability to use *both* grammatical and conceptual knowledge to achieve communicative and social purposes (as Chomsky also seems to suggest; 1980, p. 59). In this book, I have kept with the inclusion of pragmatics into the conceptual aspects of language. This tentative position may have to be revised with further empirical work and theoretical progress in characterizing more coherently the so-far somewhat scattered domain of pragmatics (assuming that it can be meaningfully unified).

9. One could argue that since true comprehension requires computing a semantic interpretation/representation mapped to the syntactic structural representation, an impaired semantics – especially one involving deficiencies in above word-level semantic structure – could result in the kinds of comprehension difficulties that Laura displays. Production, in contrast, would "look fine" since it allows for well-formed phonology, syntax, and morphology coupled with an anomalous (but invisible) semantic representation. If this were the case, it seems to me that Antony and Rick, who have serious lexical and semantic difficulties, should also display receptive grammatical problems, which is not observed. It could perhaps also be argued that as Laura's auditory-verbal short-term memory span is makedly deficient (she has a span of three items; see Chapter 6, for more detail), this might be sufficient to cause apparent comprehension-production discrepancies. But, again, Antony and Rick also have severely limited short-term memory spans (containing about four items). However, they do not exhibit comprehension difficulties akin to those of Laura. Moreover, as will be documented later (Chapters 5 and 6), Françoise, the exceptional DS subject studied here, also has a short-term memory span of four items together with a remarkably preserved receptive grammatical capacity.

10. One may wonder why Chomsky has described them the way he did. I have not found any full terminological specification on this point in Chomsky's writings. Visuals theorists use the term "computation" to imply that the brain acts "to form a symbolic representation of the visual world, with a mapping (in the mathematical sense) of certain aspects of that world onto elements in the brain" (Crick & Koch, 1992, p. 54). Perhaps (likely, in my view) the term *computational* in language is to be linked to such terms as *generative* and *generate* (i.e., *explicit* and *make explicit*; Chomsky, 1986b). The idea probably is that systems of rules may be constructed and used mentally (and, secondarily, be given mathematical or formal descriptions) that explicitly (and separately) account for the derivation of phonomorphological and morphosyntactic structures from their respective underlying forms or, in other words, that particular calculations are effected on the grammatical mental representations at various levels from deep to surface structure. [A confirmation of this may be found in Gil, 1987, n. 54, quoting from a private exchange with Chomsky, who is reported to have stated, "It has always been assumed in generative grammar . . . that the theory of grammar and its mental representation involves some elements of mathematics. That's central to the whole approach to the language faculty as a system of rules and representations, a computational system of some sort" (p. 139).] The regrouping of other language components under the denomination of "conceptual aspects" denotes the fact that they are more in relation with the conceptual systems of the mind. They might enter into extragrammatical logical structures.

11. Finer and Roeper (1989) recognize that cognitive and thematic notions are distinct and that both are necessary. At times, their formulation, it seems to me, may appear to allow for the existence of the three types of representations that, I have argued, the logic of the system as well as the observed pathological dissociations demand, i.e., cognitive categories, semantic ("nonsyntactic") categories, and thematic relations that are given a syntactic form. They state, "A cognitive notion can enter into the definitions of a word without becoming a part of the thematic grid associated with that word" (p. 206). But I may be misinterpreting their statement. Pinker (1989a) clearly states that semantic structures constitute an autonomous level of linguistic representation not reducible either to syntax or to cognition. He stresses that the lexical representations governing the applicability of argument rules are neither syntactic nor conceptual (since each language selects for linguistic encoding only some among several possible idealizations from conceptual knowledge).

4   Cognition-language relationships and modularity issues

The nature of the relationship between language and thought has been of interest to philosophers, psychologists, and linguists for a long time. One will recall the position identified in recent times as the Whorfian hypothesis, associated with the names of Sapir (1921) and Whorf (1956). According to this position, and roughly put, the language that we speak directly affects the way we think.[1] Over the years, the Whorfian hypothesis has taken two basic forms. The stronger form asserts that the categories and boundaries of language determine the categories and boundaries of perception and cognition. Consequently, people speaking unrelated languages should perceive and conceive the world in different ways. The weaker form posits that language orients our thinking in certain directions but does not actually force our thoughts to take specific forms. The Whorfian hypothesis has generated a great deal of research over the past decades in anthropological, linguistic, and psychological circles, leading to the conclusion that only its weaker form is at least partially acceptable (see R. Brown, 1968; see Bloom, 1981, for a different point of view, and R. Brown, 1986, for a reply). But even this weaker form did not go unchallenged. The opposite viewpoint, that thought processes are ontogenetically prior to language and that they constitute developmental prerequisites for language development, has found a grounding in the work of Piaget and followers. I will not consider here in detail the Vygotsky-Luria position on the problem because it pertains more particularly to the role of language and language representations in cognitive development and functioning. Suffice it to say that, for Vygotsky, language and thought processes are ontogenetically distinct until approximately 3 years of age, at which time they gradually fuse into each other, rendering speech "rational" and thought largely, if not completely, verbal (inner speech and covert mental representational mechanisms) (see Vygotsky, 1929/1962; Luria, 1958, 1961, 1978; and Sokolov, 1972, for clear presentations of the main thrust of this position). It is debatable whether Vygotsky's point of view differs fundamentally (and if yes to what extent) from the Whorfian hypothesis. The two positions are historically and epistemologically unrelated, but they are in opposition to Piaget's cognitive developmental theory (see Payne, 1968; Wozniak, 1972; and Rondal, 1975b, for presentations and discussions of the philo-

51

sophical foundations of traditional Russian psychology). But as will be seen later, the theories of Whorf, Vygotsky, and Piaget, all are in opposition with the more recent modular conceptions that claim a much larger autonomy for (at least some of) the components of language.

4.1 Piagetian and other "cognition drives grammar" hypotheses

4.1.1 Piaget's conception of the relationship between language and cognition, or to use his preferred terms, between language and intellectual operations – a (partial) modern version of Aristotle's and other Greek philosophers' so-called analogist position – is explicated in several books and articles (see, e.g., Flavell, 1963; Furth, 1969; Piaget, 1968, 1970, 1976; Sinclair, 1973; and Bronckart, 1977; for detailed presentations). Perhaps the most explicit statement on the question is found in a paper that Piaget (1963) prepared for a symposium on problems of psycholinguistics, held in 1962, under the auspices of the Association de Psychologie Scientifique de Langue Française. The paper was later translated by Hans Furth and included in his excellent book *Piaget and knowledge* (1969). In this article, Piaget reminds the reader that he had once been a strong believer in the existence of close relations between language and thought, and that he studied almost nothing but verbal thought (see Piaget, 1923) until he discovered the existence of so-called sensorimotor intelligence. It is this latter system of action schemes prefiguring aspects of the structures of classes and relations that actually supplies the ontological source of intellectual operations (Piaget, 1930, 1936, 1979a; Inhelder, 1976). Consequently, and in principle, language cannot be a sufficient condition for the formation of intellectual operations.

Piaget further argues that language can not even be considered as a necessary condition for the formation of these operations. He concedes, however, that it may be a necessary condition for the achievement of intellectual operations at the advanced level of formal or propositional structures (reached at adolescence). To set it briefly, intellectual operations, insofar as they result from the interiorization of actions and from their coordination, remain for a long developmental time relatively independent of language (Piaget, 1936). Conversely, it is language that depends on intellectual development for its ontogenetic evolution. The capacity to represent, it is claimed, depends on the same knowledge structure permitting the construction of the known object. Representative capacity gradually emerges in the second half of the sensorimotor period (12 to 18 months). It manifests itself, first, in the symbolic play and mental imagery of the child. Language is also the product of this general representational function. "Consequently," lexical, semantic, and grammatical developments are largely dependent on cognitive development. It may be useful to recall here the basic distinction between the cognitive structures and processes that underlie our specific thoughts, and the contents or concepts of these thoughts. Most people agree that language encodes particular cognitive concepts, and this is not controversial. The nature of conceptual representations is controversial, however (see Scholnicks's 1983 chapter and edited book); but that is another problem. Keeping with the present topic, Piagetian hypothesis posits not only that language is dependent on thought for its meaning contents, but also that particular (nonlinguistic) cognitive structures and processes are directly involved in the acquisition and the functioning of the whole language system, including the grammatical subsystem. In other terms, Piaget insists that grammar is not autonomous and that the general conceptual system underlies the computational as much as the conceptual aspects of language.[2] It should be noted that Piaget has never made clear exactly which conceptual structures and processes would determine grammatical development and functioning. (Some of his followers have attempted to do that, e.g., Sinclair, Ferreiro; see later.) At times, even his theoretical proposals are somewhat confusing as he seems to suggest that both operational and language-grammar developments are reflections of a third factor, for example, common "psychobiological" principles such as logico-mathematical or "reflecting" abstraction (*abstraction réfléchissante*), constructive generalization (*généralisation constructive*), and equilibration (see, e.g., Piaget, 1979b), the exact theoretical status (and actually the specific meaning) of which has remained something of a mystery.

Empirical studies with normally developing children conducted within the Piagetian tradition or outside of it have yielded little firm support for Piaget's position on the cognition-language issue, despite occasional affirmations to the contrary. Not surprisingly, general mental and intellectual development precedes or is contemporaneous with early lexical and semantic developments. Children's holophrases, for example, entail meanings that seem to correspond to what Piaget (1945) calls "action schemes, either pertaining to the subject or partially objectified." Sinclair (1970, 1973) and Edwards (1973) proposed analyses showing that basic relational semantic categories present interesting convergences with more complex action schemes developed by children in the course of the later sensorimotor (intellectual) period. It may be that the action schemes constitute a part of the common world knowledge on the basis of which semantic structures may be considered to be created, as indicated in the preceding chapter. Other work conducted in the Piagetian line convincingly demonstrates that a number of specific notions have to be mastered or, at least, to be in the process of being mastered for the child to appropriately use the linguistic structures involving these contentive aspects. For example, Ferreiro's work (1971) shows that children make progress in the understanding of temporal clauses in proportion with their cognitive evolution. Particularly, they have difficulty in decoding temporal clauses in which the presented order of the events does not match the order of the events in reality (so-called noncanonical temporal clauses; e.g., *Before having breakfast he shaved* vs. *He shaved before having breakfast*). Bronckart (1976) showed that the first temporal inflexions in children mostly have an aspectual meaning rather than a genuinely temporal one. Related to this observation may be the fact that in cognitive development the child first concentrates, so to speak, on the states and the results of the actions before being able to take into account the various physical transformations. The matter, in my opinion, is relatively trivial. As already stated, nobody contests that some elements of language (particularly acquisition of words) are in direct relation with nonlanguage concepts. However, one should keep in mind Petitto's indication that lexical knowledge (words or signs in signed languages) is not wholly derived from a general cognitive capacity to symbolize but that there are particular constraints at work in early lexical development (e.g., kind boundaries); likewise Petitto claims that linguistic communication does not simply follow in continuity with prelinguistic expression, but involves language-specific knowledge (see Petitto, 1987, 1992).

But when it comes to envisaging specific relationships between cognitive structures and processes, and particular aspects of grammatical development, things are different. On the basis of the observation that early semantic relations are related to sensorimotor schemes, Sinclair (1971) indicates, without any direct empirical evidence, that action patterns are a necessary condition for the acquisition of syntax. This type of extrapolation does not follow. Moreover, it is contradicted by observations showing that children with severe congenital motor problems do not necessarily have difficulties in their grammatical development (nor even in their intellectual development), as first stressed by Lenneberg (1967; see Mehler & Dupoux, 1990, for corresponding arguments along the same line of reasoning). Inhelder (1979) suggests that children overcome their inversion difficulty with noncanonical temporal clauses around 7 years of age, the time at which they achieve the concrete operational level of thinking and therefore are able to reverse states and actions. The argumentation is highly dubious. Ferreiro herself (1971) reports that until 8 or 9 years (i.e., well into the concrete operational stage), most children cannot correctly understand temporal clauses the sequential order of which does not correspond to the order of events in reality. A similar situation prevails with passive sentences. Sinclair and Ferreiro (1970; also see Sinclair, Sinclair, & de Marcellus, 1971) postulate the intervention of a general cognitive factor – that is, logical decentration or the ability to view an event from two different perspectives, also tied to reversibility and therefore to the concrete operational stage – in the explanation of children's evolution in passive sentence comprehension beyond the specific morphosyntactic and pragmatic characteristics of passive forms. Again, the acquisition ages do not correspond. As is known, nonreversible passives are correctly understood by children as early as 3 or 4 years of age (Beilin & Sack, 1975). But children do not need to analyze such sentences syntactically to recover their meaning. Lexical and semantic knowledge is sufficient. Full reversible passives are not usually correctly understood before approximately 9 years (depending on a number of additional factors among which is the composition of the sentence in terms of semantic transitivity; see Section 2.5), again well into the postulated cognitive stage. There even exist indications according to which the negative passive is not necessarily controlled by all normal adults irrespective of IQ considerations (see Bishop, 1983). Other examples could easily be provided (see, e.g., Cromer, 1987, 1988, 1991, for reviews of additional studies and discussions along similar lines as mine).

But even assuming that one could find strong data convincingly showing the co-occurrence of grammatical and cognitive acquisitions, one would still be left with simple correlations allowing several possible causal hypotheses. Experimental analyses of factors possibly involved in determining the course of human development are notoriously hard to come by and many cannot be realized for ethical reasons. Pathological cases are especially instructive, therefore. In aphasic patients, there is, it seems, no clear relation between intellectual dysfunctions and the gravity of language disorders. Many subjects with grossly abnormal grammatical abilities exhibit little generalized intellectual difficulties (Marshall, 1990). Mental retardation also offers natural experimental situations for studying the nature of the relationships between cognitive and language development (also Sinclair, 1975). In this respect also, the available data do not favor the Piagetian cognition hypothesis. For example, in a study by Kahn (1975), 7 of the 8 MR subjects who demonstrated combinatorial language were functioning cognitively at Piagetian sensorimotor stage VI (see Uzgiris & Hunt, 1975) (sometimes referred to as a "prerequisite" for access to the level of combinatorial language – without any clear theoretical justification, in my opinion), but one subject was not. This subject was able to produce correctly formed multiword utterances without having attained the indicated cognitive substage. Several similar exceptions were recorded by Smith and Von Tetzchner (1986) in a corresponding study conducted with 13 DS subjects. Other indications along the same line are reported and discussed in Cromer (1991). More recently, Kahn (1993) reported only minimal correspondence between Piagetian sensorimotor stages according to Uzgiris and Hunt's scales (1975) and manual sign combinations in 34 severely MR children of varied etiologies. Data of this type provide strong evidence against theoretical positions claiming that specific structural cognitive developments are necessary conditions for particular advances in grammatical development.

Of course, the most damaging, and probably fatal, blow to the Piagetian cognition-language hypothesis is caused by the observations on the exceptional cases of grammatical development reported in the preceding chapter. I do not see how the Piagetian position could account *in principle* for those facts. Given that such a position is not supported by strong data on NR children's language development and is flatly contradicted by substantial data on pathological cases constituting as many natural experiences on the problem, one may reasonably consider it to have been falsified.

Not to leave any room for misunderstanding, let me stress that what has been proven false is not the existence of a cognitive basis for some aspects or components of language (the conceptual aspects) – there is a convincing empirical literature supporting this notion and it is reflected in the preceding pages and sections – but *the idea that grammatical regulations deductively follow from cognitive regulations*. Of course, it can always be argued that a minimal level of cognitive development is necessary to "trigger" an otherwise mostly autonomous grammatical development (see later this chapter and also Chapter 6, on this point).

4.1.2 An interesting question is whether the MR data summarized in preceding sections also invalidate or cast a skeptical prospect on other theoretical frameworks assuming one way or the other that "cognition drives language" or, more precisely, that "cognition drives grammar" (as it has been indicated that a dependency between the conceptual systems of mind and the conceptual aspects of language is not controversial).

A defining characteristic of several (distinct and at times diverging) lines of work regrouped in the "cognitive approach" category (e.g., Slobin, 1973; Karmiloff-Smith, 1979; Maratsos & Chalkley, 1981; Bates & MacWhinney, 1982, 1987; MacWhinney, 1987; Bates, Bretherton, & Snyder, 1988) is an effort to explain language development in terms of underlying cognitive processes and mechanisms shared, at least in part, with other perceptual and cognitive domains. Most, if not all, of these approaches acknowledge linguistic categories as useful tools (particularly descriptively) but do not define them as domain specific and as innate primitives actually determining the course of development. Rather, they favor the possibility that general cognitive abilities (e.g., those underlying concept formation and information-processing skills) contribute in major part to language development, including the development of grammatical categories. Some cognitive models hypothesize that linguistic categories are acquired through the intervention of learning processes that are probabilistic in nature. Maratsos and Chalkley (1981), for example, suggest "correlational bootstrapping" as a solution to the question of how the child gets a proper start in forming the correct type of morphosyntactic rules. They assume that the child analyzes distributional properties of the language input, such as word serial positions and inflections, and, in so doing, constructs his grammatical categories (see Pinker, 1987, and Chapter 6, this book, for logical and empirical counterarguments against this type of position). Bates and MacWhinney (1987) and MacWhinney (1987), in their so-called competition model, also assume that distributional regularities (or "cues") available in children's input play a major role in language learning. As this model has been more elaborated theoretically than other cognitive approaches to language development, let me discuss it in more detail. The model is presented as a "neo-Tolmanian" approach to the acquisition of grammar, one that refuses to separate form and function and avoids making innatist assumptions as much as possible. It has two major distinguishing features: (1) *lexicality*, referring to the assumption that grammatical knowledge is represented by connections in the lexicon; and (2) *competitiveness*, that is, the view that lexical items compete with each other during language comprehension and expression (e.g., competition of nouns for grammatical roles). Learning is considered to take place through the shaping of connections between lexical items on the basis of positive instances from language input.

The competition model may be analyzed in two major respects from the language pathology point of view: first, lexicality, and, second, the cognitive principles and analyses involved. The insertion of grammatical knowledge in the lexicon of the language – regardless of its possible validity and sufficiency as a theoretical proposal, which I will not discuss – in no way renders the task of the regular MR child easier, so to speak, nor could it help explain the remarkable grammatical levels reached by the exceptional MR subjects. As indicated previously, lexical development, *on the whole*, is not particularly outstanding in these subjects. It is often in closer connection with the conceptual level than with morphosyntactic abilities. It is hard to see, therefore, how lexicality could "resist" the data on language-exceptional MR cases better than a Piagetian type of approach to grammatical development does. The competition model also uses a set of general cognitive principles (general in the sense of not being specific to language processing) assumed to provide the learner with the tools necessary to achieve input-sensitive language learning. Briefly stated, they are first, the *representational principles*, emphasizing the importance of the lexicon as an organizer of language knowledge (syntactic as well as semantic) and corresponding to the lexicality dimension of the model, as already indicated; second, the *processing principles*, emphasizing the ways in which lexical items compete with each other during language comprehension and expression, corresponding to the notion of competitiveness already defined and giving the model its name; and, third, the *learning principles*, working to isolate lexical items and to shape connections between them and their properties. Equipped with such principles, it is assumed that the language learner will succeed in mapping forms and functions (i.e., "vertical correlations").

Major predictive constructs in the competition model are *cue validity* and *cue strength*. Cue validity is defined as the product of *cue availability* (i.e., how often a piece of information is offered during a decision-making process) times *cue reliability* (i.e., how often a cue leads to a correct conclusion, when used). For example, Italian (or Spanish), as opposed to English (or German), is a "pro-drop" or a "null-subject" language (i.e., a language in which it is accepted and common to omit lexical subjects). As a result, the most frequent form in Italian discourse (particularly in informal speech) is not subject-verb-object (SVO), as is the case in English, but (S)VO or O(S)V. Given this combination of variation of word order plus pro-drop, the cue validity of word order or pre- and postverbal position for identifying grammatical subject and object is not high in Italian, whereas it is very high in English. Cue validity is a property of the language. Cue strength is a subjective property of the learner and language user. It is "the probability or weight that the organism attaches to a given piece of information relative to some goal" (Bates & MacWhinney, 1987, p. 164). Cue validity partially determines cue strength. Another important part of determinism of cue strength has to do with *task frequency*. Bates and MacWhinney (1987) also consider so-called horizontal correlations in language, that is, relationships between forms themselves and relationships between functions. In so doing, they seek to integrate in their functionalist theory the correlational type of grammatical learning proposed by Maratsos (1982) and Maratsos and Chalkley (1981). However, Bates and MacWhinney (1987) hasten to add that, in their view, the child does not have to consider "all possible correlations between all items in all sentences in acquiring an accurate set of form-form correlations" (p. 166). Rather, the child appears to be guided by semantic connectedness and positional patterning in acquiring the basic form-form correlations of the language.

This presentation is, obviously, very sketchy and incomplete. But it is probably sufficient to realize the importance and the ubiquity of the cognitive principles and the cognitively based analyses needed in grammar acquisition according to the competition model. This, in a sense, is natural, as one could argue, reversing Lasnik's indication (1989, p. 102) that the less structure the language acquisition device of the developing organism has, the more data of all sorts, as well as the more cognitive work to treat these data, it needs. It is easy to understand why regular moderately and severely MR subjects would fail to develop grammatical regulations properly according to the competition model, as they are mostly unable or, at best, have major difficulties in performing cognitive tasks of the type of those demanded by such a model (because of drastic working memory limitation, attentional problems, poor organization of semantic memory, retrieval difficulties, etc.). The language-exceptional MR subjects mentioned in preceding sections all have most serious cognitive shortcomings, and about to the same extent, as typical MR subjects. However, this does not prevent them from developing sophisticated (at times quasi-normal or normal) language abilities, particularly grammatical abilities. The implication is that the competition model, inasmuch as it relies heavily on cognitive principles for its implementation, can account for the exceptional cases of language development documented in MR subjects no more than the Piagetian model or other "cognition drives grammar" models. Any model postulating too important a cognitive basis for grammatical development is bound to be in serious difficulty when confronted with cases of exceptional development in such and similar subjects. This is not to deny that lexicality, competitiveness, or other concepts basic to the competition model (but not specific to this model, however) are devoid of explanatory potential. For example, it is likely that there is competition among cues when parsing sentences (Pinker, 1987).

4.2 Chomsky's point of view

Partially reminiscent of the epistemological position of Greek philosophers referred to as "anomalists" (including the Stoics and the Skeptics; see Bates et al., 1988) and considerably influenced by a number of ideas developed by Descartes and the Cartesian philosophers and linguists, as well as by von Humboldt (see de Cordemoy,

1666/1968; von Humboldt, 1836/1960; Chomsky, 1966, 1968, 1969),[3] is Chomsky's view on language, cognition, mental development, and knowledge. This position is almost completely antithetical to the one of Piaget (for a clear contrast between Chomsky's and Piaget's points of view, see the proceedings of the Piaget-Chomsky encounter, in the fall of 1975, at the Abbey of Royaumont, France, edited by Piattelli-Palmarini, 1979, 1980). The two authors may agree, as it would seem, on the necessity of rejecting philosophic and scientific empiricism in the approach to explaining human knowledge. But, even on this point, things are less than fully clear. Piaget considers himself to be an antiempiricist. He has developed a theoretical approach to the study of human knowledge that he calls constructivism or constructive interactionism. Accordingly, new knowledge is constructed by the child's own activity through interactions with the environment (mainly the physical environment). Piaget maintains that, in humans, no a priori cognitive structures exist. "Only the functioning of intelligence is inherited and it engenders structures only through an organization of successive actions performed on objects" (1979b, p. 53).[4] Chomsky believes Piaget's position to be obscure in crucial respects (see, e.g., several of Chomsky's remarks and interventions at the Royaumont encounter, as well as passages from his conversations with Mitsou Ronat; Chomsky, 1979). The preceding quotation, and many others of the same kind in Piaget's writings, certainly attests to a lack of clarity on the basic issue addressed. How can one deny the existence of innate cognitive structures and at the same time admit that the functioning of human intelligence is indeed inherited? Claiming to refuse the existence of innate cognitive structures, Piaget is led to suggest a developmental process that, according to Chomsky, in many respects falls back into something much akin to the empiricism he (Piaget) wants to reject and, for the major part, is very vague indeed. The whole theoretical endeavor seems to Chomsky "nowhere near sufficient . . . to account for the specific course of cognitive development" (1979, p. 85).

According to Chomsky, who cautions against methodological dualisms (also epistemological dualisms) of the Piagetian type, the human mind is part of nature. It is a biological system – more complex than others, but a biological system nevertheless – with its potential scope and its intrinsic limits. Regarding the human mind, or systems of it such as cognition or language, one is faced with the following apparent paradox known as Plato's problem (see the *Meno* dialogue): How can it be that human beings are able to develop knowledge systems as much as they do, given that their contacts with the world are limited and idiosyncratic? The answer given to this problem by a number of philosophers over the centuries (including Plato himself – if one corrects him for the belief in preexistence – and Descartes, and Leibniz), as well as and by Chomsky, is that when rich and complex knowledge can be found constructed in a uniform way, as is the case for cognition and language, there must exist innate structures allowing the development observed and at the same time constraining it relatively narrowly. This latter characteristic of the biological species-specific makeup is most important. If strict limits on attainable knowledge did not exist, we could never dispose of such extensive knowledge as the one displayed in human cognition or language, because without a priori limitations, we could construct a very large number of possible systems of knowledge with little possibility of determining which of these systems is the right one. Therefore, one could never observe the uniform attainment of specific knowledge systems extending far beyond experience as is the case in humans. The task of cognitive psychology is to study those systems, their biological constraints and maturational characteristics, their structures, and their modes of interaction. Linguistics is one part of cognitive psychology. It must work according to the same principles (Chomsky, 1975a, 1979).

Chomsky's basic position on language and language development follows from the epistemological principles just enunciated and from his position regarding the relative autonomy of grammar. Here is a sketch of this position. For more detail, the interested reader is referred to Chomsky's own writings (particularly 1980, 1981, 1982, 1986a, 1987, 1988) and to Hyams (1986) and Roeper and Williams (1987) for the developmental aspects.

Chomsky's current theory [government and binding (GB) theory, or better, principles and parameters theory] – markedly different from predecessor theories in a number of respects – is essentially a theory of the language faculty. Accordingly, language knowledge can be characterized by a formal system of general rules and principles of well-formedness. The theory must meet two important conditions. First, it must be compatible with existing human grammars. Second, it must be sufficiently constrained as to permit grammars to develop on the basis of rather limited input evidence (a case of Plato's problem, as just indicated). The general system designed to meet these conditions is referred to as universal grammar (UG). UG possesses four different levels of representations (D-structure, S-structure, phonetic form or PF, and logical form or LF). *D-structures* are abstract structures characterized by two components: the categorial component (involving phrasal formation rules that generate abstract syntactic structures) and the lexicon (specifying the abstract phono-morphological structure of each lexical item as well as its syntactic and semantic features). D-structures are generated through insertion of lexical items into the syntactic structures provided by the categorial component. In several respects, the rules of the categorial component resemble the phrase structure rules of earlier transformational grammars. However, they differ also in important respects, which I will not discuss here (e.g., the former conforms to X-bar theory). *S-structures* (still abstract representations) are derived from D-structures via the rule Move alpha. This rule is a single, general "movement rule" replacing the diverse transformations presented in earlier theories. When a constituent is moved, it is considered that it leaves behind an empty node coindexed with itself (a trace). For the movement rule to function properly, it must be restricted from generating ungrammatical sequences. This constraint is effected through a series of well-formedness principles (not to be developed here). *PF* provides an abstract characterization of sound or other physical forms (e.g., sign languages). The mapping from S-structure to PF includes phonological rules as well as various other operations. *LF* provides an abstract characterization of interpretation. Much of the meaning of a sentence is available from D- and S-structures, but additional rules are needed to handle potential ambiguities of reference. In addition to defining levels of representation, UG comprises a set of "submodules" (described by subtheories) serving to constrain the representations at each level. These subtheories are *bounding theory* (concerned with the restriction of movement within sentences), *government theory* (pertaining to the dominance relations existing between particular syntactic constituents), *case theory* (concerned with the assignment of abstract case – e.g., nominative, accusative – to noun phrases), *binding theory* (a theory of reference stipulating the conditions under which a given noun phrase – e.g., pronouns and anaphoras – can be interpreted as referring to the same entity as another noun phrase in the sentence), *theta theory* (concerned with the assignment of thematic roles to syntactic configurations and interacting with case theory in important ways), and finally, *control theory* [a somewhat ad hoc set of rules determining the potential reference of PRO (for pronominal), the empty subject of infinitives – e.g., *It is not clear what PRO to do*].[5]

In Chomsky's formulations, the principles of UG are considered to belong to the human species-specific endowment for language.[6] They, therefore, are innate and constitute the initial state of the language faculty in the process of language acquisition. As will be specified later, but is worth stressing here, Chomsky does not claim that human beings have "innate grammars," but rather that they are endowed with UG principles, that is, "a theory of grammars, a kind of metatheory or schematism for grammar" (1979, p. 183). It does not follow that UG must either regroup specific elements or rules common to all languages or features from all languages. Structural variation across languages is quite obvious. However, it requires explanation. Variation is accounted for by a small set of variations on each UG principle, "parameters" that can assume one of two (or more) possible values (one may think of the system as a complex network associated with a switch box containing a finite number of switches; the network is invariant but each switch can be in one of two positions, in the simpler cases). Examples of proposed parameters are the stem parameter (languages such as English permit bare stems as words – e.g., *I work, They work* – whereas other languages, such as Italian, do not – e.g., *Amo, I love*; *Ami, You love*; *Ama, He or she loves*; but never **Am*, the stem of the verb *amare*), and the so-called pro-drop, or null subject, parameter (languages such as English require overt sentence subjects, whereas in languages such as Italian and Spanish, the overt sentence subject may be absent; e.g., one may say *Parlano bene* – meaning *loro, they* – in Italian, whereas the equivalent formulation **Speak well* is ungrammatical in English). When the parameters of UG have been set in one of the permitted ways, perhaps as a consequence of early linguistic experience in a given language, the resulting grammar is said to be the "core" grammar. The notion of core grammar is meant to reflect the setting of the UG principles to those aspects of the grammar of a given language that are most lawful or "natural." Exceptions, that is, idiosyncratic properties of the language, are consigned to the periphery. They include "historical relics," foreign borrowings, and particular inventions that make the languages imperfect systems. Constructions that are in the periphery of the grammar may violate the rules and the principles of UG, but at a cost. They should be marked (Pinker, 1989b), require direct experience, and exhibit the following properties: rarity, variation from speaker to speaker, diachronic instability, and more difficulty for the language learner (Salkie, 1987).[7]

Along this line, language development is to be viewed as a process of deductive selection of one core grammar (with the appropriate fixing – not the learning[8] – of the UG parameters; see, e.g., Hyams, 1986, 1987) from a large set of linguistically possible grammars excluding a more limited set of cognitively possible grammars (computer languages, e.g., are instances of cognitively possible languages but not naturally occurring ones). The deduction is considered to be automatic, since the general rules and principles of UG are innate, given some (minimal) language experience sufficient to determine the switch settings. A proper theory of language development will specify the principles of development that are responsible for the transition from the initial state of the language faculty to the steady state of adult competence.[9]

As indicated by Chomsky (1981) and Roeper (1987a, 1987b; Finer & Roeper, 1989), cognitive concepts can bear a "trigger" relation to grammatical entities. Trigger, here, is used in a biological sense of releasing mechanism, that is, one that does not bear a deductive relation to the thing triggered.[10] It is worth noting that a theory of triggers does not contradict the Chomskyan notion of the (relative) autonomy of syntax, given that cognitive triggers are considered to be nondeductive. But it may be in opposition with a maturational perspective on syntactic development. For example, Borer and Wexler (1987) have proposed a maturational theory of syntax claiming that parts of a child's innate grammatical endowment may be unavailable at early stages of language development and become available for grammatical construction at later times. Such a view, coupled with the indication that what is at stake in those cases is not the maturation of general cognitive or perceptual abilities (which happens too), may challenge not only the triggering point of view, but also the so-called continuity hypothesis suggested by Pinker (1984). The continuity hypothesis assumes that the principles that the child uses to fix his grammar from the input data are constant over the course of development until linguistic maturity. In opposition, Borer and Wexler's assumption is that certain of these principles undergo maturation. They reason that since grammatical development is an instance of biological development, grammar ought to mature just like any other biological system. The maturation point of view seems to have the advantage over the continuity hypothesis in that it can better explain why certain language constructions develop at certain times and other constructions at other times, given that all are available in the input from the beginning and that there does not seem to exist solid ground for the existence of an acquisitional ordering in linguistic theory. But one still must consider the contribution of a properly formulated learning theory and the role learning principles would play in accounting for stages seen in acquisition. Also the question of the nature of maturational changes needs to be looked into in more detail. Is it the case that the specific constraints on learning particular to language acquisition undergo a sort of maturational development and then decay, as Borer and Wexler (1987) suggest, or do specific language learning abilities decline because of the expansion of nonlinguistic cognitive abilities? For example, the fact that children can perceive and store only component parts of complex linguistic stimuli – due to momentary limitations in short-term memory – possibly could paradoxically provide an advantage for tasks such as language learning, which involve componential analysis. Adults, who have better short-term memory capacities and more readily perceive whole complex stimuli, could be in a less advantageous position to locate langage components – although quite obviously such an indication is not sufficient in itself since MR subjects never have normal short-term memory capacities (see Chapters 5 and 6), which does not confer to them any known advantage in language acquisition (see Newport, 1990, for a discussion).

4.3 Language modularity and general modularity theory

In Chomsky's writings, the notion of language modularity appears to have two extensions, only one being of immediate interest here. There is modularity within the grammatical theory itself (i.e., internal modularity) to the extent that the subtheories (identified in the preceding section) are considered to be distinct but interacting "grammars," each one with its particular principles and functional rules (see Grodzinsky, 1984, 1986, 1990, and Rizzi, 1985, for empirical indications along such a line from observations of agrammatic aphasic patients; but also see Martin, Wetzel, Blossom-Stack, & Feher, 1989, and Druks & Marshall, 1991, for empirical reservations about Grodzinsky's particular version of the syntactic loss hypothesis in agrammatism). There is also modularity in a second sense (external grammatical), that is, the indication that "more traditional" components of the linguistic system are mostly independent from one another in terms of functional organization and, likely, in terms of organic substratum and architecture. But, of course, these components interact in what, "from the outside," appears to be an integrated "language" system. *This is the type of functional and interactive modularity that I am considering here.* As seen in preceding chapters, and as will be seen again later in the book, there is considerable evidence for its existence, even if the specification of the interactions between language components largely remains to be done. Another aspect of this modularity thesis is the distinction between conceptual and computational aspects of language together with the proviso that only conceptual language components have deductive relations with the more general conceptual system of the mind. This indication also enjoys some interesting empirical support. At a theoretical level, this distinction prolongs and refines the hypothesis of "autonomy of syntax" present in

Chomsky's writing in one form or another since the fifties (e.g., 1957a; 1965, 1955/1975b). It might appear at first glance (so to speak) that this thesis has weakened somehow in Chomsky's GB theory (e.g., Rouveret, 1987). But upon careful analysis, there is no doubt that it is still there in a strong form. Such a "strong form" obviously, and as already indicated in the preceding chapter but worth stressing, does not mean that the computational aspects of language or the syntactic module have no connection with other components. What it means is that the elements referred to in the syntactic rules are hypothesized to be purely syntactic elements. They are not semantic, conceptual, or any other kind of nonsyntactic element.

Chomsky (e.g., 1984), more generally, also proposes that the structure of mind is in fact modular. In this respect, he claims, "The human mind is just like other complex biological systems: it is composed of interacting sub-systems with their specific properties and character and with specific modes of interaction among the various parts" (1984, p. 16). System modularity (for language, vision, etc.) therefore coexists with general mind modularity. This type of organization of mind structures makes them the metaphorical mental analogs of body organs. Marshall (1990) has called this conception "the new organology" (referring back to Gall, 1809).

Fodor (1983, 1985) has also defined a modular approach to the study of mind. It is different from that of Chomsky in several respects. According to Fodor (1983), a basic functional taxonomy of psychological processes can be established that distinguishes between so-called transducers, input systems, and central processors. The transducers, or sensory organs, provide modality-specific immediate representations of proximal stimulus configurations. The role of the input analyzers is to characterize "the arrangement of things in the world" (p. 42). They are inference-performing systems having as their "premises" representations of proximal stimulus configurations, and as their "conclusions" representations of the character and distribution of distal objects. Fodor is reluctant to completely identify input systems with perceptual analyzers. This is because, first, perception is not the only psychological mechanism available for presenting the world to thought, and second, perception is a mechanism of belief fixation "par excellence," which function Fodor restricts to the central processors together with the planning of intelligent action. Most importantly for our discussion, Fodor argues that language is an input system.[11]

Input systems are modules, that is, in Fodor's sense, "informationally encapsulated subsystems of the brain" or automata composed of "subroutines" serving special objectives. A module is said to be informationally encapsulated to the extent that its data processing is limited to two basic types of information: (1) lower-level data, that is, input from the transducers, and (2) background information stored in the module itself, either innately given or having arrived there as a result of the system's previous functioning. By contrast, cognitive processors are defined as holistic or nonmodular systems (or "horizontal" faculties)[12] that may be characterized by "equipotentiality," which makes them all the more difficult to study.

Other more or less independent properties of the modules can be specified in the following way: They are *domain specific*; their modus *operandi* is *mandatory* ["You can't help hearing an utterance of a sentence (in a language you know) as an utterance of a sentence" (Fodor, 1983, p. 53)]; there is only *limited central access* to the representations that modules compute ("Not only must you hear an utterance of a sentence as such, but, to a first approximation, you can hear it *only* that way" p. 56); they are *fast*; they have "*shallow*" *outputs* (i.e., outputs confined to their domain-specific features); they are associated with *fixed neural architectures* (which may be thought of as the natural concomitant of informational encapsulation); they have *characteristic and specific breakdown patterns* when that architecture is damaged; they exhibit an ontogeny that demonstrates *characteristic pace and sequencing*; and, finally, they are *computationally autonomous*. For a subsystem to be a module, according to Fodor, all the properties have to be present at least to a "reasonable" degree.

Fodor cites various kinds of evidence in support of his modular hypothesis. I will not enter into their discussion (see my related Section 6.4). The interested reader is referred to Fodor's book as well as to detailed and critical analyses by Marshall (1984), Putnam (1984), Shallice (1984), and the *Précis of the modularity of mind* (Fodor, 1985). Major problems concern three basic issues: (1) the exact definition and neuropsychological nature of the modules (i.e., how modular are Fodorian modules?); (2) the possible existence of "weaker modules" (Schwartz & Schwartz, 1984; Shallice, 1984) or "relatively modular" processes (Gardner, 1985), i.e., information-processing systems that mediate human skills and that have some of the properties of Fodorian modules but not all; and (3) the posited nonmodular nature of central cognitive processes.

Gardner (1985) also has some interesting views to offer on the modularity problem. He broadly endorses Fodor's distinction between horizontal and vertical faculties of mind and his reading of the current literature. Gardner himself (1983) has proposed a concept of multiple intelligence formally corresponding to the Gall-Fodor notion of vertical faculties (i.e., separate "intelligences": linguistic, logico-mathematical, spatial, musical, somatic-kinesthesic, and so-called personal – i.e., intra- and interpersonal, meaning the ability to discriminate and control one's feelings and emotions and the ability to be sensible and to understand another's feelings and emotions). Returning to Fodor's modules, Gardner (1985) suggests that fully encapsulated modules in Fodor's sense are "ideals" possibly observable early in development but later only in special cases (e.g., some autistic children). With (normal) development, Gardner claims, encapsulation gradually dissolves because the highest human capabilities depend on the ability to integrate information from various sources including cultural ones or, in other words, on the ability for the modules to interact, either through a network of multiple individual connections or through a separate common system that "supervises" the communications. Although encapsulation progressively fades away, it is never completely eradicated, however. "The core"[13] may become visible again under certain conditions of brain damage (1983, p. 13), as the neuropsychological literature shows. The dissociations demonstrated in cases of brain damage, mental retardation, autism, and the like, might be thought of as suggesting lines along which the original modular entities are organized before they develop their interactive networks (in normal beings) to such an extent that their distinctive modular characteristics recede. But the modular dissolution perspective also has its limits, for some degree of encapsulation is probably necessary in the input-output systems to account for their automatic-mandatory character, their procedural rapidity, and some of the other properties listed by Fodor (1983). It could be, for example, that, in normally developing people, the integration phase proposed by Gardner either does not affect all the previously modular systems to the same extent (certain types of structures being intrinsically more modular than others) or is followed, again perhaps more for some structures than others, by a secondary modularization phase and/or function automatization, which may also come (as Sternberg, 1985, suggests) as a consequence of relatively large amounts of practice and experience.

Specific abilities, unrelated to intelligence or other mental functions, indeed exist in MR, autistic, and other pathological cases. The cases of a number of hyperlinguistic MR subjects are documented in this book. A whole series of MR and/or autistic subjects (sometimes labeled idiot savants after Langdon Down, 1887, the scientist who first described the clinical signs of what became known as Down syndrome)[14] with isolated exceptional abilities in music (improvisation, composition, and memorization), drawing (creation and graphic reproduction abilities), perception and recognition memory for shapes, calendrical calculation, and numerical ability have been studied and reported by O'Connor, Hermelin, and their associates (O'Connor & Hermelin, 1984, 1987a, 1987b, 1988, 1989, 1990; Sloboda, Hermelin, & O'Connor, 1985; Hermelin & O'Connor, 1986, 1990a, 1990b; Hermelin, O'Connor, & Lee, 1987; Hermelin, O'Connor, Lee, & Treffert, 1989; O'Connor 1989). The documented exceptional capacities in all cases are independent of general intelligence and seem to involve, at least partially, structure-based and rule-governed knowledge and skills. The exceptional abilities become apparent at an early age, and they are not improved much by practice (which suggests that they may be innate). However, corresponding exceptional talents (plus particular and isolated capacities for eidetic imagery, chess playing, mathematical talent, hyperlexia, foreign languages) in otherwise normal people have also been documented in a number of studies gathered by Obler and Fein (1988). These latter dissociations do not represent the end points of normal distributions of different faculties or states of arrested evolutions. They certainly make problems for Gardner's developmental account of modularity.[15]

Notes

1. This position actually was most clearly put forward by the Romantic philosophers and linguists of the nineteenth century (particularly von Humboldt, 1836/1960). For von Humboldt, languages largely determine human cognitive processes and world conceptions (weltanschauung); and, being a creative system, language is directly responsible for human creative thinking and thinking power. From there, it follows that translating from one language into another will entail considerable (at times, insuperable) difficulties (particularly if the languages are little related). The Romantic conception, it may be added, breaks on this point with the Cartesian tradition in which there is an almost complete identification of the language and thought processes – languages being considered as the best mirror of the human mind and the product of reason (Arnaud & Lancelot, 1660/1810; Leibniz, 1765/1927; see Harnois, 1927, for a historical perspective), and the creative character of language finding its source in creative thinking itself (Beauzée, 1767/1819); the latter remaining unaccounted for, however. See de Cordemoy (1666/1968) for an exposition of the Cartesian claim that the same basic mental processes are common to all normal humans and that languages differ only in their expressing modes but not in the thoughts that they express. It follows, in the Cartesian conception, that translating from one language into another one should not meet basic difficulties and that learning a second language is "simply" a matter of assigning new labels and expressions to ideas already associated to the first language.

2. Some of Piaget's beliefs are embodied in current so-called cognitive grammars (see Lakoff, 1987; Langacker, 1987), e.g., the ideas that language is not a separate mental function and that semantics, itself based on cognition, is the basic feature of language rather than syntax.

3. But, by far, not all of these ideas. Chomsky rejects the Cartesian belief that thought and language processes are mostly identical (see Note 1). Also, for Descartes and the Cartesian philosophers, the mind is entirely indivisible. Chomsky, on the contrary, proposes a modular approach to the study of mind (see, particularly, Chomsky, 1984, on this point and later in this chapter).

4. My literal translation.

5. In a variant formulation of GB theory (still the object of much work and controversy today) presented by Manzini (1983), control theory is subsumed under binding theory, which is reformulated accordingly.

6. Pinker and Bloom (1990) argue in favor of an explanation of the evolution of the human language faculty by Darwinian natural selection. In so doing they oppose Gould's (e.g., 1987) and other authors' (e.g., Piattelli-Palmarini, 1989) view according to which language is not the product of natural selection, but a side effect of other evolutionary forces such as an increase in overall brain size. Additionally, Gould and other so-called punctuated equilibria theorists (see Gould & Eldredge, 1977; echoed in Piattelli-Palmarini, 1989) oppose Darwinian gradualism (see Dawkins, 1986) in favor of "sudden" vast genetic reshufflings or evolutionary jumps. Regarding the origins of language, this means believing that a full-blown novelty such as (human) language can arise abruptly, for no reason, i.e., eluding strict adaptationism, and therefore that there may not be language precursors in primates or in other hominids because there are no intermediate forms to human language.

7. Although the distinction between core grammar and periphery may be seen as another logical step in Chomsky's list of idealizations and simplifying assumptions (a list that includes restricting attention to competence rather than performance, Chomsky, 1965; treating competence as perfect and neglecting sociolinguistic variation, Chomsky, 1965; and treating grammatical acquisition as instantaneous, Chomsky, 1975a) that may be necessary in any explanatory science, it could be considered that it entails some degree of tautology, since the same criteria are used to define UG and core grammar, and to reject unaccounted or contradictory language characteristics to grammatical periphery. (For tentative proposals relating to a more continuous theory of core and periphery, see Fodor, 1989, however.)

8. Chomsky's language development scheme, in its general principles, is very close to von Humboldt's (1836/1960) rationalist view on language acquisition. According to Humboldt (himself partially reminiscent of Leibniz on this point; see Leibniz, 1765/1927), language cannot really be taught. One can only present the appropriate conditions under which it will "spontaneously" develop in the mind in its own way. What Humboldt labels the "form of language" (close to the essence of Chomsky's notion of grammar) is considered to be largely given. But it will not be realized without appropriate experience that will set the language-forming process into operation.

9. Other theoretical proposals than that of Chomsky exist along corresponding lines, although much less developed. An interesting one is that of Bickerton (1981, 1984, 1986; for the more general phylogenetic context of Bickerton's ontogenetic hypothesis, see Bickerton, 1981, 1988, and 1990; also see Chapter 6 in this book, and Studdert-Kennedy, 1992, for a critical analysis), known as the *language bioprogram hypothesis*. It has been recognized for some time by creolists that Creoles render more complex the Pidgin grammars that preceded them (e.g., Hall, 1966). Bickerton claims that the innovative aspects of Creole grammars are true inventions on the part of the first generation of children starting with a Pidgin as their linguistic input and that such inventions exhibit an important degree of similarity across large variations in linguistic background. The explanation suggested by Bickerton is that they derive partly "from the structure of a species-specific program for language, genetically coded and expressed, in ways still largely mysterious, in the structures and mode of operations of the human brain" (1984, p. 173), and partly "from processes inherent in the expansion of a linear language" (1981, p. xiii). Bickerton (1984) supplies a specification of the grammatical information coded in his assumed bioprogram (e.g., notions of sentence, noun, verb, determiner, single transformational rule Move alpha – taken from Chomsky, 1981 – and a set of rewriting rules). It may be useful to stress that Bickerton's hypothesis, even if compatible with Chomsky's distinction between conceptual and computational components of language, is nonparametric and therefore an alternative to Chomsky's view of universal grammar (but not necessarily incompatible with it). There are other differences between Chomsky's and Bickerton's basic proposals (see Bichakjian, 1989, for an analysis): for example, the exact nature of what is assumed to be innate and, consequently, the role of the child in language development; and the source of empirical data attesting to the genetic determinacy of language (i.e., the inventory of linguistic universals for Chomsky, and the instructions of the bioprogram as they are instantiated in Creoles, e. g., for Bickerton).

10. This "brute-causal" triggering must be distinguished from the implicational or "rational-causal" triggering considered to be involved in parameter setting. Triggering in this second sense does not apply to the setting of the parameter value itself but rather to the unfolding of the deductive consequences of a parameter being set in a particular way (see Atkinson, 1987, and Harris & Davies, 1987, for discussions of these notions).

11. A first peculiarity of Fodor's scheme appears here. He seems to be willing to restrict language to an input function. It may be that his characterizing of the input systems applies equally well to output systems, as Marshall (1984) suggests. Nevertheless, this is a curious way of analyzing the language function (also criticized in Chomsky, 1988). Quite clearly too, language is used in speaking and thought. The output system must be linked to the input system, and both are related to systems of knowledge.

12. This distinction (but not the terms, which are Fodor's) originates in the work of Gall (1809; also see Gall & Spurzheim, 1810), for whom traditional mental faculties (e.g., judgment, volition, attention, memory) are largely a fiction. Instead, there is a set of dispositions, aptitudes that are specific to given domains (music, mathematics, language, etc.) (or "vertical faculties," in Fodor's terms). As indicated earlier in this chapter, Chomsky is not convinced that "central" cognitive processors are nonmodular (also see Chomsky, 1988).

13. "Core," here, is used in a sense different from Chomsky's core grammar.

14. Actually, a preliminary description of the major clinical signs of trisomy 21 had already been supplied by the French psychiatrist Esquirol, earlier in the nineteenth century (Esquirol, 1838).

15. The preceding accounts and discussions evidently in no way pretend to exhaust the modularity problem. As already mentioned, further discussions, particularly from language-processing and language pathology points of view, are included in Chapter 6. The interested reader might also want to consider further the *Precis of the modularity of mind* (Fodor, 1985), already referred to, as well as the more recent collection of essays on *Modularity and constraints in language and cognition*, edited by Gunnar and Maratsos (1992).

5   A case study

5.1 The subject

Françoise was 32 to 36 years old during the time of the study. Her IQ and MA are supplied in Section 5.8. She was born on April 5, 1955, 3 weeks before term, weighing 2.750 kg. Delivery was relatively rapid and normal but for some degree of cyanosis due to the umbilical cord being wrapped around the neck. Additional oxygen was given on an intermittent basis for 24 hours following birth.

The Down syndrome condition was not diagnosed until Françoise was 3 years old, at which time the parents consulted at the Pediatric Clinic of the Liège University Hospital for her slow development and complete lack of speech. A karyotype was made at the time revealing a genotype 47, XX, + free 21 in each of the metaphases studied (standard trisomy 21). In the course of the present study, suspecting a possible subetiology of mosaicism, I requested a new karyotype. It was made in July 1988 and confirmed the first one.

The mother of Françoise was 35 years old at the time of birth, and the father 32. They already had two normal children, one boy and one girl, respectively aged 5 and 7 years. The socioeconomic level of the family is upper middle class.

Françoise made her first attempts at walking unassisted around 2 years. She was toilet trained at 4 years. The parents did not report any sensory problem at the time, but no systematic examination of her visual and auditory acuity was made. The only word she was able to pronounce at 4 years was /to/ for *couteau – knife*. Little information is available on her language receptive ability at the time. She was reported as capable of understanding short concrete verbal orders or instructions in situation. At 4½, Françoise started language reeducation twice a week at the Speech Clinic of the University of Liège. She was taught to speak, read, and write (at the same time) by a team of speech pathologists (according to the so-called alphabetical-gestural method developed in Paris by Suzanne Borel-Maisonny and introduced in Liège by Denise Jarbinet). The parents as well as the professionals in charge reported good results.

At 6 years and a few months, following a failed attempt at integration in a primary school for normally developing children, Françoise started attending a special school for moderately and severely mentally handicapped children in the city of Liège. The results were satisfactory and she made regular progress. On October 9, 1962

(Françoise was 7 years and 6 months), the report of a consultation made at the Speech Clinic of the University of Liège indicates that her language, very poor at the beginning, had improved considerably and that she was exhibiting much interest for anything having to do with speech (unfortunately no further details are given). After 10 years in primary special school, she had access to a secondary special school for MR adolescents, which she attended for 3 years, again with satisfactory results. At 19 years, she started attending the courses of a state technical institute (for NR adolescents) with little satisfaction and success. As a consequence, Françoise lost much of her motivation for school. From then on, she stayed home helping her mother with the housework and taking care of three elderly women (the two grandmothers and one grandaunt) living under the same roof as the family. After the death of her two grandmothers and her grandaunt, Françoise started frequenting an occupational center for adults with DS (La Fermette), first once a week and then twice weekly, which she was still doing at the time of the study.

Françoise's medical record is relatively straightforward. She was exempt from most of the organic problems affecting DS children in substantial proportions (i.e., cardiac malformations, pneumovascular difficulties, gastroduodenal problems). From birth until early adolescence, Françoise presented the ligamentary hyperlaxity that is typical of most DS children. From the detailed report made by physicians from the Pediatric Department of the University of Liège when Françoise was 13½ years, it appears that she was enjoying good health (she was never sick but for the usual children's illnesses – measles, etc.). At the time, she weighed 37.400 kg and was 1.475 m high. Her electrocardiogram was normal. The otorhinolaryngological structures appeared to be fairly normal and functioning well. On the electroencephalography, a few slight signs of diffuse paroxysmal "suffering" were detected. They were not confirmed on subsequent examinations, however. Around 30 years, Françoise presented neurotic behavioral problems (anorexia, hypersensitivity, and social disinhibitions) possibly associated with hyperthyroidism and its treatment (by iodic complement). She had recovered taking only light neuroleptics from time to time at the beginning of the study.

5.2 General procedure

Françoise was submitted to a large number of tests and evaluation procedures over a period of 4 years (between 1988 and the beginning of 1992). Foremost in this respect was the evaluation of her expressive and receptive oral language capabilities. For assessing expressive oral language, we recorded 2 (fully sustained) hours of Françoise's conversational speech in free interaction with Jean-François Bachelet (hereafter J.F.B.). Portions of this corpus (amounting to more than 80 double-spaced manuscript pages) were analyzed using Halliday's functional grammar (Halliday, 1985). Halliday's grammar was selected because it is well adapted to discourse analysis and to describing linguistic performance, and also because, being overtly functional (i.e., "designed to account for how the language is *used*"; Halliday, 1985, p. xiii), it allows one – in this part of the study – to avoid various premises regarding the nature of linguistic competence and its origins that are inherent in a number of current theorical works [including Chomskyan grammars, already presented, Bresnan's "lexical-functional" grammar (Bresnan, 1982), Langacker's "cognitive" grammar (Langacker, 1987), and O'Grady's principles of grammar and learning (O'Grady, 1987)].

For assessing advanced receptive oral language, we used homemade tasks adapted from our psycholinguistic studies with normally developing children, devised to evaluate the comprehension of active and passive declarative sentences, relative clauses, temporal and causal subordinate clauses, and the comprehension of pronominal coreference. Receptive lexical tests and tasks for assessing Françoise's semantic-lexical organization and semantic memory were also administered. Françoise's metalinguistic ability was also examined: Sentence grammaticality and semantic acceptability judgments were obtained; phonological awareness and capacity to analyze sentences grammatically were assessed; and word definitions were proposed.

The written language examination assessed Françoise's capability for reading words, sentences, and texts, as well as for spontaneous written expression and for conventional orthography. Françoise's hemispheric specialization for speech was also tested using dichotic-listening and dual-task procedures.

The "nonlinguistic" examination evaluated Françoise's functioning on a number of tasks: working and long-term memory, selective recall, visuographic ability, visual perception, computational capacity, and others. She was tested for intellectual operational functioning in the sense of Piaget (conservation, seriation, and classification skills). She was also given the verbal and the nonverbal subscales of the Wechsler Adult Intelligence Scale (WAIS; Wechsler, 1968). Because Françoise was 32 years old at the beginning of the study and the evaluation procedure was spread over a 4-year period, it was necessary to have her general mental functioning tested twice (in May 1988 and in 1991) to establish (and in that case to deal properly with) or to rule out a possible age-related cognitive decline. Such a decline, often tied to Alzheimer-like neuropathologic features (Wisniewski, Dalton, Crapper-McLachlan, Wen, & Wisnieswki, 1985; see Oliver & Holland, 1986, and, more recently, Schellenberg, Kamino, Bryant, Moore, & Bird, 1992, for reviews of the specialized literature), affects a significant proportion of DS persons past the age of 40 (Thase, 1988). The WAIS given in 1988 and that in 1991 yielded similar results (see Section 5.8, for more detail). All the analytical procedures are fully explained in the following sections.

5.3 Conceptual rationale

I hypothesize that upon careful analysis Francoise's language will prove close to normal concerning the basic phonological and morphosyntactic aspects, but that it will depart from normal with respect to (advanced) lexical aspects (particularly, word semantics, i.e., word meaning and reference) and textual cohesion (to be defined later). The strategy adopted is as follows. I will assume that a major descriptive grammar such as Halliday's (1985) – see the later systematic presentation – captures many significant grammatical and discursive facts of the English language (and mutatis mutandis of the French language, given the structural similarities of the two languages). Comparing Francoise's language with the specifications of Halliday's grammar, it should be possible to indicate to what extent her language organization is normal or normallike. Halliday's grammar had to be adapted for French. I have done so, using two descriptive sources as a guide: the *Eléments de linguistique française* of Dubois and Dubois-Charlier (1970), and the *Grammaire Larousse du XXè. siècle* of Gaiffe, Maille, Breuil, Jahan, Wagner, and Marijon (1936). Halliday's scheme, of course, does not cover everything in language organization. It was extended with a series of observational probes of her spoken capacities, derived mainly from Françoise's corpus. On the receptive language side, various tests and psycholinguistic tasks were used to specify the extent of Françoise's lexical, semantic, and morpho-syntactic capabilities. The language picture, then, was to be assessed along with extensive data gathered on Françoise's (nonverbal) cognitive functioning.

5.4 Oral language assessment

5.4.1 Conversational speech

Françoise's 2 hours of free conversational speech with one of my assistants (J.F.B.) was transcribed verbatim and divided into utterances by the interlocutor himself. For segmenting into utterances, we used the procedure described in Rondal, Bachelet, and Perée (1986). This procedure is based on the five criteria defined in Table 5–1.

Rondal et al.'s procedure for utterance segmentation is not basically different from the one described in Siegel (1963), except in one respect. An utterance or vocal response unit was defined according to Siegel as "a unit of spoken language marked off on either side by a pause or by some change in inflection" (1963, App. H, p. 101). Such a criterion has two major disadvantages. First, it is difficult to apply. Second, it leads to segmenting what constitutes a grammatical sentence into two or several utterances in cases where the sentence is interrupted by pauses (e.g., /He said . . . /that he could not reveal . . . /that secret to you/). The second problem is particularly unwelcome in analyses that are interested in the grammatical structure of discourse, since the primary data segmented in such analyses (i.e., the utterances identified in Siegel's way) may not do justice to the grammatical capability of the speaker. The scheme supplied in Table 5–1 corrects this bias in subordinating the prosodic criterion to the grammatical one.

Randomly selected portions of the corpus amounting to one-fourth of conversational speech were independently transcribed and segmented by a neutral observer. Interobserver agreement reached .96 for transcription and .92 for utterance segmen-

Table 5–1. *Criteria for corpus segmentation into utterances*

Criterion 1

Each time a sentence is identified, it automatically constitutes an utterance. A sentence is defined as being composed minimally of a conjugated verb and a grammatical subject. The two elements must be properly distributed sequentially according to the normative rules of the language. Imperative sentences represent exceptions in that they do not necessarily express the grammatical subject in surface structure. Maximally, a sentence may contain one or several clauses explicitly coordinated or subordinated.

Criterion 2

When the isolated lexeme or the sequence of lexemes do not form a sentence but are separated from the rest of the discourse by a clearly distinguishable pause or interruption in the speech flow, they will be considered as constituting an utterance.

Criterion 3

When verbal elements are repeated within the boundaries of a sentence, the sentence will count for one utterance. In other cases, the repeated element(s) will be counted as (a) distinct utterance(s), e.g., /more water/more water/more water/.

Criterion 4

In all other cases, one will use the pauses for identifying utterances.

Criterion 5

The interjections and the lexical elements *yes* and *no* will not be considered as constituting an utterance unless they represent the only response supplied to a previous piece of information, clarification, or confirmation request by the interlocutor, or the only comment produced in direct response to a previous production by the interlocutor.

Source: After Rondal, Bachelet, and Perée, 1986.

tation (Fliess's kappa statistics were .92 and .84, respectively, both significant at $p <$ .00001, one-tailed α).

Three hundred and sixty-six speech turns were identified in Françoise's subcorpus. Among those, 10 speech turns randomly selected from the 72 speech turns counting more than five utterances (arbitrary criterion) were chosen for the detailed analyses presented later in the chapter. The selected turns numbered from 1 to 10 (randomly divided into two samples of 5) are presented in Appendix 1 together with their immediate verbal contexts. Appendix 2 supplies the English translation of the 10 selected turns. It was decided to center the analyses on sequences of related utterances in order to have a better chance of properly capturing whatever semantic, grammatical, and discursive organization the speech of Françoise could contain.

5.4.1.1 Mean length of utterance

Mean length of utterance (MLU) was computed using the procedure defined in Rondal, Bachelet, and Perée (1986). According to this procedure, MLU is the ratio of the number of words plus bound grammatical morphemes identified in the utterances analyzed to the total number of these utterances. The bound grammatical morphemes considered are only those serving to mark gender and number on the nouns, pronouns, articles, and adjectives, and to mark person, tense and/or aspect, and grammatical mode on the verbs. One unit is counted for each word-root. One or several additional units are counted for the bound grammatical morpheme(s) added to the word-root. Furthermore, it is necessary that the grammatical morphological markers counted be overtly (i.e., phonetically) realized in the oral language and be fully audible in the speech of the speaker. The following examples illustrate the counting procedure:

- – *berger* (*shepherd*): one unit (word-root).
- – *bergère* (*shepherd*, feminine form): one unit (word-root) and 1 bound grammatical morpheme (expressing feminine gender), that is, two units for the MLU count.
- – *les bergères* (*the shepherds*, feminine forms): two units for *les* (word root + plural marker), two units for *bergères* (word-root + feminine marker) – the plural marker on *bergères*, that is, /s/, is not counted as it is not overtly realized in the oral language.
- – *jolies* (*beautiful,* plural feminine form): two units (word-root + feminine marker) – the plural marker, that is, /s/, is not counted as it is not overtly realized in the oral language.
- – *manger* (*eat*, infinitive form): two units (word-root + mode marker).
- – *mangera* (*will eat*, third-person singular of the future in the indicative): three units (word-root + tense + person).
- – *mangeront* (*will eat*, third-person plural of the future in the indicative): three units (word-root + tense + person).
- – *elles auront mangé* (*they* – feminine form – *will have eaten*): three units for *elles* (word-root + feminine form + plural marker – realized phonetically for need of chaining with following word); three units for *auront* (word-root + tense + person); two units for *mangé* (word-root + mode marker).

Rondal et al.'s procedure for calculating MLU also includes the following rules borrowed from R. Brown (1973, p. 54):

1. Only fully transcribed utterances are used; none with blanks.
2. All exact word repetitions or stuttering and stutteringlike phenomena are counted only once in the most complete form produced.
3. Fillers such as *mm* or *oh* (or their "French" equivalents) are not counted, but *see*, *yeah*, *yes*, and *hi* (or their "French" equivalents) are counted.
4. All compound words (two or more free morphemes), proper names, and ritualized reduplications (e.g., *bow-wow*; *wou-wou* in "French") count as single words.

Our procedure for calculating MLU differs from Brown's only in that we count as separate units the words and the bound grammatical morphemes as previously indicated when they are integrated into the word, whereas Brown does not. His procedure was primarily intended to quantify gross linguistic evolution in the young child. Ours applies to later language functioning, and this justifies the modification introduced in the MLU counting procedure.

Françoise's MLU count was made on 753 utterances (i.e., all the utterances transcribed on the pair-numbered pages of the whole corpus of speech). This is more than sufficient for deriving a reliable MLU index (100 utterances are enough to warrant an MLU reliability of .80 or more in children according to the analyses performed by Rondal & Defays, 1978). The MLU obtained is 12.24 with an SD of 9.65 (range 1–58; this latter figure gives the upper bound, according to R. Brown, 1973). No tables exist for interpreting MLU values in NR adults, although 12 or so is sometimes cursorily referred to as the average value for most conversational nonnarrative speech. It would appear that Françoise is able to construct utterances that conform in mean length to the ones usually observed in normal adults placed in corresponding language contexts.

MLU, of course, only supplies a rough indication on the global envelope of speech (see the remarks on MLU in Chapter 3). It is necessary to analyze much further the structural organization of Françoise's language.

5.4.1.2 Grammatical, semantic, and textual organization

5.4.1.2.1 Halliday's scheme

A detailed presentation of the guiding principles and the major analytical dimensions of Halliday's functional grammar is in order. The following pages are mostly borrowed from Halliday (1985), which the interested reader should consult for more detail. Many examples are taken from Halliday's presentation. Halliday's grammar is said to be functional in the sense that it is assumed to be ultimately "explained" by reference to how language is used.

Structurally, the fundamental unit of organization is the *clause*. This is the same unit whether it is functioning in isolation (as a *simple sentence*) or as part of a clause complex (a *compound/complex sentence*). Halliday's analysis proceeds through related parts: clause level, below the clause (groups and phrases), above the clause (clause complex and sentences), beside the clause (information unit), and around the clause (cohesion and discourse).[1]

Halliday defines the clause as a unit in which meanings of three different kinds are combined and mapped on to one another to produce a single sequential wording. A clause may be considered simultaneously as a *message*, an *exchange*, and a *representation*. Each of these three kinds of meaning is expressed by means of certain structures (more exactly substructures). Let us see the particulars of the above analytical categories.

Clause as message

In all languages, the clause has the character of a message.[2] This form of organization that gives it the status of a communicative event is labeled the *thematic structure* (in a sense different from thematic relations or theta theory in preceding sections). This structure corresponds to the following organization: One element in the clause is enunciated as the theme. This element then combines with the remainder of the clause so that the two parts together constitute a message. The *theme* is the element that serves as the point of departure of the message. It is that with which the clause is concerned (e.g., *the duke*, in the clause *The duke has given my aunt that teapot*). The remainder of the message is called the *rheme* (Halliday, here, is borrowing from the Prague school terminology). As a message structure, therefore, a clause consists of a theme that always comes in first position, whatever it is, accompanied by a rheme (in the preceding example, *The duke* is the theme, *has given my aunt that teapot* is the rheme; other thematicorhematic configurations might be *My aunt* – theme – *has been given that teapot by the duke* – rheme; *That teapot* – theme – *the duke has given to my aunt* – rheme). In the theme-rheme structure, it is the theme that is the prominent element. It receives particular attention in Halliday's analysis. Some grammarians have used the terms *topic* and *comment* instead of theme and rheme. The topic-comment dichotomy, however, carries different connotations (see François, 1987, for an analysis). With respect to Halliday's presentation, the label "topic" usually refers to one particular kind of theme (see "topical theme" discussed later).

The theme is not necessarily a nominal group introduced by a locution like *as for, with regard to* (e.g., *As for my aunt, the duke has given her that teapot*), as in the preceding examples. It may belong to a number of other grammatical classes. Those major ones are indicated and illustrated here:

- Adverbial group (*once* in *Once I was a real turtle*).
- Prepositional phrase (*on Friday night* in *On Friday night I go backward to bed*).
- Clause (*what happened* in *What happened was that the duke gave my aunt that teapot*).
- Conjunctive adjunct [those elements that relate the clause to the preceding text or to the (extralinguistic) context, e.g., conditional adjuncts: *in that case, otherwise*].
- Modal adjunct (those elements that express the speaker's judgment regarding the relevance of the message, e.g., opinion or comment adjuncts: *from my point of view, in my opinion*).
- Conjunction (coordinator, subordinator).
- WH-item (interrogative, relative).
- TH-item (demonstrative, personal pronoun).
- Finite verb in yes/no questions (e.g., *is, isn't, do, don't, can, can't*). These verbs are so labeled because their function is to make the proposition finite (see later for a specification of the notion of "proposition").
- *You, let's*, finite verb *do* (or *don't*) in imperative clause (e.g., *You keep quiet, Let's go home, Don't argue*).

The element that is typically chosen as theme in a clause will vary with the mood. Major clauses are either indicative or imperative. If indicatives, they are either declarative (or exclamative) or interrogative. If interrogatives, they are either polar interrogative (yes/no questions) or content interrogative (WH-questions). In a *declarative clause*, the typical pattern is one in which theme is conflated with (grammatical) subject. When this situation prevails, the theme of the declarative clause is said to be unmarked. Any other element selected as theme (e.g., prepositional phrase, adverbial group, complement, or exclamatory WH-element – in the exclamative clauses, e.g., *How cheerfully he seems to grin*) is a marked theme. In yes/no *interrogative clauses*, the unmarked theme is the group formed by the finite verb plus subject (*Is anybody at home?*). In WH-questions, it is the WH-element, that is, the element specifying the nature of the requested information. But marked themes do sometimes occur in interrogative clauses, for example, in *After tea, will you tell me a story?* Finally, in *imperative clauses*, the unmarked theme is either, *you* or *let's* (*You keep quiet, Let's go home*), the finite verb *do* (*Do keep quiet*), the negative forms *don't* or *let's not*, or the imperative verb itself (*Sing a song, Close the door*).

Themes may be structurally *simple* or *multiple*. Unlike simple themes, multiple themes have "an internal structure of their own." The internal structure of a multiple theme is based on the principle that a clause is the product of three simultaneous semantic processes: It is a representation of experience (*ideational function*), an interactive exchange (*interpersonal function*), and a message (*textual function*). There is always (i.e., in all nonelliptical clauses) an ideational element in the theme, and there may be, but need not be, interpersonal and/or textual elements as well. Simple themes, therefore, have only an ideational element. Ideational meaning is the representation of experience, that is, anything representing a process, a participant in a process (person, thing), or a circumstance bearing on that process (time, place, manner, etc.). Foremost within the ideational element is the so-called topical theme, that is, the subject, complement, or circumstantial adjunct. It is labeled "topical" because it corresponds well to the element identified as "topic" in conventional topic-comment analysis. Interpersonal meaning is meaning as a form of action performed by the speaker on the hearer by means of language (statements, offers, requests). Within the interpersonal element, one may have (1) a modal theme, that is, one of the modal adjuncts already defined; (2) the finite verb in a yes/no interrogative clause; or (3) a vocative element. Textual meaning is relevant to the message function of the clause, that is, its insertion between a preceding and a following text and within a situational context. The textual element may have any combination of (1) continuative, (2) structural, and (3) conjunctive themes, in that order. Continuatives are small items such as *yes, no, well*, which constitute a response in dialogue or indicate a new move if the same speaker is continuing. A structural theme is a conjunction, a proposition, or an adverb. A conjunctive theme is one of the conjunctive adjuncts as previously defined. The typical sequence of the theme elements is textual-interpersonal-ideational. The sequence textual-interpersonal may be reversed, but the ideational element is always the final one and therefore precedes the rheme.

Examples:

on the other hand	may be	on a weekday	it would be less crowded
conjunctive textual theme	modal interpersonal	topical ideational	rheme

and

girls and boys	come out	to play
vocative interpersonal theme	topical ideational	rheme

Considered so far have been mostly theme and rheme in independent clauses. What about the thematic organization of nonindependent clauses? *Finite (i.e., complete) dependent clauses* typically have a conjunction as structural theme followed by a topical theme:

(1) (He left)

because	his work	was done
structural theme	topical	rheme

But if the dependent clause begins with a WH-element, that element constitutes the topical theme:

(2) (I asked)

why	no one was around
topical theme	rheme

In *nonfinite dependent clauses*, there may be a preposition as structural theme, which may be followed by a subject as topical theme; but many nonfinite clauses have neither and consist of rheme only.

Example:

with	every door	being locked (we had no choice)
structural theme	topical	rheme

Embedded clauses have a thematic structure that is the same as that of dependent clauses. Finally, *elliptical clauses* fall into three categories. Anaphoric elliptical clauses presuppose a part or the whole of what has been said before. If the latter, these clauses have no thematic structure (e.g., *Yes* or *No* in response to a question). In the former case, the specification of the thematic structure will depend on which part of the preceding clause is presupposed. In cataphoric elliptical clauses, the topical theme is left to the following clause. In exophoric elliptical clauses, the unexpressed part of the clause (subject and sometimes finite verb) may be understood from the context. These clauses consist of rheme only (e.g., *Thirsty?* for *Are you thirsty?*).

Clause as exchange

Simultaneously with its organization as a message, the clause is also organized as an interactive event involving speaker and audience – hearer(s) or listener(s). In this respect, four primary speech functions can be defined: offer, command, statement, question. The corresponding set of desired responses consists of accepting an offer, carrying out a command, acknowledging a statement, and answering a question. Cutting across these differences is another distinction that concerns the nature of the "commodity" being exchanged. It is either "goods and/or services," or (verbal) exchange of information. When language is used to exchange information, the clause takes on the form of a *proposition* (in the everyday sense of the word). When the function of the clause resides in the exchange of goods and/or services, it is a *proposal*.

The difference between proposition and proposal is that the former can be affirmed or denied (also doubted, tempered, qualified, etc.) whereas the latter can not. As expected, propositions have a more elaborated grammar than do proposals. The pivotal structure of these clauses is the *mood* element; the remaining is the *residue*. The mood consists of two parts: (1) the (grammatical) subject (nominal group, which may contain one or several embedded clauses) and (2) the finite element (which is part of the verbal group). The finite element is one of a small number of verbal operators expressing person, number, tense (e.g., *is*, *has*), aspect (e.g., *-ing*), modality (e.g., *can*, *must*), and polarity (affirmative or negative). In many instances, however, the finite element and the lexical verb are "fused" into a single word (e.g., *loves*). The grammatical category that is characteristically used to exchange information is the indicative [statements being expressed through declarative (or exclamative) clauses, and questions through interrogative ones]. This feature is typically realized in the following way:

1. The mood element consisting of subject plus the finite element realizes the feature indicative.
2. Within the indicative, the order of subject and finite is the significant aspect: (a) the order subject-finite specifies declarative (or exclamative); (b) the order finite-subject specifies yes/no interrogative; (c) in WH-interrogatives, the order is subject-finite if the WH-element is the subject, finite-subject, otherwise.

Imperative clauses may have a mood element consisting of finite plus subject (e.g., *Don't you believe it*), finite only (*Don't believe it*), subject only (*You believe it*), or have no mood element at all (*Believe it*). The subject specifies the one by reference to which the proposition can be affirmed or denied or the one who is responsible for the success of the proposal. This is not necessarily the same thing as actor, sensor, identifier, behaver, or sayer (to be defined later), since propositions and proposals can be passive. One factor is determinant in the speaker's choice of the particular item that will serve as subject of a proposition. Other things being equal, the same item will function as subject and as theme. In a declarative clause, the unmarked theme is the subject. If the speaker wants to change theme without the additional contrast of using a marked theme, he will use the passive option (e.g., *That teapot was given to my aunt by the duke* instead of *That teapot the duke gave to my aunt*).

The residue consists of functional elements of three kinds: (1) *predicator*, (2) *complement*, and (3) *circumstantial adjuncts*. There can be only one predicator, one or two complements, and a larger number of adjuncts (up to seven, in principle). The *predicator* is present in all nonelliptical clauses. It is realized by a verbal group minus the temporal-aspectual, the modal operator, or the polarity operator. These function as finite in the mood element. A complement is typically realized by a nominal group (e.g., in *The duke gave my aunt that teapot*, there are two complements: *my aunt* and *that teapot*). But there are also attributive complements (e.g., *China-blue* in *The teapot was China-blue*). A circumstantial adjunct is typically realized by an adverbial group or a prepositional phrase. In the clause *My aunt was given that teapot yesterday by the duke*, there are two circumstantial adjuncts: the adverbial group *yesterday* and the prepositional phrase *by the duke*. The typical (but in no way absolute) order of elements in the residue is predicator-complement(s)-circumstantial adjunct(s).

As already noted, other types of adjuncts exist besides circumstantial ones. Conjunctive adjuncts are outside the mood-residue organization. They have no function in the clause as exchange. Modal adjuncts are of two subtypes: (1) Mood adjuncts (expressing probability, usuality, obligation, inclination, presumption, time, degree, intensity) form part of the mood element (e.g., *gladly* in *I'd gladly help*); (2) comment adjuncts are not themselves part of the proposition and therefore fall outside the mood-residue structure. The following examples illustrate various types of adjuncts occurring in the same clause:

unfortunately	however	he	can't	usually
comment adjunct	conjunctive adjunct	subject	finite	mood adjunct
		mood		

and

hear	clearly	on the telephone
predicator	circumstantial adjunct	circumstantial adjunct
residue		

Either the mood or the residue may be absent in elliptical clauses. The residue may be established at the start and be left out of the clause or substituted with do [e.g., *(Will you join the party?) I might (do)*]. In exchanges involving the WH-variable, where just one element is under discussion, everything may be omitted except that element. There are also forms of ellipsis of the mood, either the subject and the finite element [*(Shall I) carry your bag?*)] or the subject alone [*(Have you) seen Fred?*]. In a giving clause (offer or statement), the unmarked subject is *I* or *we*. In a demanding clause, it is *you*. Therefore, in a giving clause without subject, the listener will understand the subject as *I* or *we*. In a demanding clause, the listener will understand the subject as *you*.

Clause as representation

According to Halliday, our conception of reality consists of doing, happening, feeling, being, and so on. These "goings-on" are organized in the semantic system of the language and expressed through the grammar of the clause. They constitute the system of *transitivity*. Transitivity specifies the different types of processes that are recognized in the language and the structures that serve to express them. A process potentially consists of three components: (1) the *process* itself, (2) the *participants* in the process, and (3) the *circumstances* associated with the process. Such an interpretation of processes lies behind the grammatical sorting of words into phrase classes: verbal group, nominal group, adverbial group, attributive group, and prepositional phrase. It is possible to specify further the different types of processes and the kinds of participant role associated with each.

MATERIAL PROCESSES (DOING). They express the notion that some entity (traditionally referred to as the *agent*) does something that may be done (in the case of transitive verbs or, more accurately, transitive clauses) to some other entity (referred to as the *goal* or the *patient*). Material processes can be further distinguished between dispositive and creative types (the latter occurring if the goal, not preexisting, is brought into being by the process, as e.g., in *She prepared the cocktails*). Material processes are not necessarily physical events. There are abstract doings (e.g., *The major resigned*).

MENTAL PROCESSING (FEELING, PERCEIVING, THINKING). They express the notion that a participant who is human or humanlike "senses," in the large sense, a *phenomenon* (i.e., feels, perceives, or thinks); hence, he will be referred to as the *senser*. Material processes fall into two types: transitive (those with two participants) and intransitive ones (those with one participant). Mental processes are of one type only. They all involve a senser and a phenomenon; this does not mean that both are always expressed in the clause.

RELATIONAL PROCESSES (BEING). The central meaning of an important number of clauses in the language is that "something is." This general meaning can be accommodated in at least three different ways (types): (1) *intensive* (*X* is *A*), (2) *circumstantial* (*X* is at *A*), and (3) *possessive* (*X* has *A*). Each of these comes in two modes: (1) *attributive* (*A* is an attribute of *X*), and (2) *identifying* (*A* is the identity of *X*). This gives six types of relational processes. In the attributive mode, an attribute is ascribed to some entity, either as a quality (intensive), a circumstance (time, place, etc.), or a possession. This defines the two elements: *attribute* and *carrier* [e.g., in *Sarah is wise*, *Sarah* is the carrier and *wise* is the attribute (intensive)]. In the identifying mode, the structural functions are *identifier* and *identified* [in *The piano is Peter's*, *piano* is the identified, and *Peter's* is the identifier (possessive)]. These functions are conflated with another pair of grammatical functions: those of *token* (sign, name, form, holder, occupant) and *value* (meaning, referent, function, status, role). The conflation can go either way. Either the token or the value can serve as identifier. It is this feature that determines the voice in an identifying clause. If the subject is the same as the token, then the clause is active (e.g., *Mr. Garrick played Hamlet*). If the subject is the same as the value, then the clause is passive (e.g., *Hamlet was played by Mr. Garrick*).

SUBSIDIARY TYPES OF PROCESS (BEHAVING, SAYING, HAPPENING). Behavioral processes, grammatically, are intermediate between material and mental processes. The *behaver* typically is a conscious being like the sensor, but the process functions more like one of *doing*. In verbal processes, everything (conscious or not) that puts out a signal, let's say the *sayer*, expresses a "verbalization." Existential processes typically have the verb *be* or some other verb expressing *existence* (*exist*, *arise*, etc.) followed by a nominal group functioning as *existent* (e.g., *On the wall – there – was a picture*).

OTHER PARTICIPANT FUNCTIONS. The participants envisaged so far are those that are directly involved in the process. Grammatically, they typically are directly related to the verb. There are other participant functions in the clause also specific to each particular process type. However, they may be grouped together into two general functions common to all clauses: the *beneficiary* and the *range*. Beneficiary and range are the indirect participants. They are not so much inherent elements in the process as the direct participants. For example, in a material process, the beneficiary is either *recipient* (the one that goods are given to) or *client* (the one that services are done for) – for example, *She sent her best wishes to John*. In a verbal process, the beneficiary is the one being addressed (*receiver*) – for example, *Mary* in *John told Mary a story*. The range is the element that specifies the scope of the process. For example, in a material process, the range may express the domain over which the process takes place (e.g., *the mountain* in *Mary climbed the mountain*). In a verbal process, the range is the element expressing the class, quantity, or quality of what is said (e.g., *a silly question* in *John asked a silly question*).

CIRCUMSTANTIAL ELEMENTS. The major types of circumstantial elements are as follows: (1) *extent and location in time* (i.e., *duration* and *time*), and *space* (i.e., *distance* and *place*), including *abstract space*; (2) *manner*, with four subcategories: (a) *means* (typically expressed by a prepositional phrase – e.g., *The pig was beaten with the stick*), (b) *quality* or (c) *quantity* (typically expressed by an adverbial group – e.g., *It was snowing heavily*), and (d) *comparison* (typically expressed by a prepositional phrase – e.g., *It went through my head like an earthquake*); (3) *cause*, also with three subcategories: *reason*, *purpose*, and *behalf*; (4) *accompaniment*, which is a form of joint participation in the process; (5) *matter* (e.g., *I worry about her health*); and (6) *role* (e.g., *I come here as a friend*). Figure 5–1 summarizes the major aspects of clause organization (message, exchange, representation) according to Halliday's analysis.

Below the clause

Eight structures constituting the clause may be distinguished: nominal group, verbal group, attributive group, adverbial group, conjunction and preposition groups, conjunction and prepositional phrases. The difference between group and phrase is that a group is an expansion of a word (a "word complex," i.e., a head word together with other words that modify it), whereas a phrase is a contraction of a clause. The most important component in these structures is the so-called experiential one.

NOMINAL GROUP. The experiential structure of the nominal group has the function of specifying (1) a class of thing or (2) some category of membership within this class. The element specifying the class will be labeled *the thing*. It is the semantic core and the syntactic head of the nominal group. It may be common noun, proper noun, or personal pronoun. Membership within the class is typically expressed by one or more of the following elements (premodifiers): (1) *deictic*, (2) *quantifier*, (3) *epithet*, and (4) *classifier*.

The deictic elements indicate whether some specific subset of the thing is intended. They are the article *the*, the demonstrative and the possessive pronouns, the Saxon genitive (e.g., *my father's* . . .), the interrogative pronouns *which (ever)*, *what (ever)*, *whose (ever)*, as well as a number of nonspecific items such as *each*, *every*, *both*, *all*, *some*. There are also postdeictic elements, that is, a second element in the nominal group that adds further specification to the identification of the subset in question (e.g., *well-known* in *the well-known Mr. John Smith*). The quantifier indicates some quantitative or numerical feature of the subset: either quantity (cardinal numerals or other quantity indicators) or order (ordinal numerals). The epithet indicates some quality (objective or subjective) of the subset. The classifier indicates a particular subclass of the thing in question (e.g., *electric trains* vs. *toy trains*).

In terms of ordering, there is a progression in the nominal group from the kind of element that has the greatest specifying potential (the deictic) to that which has relatively less (i.e., postdeictic, quantifier, epithet, and classifier) – for example, *those same two white tennis balls*. In French, however, the classifier typically is placed after the thing. It is either introduced by a preposition (usually *de*) – for example, in *balle de tennis* – or not – for example, in *train-jouet*. In French again, the epithet may be placed either before the thing (*une belle maison*) or after the thing or the group thing-classifier (*une maison belle*, *une balle de tennis jaune*). Particular rules exist, however. For example, epithets expressing color are always placed after the thing that they specify (e.g., *un livre rouge*). There also may be noticeable differences of meaning depending on whether the epithet precedes or follows the thing. For example, *un homme grand* means a man who is of an elevated stature, whereas *un grand homme* means a man of exceptional qualities. It is often the case that the anteposited epithet expresses a meaning that is not literal.[3]

Following the thing, in English, is the *qualifier* (postmodifier). These are embedded relative clauses, participial or infinitive clauses, or prepositional phrases (e.g., *with the luminous nose*, in *the dong with the luminous nose*). In French, the qualifier follows the thing or the epithet whenever it is placed after the thing. Participial clauses may be introduced by a preposition (e.g., *He is good at playing cards*); the corresponding form in French is the infinitive clause (e.g., *Il est bon pour jouer aux cartes*). This is an area of overlap between prepositional phrases and nonfinite clauses of this type.

VERBAL GROUP. A verbal group consists of a sequence of words of the primary class of verb. For example, in the clause *Someone has been eating my porridge*, the verbal group is *has been eating*. It contains a lexical verb *eat*, which comes last, a finite verb *has*, which comes first, and an auxiliary verb *been*, which comes in between. The experiential structure of the finite verbal group is *finite* plus *event* with one or more optional *auxiliary(ies)*. There is a formal parallelism between the nominal and the verbal group. The verbal group begins with the finite, which is the verbal equivalent of the deictic, relating the process to the "speaker-now." The finite does

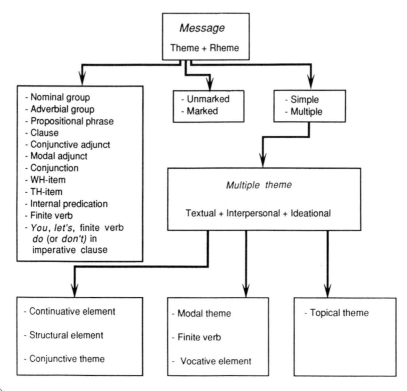

(a)

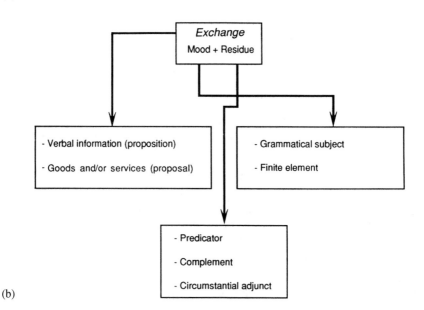

(b)

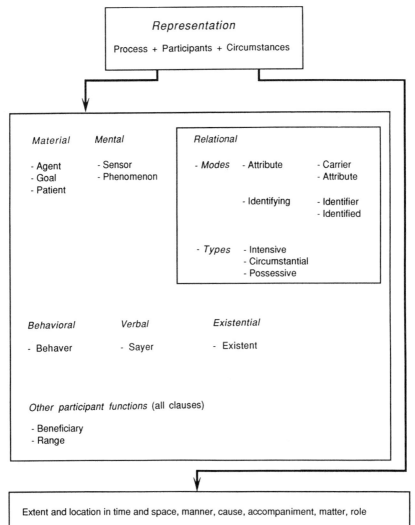

Figure 5–1. Summary of Halliday's clause analysis: (a) message, (b) exchange, (c) representation (Halliday, 1985).

so by tense or modality (i.e., the intermediate degrees between positivity and negativity in the meaning of a clause), whereas the deictic does so by person or proximity. The verbal group ends with the *event*, which is the verbal equivalent of the thing.

ATTRIBUTIVE GROUP. The attributive group has an attribute (of the grammatical subject) as head, which may be accompanied by modifying elements (premodifiers and/or postmodifiers). The attribute may be a noun, an adjective, a participle, a pronoun (e.g., *myself* in *I am myself again*), an infinitive (e.g., *to come* in *The best is yet to come*), an adverb, or a clause.

ADVERBIAL GROUP. The adverbial group has an adverb as head, which may be accompanied by modifying elements (premodifiers: *not, so, more –* e.g., *not so easy*; embedded postmodifiers: e.g., *than I could count* in *more quickly than I could count*).

CONJUNCTION GROUP. Conjunctions also form word groups by modification (e.g., *if only, not until*).

PREPOSITION GROUP. Prepositions form groups by modification in the same way as conjunctions (e.g., *not without* and *right behind*, in *not without some misgivings* and *right behind the door*).

CONJUNCTION PHRASE. A conjunction phrase consists of a conjunction (or conjunction group) plus a nominal group (e.g., *like that*) or an adverbial group (e.g., *like here*).

PREPOSITIONAL PHRASE. A propositional phrase consists of a preposition (or preposition group) plus a nominal group (e.g., *on the burning deck*) or an adverbial group (e.g., *nearby here*).

Table 5–2 summarizes the major aspects of below-the-clause organization according to Halliday's scheme.[4]

Above the clause

In the same way as a group can be interpreted as a word complex, a sentence can be interpreted as a "clause complex," that is, a head clause with other clauses that modify it. Of first importance here are the types of relationship holding between clauses. Two separate dimensions need to be considered: (1) the type of interdependency between clauses, or "taxis," and (2) the logicosemantic relations between clauses.

When two (or more) clauses have equal grammatical status, one *initiating* and the other(s) *continuing*, this is *parataxis*. Contrasting with this, is *hypotaxis*, where one or several clauses modify another one. The modifying clause(s) is(are) *dependent* on the one modified (*dominant*). For example, there is a paratactic relationship between *I would if I could* and *but I can't*, and a hypotactic relationship between *I would* and *if I could*.

For the sake of descriptive facility, the members of a pair of related clauses in "tactic" relation are referred to as *primary* and *secondary*. The primary is the initiating clause in a paratactic structure, and the dominant clause in a hypotactic one. The secondary is the continuing clause in a paratactic structure, and the dependent clause in a hypotactic one.

Table 5–2. *Summary of Halliday's below-the-clause analysis*

---

1. Nominal group

    Thing: common noun, proper noun, or personal pronoun

    Premodifiers: deictic, quantifier, epithet, or classifier

    Postmodifiers: qualifier (may be a numerative, an epithet, a classifier, an embedded relative clause, a participial or an infinitive clause, or a prepositional phrase)

2. Verbal group

    Finite

    Event

    Auxiliary

3. Attributive group

    Attributive

    Modifying elements (premodifiers and/or postmodifiers)

4. Adverbial group

    Adverb

    Modifying elements

5. Conjunction group

    (modified) conjunction or preposition

6. Preposition group

7. Conjunction phrase

    Conjunction (group)

    Nominal group

    Adverbial group

8. Prepositional phrase

    Preposition (group)

    Nominal group

    Adverbial group

Source: After Halliday, 1985.

There is a wide range of different logicosemantic relations any of which may hold between a primary and a secondary member of a clause complex. They can be classified in two fundamental types: (1) *expansion* and (2) *projection*. In expansions, the secondary clause expands the primary one by (1) *elaborating* it (i.e., restating it in other words, commenting, or exemplifying; e.g., hypotactic: *John ran away, which surprised everyone*; paratactic: *John didn't wait; he ran away and Fred stayed behind* – example of explicit co-ordination between clauses), (2) *enhancing* it (i.e., qualifying it with some circumstantial feature of time, place, cause, explanation, comparison, or condition; e.g., hypotactic: *John ran away because he was scared*; paratactic: *John was scared; so he ran away*), or (3) *extending* it (i.e., extending the meaning of the primary clause by adding something new to it, e.g., an addition, a replacement, or an alternative).

In projections, the secondary clause is projected through the primary one, which instates it (1) as *a report* (i.e., a construction of wording; e.g., hypotactic: *John said he was running away*; paratactic: *John said, "I'm running away"*), (2) as an *idea* (i.e., a construction of meaning; e.g., hypotactic: *John thought he would run away*; paratactic: *John thought to himself, "I'll run away"*), or (3) as a *fact* (i.e., one type of construction that involves neither mental nor verbal process but comes as if it were ready packaged in projected form, e.g., the attributive clause *that Caesar was dead* in *That Caesar was dead was obvious to all*). Subtypes for these above categories are given and defined in Halliday (1985). They will not be presented here or utilized in the analysis that follows.

In hypotaxis, the two clauses, primary and secondary, can occur in either order (e.g., *John ran away because he was scared*; *Because he was scared John ran away*). Order does not modify the dominant, dependent relationship. In parataxis, the two clauses can occur in either order, but, of course, the initiating clause is always the one that comes first. Figure 5–2 summarizes the major principles of the clause complex organization.

Beside the clause

This section relates to the information structure of the language. An information unit does not correspond exactly to any unit in the clause grammar. It may correspond to the clause, and this may be regarded as the unmarked condition, but not necessarily. A single clause may be mapped onto two or more information units, or a single information unit into two or more clauses. *Information* is defined here as a process of interaction between what is already known or can be predicted, and what is new or can not be predicted. Structurally, an information unit consists of an obligatory *new* element plus an optional *given* element. If the given element is not expressed (ellipsis), it must refer to something already present in the verbal or the nonverbal context. The information structure is realized as follows. The new is marked by tonic prominence or stress, and the given typically precedes the new. Each information unit is realized as a pitch contour (falling, rising, or mixed). Within the unit, one foot (and in particular its first syllable) carries the main pitch movement. The tonic foot specifies the end portion of what is new (focus) in the utterance (e.g., *The boy stood on the burning **deck*** – where the bold italics indicate tonic prominence or stress). However, nothing usually indicates where the new begins. This has to be established with the help of the verbal or the nonverbal context. The typical sequence of informational elements is the given followed by the new, but it is possible to have given material following the new (e.g., *They **see** it as beautiful*). At this stage, the notion of discursive newness needs specification. A new element may be

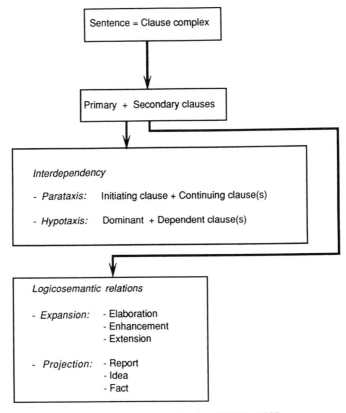

Figure 5–2. Summary of clause complex organization. (Halliday, 1985)

something that has not been mentioned before and that is not predictable from the nonverbal context, but it may also be something unexpected (contrastive emphasis), whether previously mentioned or not. Also, there are items in the language that are inherently given like the anaphoric elements (referring to things mentioned before) and the deictic elements. Typically these elements do not carry information focus. If they do, they are contrastive. The French language has the same information structure and pitch contour system as the English language.

Although there is a close semantic relationship between information structure and thematic structure (i.e., the theme will most often be selected from within what is in the given and the focus will be located within the rheme), they are not the same thing. The theme is what the speaker chooses as point of departure. The theme-rheme structure, therefore, is speaker oriented. The given is what the listener already knows, has access to, or does expect. The given-new structure is listener oriented. The unmarked pattern is for theme to go with given, and new with rheme, but there exist environmental conditions and rhetorical maneuvers that have the consequence of overriding this pattern.

Around the clause (textual dimension)

The preceding sections concern the organization of the clause (thematic and information structures). But for a sequence of clauses to constitute a text, it is also necessary to make explicit the relationships between clauses, clause complexes, or larger entities (paragraphs) that allow for textual cohesion (particularly at the "micro" level of the speech turn). There are four ways by which cohesion is created in English (as well as in French): (1) reference, (2) ellipsis, (3) conjunction, and (4) lexical cohesion.

REFERENCE.   A participant or circumstantial element introduced at one place in the text can be taken as a reference point for something that follows (e.g., *The boy who looks after the sheep ... he ... him ... he*).

ELLIPSIS.   A clause, part of a clause, or part of a nominal or verbal group may be presupposed at a subsequent place in text. Either the element is omitted or it is replaced by a substitutive element (e.g., the *do* in *I will not wake him up for if I do ...*).

CONJUNCTION.   A clause, clause complex, or some longer portion of text may be related to what follows by one of a set of semantic relations. These relations are fundamentally of the same kind as those that obtain between clauses in an expanded clause complex, as previously described.

LEXICAL COHESION.   Textual continuity may also be established by the choice of words. This may take the form of word repetition, the choice of a word that is related semantically or collocationally to a previous one, or the presence of "key words," that is, words having special significance for the meaning of the particular text.

Textual *cohesion* (in the sense just indicated) should not be confused with discursive *coherence* (i.e., connectedness of production or conversation at a macro level – over series of speech turns, and also between verbal and nonverbal acts). (For a further specification of these concepts, see Craig & Tracy, 1983; van Balkom, 1991.)

5.4.1.2.2 Data analysis

We now are in a position to apply Halliday's scheme to Françoise's corpus. Given the extent of the analysis, only the first sample of speech was analyzed. It appears that the second speech sample does not differ from the first one in terms of basic language structures. This minimizes the usefulness of performing and reporting very time- and space-consuming additional analyses.

First speech sample

The utterances analyzed in the first speech sample and constituting five speech turns of Françoise are numbered from 1 to 62. As Halliday's analytical scheme is largely based on the notion of major clause, only those utterances exhibiting a clear thematicorhematic structure were considered. This leaves out 10 utterances not qualifying as (major) clauses, the role of which seems to be mostly conversational (ellipses, additional qualifications or specifications of previous statements, emphasis expressed in relationship with previous statements, and interrupted clauses). These utterances were taken into account, however, at the "around-the-clause" level of analysis, which is particularly concerned with textual cohesion. The 52 remaining utterances (containing major clauses) were analyzed according to the three levels of clause structuring, that is, clause as message, clause as exchange, and clause as representation, as well as the other levels of analysis explained in the preceding section. The ordering numbers of these major-clause utterances bear the asterisk as they appear in the speech excerpts in Appendix 1, as well as in their translation in Appendix 2. Such number asterisks, therefore, do not indicate the ungrammatical status of the utterance as is the case in the rest of the book.

In what follows, the analytical data are first exposed. The reader will notice that the results of the above-the-clause analysis are presented in two separate blocks. The clause interdependency analysis is exposed within the clause-as-message level of characterization (where it is primarily relevant), whereas the analysis of the logicosemantic relations between clauses is the subject of a distinct section. The around-the-clause analysis dealing with the textual dimension of speech is not presented utterance per utterance but once at the end of each one of the five blocks of connected utterances produced by Françoise. The conclusions of the analyses are then provided.

Summary of analysis

WARNING TO THE ENGLISH-SPEAKING READER. For reasons having to do with the existence of subtle differences between French and English (particularly at the level of morpho-syntax), it has not always been possible to provide an exact correspondence between the French data and their English counterparts. This is exemplified on several occasions in the clause analysis, particularly as to the exchange dimension (where the decomposition of the clause elements and their classification into finite, predicator, complement, and circumstantial adjunct do not always correspond exactly in the two languages). I have tried to acknowledge those differences in the analysis at least on their first appearance. However, it would be tedious to repeat the same remark every time. The reader is invited to keep in mind that the primary data for the analysis are the French-language ones and that the English translations and correspondences are supplied only for his convenience.

Speech turn 1

UTTERANCE 2

et mon frère il habite sur les *roches*
(and my brother he lives on the rocks)

1. Clause level

MESSAGE.   Independent declarative[5] clause introduced by continuative theme (conjunction *et – and*), continued with unmarked topical theme as grammatical subject (*mon frère – my brother*), and rheme (*il habite sur les roches – he lives on the rocks*).

EXCHANGE.   Statement: Declarative with mood element consisting of grammatical subject (*mon frère – my brother*; and, in a subsidiary way, the immediately following recast of this nominal in the form of personal pronoun *il – he*), and finite element, integrated within the lexical verb (*habite – lives*); followed by residue consisting of predicator (*habite – lives*), and circumstantial adjunct (prepositional phrase *sur les roches – on the rocks*).

REPRESENTATION.   Intransitive material process *habiter – live* (participant: agent *mon frère – my brother*; circumstance: space *sur les roches – on the rocks*).

2. Below the clause

Conjunction group (conjunction *et – and*), nominal group (noun *frère – brother*, deictic *mon – my*, pronominal recast of noun head *il – he*), verbal group (finite-event *habite – lives*), prepositional phrase [preposition *sur*, nominal group (noun *roches – rocks*, deictic *les – the*)].

3. Beside the clause

Given information (*mon frère – my brother*) followed by new information (*il habite sur les **roches** – he lives on the rocks*), bold italics indicating (major) tonic prominence or stress. Notice that only the word in which tonic prominence is expressed was marked off that way; no attempt was made to specify more narrowly the localization of stress within the word.

UTTERANCE 3

quand vous venez donc de la vallée entre Verviers et ***Liège*** comme ça
mon frère habite juste au-dessus dans un chalet juste sur les ***roches***
(when you come therefore from the valley between Verviers and Liège
like that my brother lives right above in a chalet right on the rocks)

1. Clause level

MESSAGE. Hypotactic chaining: independent declarative clause with unmarked topical theme (*mon frère – my brother*) and rheme (*habite juste au-dessus dans un chalet juste sur les roches – lives right above in a chalet right on the rocks*); preceded by finite dependent clause with structural theme (conjunction *quand – where*), unmarked topical theme (personal pronoun *vous* – polite form for *you*), and rheme (*venez donc de la vallée entre Verviers et Liège comme ça – come therefore from the valley between Verviers and Liège like that*).

EXCHANGE. Statements: First declarative with mood element consisting of grammatical subject (*vous – you*) and finite element integrated into the lexical verb (*venez – come*); residue consisting of predicator (*venez – come*) and circumstantial adjuncts (prepositional phrase *de la vallée entre Verviers et Liège – from the valley between Verviers and Liège*, adverbial group *comme ça – like that*); conjunctive adjunct (*donc – therefore*) occurring in the middle of the clause coincides with a boundary between mood and residue (keeping in mind the fact that the lexical verb *venez – come* incorporates both the finite element and the predicator). Second declarative with mood element consisting of grammatical subject (*mon frère – my brother*) and finite element "fused" into the lexical verb (*habite – lives*); residue consisting of predicator (*habite – lives*) and a series of circumstantial adjuncts (adverbial group *juste au-dessus – right above*, prepositional phrase *dans un chalet – in a chalet*, and other prepositional phrase *juste sur les roches – right on the rocks* with anteposition of the adverbial modifier).

REPRESENTATION. First clause (in the linear order): intransitive material process *venir – come* (participant: agent *vous – you*; circumstance: space *de la vallée entre Verviers et Liège – from the valley between Verviers and Liège*). Second clause: intransitive material process *habiter – live* (participant: agent *mon frère – my brother*; circumstances: space *juste au-dessus – right above*, *dans un chalet – in chalet*, *juste sur les roches – right on the rocks*).

2. Below the clause

First clause: conjunction group (conjunction *quand – when*), nominal group (pronoun *vous – you*), verbal group (finite-event *venez – come*), prepositional phrase [preposition *de – from*, nominal group (noun *vallée – valley*, deictic *la – the*)], prepositional phrase [preposition *entre – between*, nominal group (proper nouns *Liège, Verviers*)], conjunction phrase [conjunction *comme – like*, nominal group (pronoun *ça – that*)]. Second clause: nominal group (noun *frère – brother*, deictic *mon – my*), verbal group (finite-event *habite – lives*), adverbial group (adverb *au-dessus – above*, premodifier *juste – right*), prepositional phrase [preposition *dans – in*, nominal group (noun *chalet – chalet*, deictic *un – a*)], prepositional phrase [preposition *sur – on*, premodifier *juste – right*, nominal group (noun *roches – rocks*, deictic *les – the*)].

3. Above the clause (logicosemantic relations)

Secondary clause *enhances* the meaning of the primary one by qualifying it with a circumstantial feature of *place*.

4. Beside the clause

First clause: given information (*vous – you*) followed by new information (*venez donc de la vallée entre Verviers et **Liège** comme ça – come therefore from the valley between Verviers and Liège like that*). Second clause: given (*mon frère – my brother*), new (*habite juste au-dessus dans un chalet juste sur les **roches** – lives right above in a chalet right on the rocks*).

UTTERANCE 5

il faut faire très attention ***là*** parce que il y a un grand ***tournant*** et alors pour tourner il faut bien tout ***ça***
(one must be very cautious there because there is a large turn and then in order to turn one really needs every caution)

1. Clause level

MESSAGE.   Paratactic chaining of two clause complexes tied by conjunction *et* (*and*): initiating clause complex is made of independent declarative clause with pronoun *il* (*one*) as unmarked topical theme plus rheme (*faut faire très attention là – must be very cautious there*) and finite dependent clause with structural theme (conjunction *parce que – because*), unmarked topical theme (pronoun *il y – there*), and rheme (*a un grand tournant – is a large turn*). Continuing clause complex is made of independent declarative clause with conjunctive theme (temporal adverb *alors – then*), unmarked topical theme (*il – one*), and rheme (*faut bien tout ça – really needs every caution*), and embedded nonfinite clause with preposition *pour* (*in order to*) as structural theme, plus rheme (*tourner – turn*).

EXCHANGE.   Statements: First declarative with mood (subject *il – one*, finite *faut – must*), and residue (predicator *faire attention – be cautious*; circumstantial adjuncts: quantitative adverb *très – very* inserted between the two lexical elements forming the predicator, locative adverb *là – there*). Second declarative with mood (subject *il y – there*, finite *a – is*) and residue (predicator *a – is*, complement *un grand tournant – a large turn*). Third declarative (elliptical) consisting of residue only (lexical verb *tourner – turn* as predicator). Fourth declarative consisting of mood (subject *il – one*, finite *faut – needs*) and residue (predicator *faut – needs*, adverb *bien* – *really*, complement *tout ça* – translated, in this context into *every caution*). Notice that the meaning and the interpersonal function of *faut* differs in the first declarative where it is a modal element meaning *must*, and in the fourth declarative where it is a lexical verb fused with finite element with the sense of *needs*.

REPRESENTATION. First clause: mental process *faire attention* – *be cautious* (participant: senser *il* – *one*; circumstance: space *là* – *there*). Second clause: happening process *(il y) a* – *(there) is* (participant: existent *un grand tournant* – *a large turn*; circumstance: space *y* – *there*). Third clause (relational processes): intensive *bien falloir* – *need* (participants: carrier *il* – *one*, attribute *tout ça* – *every caution*; circumstances: time *alors* – *then*, purpose *pour tourner* – *in order to turn*).

2. Below the clause

First clause: nominal group (pronoun *il* – *he*), verbal group (finite *faut* – *must*, event *faire attention* – *be cautious*), adverbial group (adverb *très* – *very*), adverbial group (adverb *là* – *there*). Second clause: conjunction group (conjunction *parce que* – *because*), nominal group (pronoun *il y* – *there*), verbal group (finite-event *a* – *is*), nominal group (noun *tournant* – *turn*, deictic *un* – *a*, deictic *grand* – *large*). Third clause (elliptical): conjunction group (conjunction *et* – *and*), adverbial group (adverb *alors* – *then*), preposition group (preposition *pour* – *in order to*), verbal group (event *tourner* – *turn*). Fourth clause: nominal group (pronoun *il* – *one*), verbal group (finite-event *faut* – *needs*), nominal group (pronoun *ça*, epithet *tout* – *every*), adverbial group (adverb *bien* – *really*).

3. Above the clause (logicosemantic relations)

Secondary clause in first clause complex *enhances* the meaning of the primary one by qualifying it with a circumstantial feature of *cause*. Secondary clause in second clause complex *enhances* the meaning of the primary one by qualifying it with a circumstantial feature of *condition*. The secondary clause complex *elaborates* the meaning of the primary one by *restating it* in other words.

4. Beside the clause

First clause: given information (*il* – *one*), new information (*faut faire très attention **là*** – *must be very cautious there*). Second clause: given (*il y* – *there*), new (*a un grand **tournant*** – *is a large turn*). Third clause: given (*alors pour tourner* – *then in order to turn*) new (*il faut bien tout **ça*** – *one really needs every caution*).

Speech turn 1 – Around the clause

The speech turn centers around the specification of the location of the house of Françoise's brother. *Lexical cohesion* appears to be the major way through which a degree of textual organization is achieved (explicit interutterance conjunction, ellipsis, and reference are little used). Lexical cohesion is maintained through the repetitive use of *mon frère – my brother, habite – lives*, and semantically related words such as *venir – come, route – way, tournant – turn, tourner – (to) turn*, and *rencontrer – encounter*, all suggesting an itinerarylike representation.

Utterance 4 (*une grande un grande morceau d'route comme ça – a large a large piece of road like that*) does not directly follow from the preceding utterance. It begins with a false start probably attesting to some (minor) degree of local difficulty in textual organization.

Speech turn 2

UTTERANCE 8

j'ai une *amie* qui habite juste sur la place de Fraipont la place de
l'*église*
(I have a girlfriend who lives right on Fraipont Square church square)

1. Clause level

MESSAGE. Hypotactic chaining: independent declarative clause with unmarked topical theme conflated with personal pronoun as grammatical subject (*j' – I*) and rheme (*ai une amie – have a girlfriend*), followed by relative clause with relative pronoun subject (*qui – who*) as topical theme and rheme (*habite juste sur la place de Fraipont la place de l'église – lives right on Fraipont Square church square*).

EXCHANGE. Statements: First declarative with mood subject (*j' – I*, finite *ai – have*) and residue (predicator *ai – have*, complement *une amie – a girlfriend*). Second declarative with mood (subject *qui – who*, finite *habite – lives*) and residue (predicator *habite – lives*; circumstantial adjuncts: adverb *juste – right*, elaborated prepositional phrase *sur la place de Fraipont la place de l'église – on Fraipont Square church square*).

REPRESENTATION. First clause (relational process): possessive *avoir – have* [participants: identifier (possessor) *j' – I*, identified (possessed) *une amie – a girlfriend*]. Second clause: intransitive material process *habiter – live* (participant: agent *qui -who*; circumstance: space *juste sur la place de Fraipont la place de l'église – right on Fraipont Square church square*).

2. Below the clause

First clause: nominal group (pronoun *j' – I*), verbal group (finite-event *ai – have*), nominal group (noun *amie – girlfriend*, deictic *une – a*). Second clause: nominal group (pronoun *qui – who*), verbal group (finite-event *habite – lives*), adverbial group (adverb *juste – right*), prepositional phrase [{[preposition *sur – on*, nominal group [noun *place – square*, premodifier: deictic *la*, postmodifier: prepositional phrase [preposition *de*, nominal group (noun *Fraipont*)]}, nominal group {[noun *place – square*, premodifier: deictic *la*, postmodifier: prepositional phrase [preposition *de*, nominal group (noun *église – church*, deictic *l'*)]}}].

3. Above the clause (logicosemantic relations)

Secondary clause *extends* the meaning of the primary one by *adding new information*.

4. Beside the clause

First clause: given information (*j' – I*), new information (*ai une **amie** – have a girlfriend*). Second clause: given (*qui – who*), new (*habite juste sur la place de Fraipont la place de l'**église** – lives right on Fraipont Square church square*).

UTTERANCE 9

c'est bien bien *simple*
(that is fairly simple)

1. Clause level

MESSAGE. Independent declarative clause with unmarked topical theme conflated with demonstrative pronoun as subject (*c'* – contracted from for *this* or *that*) and rheme (*c'est bien simple – is fairly simple*).

EXCHANGE. Statement: Declarative with mood (subject *c'* – *that*, finite *est – is*) and residue (predicator *est – is*, attributive complement *bien simple – fairly simple*).

REPRESENTATION. Relational process: intensive *être – be* (participants: carrier *c'* – *that*, attribute *bien simple – fairly simple*).

2. Below the clause

Nominal group (pronoun *c'* – *that*), verbal group (finite-event *est – is*), and attributive group (attribute *simple – simple*, premodifier *bien – fairly*).

3. Beside the clause

Given information (*c'* – *that*), new information (*est bien **simple** – is fairly simple*).

UTTERANCE 10

il y a une église juste dans l'*fond* et alors vous montez un peu plus haut comme ça en traversant le un grand *pont* parce qu'il y a un petit et un

grand à côté d'une épicerie le petit et l'autre pour aller pour monter alors la route du **Haveigné**
(there is a church right at the bottom and then you go up a little more like that crosssing the a large bridge because there is a small one and a large one next to a grocery store the small one and the other one to go to go up then Haveigné Road)

1. Clause level

MESSAGE.   Paratactic chaining of one clause and one clause complex tied by conjunction *et* (*and*). Initiating clause is introduced by unmarked topical theme (*il y – there*) followed by rheme (*a une église juste dans l'fond – is a church right at the bottom*). Continuing clause complex (hypotactic) is made of independent declarative clause with conjunctive theme (*alors – then*), unmarked topical theme (*vous – you*), plus rheme (*montez un peu plus haut comme ça en traversant le un grand pont – go up a little more like that crossing the a large bridge*), and finite dependent clause with structural theme (conjunction *parce qu'* – contracted form for *because*), unmarked topical theme *il y* (*there*), and rheme (*a un petit et un grand à côté d'une épicerie le petit et l'autre pour aller pour monter alors la route du Haveigné – is a small one and a large one next to a grocery store the small one and the other one to go to go up then Haveigné Road*).

EXCHANGE.   Statements: First declarative (mood: subject *il y – there*, finite: *a – is*; residue: predicator *a – is*, complement *une église – a church*, circumstantial adjunct *juste dans l'fond – right at the bottom*). Second declarative (mood: subject *vous – you*, finite *montez – go*; residue: predicator *montez – go up*, circumstantial adjuncts *un peu plus haut – a little more*, *comme ça – like that*, *en traversant le un grand pont – crossing the a large bridge*). Third declarative (mood: subject *il y – there*, finite *a – is*; residue: predicator *a – is*, complement *un petit et un grand – a small one and a large one*). Fourth declarative (elliptical) (mood: subject *le petit – the small one*, no finite; residue: no predicator, circumstantial adjunct *à côté d'une épicerie – next to a grocery store*). Fifth declarative (elliptical) [mood: subject *l'autre – the other*, no finite; residue: no predicator, complement consisting itself of a sixth declarative (elliptical) with residue only: predicator formulated twice *aller – go*, *monter – go up*, circumstantial adjunct *alors – then*, complement *la route du Haveigné – Haveigné Road*].

REPRESENTATION.   First clause: happening process (*il y*) *a – (there) is* (participant: existent *une église – a church*; circumstances: space *y – there*, *juste dans le fond – right at the bottom*). Second clause: intransitive material process *monter – go up* (participant: agent *you – vous*; circumstances: space *un peu plus haut – a little more*, comparison *comme ça – like that*, space *en traversant un grand pont – crossing a large bridge*). Third clause: happening process (*il y*) *a – (there) is* [participants: existents *un petit et un grand (pont)* – *a small one and a large one*; circumstances: space *à côté d' une épicerie* – *next to a grocery store* (*le petit* – *the small one*, repetition of the existent), (*l'autre* – *the other one*, repetititon of the existent) *pour monter la route du Haveigné* – *to go up Haveigné Road*, time *alors* – *then*].

2. Below the clause

First clause: nominal group (pronoun *il y* – *there*), verbal group (finite-event *a* -*is*), nominal group (noun *église* – *church*, deictic *une* – *a*), adverbial group (adverb *juste* – *right*), prepositional phrase [preposition *dans* – *at*, nominal group (noun *fond* – *bottom*, deictic *le* – *the*)]. Second clause: conjunction group (conjunction *et* – *and*), adverbial group (adverb *alors* – *then*), nominal group (pronoun *vous* – *you*), verb group (finite-event *montez* – *go up*), adverbial group (adverb *plus haut* – *more*, premodifying locution *un peu* – *a little*), conjunction phrase [conjunction *comme* – *like*, nominal group (pronoun *ça* – *that*], verbal group (finite-event *travers-ant* – *crossing*), nominal group (noun *pont* – *bridge*, deictic *un* – *a*, epithet *grand* – *large*). Third clause: conjunction group (conjunction *parce que* – *because*), nominal group (pronoun *il y* – *there*), verbal group (finite-event *a* – *is*), nominal group (elliptical) (head noun not produced, deictic *un* – *a*, epithet *petit* – *small*), conjunction group (conjunction *et* – *and*), nominal group (elliptical) (head noun not produced, deictic *un* – *a*, epithet *grand* – *large*), prepositional phrase [preposition *à côté de* – *next to*, nominal group (noun *épicerie* – *grocery store*, deictic *une* – *a*), nominal group (elliptical) (head noun not produced, deictic *le* – *the*, epithet *petit* – *small*)], conjunction group (conjunction *et* – *and*), nominal group (elliptical) (head noun not produced, deictic *l'* – *the*, epithet *autre* – *other*). Fourth clause (infinitive): subject not expressed, verbal group (event *aller* – *go*, *monter* – *go up*), nominal group {[noun *route* – *route*, premodifier: deictic *la* – *the*, postmodifier: prepositional phrase [preposition *du*, nominal group (noun *Haveigné*)]}, adverbial group (adverb *alors* – *then*).

3. Above the clause (logicosemantic relations)

Clause complex *extends* the meaning of clause by *adding new information*. Secondary clause in clause complex *enhances* the meaning of the primary one by qualifying it with a circumstantial feature of *explanation*, bearing more specifically on the use in the primary clause of the epithet *grand* – *large* next to the word *pont* – *bridge*.

4. Beside the clause

First clause: given information (*il y* – *there*), new information (*a une église juste dans le **fond*** – *is a church right at the bottom*. Second clause: given (*alors vous* – *then you*), new (*montez un peu plus haut comme ça en traversant le un grand **pont***

– go up a little more like that crossing the a large bridge). Third clause: given (*il y –* *there*), new (*a un petit et un grand à côté d' une épicerie le petit et l' autre pour aller* *pour monter alors la route du* **Haveigné** *– is a small one and a large one next to a* *grocery strore the small one and the other one to go to go up then Haveigné Road*).

UTTERANCE 11

alors ça commence déjà à ce moment **là**
(then that begins already at that moment)

1. Clause level

MESSAGE. Independent declarative clause with conjunctive theme (*alors – then*), unmarked topical theme conflated with demonstrative pronoun subject *ça* (*that*), and rheme (*commence déjà à ce moment là – begins already at that moment*).

EXCHANGE. Statement: Declarative with mood (subject *ça – that*, finite *commence – begins*), and residue (predicator *commence – begins*; circumstantial adjuncts: adverb *déjà – already*, prepositional phrase *à ce moment là – at that moment*).

REPRESENTATION. Happening process, *commencer – begin* (participant: existent *ça – that*; circumstances: time *alors – then*, quality *déjà – already*, time *à ce moment là – at that moment*).

2. Below the clause

Adverbial group (adverb *alors – then*), nominal group (pronoun *ça – that*), verbal group (finite-event *commence – begins*), adverbial group (adverb *déjà – already*), prepositional phrase [preposition *à – at*, nominal group (noun *moment – moment*, premodifier: deictic *ce – that*, postmodifier: adverb *là*)].

3. Beside the clause

Given information (*ça – that*), new information (*commence déjà à ce moment là – begins already at that moment*).

UTTERANCE 12

mais alors du côté pour donc on **va** parce qu'il y a beaucoup de **tournants** comme ça et alors on **arrive**
(but then on the side to therefore one goes because there are many turns like that and then one is arrived)

1. Clause level

MESSAGE. Paratactic chaining of one clause complex and one clause tied by conjunction *et* (*and*). Initiating clause complex (hypotactic) is made of independent declarative clause introduced by what appears to be a poorly organized multiple theme, some elements of which being (in the following linear order) continuative (oppositive) theme (*mais* – *but*), conjunctive theme (*alors* – *then*), unmarked topical theme (*on* – *one*), and rheme (*va* – *goes*); followed by finite dependent clause with structural theme (*parce qu'* – *because*), unmarked topical theme (*il y* – *there*), and rheme (*a beaucoup de tournants comme ça* – *are many turns like that*). Continuing clause is an independent declarative clause with conjunctive theme (*alors* – *then*), unmarked topical theme (*on* – *one*), and rheme (*arrive* – *is arrived*).

EXCHANGE. Statements: First declarative (mood: subject *on* – *one*, finite *va* – *goes*; residue: predicator *va* – *goes*). Second declarative (mood: subject *il y* – *there*, finite *a* – *are*; residue: predicator *a* – *are*, complement (*beaucoup de tournants* – *many turns*). Third declarative (mood: subject *on* – *one*, finite *arrive* – *is*; residue: predicator *arrive* – *arrived*).

REPRESENTATION. First clause: intransitive material process *aller* – *go* [participant: agent *on* – *one*; circumstances: time *alors* – *then*, space (incomplete) *du côté* – *on the side*]. Second clause: happening process (*il y*) *a* – (*there*) *are* (participant: existent *beaucoup de tournants* – *many turns*; circumstance: comparison *comme ça* – *like that*). Third clause: intransitive material process *arriver* – *arrive* (participant: agent *on* – *one*; circumstance: time *alors* – *then*).

2. Below the clause

First clause: nominal group (pronoun *on* – *one*) (preceded by dysfluent sequence), verbal group (finite-event *va* – *goes*), adverbial group (adverb *alors* – *then*). Second clause: conjunction group (conjunction *parce qu'* – *because*), nominal group (pronoun *il y* – *there*), verbal group (finite-event *a* – *is*), nominal group (noun *tournants* – *turns,* deictic *de,* quantifier *beaucoup* – *many*), conjunction phrase [conjunction *comme* – *like,* nominal group (pronoun *ça* – *that*)]. Third clause: conjunction group (conjunction *et* – *and*), adverbial group (adverb *alors* – *then*), nominal group (pronoun *on* – *one*), verbal group (finite-event *arrive* – *is arrived*).

3. Above the clause (logicosemantic relations)

Secondary clause in clause complex *enhances* the meaning of the primary one by qualifying it with a circumstantial feature of *cause*. Secondary clause in paratactic chaining *extends* the meaning of the clause complex by *supplying new information*.

4. Beside the clause

First clause: given information (*on – one*), new information (***va** – goes*). Second clause: given (*il y – there*), new (*a beaucoup de **tournants** comme ça – are many turns like that*). Third clause: given (*on – one*), new (***arrive** – is arrived*).

UTTERANCE 13

il y a encore une maison sur le ***coin*** et vous montez un peu plus ***haut*** et c'est là que j'***habite***
(there is one more house on the corner and you go a little upper and that is there that I live)

1. Clause level

MESSAGE.   Paratactic chaining of two independent declarative clauses and one hypotactic clause complex tied by conjunctions (*et – and*). Initiating clause is introduced by unmarked topical theme *il y – then*) followed by rheme (*a encore une maison sur le coin – is one more house on the corner*). First continuing clause is made of unmarked topical theme (*vous – you*) and rheme (*montez un peu plus haut – go upper a little more*). Second continuing clause (i.e., hypotactic clause complex) is made of independent declarative clause with unmarked topical theme (*c' – this* or *that*) and rheme (*est là – is there*); followed by finite dependent clause with structural theme (*que – that*), unmarked topical theme (*j' – I*), and rheme (*habite – live*).

EXCHANGE.   Statements: First declarative (mood: subject *il y – there*, finite *a – is*; residue: predicator *a – is*, circumstantial adjunct *encore – more*, complement *une maison – one house*, circumstantial adjunct: prepositional phrase *sur le coin – on the corner*). Second declarative (mood: subject *vous – you*, finite *montez – go*; residue: predicator *montez – go upper*, circumstantial adjunct *un peu plus haut – a little upper*). Third declarative (mood: subject *c' – that*, finite *est – is*; residue: predicator *est – is*, circumstantial adjunct: adverb *là – there*). Fourth declarative (mood: subject *j' – I*, finite *habite – live*; residue: predicator *habite – live*).

REPRESENTATION.   First clause: happening process (*il y) a – (there) is* (participant: existent *une maison – one house*; circumstances: quality *encore – more*, space *sur le coin – on the corner*). Second clause: intransitive material process *monter – go up* (participant: agent *vous – you*, circumstance: space *un peu plus haut – a little upper*). Third clause relational process: intensive *être – be* (participants: carried *c' – that*, attribute *là – there*). Fourth clause: intransitive material process *habiter – live* (participant: agent *je – I*; circumstance: space *que – that*).

2. Below the clause

First clause: nominal group (pronoun *il y – there*), verbal group (finite-event *a -is*), nominal group (noun *maison – house*, deictic *une – a*), adverbial group (adverb *encore – more*), prepositional phrase [preposition *sur – on*, nominal group (noun *coin – corner*, deictic *le – the*)]. Second clause: conjunction group (conjunction *et – and*), nominal group (pronoun *vous – you*), verbal group (finite-event *montez – go up*), adverbial group (adverb *plus haut – upper*, quantifier *un peu – a little*). Third clause: conjunction group (conjunction *et – and*), nominal group (pronoun *c' – that*), verbal group (finite-event *est – is*), attributive group (attribute *là – there*). Fourth clause: nominal group (pronoun *j' – I*), verbal group (finite-event *habite – live*).

3. Above the clause (logicosemantic relations)

First and second continuing clauses in paratactic chaining *extend* each other's meaning and the meaning of the primary clause by *adding new information*. Second clause in hypotactic clause complex *extends* the primary clause by specifying the meaning of the locative adverb *là – there*.

4. Beside the clause

First clause: given information (*il y a encore une maison – there is one more house*), new information (*sur le **coin** – on the corner*). Second clause: given [*vous montez – you go (a little) upper*)], new (*un peu plus **haut** – a little upper*). Third clause: given (*c'est là – that is there*), new (*j'**habite** – I live*).

UTTERANCE 14

moi j'habite par *là*
(me I live over there)

1. Clause level

MESSAGE. Independent declarative clause with unmarked topical theme (*moi – me*), and rheme (*j'habite par là – I live over there*). (N.B. This clause is perfectly correct in French, unlike its English literal translation.)

EXCHANGE. Statement: Declarative with mood (subject *moi j' – me I*, finite *habite – live*) and residue (predicator *habite – live*, prepositional phrase *par là – over there*).

REPRESENTATION. Intransitive material process: *habiter – live* (participant: agent *j' – I*; circumstance: space *par là – over there*).

2. Below the clause

Nominal group (pronouns *moi je – me I*), verbal group (finite-event *habite – live*), adverbial group (adverb *par là – over there*).

3. Beside the clause

Given information (*moi j'habite – me I live*), new information (par *là – over there*).

Speech turn 2 – Around the clause

The whole speech turn answers J.F.B.'s question as to Françoise living in the valley or in the upper village. Françoise starts her verbal description from the church village in the valley, whereby she is side tracked into mentioning the place of her girlfriend, and then she moves gradually up until the location of her house.

Textual cohesion is ensured through the use of *lexical cohesion, reference,* and *conjunction.* A number of related spatial lexical terms and expressions are used that suggest the itinerary that follows (*fond – bottom, montez un peu plus haut – go up a little more, en traversant – crossing, à côté de – next to, épicerie – grocery store, pour monter – to go up, tournants – turns, on arrive – one is arrived, maison – house, le coin – the corner, vous montez – you go up.* Participants or circumstantial elements introduced at one place in the text are taken as reference points for information that follows [*un petit – a small one* and *un grand – a large one* referring back to bridges, *ça – that* referring back to *la route du Haveigné – Haveigné Road, il y a – there is* (two times), and *là – there* (two times) referring back to itinerary elements]. A relatively large number of loose coordination elements (conjunctions, temporal adverbs) are also used as text organizers (*et alors – and then, comme ça – like that, alors – then, mais alors – but then, et alors – and then, et . . . et – and . . . and*).

Utterance 12 begins with a false start (*mais alors du côté pour donc on va – but then on the side to therefore one goes*). Françoise appears to have wanted to supply an additional information on direction only to end up with a causally introduced statement on the quantity of turns (*parce qu'il y a beaucoup de tournants – because there are many turns*).

Speech turn 3

UTTERANCE 16

alors on doit faire ***attention*** parce qu'ils sont forts pour entrer dans les ***maisons***
(then one must be cautious because they are clever at breaking into the houses)

1. Clause level

MESSAGE. Hypotactic chaining: clause complex made of independent declarative clause with conjunctive theme (*alors – then*), unmarked topical theme (pronoun *on – one*), and rheme (*doit faire attention – must be cautious*); followed by finite dependent clause with structural theme (conjunction *parce qu'* – *because*), unmarked topical theme (*ils* – *they*), and rheme (*sont forts pour entrer dans les maisons* – *are clever at breaking into the houses*).

EXCHANGE. Statements: First declarative (mood: subject *on* – *one*, finite *doit* – *must*; residue: predicator *faire attention* – *be cautious*). The English translation of *faire attention* into *be cautious*, if analyzed literally, calls for a decomposition of residue into predicator *be* and attributive complement *cautious*. Second declarative (mood: subject *ils* – *they*, finite *sont* – *are*; residue: predicator *sont* – *are*, attributive complement (*forts pour entrer dans les maisons* – *clever at breaking into the houses*).

REPRESENTATION. First clause: mental process *faire attention* – *be cautious* (participant: senser *on* – *one*, circumstance: time *alors* – *then*). Second clause (relational process): intensive *être* – *be* (participants: carrier *ils* – *they*, attribute *forts* – *clever*, circumstance: reason *pour entrer dans les maisons* – *at breaking into the houses*).

2. Below the clause

First clause: adverbial group (adverb *alors* – *then*), nominal group (pronoun *on* – *one*), verbal group (finite *doit* – *must*, event *faire attention* – *be cautious*). Second clause: conjunction group (conjunction *parce qu'* – *because*), nominal group (pronoun *ils* – *they*), verbal group (finite-event *sont* – *are*), attributive group [attribute *forts* – *clever*, qualifier: infinitive clause introduced by preposition *pour* – *at* (*entrer dans les maisons* – *breaking into the houses*)]. This (third) clause (elliptical) is made of verbal group (event *entrer* – *break*), prepositional phrase [preposition *dans* – *into*, and nominal group (noun *maison* – *houses*, deictic *les* – *the*)].

3. Above the clause (logicosemantic relations)

Secondary clause *enhances* the meaning of the primary one by qualifying it with a circumstantial feature of *time*.

4. Beside the clause

First clause: given information (*on* – *one*), new information (*doit faire* **attention** – *must be cautious*). Second clause: given (*ils sont forts* – *they are clever*), new (*pour entrer dans les* **maisons** – *at breaking into the houses*).

UTTERANCE 17
alors moi je m'***méfie***
(then me I am wary)

1. Clause level

MESSAGE. Independent declarative clause with conjunctive theme (*alors* – *then*), unmarked topical theme *moi* (*me*), and rheme (*je m'méfie* – *I am wary*).

EXCHANGE. Statement: Declarative with mood (subject *moi je* – *me I*, finite *m'méfie* – *am*) and residue (predicator *me méfie* – *wary*). The lexical verb is pronominal (*se méfier*).

REPRESENTATION. Mental process *se méfier* – *be wary* (participant: senser *je* – *I*; circumstance: time *alors* – *then*).

2. Below the clause

Adverbial group (adverb *alors* – *then*), nominal group (pronouns *me* – *je*, *me* – *I*), verbal group (finite-event *méfie* – *am wary*).

3. Above the clause

Given information (*moi* – *me*), new information (*je m'**méfie*** – *I am wary*).

UTTERANCE 18

chaque fois que je suis souvent enfin rarement mais enfin mon père est
ici *lui* et il fait son *tour*
(each time that I am often that is rarely but in the end my father is here
him and he makes his turn)

1. Clause level

MESSAGE. Paratactic chaining of one clause complex and one clause tied by conjunction *et* (*and*). Initiating clause complex (hypotactic) is made of a finite dependent clause that could not be properly completed – in its given state, it encompasses structural theme (conjunction *chaque fois que* – *each time that*), unmarked topical theme (*je* – *I*), and rheme (*suis* – *am*); followed by independent declarative clause with unmarked topical theme (*mon père* – *my father*) and rheme (*est ici lui* – *is here him*). Continuing clause is independent declarative clause with unmarked topical theme (*il* – *he*), and rheme (*fait son tour* – *makes his turn*).

EXCHANGE. Statements: First declarative (incomplete) (mood: subject *je* – *I*, finite *suis* – *am*; residue: predicator *suis* – *am*). Second declarative (mood: subject *mon père* – *my father*, finite *est* – *is*; residue: predicator *est* – *is*, circumstantial adjunct *ici* – *here*). Third declarative (mood: subject *il* – *he*, finite *fait* – *makes*; residue: predicator *fait* – *makes*, complement *son tour* – *his turn*).

REPRESENTATION. First clause is incomplete and cannot be properly analyzed from the representational point of view. Second clause (relational process):

circumstantial *être ici – be here* (participants: carrier *mon père – my father*, attribute *ici – here*). Third clause (transitive material process): *faire – make* (participants: agent *il – he*, range: *son tour – his turn*).

2. Below the clause

First clause: conjunction group (conjunction *chaque fois que – each time that*), nominal group (pronoun *je – I*), verbal group (finite-event *suis – am*), adverbial groups (adverbs *souvent – often*, *enfin, – then*, *rarement – rarely*). Second clause: conjunction group (conjunction *mais – but*), adverbial group (adverb *enfin – in the end*), nominal group (noun *père – father*, deictic *mon – my*), verbal group (finite-event *est – is*), adverbial group (adverb *ici – here*), followed by pronominal recast (*lui – him*) of nominal group *mon père – my father*. Third clause: conjunction group (conjunction *et – and*), nominal group (pronoun *il – he*), verbal group (finite-event *fait – makes*), nominal group (noun *tour – turn*, deictic *son – his*).

3. Above the clause (logicosemantic relations)

Clause complex *extends* the meaning of the primary clause in hypotactic chaining by *adding new information*. The same logicosemantic relation holds between primary and secondary clauses within the clause complex.

4. Beside the clause

First (complete) clause: given information (*est ici – is here*), new information (*mon père ... **lui** – my father ... him*). Second clause: given (*il – he*), new (*fait son **tour** – makes his turn*).

UTTERANCE 19
mais il ne revient que le *soir*
(but he comes back only at night)

1. Clause level

MESSAGE. Independent declarative clause with continuative (oppositive) theme (*mais – but*), unmarked topical theme (*il – he*), and rheme (*ne revient que le soir – comes back only at night*).

EXCHANGE. Statement: Declarative with mood (subject *il – he*, finite *ne revient – comes*) and residue (predicator *revient – comes back*, circumstantial adjuncts: adverb *que – only*, prepositional phrase *le soir – at night*).

REPRESENTATION. Intransitive material process *revenir – come back* (participant: agent *il – he*; circumstances: quality *ne que – only*, time *le soir – at night*).

2. Below the clause

Conjunction group (conjunction *mais – but*), nominal group (pronoun *il – he*), verbal group (finite-event *ne revient que – comes back only*), adverbial group (adverbial locution *le soir – at night*).

3. Beside the clause

Given information (*il – he*), new information (*ne revient que le **soir** – comes back only at night*).

UTTERANCE 20

alors souvent le *jeudi* nous autres on se réunit vous savez toutes des
(then often on Thursdays we get together you know all)

1. Clause level

MESSAGE. Independent declarative clause with conjunctive theme (*alors – then*), modal theme (*souvent – often*), and marked topical theme conflated with temporal circumstantial adjunct (*le jeudi – on Thursdays*), followed by rheme (*nous autres on se réunit vous savez toutes des – we get together you know all*).

EXCHANGE.   Statements: Declarative with mood (subject *nous autres on – we*, finite *se réunit – get*) and residue (circumstantial adjuncts *alors – then*, *souvent – often*, *le jeudi – on Thursdays*, predicator *se réunit – get together*). There are two other declaratives formulated within this utterance. One is a sort of conversational interjection *vous savez – you know* (mood: subject *vous – you*, finite *savez – know*; residue: predicator *savez – know*). The other one is incomplete (false start for utterance 21) *toutes des – all* for *nous sommes toutes des femmes – we are all women*. It consists of the attributive complement only.

REPRESENTATION.   Intransitive material process *se réunir – get together* (participant: agent *nous – we*; circumstances: time *alors – then*, quality *souvent – often*, time *le jeudi – on Thursdays*).

2. Below the clause

First clause: nominal group (pronoun *nous autres – we*), verbal group (finite-event *se réunit – get together*), adverbial groups (adverbs *alors – then*, *souvent – often*, *le jeudi – on Thursdays*). Second clause: nominal group (head: pronoun *vous – you*), verbal group (finite-event *savez – know*). Third clause (elliptical): nominal group subject and verbal group not produced, attributive group (attribute missing, quantifier *toutes – all*, deictic *des*).

3. Beside the clause

Given information (*nous autres on se réunit – we get together*), new information (le ***jeudi** – on Thursdays*).

UTTERANCE 21

nous sommes toutes des ***femmes*** et on se réunit en petit nombre pour le goûter et tout ***ça***
(we are all women and one gets together in small number for tea and all that)

1. Clause level

MESSAGE. Paratactic chaining of two independent declarative clauses tied by conjunction *et* (*and*). Initiating clause is made of unmarked topical theme (personal pronoun subject *nous – we*) followed by rheme (*sommes toutes des femmes – are all women*). Continuing clause is formed of unmarked topical theme (pronoun subject *on – one*) followed by rheme (*se réunit en petit nombre pour le goûter et tout ça – gets together in small number for tea and all that*).

EXCHANGE. Statements: First declarative (mood: subject *nous – we*, finite *sommes – are*; residue: predicator *sommes – are*, attributive complement *toutes des femmes – all women*). Second declarative (mood: subject *on – one*, finite *se réunit – get*; residue: predicator *se réunit – get together*, circumstantial adjunct *pour le goûter et tout ça – for tea and all that*).

REPRESENTATION. First clause (relational process): intensive *être – be* (participants: carrier *nous – we*, attribute *des femmes – women*; circumstance: quantity *toutes – all*). Second clause: intransitive material process *se réunir – get together* (participant: agent *on – one*; circumstances: quantity *en petit nombre – in small number*, purpose *pour le goûter et tout ça – for tea and all that*).

2. Below the clause

First clause: nominal group (pronoun *nous – we*), verbal group (finite-event *sommes – are*), attributive group (attribute *femmes – women*, quantifier *toutes – all*, deictic *des*). Second clause: nominal group (pronoun *on – one*), verbal group (finite-event *se réunit – gets together*), prepositional phrase [preposition *en – in*, nominal group (noun *nombre – number*, epithet *petit – small*], prepositional phrase [preposition *pour – for*, nominal group (noun *goûter – lunch*, deictic *le*)], conjunction group (conjunction *et – and*), nominal group (pronoun *ça – that*, quantifier *tout – all*).

3. Above the clause (logicosemantic relations)

Secondary clause *extends* the meaning of the primary one by *adding new information.*

4. Beside the clause

First clause: given information (*nous – we*), new information (*sommes toutes des femmes – are all women*). Second clause: given (*on se réunit – one gets together*), new (*en petit nombre pour le goûter et tout ça – in small number for tea and all that*).

UTTERANCE 22

alors donc on on s'amuse **bien**
(then therefore one has a good time)

1. Clause level

MESSAGE. Independent declarative clause with conjunctive theme (*alors – then*), another conjunctive theme (conjunctive adjunct *donc – therefore*), unmarked topical theme (*on – one*), and rheme (*s'amuse bien – has a good time*).

EXCHANGE. Statement: Declarative with mood (subject *on – one*, finite *s'amuse – has*) and residue (predicator *s'amuse – has* circumstantial adjunct *bien – a good time*).

REPRESENTATION. Mental process *bien s'amuser – have a good time* (participant: senser *on – one*; circumstance: time *alors – then*).

2. Below the clause

Adverbial group (adverb *alors – then*), conjunction group (conjunction *donc – therefore*), nominal group (pronoun *on – one*), verbal group (finite-event *s'amuse – has a good time*), adverbial group (adverb *bien*).

3. Beside the clause

Given information (*on – one*), new information (*s'amuse bien – has a good time*).

UTTERANCE 23

des fois on joue aux **cartes** et des fois **pas**
(sometimes one plays cards and sometimes not)

1. Clause level

MESSAGE. Paratactic chaining of two independent declarative clauses tied by conjunction *et* (*and*). Initiating clause is made of modal theme (modal adjunct *des fois – sometimes*), unmarked topical theme (*on – one*), and rheme (*joue aux cartes – plays cards*). Continuing clause is elliptical (partial anaphora). It is only formed (lawfully) of interpersonal element (modal theme *des fois – sometimes*) and rheme (*pas – not*).

EXCHANGE. Statements: First declarative (mood: subject *on – one*, finite *joue -plays*; residue: circumstantial adjunct *des fois – sometimes*, predicator *joue – plays*, complement *aux cartes – cards*). Second declarative (elliptical) (mood: finite *pas – not*; residue: circumstantial adjunct *des fois – sometimes*).

REPRESENTATION. Intransitive material process *jouer – play* (participant: agent *on – one*; circumstances: time *des fois – sometimes*, means *aux cartes – cards*).

2. Below the clause

First clause: adverbial group (*des fois – sometimes*), nominal group (pronoun *on – one*), verbal group (finite-event *joue – plays*), prepositional phrase [contracted preposition *à*, nominal group (noun *cartes – cards*, contracted deictic *les*)]. Second clause (elliptical): conjunction group (conjunction *et – and*), negative adverb *pas – not*, adverbial group (*des fois – sometimes*).

3. Above the clause (logicosemantic relations)

Secondary clause *extends* the meaning of the primary one by *adding new information*.

4. Beside the clause

First clause: given information (*des fois – sometimes*), new information (*on joue aux **cartes** – one plays cards*). Second clause: given (*des fois – sometimes*), new (***pas** – not*).

UTTERANCE 24

des fois comme on ***dit*** on passe sa ***flemme***
(sometimes as they say one just passes the time)

1. Clause level

MESSAGE. Hypotactic chaining: independent declarative clause with modal theme (*des fois – sometimes*), unmarked topical theme (*on – one*), and rheme (*passe sa flemme – just passes the time*); embedded finite dependent clause with structural theme (comparative conjunction *comme – as*), unmarked topical theme (*on – they*), and rheme (*dit – say*).

EXCHANGE. Statements: Declarative [mood: subject *on – one*, finite *passe – passes*; residue: predicator *passe – passes*, first circumstantial adjunct *des fois – sometimes*, second circumstantial adjunct itself a declarative with mood (subject *on – they*, finite *dit – say*) and residue (predicator *dit – say*, and complement *sa flemme – the time*)].

REPRESENTATION. Intransitive material process *passer sa flemme – pass the time* (participant: agent *on – one*; circumstances: time *des fois – sometimes*, comparison *comme on dit – as they say*).

2. Below the clause

First clause: adverbial group (*des fois – sometimes*), nominal group (pronoun *on – they*), verbal group (finite-event *dit – say*). Second clause: nominal group (pronoun *on – one*), verbal group (finite-event *passe – passes*), nominal group (noun *flemme – time*, deictic *sa*).

3. Above the clause (logicosemantic relations)

Secondary clause *enhances* the meaning of the primary one by qualifying it with a circumstantial feature of *comparison*.

4. Beside the clause

First clause: given information (*on – they*), new information (**dit** – *say*). Second clause: given (*des fois – sometimes*), new (*on passe sa **flemme** – one just passes the time*).

UTTERANCE 25

on *s'assied* et puis c'est **tout**
(one sits down and then that is all)

1. Clause level

MESSAGE. Paratactic chaining of two independent declarative clauses tied by *et* (*and*). Initiating clause is made of unmarked topical theme (*on – one*) and rheme (*s'assied – sits down*). Continuing clause is formed of conjunctive adjunct (temporal adverb *puis – then*), unmarked topical theme (*c' – that*) and rheme (*c'est tout – is all*).

EXCHANGE. Statements: First declarative (mood: subject *on – one*, finite *s'assied – sits*; residue: predicator *s'assied – sits*). Second declarative (mood:

subject *c'* – *that*, finite *est* – *is*; residue: predicator *est* – *is*, attributive complement *tout* – *all*).

REPRESENTATION. First clause: intransitive material process *s'asseoir* – *sit down* (*participant*: agent *on* – *one*). Second clause (relational process): intensive *être* – *be* (participants: carrier *c'* – *that*, attribute *tout* – *all*; circumstance: time *puis* – *then*).

2. Below the clause

First clause: nominal group (pronoun *on* – *one*), verbal group (finite-event *s'assied* – *sits down*). Second clause: conjunction group (conjunction *et* – *and*), adverbial group (adverb *puis* – *then*), nominal group (pronoun *c'* – *that*), verbal group (finite-event *est* – *is*), attributive group (attribute *tout* – *all*).

3. Above the clause (logicosemantic relations)

Secondary clause *extends* the meaning of the primary one by *adding new information*.

4. Beside the clause

First clause: given information (*on* – *one*), new information (**s'assied** – *sits*). Second clause: given (*c'* – *that*), new (*est **tout** – is all*).

UTTERANCE 26

oui on doit bien de temps en ***temps***
(yes one must from time to time)

1. Clause level

MESSAGE. Independent declarative clause with continuative theme (*oui* – *yes*), unmarked topical theme (*on* – *one*), and rheme (*doit bien de temps en temps* – *must from time to time*).

EXCHANGE. Statement: Declarative (mood: subject *on* – *one*, finite *doit* – *must*; residue (circumstantial adjuncts): adverb *bien*, prepositional phrase *de temps en temps* – *from time to time*). This utterance does not appear to have a predicator. It may be considered, however, that the statement is elliptical (predicator *faire* – *do*, as well as complement *le* ou *ça* – *it*, being left unexpressed).

REPRESENTATION. (assuming ellipsis of *le faire* – *do it*). Transitive material process *faire* – *do* (participants: agent *on* – *one*, goal *le* – *it*; circumstance: time *de temps en temps* – *from time to time*).

2. Below the clause

Affirmative adverb *oui – yes*, nominal group (pronoun *on – one*), verbal group (finite *doit – must*), adverbial group (adverb *bien*), prepositional phrase [prepositions *de . . . en – from . . . to*, nominal groups (nouns *temps – time*)].

3. Beside the clause

Given information (*on – one*), new information (*doit bien de temps en* **temps** *– must from time to time*).

UTTERANCE 27

tandis que moi quand il fait des chaleurs comme **ça** moi on me voit très rarement à la porte en tous **cas**
(whereas me when it is hot like that me one sees me very rarely outdoors anyway)

1. Clause level

MESSAGE. Hypotactic chaining: independent declarative clause with continuative (oppositive) theme (*tandis que – whereas*), marked topical theme (personal pronoun as grammatical object *moi – me*) repeated twice on each side of the temporal clause, and rheme (*on me voit très rarement à la porte en tous cas – one sees me very rarely outdoors anyway*); embedded finite dependent clause introduced by temporal conjunction *quand* (*when*) as structural theme, followed by unmarked topical theme (*il – it*) and rheme (*fait des chaleurs comme ça – is hot like that*).

EXCHANGE. Statements: First declarative (mood: subject *il – it*, finite *fait – is*; residue: predicator *fait – is*, complement *des chaleurs – hot*, circumstantial adjunct *comme ça*). Second declarative (mood: subject *on – one*, finite *voit – sees*; residue: predicator *voit – sees*, complement *me – me*, circumstantial adjuncts: adverbial group *très rarement – very rarely*, prepositional phrase *à la porte – outdoors*, prepositional phrase *en tous cas – anyway*). According to French syntax, the complement personal pronoun (*me*, in this case) is correctly placed before the finite verbal element in the second declarative.

REPRESENTATION. First clause: happening process *faire – be* (participant: existent *des chaleurs – hot*; circumstance: comparison *comme ça – like that*). Second clause: mental process *voir – see* (participants: senser *on – one*, phenomenon *me – me*; circumstances: quality *très rarement – very rarely*, space *à la porte – outdoors*, quality *en tous cas – anyway*).

2. Below the clause

First clause: conjunction group (conjunction *tandis que – whereas*), nominal group (pronoun *moi – me*), nominal group (pronoun *on – one*), verbal group (finite-event *voit – sees*), nominal group (pronoun *me – me*), adverbial group (adverb *rarement – rarely*, premodifier *très – very*), prepositonal phrase [preposition *à*, nominal group (noun *porte*, deictic *la*)], prepositional phrase [preposition *en*, nominal group (noun *cas*, quantifier *tout*)]. Second clause: conjunction group (conjunction *quand – when*), nominal group (pronoun *il – it*), verbal group (finite-event *fait – is*), nominal group (noun *chaleurs*, deictic *des*), conjunction phrase [conjunction *comme – like*, nominal group (pronoun *ça – that*)].

3. Above the clause (logicosemantic relations)

Secondary clause *enhances* the meaning of the primary one by qualifying it with a circumstantial feature of *condition*.

4. Beside the clause

First clause: given information (*il – it*), new information (*fait des chaleurs comme ça – is hot like that*). Second clause: given (*moi – me*), new (*on me voit très rarement à la porte en tous **cas** – one sees me very rarely outdoors anyway*).

UTTERANCE 31

et ça ne m'étonne **pas** parce que les chiens ont toujours trop **chaud** quand ils vont à la **porte**
(and that does not surprise me because dogs are always too warm when they go outdoors)

1. Clause level

MESSAGE.   Double hypotactic chaining: independent declarative clause with continuative theme (*et – and*), unmarked topical theme (demonstrative pronoun *ça – that*), and rheme (*ne m'étonne pas – does not surprise me*); followed by finite dependent clause with structural theme (*parce que – because*), unmarked topical theme (*les chiens – dogs*), and rheme (*ont toujours trop chaud – are always too warm*). This dependent clause is followed by another finite dependent clause with structural theme (conjunction *quand – when*), unmarked topical theme (*its – they*), and rheme (*vont à la porte – go outdoors*).

EXCHANGE.   Statements: First declarative (mood: subject *ça - that*, finite *ne m'étonne pas – does not*; residue: predicator *étonne – surprise*, complement *m' – me*). Second declarative (mood: subject *les chiens – dogs*, finite *ont – are*; residue: predicator *ont – are*, circumstantial adjunct *toujours – always*, complement *trop chaud – too warm*). Third declarative (mood: subject *ils – they*, finite *vont – go*; residue: predicator *vont – go*, circumstantial adjunct *à la porte – outdoors*).

REPRESENTATION.   First clause: mental process *étonner – surprise* (participants: senser *m' – me*, phenomenon *ça – that*). Second clause (relational process): intensive *avoir – be* (participants: carrier *les chiens – dogs*, attribute *chaud – warm*; circumstances: time *toujours – always*, quantity *trop – too*). Third clause: intransitive material process *aller – go* (participant: agent *ils – they*; circumstance: space *dehors – outdoors*).

2. Below the clause

First clause: conjunction group (conjunction *et – and*), nominal group (pronoun *ça – that*), verbal group (finite-event *ne m'étonne pas – does not surprize*), nominal group (pronoun *m' – me*). Second clause: conjunction group (conjunction *parce que – because*), nominal group (noun *chiens – dogs*, deictic *les*), verbal group (finite-event *ont – are*), attributive group (attribute *chaud – warm*, premodifier *trop – too*), adverbial group (adverb *toujours – always*). Third clause: conjunction group (conjunction *quand – when*), nominal group (pronoun *ils – they*), verbal group (finite-event *vont – go*), prepositional phrase [preposition *à*, nominal group (noun *porte*, deictic *là*)].

3. Above the clause (logicosemantic relations)

The meaning of primary clause is *enhanced* in the following clause by qualifying it with a circumstantial feature of *cause*. The meaning of the latter clause is itself *enhanced* in what follows by qualifying it with a circumstantial feature of *condition*.

4. Beside the clause

First clause: given information (*ça – that*), new information (*ne m'étonne* **pas** *– does not surprise me*). Second clause: given (*les chiens – dogs*), new (*ont toujours trop* **chaud** *– are always too warm*). Third clause: given (*ils – they*), new (*vont à la* **porte** *– go outdoors*).

Speech turn 3 – Around the clause

The speech turn centers around four loosely connected issues corresponding to four paragraphs not clearly separated from each other: (1) the potential danger represented by the momentary presence of gypsies in the vicinity; (2) the absence of Francoise's father during the daytime; (3) women meeting in Françoise's home on Thursdays to spend the afternoon together; and (4) the fact that Françoise, in the same way as her dog, does not like to be outside when the weather is hot.

Utterances 15, 16, and 17 are related to paragraph 1. Paragraphic *cohesion* is realized through the use of the causal conjunction *parce que – because* and pronominal coreference (*ils – they*). Utterance 18 begins with a false start. Apparently Françoise was going to elaborate on the fact that she is wary of gypsies particularly when alone at home (which, she says first, happens often – she then corrects herself, saying that happens only rarely). She ends up indicating that her father is at home but that he goes out and returns only at night. The meanings intended in the paragraph are contradictory, and correspondingly, the wording lacks cohesion with opposite expressions (e.g., *souvent enfin rarement – often that is rarely*; *mon père est ici . . . mais il ne revient que le soir – my father is here . . . but he comes back only at night*). Paragraph 3 on women meeting is made of a series of seven loosely connected utterances each one extending the meaning of the previous one(s). Conjunctions and temporal adverbs are used to strengthen paragraphic *cohesion* (*alors – then*, *et – and*, *et – and*, *alors donc – then therefore*, *et – and*, *et puis – and then*). Paragraph 4 is made of five utterances simply juxtaposed or conjoined with the conjunction *et – and*. This paragraph is introduced by the contrastive conjunction *tandis que – whereas,* which is used out of context since paragraph 4 is in no opposite relationship with any utterance in paragraph 3.

Speech turn 4

UTTERANCE 32

c'est si j'peux l'*dire* c'est un peu comme *ici* enfin
(that is if I may say it that is a bit like here in the end)

1. Clause level

MESSAGE. Hypotactic chaining: independent declarative clause with unmarked topical theme (demonstrative pronoun subject *c' – that*) and rheme (*est un peu comme ici enfin – is a bit like here in the end*); embedded finite dependent clause with structural theme (conditional conjunction *si – if*), unmarked topical theme *j' (I)*, and rheme (*peux l'dire – may say it*). The first two elements of the independent clause are reproduced following the conditional clause, and the rheme of the former clause receives further development.

EXCHANGE. Statements: First declarative (mood: subject *c' – that*, finite *est – is*; residue: predicator *est – is*). Second declarative (conditional) (mood: subject *j – I*, finite *peux – may*; residue: predicator *dire – say*, complement *l' – it*). Third declarative (mood: subject *c' – that*, finite *est – is*; residue: predicator *est – is*, attributive complement *un peu comme ici – a bit like here*, circumstantial adjunct *enfin – in the end*.

REPRESENTATION. First clause (relational process): intensive *être – be* (participants: carrier *c' – that*, attribute *un peu comme ici – a bit like here*; circumstance: time *enfin – in the end*). Second clause: transitive material process *dire – say* (participants: agent *je – I*, goal *le – it*).

2. Below the clause

First clause: nominal group (pronoun *j – I*), verbal group (finite *peux – may*, event *dire – say*), nominal group (pronoun *l – it*). Second clause: nominal group (pronoun *c' – that*), verbal group (finite-event *est – is*), adverbial groups (adverbs *un peu – a bit, enfin – in the end*), conjunction phrase [conjunction *comme – like*, adverbial group (adverb *ici – here*)].

3. Above the clause (logicosemantic relations)

Secondary clause *enhances* the meaning of the primary one by qualifying it with a circumstantial feature of *condition*.

4. Beside the clause

First clause: given information (*j' – I*), new information (*peux l'**dire** – may say it*). Second clause: given (*c' – that*), new (*est un peu comme **ici** enfin*).

UTTERANCE 33

que vous *voyez*
(that you see)

1. Clause level

MESSAGE.   Independent declarative clause with structural theme *que* (*that*), unmarked topical theme *vous* (*you*), and rheme (*voyez – see*). It is likely that this utterance is something of a false start for utterance 34.

EXCHANGE.   Statement: Declarative (mood: subject *vous – you*, finite *voyez – see*; residue: predicator *voyez – see*, complement *que – that*).

REPRESENTATION.   Mental process *voir – see* (participants: senser *vous – you*, phenomenon *que – that*).

2. Below the clause

Nominal group (pronoun *vous – you*), verbal group (finite-event *voyez – see*), nominal group (pronoun *que – that*).

3. Beside the clause

Given information (*vous – you*), new information (*voyez – see*).

UTTERANCE 34

même à *Liège* que vous voyez même des des drôles de gens
drôl'dement si j'peux l'dire *platement* drôl'dement habillés

(even in Liège that you see even funny people in a funny way if I may
say it flatly dressed in a funny way)

1. Clause level

MESSAGE. Hypotatic chaining: independent declarative made of conjunctive theme (*même – even*), marked topical theme (prepositional phrase *à Liège –
in Liège*), and rheme (*que vous voyez même des des drôles de gens drôl' dement . . .
drôl' dement habillés – that you see even funny people in a funny way . . . dressed in
a funny way*). Relative element *que* (*that*) is not necessary. Actually it renders the
clause incorrect according to strict normative French grammatical standards
(although superfluous relative elements of this sort are commonly heard in familiar
exchanges). Embedded finite dependent clause with structural theme (conditional
conjunction *si – if*), unmarked topical theme *j' – I*, and rheme (*peux l' dire platement
– may say it flatly*).

EXCHANGE. Statements: First declarative (mood: subject *vous – you*,
finite *voyez – see*; residue: predicator *voyez – see*, circumstantial adjuncts: *à Liège –
in Liège*, complements: *que – that, des drôles de gens . . . drôl' dement habillés –
funny people . . . dressed in a funny way*). Second declarative (conditional) (mood:
subject *j' – I*, finite *peux – may*; residue: predicator *dire – say*, complement *l' – it*).

REPRESENTATION. First clause: mental process *voir – see* (participants: senser *vous – you*, phenomenon *des drôles de gens . . . drôl' dement habillés –
funny people . . . dressed in a funny way*; circumstance: space *à Liège – in Liège*).
Second clause: verbal process *dire – say* (participants: sayer *je – I*, signal *le – it*).

2. Below the clause

First clause: adverbial group (adverb *même – even*), prepositional phrase
[preposition *à – in*, nominal group (head: noun *Liège*)], conjunction group (conjunction *que – that*), nominal group (pronoun *vous – you*), verbal group (finite-event
voyez – see), nominal group (noun *gens – people*, premodifiers: deictic *des*, epithet
drôles – funny, postmodifier: epithet *habillés – dressed*), adverbial group (adverb
drôl' dement – in a funny way). Second clause: conjunction group (conjunction *si –
if*), nominal group (pronoun *j – I*), verbal group (finite *peux – may*, event *dire – say*),
nominal group (pronoun *l' – it*), adverbial group (adverb *platement – flatly*).

3. Above the clause (logicosemantic relations)

Secondary clause *enhances* the meaning of the primary one by qualifying it
with a circumstantial feature of *condition*.

4. Beside the clause

First clause: given information (*vous voyez même des des drôles de gens . . . drôl' dement habillés – you see even funny people in a funny way . . . dressed in a funny way*), new information (*même à **Liège** – even in Liège*). Second clause: given (*j' – I*), new (*peux l'dire **platement** – may say it flatly*).

UTTERANCE 35

toute façon ici à Liège c'est comme ça *aussi*
(anyway here in Liège that is like that too)

1. Clause level

MESSAGE. Independent declarative clause with conjunctive theme (*toute façon – anyway*), marked topical theme (locative locution *ici à Liège – here in Liège*), and rheme (*c'est comme ça aussi – that is like that too*).

EXCHANGE. Statement: Declarative (mood: subject *c' – that*, finite *est – is*; residue: predicator *est – is*, attributive complement *comme ça – like that*, circumstantial adjuncts: *ici – here*, *à Liège – in Liège*, *aussi – too*).

REPRESENTATION. Relational process: intensive *être – be* (participants: carrier *c' – that*, attribute *comme ça aussi – like that too*; circumstances: space *ici – here*, *à Liège – in Liège*).

2. Below the clause

Nominal group (pronoun *c' – that*), verbal group (finite-event *est – is*), conjunction group (conjunction *comme – like*, modifier *ça – that*), adverbial groups (adverbs *toute façon – anyway*, *ici – here*, *aussi – too*), prepositional phrase [preposition *à – in*, nominal group (noun *Liège*)].

3. Beside the clause

Given information (*ici à Liège – here in Liège*), new information (*c'est comme ça **aussi** – that is like that too*).

UTTERANCE 36

je prends ***Amsterdam*** comme je prends Liège enfin
(I take Amsterdam as I take Liège in the end)

1. Clause level

MESSAGE. Hypotactic chaining: independent declarative clause with unmarked topical theme (*je – I*) and rheme (*prends Amsterdam – take Amsterdam*); followed by finite dependent clause with structural theme (comparative conjunction *comme – as*), unmarked topical theme (*je – I*), and rheme (*prends Liège enfin – take Liège in the end*).

EXCHANGE. Statements: First declarative (mood: subject *je – I*, finite *prends – take*); residue: predicator *prends – take*, complement *Amsterdam*). Second declarative (mood: subject *je – I*, finite *prends – take*; residue: predicator *prends – take*, complement *Liège*, circumstantial adjunct *enfin – in the end*).

REPRESENTATION. First clause: transitive material process (abstract) *prendre – take* (participants: agent *je – I*, goal *Amsterdam*). Second clause: transitive material process (abstract) *prendre – take* (participants: agent *je – I*, goal *Liège*, circumstance: comparison *comme – as*).

2. Below the clause

First clause: nominal group (pronoun *je – I*), verbal group (finite-event *prends – take*), nominal group (noun *Amsterdam*). Second clause: conjunction group (conjunction *comme – as*), nominal group (pronoun *je – I*), verbal group (finite-event *prends – take*), nominal group (noun *Liège*), adverbial group (adverb *enfin – in the end*).

3. Above the clause (logicosemantic relations)

Secondary clause *enhances* the meaning of primary one by qualifying it with a circumstantial feature of *comparison*.

4. Beside the clause

Given information (*comme je prends Liège enfin – as I take Liège in the end*), new information (*je prends Amsterdam – I take Amsterdam*).

UTTERANCE 37
c'est une grande *ville*
(that is a big city)

1. Clause level

MESSAGE. Independent declarative clause with unmarked topical theme (*c' – that*) and rheme (*c'est une grande ville – is a big city*).

EXCHANGE. Statement: Declarative (mood: subject *c' – that*, finite *est – is*; residue: predicator *est – is*, attributive complement *une grande ville – a big city*).

REPRESENTATION. Relational process: intensive *être – be* (participants: carrier *c' – that*, attribute *une grande ville – a big city*).

2. Below the clause

Nominal group (pronoun *c'* – *that*), verbal group (finite-event *est* – *is*), nominal group (noun *ville* – *city*, deictic *une* – *a*, epithet *grande* – *big*).

3. Beside the clause

Given information (*c'* – *that*), new information (*est une grande **ville*** – *is a big city*).

UTTERANCE 38

c'est ***vrai***
(that is true)

1. Clause level

MESSAGE.   Independent declarative clause with unmarked topical theme (*c'* – *that*) and rheme (*est vrai* – *is true*).

EXCHANGE.   Statement: Declarative (mood: subject *c'* – *that*, finite *est* – *is*; residue: predicator *est* – *is*, attributive complement *vrai* – *true*).

REPRESENTATION.   Relational process: intensive *être* – *be* (participants: carrier *c'* – *that*, attribute *vrai* – *true*).

2. Below the clause

Nominal group (pronoun *c'* – *that*), verbal group (finite-event *est* – *is*), attribute group (attribute *vrai* – *true*).

3. Beside the clause

Given information (*c'* – *that*), new information (*est **vrai*** – *is true*).

UTTERANCE 39

mais vous voyez tout l'monde habillé si je peux l'dire tout ***platement***
aussi habillé comme ***l'as de pique*** enfin
(but you see everyone dressed if I may say it bluntly also dressed like "l'as de pique" in the end)

1. Clause level

MESSAGE.   Hypotactic chaining: independent declarative clause with continuative theme (*mais* – *but*), unmarked topical theme (*vous* – *you*), and rheme (*voyez tout l'monde habillé . . . aussi habillé comme l'as de pique enfin* – *see everyone dressed also . . . dressed like "l'as de pique" in the end*); embedded finite dependent clause with structural theme (conditional conjunction *si* – *if*), unmarked topical theme (*je* – *I*), and rheme (*peux l'dire tout platement* – *may say it bluntly*).

EXCHANGE. Statements: First declarative (mood: subject *vous* – *you*, finite *voyez* – *see*; residue: predicator *voyez* – *see*, complement *tout l'monde habillé comme l'as de pique* – *everyone dressed like "l'as de pique,"* circumstantial adjunct *enfin* – *in the end*). Second declarative (conditional) (mood: subject *je* – *I*, finite *peux* – *may*; residue: predicator *dire* – *say*, complement *l'* – *it*, circumstantial adjunct *tout platement* – *bluntly*).

REPRESENTATION. First clause: mental process *voir* – *see* (participants: senser *vous* – *you*, phenomenon *tout l'monde habillé . . . comme l'as de pique* – *everyone . . . dressed like "l'as de pique"*; circumstance: time *enfin* – *in the end*). Second clause: verbal process *dire* – *say* (participants: sayer *je* – *I*, signal *l'* – *it*; circumstance: quality *tout platement* – *bluntly*).

2. Below the clause

First clause: conjunction group (conjunction *mais* – *but*), nominal group (pronoun *vous* – *you*), verbal group (finite-event *voyez* – *see*), nominal group (nominal locution *tout l' monde* – *everyone*, epithet *habillé* – *dressed*), adverbial groups (adverbs *aussi* – *also, enfin* – *in the end*), conjunction phrase [conjunction *comme* – *like*, nominal group {noun *as*, premodifier *l'*, postmodifier: prepositional phrase [preposition *de*, nominal group (noun *pique*)]}]. Second clause: conjunction group (conjunction *si* – *if*), nominal group (pronoun *je* – *I*), verbal group (finite *peux* – *may*, event *dire* – *say*), nominal group (pronoun *l'* - *it*), adverbial group (adverb *platement* – *bluntly*, premodifier *tout*).

3. Above the clause (logicosemantic relations)

Secondary clause *enhances* the meaning of the primary one by qualifying it with a circumstantial feature of *condition*.

4. Beside the clause

First clause: given information (*vous voyez tout l'monde* – *you see everyone*), new information (*habillé comme **l'as de pique** enfin* – *dressed like "l'as de pique" in the end*). Second clause: given (*je* – *I*), new (*peux l'dire tout **platement*** – *may say it bluntly*).

UTTERANCE 42

au lieu d'être coiffés comme tout le ***monde*** les hommes ont à la
(instead of being hairdressed like everyone men have)

1. Clause level

MESSAGE.   Hypotactic chaining: independent declarative clause (incomplete) with unmarked topical theme (*les hommes – men*) and rheme (*ont à la – have* ...); preceded by elliptical (cataphoric) dependent clause with structural theme (*au lieu d' – instead of*) and rheme (*être coiffés comme tout le monde – being hairdressed like everyone*).

EXCHANGE.   Statements: First declarative (elliptical) (mood: finite *être coiffés – being hairdressed*; residue: predicator *être coiffés – being hairdressed,* circumstantial adjunct *comme tout le monde – like everyone*). Second declarative (incomplete) (mood: subject *les hommes – men*, finite *ont – have*; residue: *ont – have*).

REPRESENTATION.   First clause (elliptical) (relational process): intensive *être – be* (participants: carrier not produced, attribute *coiffés – hairdressed*; circumstance: comparison comme *tout le monde – like everyone*).

2. Below the clause

First clause (elliptical): conjunction group (conjunction *au lieu de – instead of*), nominal group subject not expressed, verbal group (finite-event *être coiffés – being hairdressed*), conjunction phrase [conjunction *comme – like*, nominal group (nominal locution *tout le monde – everyone*)]. Second clause (incomplete): nominal group (*hommes – men*, deictic *les*), verbal group (finite-event *ont – have*).

3. Above the clause (logicosemantic relations)

Secondary clause *enhances* the meaning of the primary one by qualifying it with a circumstantial feature of *comparison*.

4. Beside the clause

Given information (*les hommes ont – men have*), new information (*au lieu d' être coiffés comme tous le **monde** – instead of being hairdressed like everyone*).

UTTERANCE 43

comment ça *s'appelle* donc
(how do you call that again)

1. Clause level

MESSAGE.   Content interrogative clause with an unmarked theme (WH-element) (*comment – how*) and rheme (*ça s'appelle donc – do you call that again*). According to French normative grammar, the subject element in a WH-interrogative of this type must be placed after the verb unless it is recast in pronominal form following the verb (e.g., *comment ça s'appelle-t-il donc?*). Contemporary usage, particularly a familiar one, however, practices the inversion and/or the pronominal recast less and less often.

EXCHANGE. Question: WH-interrogative (mood: subject *ça – that*, finite *s'appelle – do*; residue: predicator *s'appelle – call*).

REPRESENTATION. Verbal process (abstract): *appeler – call* (participants: sayer *ça – that*, signal *c' – that*).

2. Below the clause

Conjunction group (conjunction *comment – how*), nominal group (pronoun *ça – that*), verbal group (finite-event *s'appelle – call*), conjunction group (conjunction *donc – again*).

3. Beside the clause

Given information (*ça – that*), new information (***s'appelle** donc*).

UTTERANCE 44

vous ça va ***encore***
(you that may go)

1. Clause level

MESSAGE. Independent declarative clause with conjunctive theme [*vous – (as for) you*], unmarked topical theme (*ça – that*), and rheme (*va encore – may go*).

EXCHANGE. Statement: Declarative (mood: subject *ça – that*, finite *va – may*; residue: predicator *va – go*, vocative complement (anteposited) *vous – you*).

REPRESENTATION. Literal representation: intransitive material process: *aller – go* (participant: agent *vous – you*). Actually the clause is an idiomatic equivalent of something like "*you that is acceptable,*" that is, a relational process (intensive).

2. Below the clause

Nominal group (pronoun *vous – you*), nominal group (pronoun *ça – that*), verbal group (finite-event *va – may go*), adverbial group (adverb *encore*).

3. Beside the clause

Given information (*vous – you*), new information (*ça va **encore** – that may go*).

UTTERANCE 45

vous n'êtes pas encore comme ***ça***
(you are not yet like that)

1. Clause level

MESSAGE.   Independent declarative clause with unmarked topical theme (*vous – you*) and rheme (*n'êtes pas encore comme ça – are not yet like that*).

EXCHANGE.   Statement: Declarative (mood: subject *vous – you*, finite *n'êtes pas – are not*; residue: predicator *êtes – are*, circumstantial adjunct *encore – yet*, attributive complement *comme ça – like that*).

REPRESENTATION.   Relational process: intensive *être – be* (participants: carrier *vous – you*, attribute *comme ça – like that*; circumstance: time *pas encore – not yet*).

2. Below the clause

Nominal group (pronoun *vous – you*), verbal group (finite-event *n'êtes pas – are not*), adverbial group (adverb *encore – yet*), conjunction phrase [conjunction *comme – like*, nominal group (pronoun *ça – that*)].

3. Beside the clause

Given information (*vous – you*), new information (*n'êtes pas encore comme ça – are not yet like that*).

UTTERANCE 46

enfin excusez-***moi*** quand même mais enfin
(then excuse me for the rest but then)

1. Clause level

MESSAGE.   Imperative clause with conjuctive theme (*enfin – then*), unmarked theme (imperative verb *excusez – excuse*), and rheme (*moi quand même mais enfin – me for the rest but then*). At the end of the imperative clause, there is an attempt at coordination that was cut by the interlocutor hastening to ensure Françoise that he was not irritated by her casual comparative remark on his dressing (see Appendices 1 and 2 for full transcriptions of the conversational exchange).

EXCHANGE.   Command: Imperative (mood: finite *excusez – excuse*; residue: predicator *excusez – excuse*, complement *moi – me*).

REPRESENTATION.   Mental process *excusez – excuse* (participants: senser not produced (imperative form), phenomenon *moi – me*; circumstance: time *enfin – in the end*).

2. Below the clause

Verbal group (finite-event *excusez – excuse*), nominal group (pronoun *moi – me*), adverbial groups (adverbs *enfin – then, quand même – for the rest, enfin – then*), conjunction group (conjunction *mais – but*).

3. Beside the clause

Given information (unexpressed in imperative form), new information (*excusez-**moi** – excuse me*).

Speech turn 4 – Around the clause

This speech turn illustrates Françoise's opinion on some aspects of Amsterdam, particularly as to people's dressing and hairdressing habits. The last three utterances are directed toward the interlocutor (J.F.B.), with two somewhat direct statements on his hairdressing style, remarks for which Françoise apologizes in the end.

Textual cohesion is realized through the use of *reference, ellipsis, conjunction,* and *lexical cohesion.* Central lexical terms that are repeated as such or in a synonymous way are *(ici) à Liège – (here) in Liège, habillés – dressed, coiffés – hairdressed, vous voyez – you see.* Participant or circumstantial elements introduced at one place in the text and taken as a reference point for things that follow are: *ici . . . que vous voyez – here . . . that you see, à Liège que vous voyez – in Liège that you see, ici à Liège c'est comme ça aussi – here in Liège that is like that too, c'est une grande ville – that is a big city, c'est vrai – that is true, si je peux l'dire – if I may say it, comme ça – like that, comment ça s'appelle – how do you call that, vous ça va encore – you that may go, comme ça – like that.* Utterance 41 is elliptical: The nominal group ("*tout le monde à Amsterdam*" – "*everyone in Amsterdam,*" or something of the kind) may be presupposed on the basis of what precedes. Only one utterance-connecting conjunction and one temporal adverb are used since the utterance matrix in the speech turn is predominantly juxtapositive from a formal point of view.

Speech turn 5

UTTERANCE 47

c'est ça *oui*
(that is it yes)

1. Clause level

MESSAGE.   Independent declarative clause with unmarked topical theme (*c' – that*) and rheme *est ça oui – is it yes*).

EXCHANGE.   Statement: Declarative (mood: subject *c' – that*, finite *est – is*; residue: predicator *est – is*, attributive complement *ça – it*).

REPRESENTATION. Relational process: intensive *être* – *be* (participants: carrier *c'* – *that*, attribute *ça* – *it*).

2. Below the clause

Nominal group (pronoun *c'* – *that*), verbal group (finite-event *est* – *is*), nominal group (pronoun *ça* – *it*), adverbial group (adverb *oui* – *yes*).

3. Beside the clause

Given information (*c'* – *that*), new information (*est ça oui*).

UTTERANCE 48

mais mon beau-frère il fumait *avant*
(but my brother-in-law he smoked before)

1. Clause level

MESSAGE. Independent declarative clause with continuative theme (*mais* – *but*), unmarked topical theme (*mon beau-frère* – *my brother-in-law*), and rheme (*il fumait avant* – *he smoked before*).

EXCHANGE. Statement: Declarative (mood: subject *mon beau-frère il* – *my brother-in-law he*), finite *fumait* – *smoked*; residue: predicator *fumait* – *smoked*, circumstantial adjunct *avant* – *before*).

REPRESENTATION. Transitive material process *fumer* – *smoke* (participants: agent *mon beau-frère* – *my brother-in-law*, goal not expressed (as is usually the case in familiar speech with this type of verb); circumstance: time *avant* – *before*).

2. Below the clause

Conjunction group (conjunction *mais* – *but*), nominal group (noun *beau-frère* – *brother-in-law*, deictic *mon* – *my*), nominal group (pronoun *he* – *il*), verbal group (finite-event *fumait* – *smoked*), adverbial group (adverb *avant* – *before*).

3. Beside the clause

Given information (*mon beau-frère* – *my brother-in-law*), new information (*il fumait avant* – *he smoked before*).

UTTERANCE 49

maintenant il n'fume *plus*
(now he does not smoke anymore)

1. Clause level

MESSAGE. Independent declarative clause with conjunctive theme (temporal adverb *maintenant – now*), unmarked topical theme (*il – he*), and rheme (*n'fume plus – does not smoke anymore*).

EXCHANGE. Statement: Declarative (mood: subject *il – he*, finite *n'fume plus – does not anymore*; residue: predicator *fume – smoke*, circumstantial adjunct *maintenant – now*).

REPRESENTATION. Transitive material process *fumer – smoke* (participants: agent *il – he*, goal not expressed; circumstance: time *maintenant – now*).

2. Below the clause

Adverbial group (adverb *maintenant – now*), nominal group (pronoun *il – he*), verbal group (finite-event *n'fume plus – does not smoke anymore*).

3. Beside the clause

Given information (*il – he*), new information (*n'fume **plus** – does not smoke anymore*).

UTTERANCE 50

mais le pire comme dit ma ***soeur***
(but the worse as says my sister)

1. Clause level

MESSAGE. Hypotactic chaining: independent declarative clause (with missing lexical verb) introduced by continuative theme (*mais – but*) and followed by unmarked topical theme (*le pire – the worse*); and finite dependent clause with structural theme (comparative conjunction *comme – as*), marked topical theme (verb *dit – says*), and rheme (*ma soeur – my sister*).

EXCHANGE. Statements: First declarative (elliptical) (mood: subject *le pire – the worse*; no finite and no residue). Second declarative (mood: subject *ma soeur – my sister*, finite *dit – says*; residue: predicator *dit – says*).

REPRESENTATION. First clause (incomplete) (relational process): intensive *être – be* (not expressed) (participant: carrier *le pire – the worse*, attribute not expressed). Second clause: verbal process *dire – say* (participant: sayer *ma soeur – my sister*; circumstance: comparison *comme – as*).

2. Below the clause

First clause (incomplete): conjunction group (conjuction *mais – but*), nominal group (noun *pire – worse*, deictic *le – the*). Second clause: conjunction group (conjunction *comme – as*), nominal group (noun *soeur – sister*, deictic *ma – my*), verbal group (finite-event *dit – says*).

3. Above the clause (logicosemantic relations)

Secondary clause *enhances* the meaning of the primary one by qualifying it with a circumstantial feature of *comparison*.

4. Beside the clause

Complete clause: given information (*dit – says*), new information (*ma soeur – my sister*).

UTTERANCE 51

il est marié
(he is married)

1. Clause level

MESSAGE. Independent declarative clause with unmarked theme (*il – he*) and rheme (*est marié – is married*).

EXCHANGE. Statement: Declarative (mood: subject *il – he*, finite *est marié – is married*; residue: predicator *marié – married*).

REPRESENTATION. Relational process: intensive *être – be* (participants: carrier *il – he*, attribute *marié – married*).

2. Below the clause

Nominal group (noun *il – he*), verbal group (finite-event *est marié – is married*).

3. Beside the clause

Given information (*il – he*), new information (*est **marié** – is married*).

UTTERANCE 52

mais il a une de ces ***panses*** qu'elle dit mais en ***riant*** maintenant
(but he has one of those bellies that she says but laughing now)

1. Clause level

MESSAGE. Hypotactic chaining: independent declarative clause with continuative theme (*mais – but*), unmarked topical theme (*il – he*), and rheme (*a une de ces panses – has one of those bellies*); followed by finite independent clause with marked topical theme (TH-item *qu' – that*) and rheme (*elle dit mais en riant maintenant – she says but laughing now*).

EXCHANGE. Statements: First declarative (mood: subject *il – he*, finite *a – has*; residue: predicator *a – has*, complement *une de ces panses – one of those bellies*). Second declarative (mood: subject *elle – she*, finite *dit – says*; residue: predicator *dit – says*, circumstantial adjuncts: *mais en riant – but laughing, maintenant – new*).

REPRESENTATION. First clause (relational process): possessive *avoir – have* (participants: possessor *il – he*, possessed *une de ces panses – one of those bellies*). Second clause: verbal process *dire – say* (participants: sayer *elle – she*, signal *que – that*; circumstances: quality *en riant – laughing*, time *maintenant – now*).

2. Below the clause

First clause: conjunction group (conjunction *mais – but*), nominal group (pronoun *il – he*), verbal group (finite-event *a – has*), nominal group (standard elliptical expression) {noun not produced, deictic *une – one*, prepositional phrase [preposition *de – of*, nominal group (noun *panses – bellies*, deictic *ces – those*)]}. Second clause: nominal group (pronoun *elle – she*), verbal group (finite-event *dit – says*), nominal group (pronoun *qu' – that*). Third clause: conjunction group (conjunction *mais – but*), verbal group (finite-event *en riant – laughing*), adverbial group (adverb *maintenant – now*).

3. Above the clause (logicosemantic relations)

Secondary clause *elaborates* the meaning of the primary one by *commenting* on the last element of the primary clause.

4. Beside the clause

First clause: given information (*il – he*), new information (*a une de ces **panses** – has one of those bellies*). Second clause: given (*qu' – that*), new (*elle dit mais en **riant** maintenant – she says but laughing now*).

UTTERANCE 53

mais évidemment bon quand il *fumait* ça *allait*
(but of course all right when he smoked that could go)

1. Clause level

MESSAGE. Hypotactic chaining introduced by a series of continuative themes (*mais – but, évidemment – of course, bon – all right*) and made of independent declarative clause with unmarked topical theme (*ça – that*), followed by rheme (*allait – could go*); preceded by finite dependent clause with structural theme (temporal conjunction *quand – when*), unmarked topical theme (*il – he*), and rheme (*fumait – smoked*).

EXCHANGE.   Statements: First declarative (mood: subject *il – he*, finite *fumait – smoked*; residue: predicator *fumait – smoked*). Second declarative (mood: subject *ça – that*, finite *allait – could*; residue: predicator *allait – go*).

REPRESENTATION.   First clause: transitive material process *fumer – smoke* (participants: agent *il – he*, goal not expressed; circumstances: quality *évidemment – of course*, *bon – all right*). Second clause: intransitive material process (abstract) *aller – go*, in the sense of *be acceptable* or something similar (participant: agent *ça – that*).

2. Below the clause

First clause: conjunction group (conjunction *quand – when*), nominal group (pronoun *il – he*), verbal group (finite-event *fumait – smoked*). Second clause: conjunction group (conjunction *mais – but*), adverbial groups (adverbs *évidemment – of course*, *bon – all right*), nominal group (noun *ça – that*), verbal group (finite-event *allait – could go*).

3. Above the clause (logicosemantic relations)

Secondary clause *enhances* the meaning of the primary one by qualifying it with a circumstantial feature of *time*.

4. Beside the clause

First clause: given information (*il – he*), new information (**fumait – smoked**). Second clause: given (*ça – that*), new (**allait – could go**).

UTTERANCE 54

il prenait la **pipe**
(he was taking the pipe)

1. Clause level

MESSAGE.   Independent declarative clause with unmarked topical theme (*il – he*) and rheme (*prenait la pipe – was taking the pipe*).

EXCHANGE.   Statement: Declarative (mood: subject *il – he*; finite *prenait – was taking*; residue: predicator *prenait – taking*, complement *la pipe – the pipe*).

REPRESENTATION. Transitive material process *prendre – take* (participants: agent *il – he*, goal *la pipe – the pipe*).

2. Below the clause

Nominal group (pronoun *il – he*), verbal group (finite-event *prenait – was taking*), nominal group (noun *pipe – pipe*, deictic *la – the*).

3. Beside the clause

Given information (*il – he*), new information (*prenait la **pipe** – was taking the pipe*).

UTTERANCE 55

un petit coup et on la ***reposait***
(a little stroke and one was putting it aside)

1. Clause level

MESSAGE. Paratactic chaining of presumably independent declarative (semantic) anaphoric ellipsis with rheme only (*un petit coup – a little stroke*); and continuing independent declarative clause with unmarked topical theme (*on – one*) and rheme (*la reposait – was putting it aside*).

EXCHANGE. Statement: Declarative (mood: subject *on – one*, finite *reposait – was putting*; residue: predicator *reposait – putting aside*, complement *la – it*).

REPRESENTATION. Transitive material process *reposer – put aside* (participants: agent *on – one*, goal *la – it*).

2. Below the clause

First clause (elliptical): nominal group (noun *coup – stroke*, deictic *un – a*, epithet *petit – little*). Second clause: conjunction group (conjunction *et – and*), nominal group (pronoun *on – one*), verbal group (finite-event *reposait – was putting aside*), nominal group (pronoun *la – it*).

3. Above the clause (logicosemantic relations)

Secondary clause *extends* the meaning of the primary one by *adding new information*.

4. Beside the clause

Given information (*on – one*), new information (*la **reposait** – was putting it aside*).

UTTERANCE 56

on reprenait la ***pipe*** et on refumait deux trois petits ***coups*** comme vous
faites
(one was taking the pipe back and one was smoking again two three little strokes like you do)

1. Clause level

MESSAGE.   Paratactic chaining of one independent declarative clause
and one clause complex tied by conjunction *et* (*and*). Initiating clause is made of
unmarked topical theme (*on – one*) and rheme (*reprenait la pipe – was taking the
pipe back*). Continuing clause complex (hypotactic) is made of independent declarative clause with unmarked topical theme (*on – one*) and rheme (*refumait deux trois
petits coups – was smoking again two three little strokes*); followed by finite dependent clause with conjunctive theme (comparative conjunction *comme – like*),
unmarked topical theme (*vous – you*), and rheme (*faites – do*).

EXCHANGE.   Statements: First declarative (mood: subject *on – one*,
finite *reprenait – was taking*; residue: predicator *reprenait – taking back*, complement *la pipe – the pipe*). Second declarative (mood: subject *on – one*, finite *refumait
– was smoking*; residue: predicator *refumait – smoking again*, circumstantial adjunct
deux trois petits coups – two three little strokes). Third declarative (mood: subject
vous – you, finite *faites – do*; residue: predicator *faites – do*).

REPRESENTATION.   First clause: transitive material process *reprendre
– take back* (participants: agent *on – one*, goal *la pipe – the pipe*). Second clause:
transitive material process *fumer – smoke* (participants: agent *on – one*, goal not
expressed; circumstance: quantity *deux trois petits coups – two three little strokes*).
Third clause: intransitive material process *faire – do* (participant: agent *vous – you*;
circumstance: comparison *comme – like*).

2. Below the clause

First clause: nominal group (pronoun *on – one*), verbal group (finite-event
reprenait – was taking back), nominal group (noun *pipe – pipe*, deictic *la – the*). Second clause: conjunction group (conjunction *et – and*), nominal group (pronoun *on –
one*), verbal group (finite-event *refumait – was smoking again*), nominal group
(noun *coups – strokes*, quantifiers *deux – two, trois – three*, epithet *petits – little*).
Third clause: conjunction group (conjunction *comme – like*), nominal group (pronoun *vous – you*), verbal group (finite-event *faites – do*).

3. Above the clause (logicosemantic relations)

Secondary clause in paratactic chaining *extends* the meaning of the primary
one by *adding new information*. Secondary clause in clause complex *enhances* the

meaning of the primary clause in clause complex by qualifying it with a circumstantial feature of *comparison*.

4. Beside the clause

First clause: given information (*on – one*), new information (*reprenait la* **pipe** *– was taking the pipe back*). Second clause: given (*on – one*), new (*refumait deux trois petits* **coups** *– was smoking again two three little strokes*). Third clause: given (*vous – you*), new (**faites** *– do*).

UTTERANCE 57

on la ***reposait***
(one was putting it aside)

1. Clause level

MESSAGE.   Independent declarative clause with unmarked topical theme (*on – one*) and rheme (*la reposait – was putting it aside*).

EXCHANGE.   Statement: Declarative (mood: subject *on – one*, finite *reposait – was putting*; residue: predicator *reposait – putting aside*, complement *la – it*).

REPRESENTATION.   Transitive material process *reposer – put aside* (participants: agent *on – one*, goal *la – it*).

2. Below the clause

Nominal group (pronoun *on – one*), verbal group (finite-event *reposait – was putting aside*), nominal group (pronoun *la – it*).

3. Beside the clause

Given information (*on – one*), new information (*la* **reposait** *– was putting it aside*).

UTTERANCE 58

oui mais maintenant c'est ***pire*** parce que maintenant toutes les tous les ***chemises*** qu'il a vraiment sur son estomac qu'elle dit ma ***soeur***
(yes but now that is worse because now all the all the shirts that he really has on his belly that she says my sister)

1. Clause level

MESSAGE.   Hypotactic chaining: independent clause complex and finite-dependent clause. Clause complex (itself hypotactic) is introduced by independent declarative clause made of two continuative themes (*oui* – *yes*) (oppositive *mais* – *but*), followed by conjunctive theme (temporal adverb *maintenant* – *now*), unmarked topical theme (*c'* – *that*), and rheme (*est pire* – *is worse*). This clause is followed by what should have been a finite dependent clause but actually is (incorrectly so) a nonfinite dependent clause with structural theme (conjunction *parce que* – *because*), conjunctive theme (*maintenant* – *now*), unmarked topical theme (*toutes les tous les chemises* – *all the all the shirts*), and no rheme. This dependent clause is itself followed by a another finite dependent clause (which should have been embedded) with TH-item as marked topical theme (*qu'* – *that*) and rheme (*il a vraiment sur son estomac* – *he really has on his belly*). The clause complex is followed by a finite dependent clause with marked topical theme (TH-item *qu'* – *that*) and rheme (*elle dit ma soeur* – *she says my sister*).

EXCHANGE. Statements: First declarative (mood: subject *c* – *that*, finite *est* – *is*; residue: predicator *est* – *is*, attributive complement *pire* -*worse*, circumstantial adjunct *maintenant* -*now*). Second declarative (incomplete) (mood: subject *toutes les chemises* – *all the shirts*, no finite; residue: no predicator, circumstancial adjunct *maintenant* – *now*). Third declarative (mood: subject *il* – *he*, finite *a* – *has*; residue: predicator *a* – *has*, complement *qu'* – *that*, circumstantial adjuncts: *vraiment* – *really*, *sur son estomac* – *on his belly*). Fourth declarative (mood : subject *elle* – *she*, finite *dit* – *says*; residue: predicator *dit* – *says*, complement *qu'* – *that*). The coreferent of pronoun *elle* – *she*, that is, *ma soeur* – *my sister*, is reproduced at the end of the fourth declarative probably for the sake of discursive clarity.

REPRESENTATION. First clause (relational process): intensive *être* – *be* (participants: carrier *c'* – *that*, attribute *pire* – *worse*; circumstance: time *maintenant* – *now*). Second clause (incomplete). Third clause: relational process: possessive *avoir* – *have* (participants: possessor *il* – *he*, possessed *qu'* – *that*; circumstance: quality *vraiment* – *really*, space *sur son estomac* – *on his belly*). Fourth clause: verbal process *dire* – *say* (participants: sayer *elle* – *she*, signal *qu'* – *that*).

2. Below the clause

First clause: adverbial group (adverb *oui* – *yes*), conjunction group (conjunction *mais* – *but*), adverbial group (adverb *maintenant* – *now*), nominal group (pronoun *c* – *that*), verbal group (finite-event *est* – *is*), attribute group (attribute *pire* – *worse*). Second clause (incomplete): conjunction group (conjunction *parce que* – *because*), nominal group (noun *chemises* – *shirts*, quantifier *toutes* – *all*, deictic *les* – *the*), adverbial group (adverb *maintenant* – *now*). Third clause: nominal group (pronoun *il* – *he*), verbal group (finite-event *a* – *has*), nominal group (pronoun *qu'* – *that*), adverbial group (adverb *vraiment* – *really*), prepositional phrase [preposition *sur* – *on*, nominal group (noun *estomac* – *belly*, deictic *son* – *his*)]. Fourth clause:

nominal group (noun *soeur* – *sister*, deictic *ma* – *my*), verbal group (finite-event *dit* – *says*), nominal group (pronoun *qu'* – *that*).

3. Above the clause (logicosemantic relations)

Secondary clause in clause complex *elaborates* the meaning of the primary one by *commenting* upon it. First dependent clause in hypotactic chaining *enhances* the meaning of the primary clause complex by qualifying it with a circumstantial feature of *cause*. The meaning of this first dependent clause is itself *elaborated* by a second dependent clause *commenting* on the element *chemises* (*shirts*).

4. Beside the clause

First clause: given information (*c'* – *that*), new information (*est **pire** – is worse*). Second clause: given (*qu'il a vraiment sur son estomac* – *that he really has on his belly*), new (*toutes les **chemises** – all the shirts*). Third clause: given (*qu'* – *that*), new (*elle dit ma **soeur** – she says my sister*).

UTTERANCE 59

et bien oui mais c'est une ***pénitence*** qu'elle ***dit*** parce que ma mère est toujours en train de soit de l'élargir sur les ***pinces***
(and well yes but that is a punishment that she says because my mother is always busy either enlarging it on the pinches)

1. Clause level

MESSAGE. Hypotactic chaining: independent declarative clause and two finite dependent clauses. Independent clause is made of a series of chained continuative themes (*et bien oui mais* – *and well yes but*), followed by unmarked topical theme (*c'* – *that*) and rheme (*est une pénitence* – *is a punishment*). First dependent clause is made of topical theme (*qu'* – *that*) and rheme (*elle dit* – *she says*). Second finite dependent clause is made of structural theme (*parce que* – *because*), unmarked topical theme (*ma mère* – *my mother*), and rheme (*est toujours en train de soit de l'élargir sur les pinces* – *is always busy either enlarging it on the pinches*). Notice that the second branch of the alternative initiated by *soit* (*either*) in the rheme of the second finite dependent clause is missing.

EXCHANGE. Statements: First declarative (mood: subject *c'* – *that*, finite *est* – *is*; residue: predicator *est* – *is*, attributive complement *une pénitence* – *a punishment*). Second declarative (mood: subject *elle* – *she*, finite *dit* – *says*; residue: predicator *dit* – *says*, complement *qu'* – *that*). Third declarative (mood: subject *ma mère* – *my mother*, finite *est* – *is*; residue: predicator *est en train de* – *is busy*, complement *l'élargir sur les pinces* – *enlarging it on the pinches*, circumstantial adjunct *toujours* – *always*).

REPRESENTATION. First clause (relational process): intensive *être* – *be* (participants: carrier *c'* – *that*, attribute *une pénitence* – *a punishment*). Second clause: verbal process *dire* – *say* (participants: sayer *elle* – *she*, signal *qu'* – *that*). Third clause: transitive material process *élargir* – *enlarge* (participants: agent *ma mère* – *my mother*, goal *l'* – *it*; circumstances: time *toujours* – *always*, space *sur les pinces* – *on the pinches*).

2. Below the clause

First clause: conjunction group (conjunction *et* – *and*), adverbial groups (adverbs *bien* – *well*, *oui* – *yes*), conjunction group (conjunction *mais* – *but*), nominal group (pronoun *c'* – *that*), verbal group (finite-event *est* – *is*), attributive group [attribute: nominal group (noun *pénitence* – *punishment*, deictic *une* – *a*)]. Second clause: nominal group (pronoun *elle* – *she*), verbal group (finite-event *dit* – *says*), nominal group (pronoun *qu'* – *that*). Third clause (incomplete): conjunction group (conjunction *parce que* – *because*), nominal group (noun *mère* – *mother*, deictic *ma* – *may*), verbal group (finite-event *est en train de* – *is busy*), adverbial group (adverb *toujours* – *always*), conjunction group (conjunction *soit* – *either*), nominal group (pronoun *l'* – *it*), verbal group (finite-event *élargir* – *enlarging*), prepositional phrase [preposition *sur* – *on*, nominal group (noun *pinces* – *pinches*, deictic *les* – *the*)].

3. Above the clause (logicosemantic relations)

The meaning of primary clause in the hypotactic chaining is *elaborated* by the first dependent clause *commenting* on it, and it is *enhanced* by the second dependent clause qualifying it with a circumstantial feature of *cause*.

4. Beside the clause

First clause: given information (*c'* – *that*), new information (*est une* **pénitence** – *is a punishment*). Second clause: given (*qu'* – *that*), new (*elle* **dit** – *she says*). Third clause: given (*ma mère* – *my mother*), new (*est toujours en train de soit de l' élargir sur les* **pinces** – *is always busy either enlarging it on the pinches*).

UTTERANCE 60

oui mais c'est un ouvrage *ça*
(yes but that is quite a work)

1. Clause level

MESSAGE. Independent declarative clause with continuative themes (*oui*- *yes*) (*mais* – *but*), unmarked topical theme (*c'* – *that*), and rheme (*est un ouvrage ça* – *is quite a work that*).

EXCHANGE. Statement: Declarative (mood: subject *c' – that*, finite *est – is*; residue: predicator *est – is*, complement *un ouvrage – a work*, circumstantial adjunct *ça – quite*).

REPRESENTATION. Relational process: intensive *être – be* (participants: carrier *c' – that*, attribute *un ouvrage – a work*; circumstance: quality *ça – quite*).

2. Below the clause

Adverbial group (adverb *oui – yes*), conjunction group (conjunction *mais – but*), nominal group (pronoun *c' – that*), verbal group (finite-event *est – is*), attributive group [attribute: nominal group (noun *ouvrage – work*), deictic *un – a*], nominal group (pronoun *ça*).

3. Beside the clause

Given information (*c' – that*), new information (*est un ouvrage **ça** – is quite a work*).

UTTERANCE 61

enfin maman le **fait** bon j'vais vous l'**dire** parce que c'est son **beau-fils** enfin
(then mother does it well I will tell it to you because he is her son-in-law in the end)

1. Clause level

MESSAGE. Clause complex made of independent declarative clause with continuative theme (*enfin – then*), unmarked topical theme (*maman – mother*), and rheme (*le fait – does it*), and finite dependent clause with conjunctive theme (*parce que – because*), unmarked topical theme (*c' – he*), and rheme (*est son beau-fils enfin – is her son-in-law in the end*). There is an independent declarative clause interspersed between the two clauses forming the clause complex, made of continuative theme (*bon – well*), unmarked topical theme (*j' – contracted form for je – I*), and rheme (*vais vous l'dire – will tell it to you*). This latter clause may be considered to be paratactically chained (by simple juxtaposition) to the preceding independent clause.

EXCHANGE. Statements. First declarative (mood: subject *maman – mother*, finite *fait – does*; residue: predicator *fait – does*, complement *le – it*). Second declarative (mood: subject *j' – I*, finite *vais – will*; residue: predicator *dire – tell*, complements: *l' – it*, oblique object *vous – you*). Third declarative (mood: subject *c'* – *he*, finite *est* – *is*; residue: predicator *est* – *is*, attributive complement *son beau-fils* – *her son-in-law*, circumstantial adjunct *enfin* – *in the end*).

REPRESENTATION.   First clause: transitive material process *faire* – *do* (participants: agent *maman* – *mother*, goal *le* – *it*; circumstance: time *enfin* – *in the end*). Second clause: verbal process *dire* – *say* (participants: sayer *je* – *I*, signal *l'* – *it*, beneficiary *vous* – *you*; circumstance: quality *bon* – *well*). Third clause (relational process): intensive *être* – *be* (participants: carrier *c'* – *he*, attribute *son beau-fils* – *her son-in-law*; circumstance: time *enfin* – *in the end*).

2. Below the clause

First clause: adverbial group (adverb *enfin* – *then*), nominal group (noun *maman* – *mother*), verbal group (finite-event *fait* – *does*), nominal group (pronoun *le* – *it*). Second clause: adverbial group (*bon* – *well*), nominal group (pronoun *j'* – *I*), verbal group (finite-event *vais* – *will*), verbal group (event *dire* – *tell*), nominal group (pronoun *vous* – *you*), nominal group (pronoun *l'* – *it*). Third clause: conjunction group (conjunction (*parce que* – *because*), nominal group (pronoun *c'* – *he*), verbal group (finite-event *est* – *is*), nominal group (noun *beau-fils* – *son-in-law*, deictic *son* – *her*), adverbial group (adverb *enfin* – *in the end*).

3. Above the clause (logicosemantic relations)

The meaning of first independent clause is *elaborated* by the second independent clause *commenting* on it. The meaning of primary clause in clause complex is *enhanced* in the secondary clause by qualifying it with a circumstantial feature of *cause*.

4. Beside the clause

First clause: given information (*maman* – *mother*), new information (*le **fait*** – *does it*). Second clause: given (*j'* – *I*), new (*vais vous l'**dire*** – *will tell it to you*). Third clause: given (*c'* – *he*), new (*est son **beau-fils** enfin* – *is her son-in-law in the end*).

UTTERANCE 62

donc elle le fait quand même par ***plaisir*** mais au total
(thus she does it even for fun but in the whole)

1. Clause level

MESSAGE.   Independent declarative clause made of continuative theme (*donc* – *thus*), unmarked topical theme (*elle* – *she*), and rheme (*le fait quand même par plaisir* – *does it even for fun*). As the full transcript shows (see Appendix 1), the final portion of this utterance (i.e., *mais au total* – *but in the whole*), probably meant as the beginning of another independent declarative clause (oppositive to the first one shown), could not be developed because it was interrupted by the continuative comment of the interlocutor.

EXCHANGE. Statement: Declarative (mood: subject *elle – she*, finite *fait – does*; residue: predicator *fait – does*, complement *le – il*, circumstantial adjunct *quand même par plaisir – then even for fun*).

REPRESENTATION. Transitive material process *faire – do* (participants: agent *elle – she*, goal *le – it*; circumstances: quality *quand même par plaisir – even for fun*).

2. Below the clause

Conjunction group (conjunction *donc – thus*), nominal group (pronoun *elle – she*), verbal group (finite-event *fait – does*), nominal group (pronoun *le – it*), adverbial group (adverb *quand même – even*), prepositional phrase [preposition *par – for*, nominal group (noun *plaisir – fun*)], conjunction group (conjunction *mais – but*), adverbial group (adverbial locution *au total – in the whole*).

3. Beside the clause

Given information (*elle – she*), new information (*le fait quand même par* **plaisir** *– does it even for fun*).

Speech turn 5 – Around the clause

The speech turn relates to Françoise's brother-in-law's smoking and non-smoking habits together with the usual consequences of his having relatively recently quit smoking.

Textual cohesion is realized through *lexical cohesion, reference*, and *conjunction*. Basic items for maintaining lexical cohesion are: conjugated verb forms of *fumer – to smoke, estomac – belly, le pire – the worse*. Coreference is largely used throughout the speech turn (*mon beau-frère il . . . il, my brother-in-law he . . . he, ma soeur . . . elle – my sister . . . she, la pipe . . . la – the pipe . . . it, les chemises . . . l' (élargir) – the shirts . . . it* (which, in this last case, is a grammatical mistake since the plural pronoun *les* should have been used instead of singular *le* elided into *l'*), *un ouvrage . . . le – quite a work . . . it, c'est – that is, ça – that*. A number of conjunctions and adverbs are used in a probable attempt to maintain and/or reinforce textual cohesion (*mais – but, maintenant – now, et – and, mais maintenant – but now, et bien oui mais – and well yes but, oui mais – yes but, enfin – then, bon – well, donc – thus, mais au total – but in the whole*). Most of the uses of the contrastive conjunction *mais – but* are not really contrastive. They seem to function as loose connectors between successive utterances giving the text its simple and somewhat taxing (on the interlocutor's short-term memory) serial chaining structure.

5.4.1.2.3 Conclusions of the analysis

The overall conclusion of the preceding analysis is that Françoise's conversational speech conforms itself nicely to the specifications of Halliday's functional grammar, which may be interpreted as confirming the impression of normality that one develops when listening to the tape or reading the transcription. A summary of the major findings derived from the analysis component by component follows.

At *the level of the message*, Françoise's productions correspond to the canonical thematicorhematic structure of French whether in independent or in dependent clauses. Most clauses are indicative declarative, which is natural given the nature of the conversational exchange. When imperatives or interrogatives are used, they also conform to the canonical-grammatical organization. Simple as well as multiple themes are expressed. With multiple themes, the sequential indications supplied by Halliday, and validated for French, are followed correctly (i.e., typical sequences of thematic elements: textual-interpersonal-ideational or interpersonal-textual-ideational; typical order of elements within the textual theme: continuative-structural-conjunctive). Elliptical clauses are used from time to time (mostly anaphoric ellipses) and correctly so, denoting an excellent control over the regular conversational mechanisms.

At *the exchange level*, the basic mood-residue organization is present everywhere. Given the nature of the verbal exchange recorded, all the clauses take the form of propositions. But there is no doubt that Françoise is perfectly able to negotiate the exchange of goods and/or services dimension, that is, to produce correctly formed proposals (in Halliday's sense), as well. Within the mood element, the grammatical subject and the finite verbal constituents regularly appear. They are properly ordered sequentially with one apparent exception (in utterance 43, a WH-interrogative, the observed order is subject-finite with the WH-element not being the clause grammatical subject – such a construction, however, is fairly common and fully accepted in colloquial French). In the declaratives, the unmarked topical theme supplies the grammatical subject in all cases. Verbal concord is correctly marked with no exception.

Within the residue, the predicator is present in all nonelliptical clauses as it should. Depending on the clause, complement(s) and/or circumstantial adjuncts appear. Complements are typically realized by nominal groups but a few attributive complements may be noted. Circumstantial adjuncts are typically realized by adverbial groups or prepositional phrases. The typical order of the elements in the residue, that is, predicator-complement(s)-circumstantial adjunct(s), is followed most of the time (exceptions concern utterances 10 and 31, where the adjunct element precedes the complement, a freedom allowed by the French syntax, which is not exceptional in English either). When conjunctive adjuncts are produced in the middle of the clause, they tend to coincide with the boundary between mood and residue (e.g., utterance 3).

At *the representation level*, a number of transitivity processes are exemplified (predominantly material, mental, and relational processes, but so-called subsidiary types of processes such as saying and happening also appear). The process components are regularly expressed, that is, the process itself, the participant(s) in the process and, depending on the clause, the circumstances associated with the process. Among these, there is a relatively large number of items formally pertaining to the temporal and the comparative circumstantial elements that are actually stereotyped conversational fillers (e.g., *alors – then, enfin – in the end, comme ça – like that*).

At *the below-the-clause level of analysis*, the eight basic structures identified in Halliday's grammar are all correctly used. Nominal groups have a common noun, a personal pronoun, or a proper noun as their syntactic head. Premodifiers (deictics, quantifiers, and epithets) are used. They are correctly ordered sequentially from the deictic to the epithet. Deictics and quantifiers are correctly marked for grammatical gender and for number where applicable. Their referential dependencies may be easily coindexed with an antecedent in the linguistic context. There are only two errors in this respect within the corpus: In utterance 58, Françoise produces *tous les chemises* instead of the correct *toutes les chemises (all the shirts)*. The incorrectly marked quantifier *tous*, however, is immediately preceded by *toutes (les)*. This means that the correctly marked quantifier was first produced only to be self-corrected in the wrong way for unknown reasons; in utterance 59, the object pronoun located before the verb *élargir (enlarge)* should be *les* instead of *l' (it)* since it refers back to the plural noun *les chemises (the shirts)*. It is possible, in this case, that the relatively long distance between the pronoun and its antecedent is responsible for the error (unless, of course, this is a simple speech error).

The definite-indefinite contrast on the article (opposition *un, une/le, la* for the singular; opposition *des/les* for the plural form) is correctly marked with no exceptions. In utterance 10, there is an interesting self-correction to be noted. Françoise first produced *et alors vous montez un peu plus haut comme ça en traversant le (and then you go up a little more like that crossing the)*, only to modify the definite article into an indefinite one, *un grand pont (a large bridge)*, as it should be, given, *first*, that this is the first mention of the bridge to the interlocutor who has no prior knowledge of the place, and, *second*, that the bridge is not otherwise specified in the nominal group.

Epithets are correctly marked for grammatical gender. They are properly positioned with respect to the head noun of the nominal groups according to the provisos of French syntax. Postmodifiers appear depending on particular clauses. They may be an epithet, an embedded relative clause, a participial or an infinitive clause, or a prepositional phrase.

Verbal groups consist of properly ordered sequences of words of the class of verbs. They begin with the finite and end with the event. The finite correctly relates the process to the speaker-now by person, number, modality, tense, and aspect, with only one exception: In an utterance situated without the speech turns analyzed (see two speech turns by Françoise before speech turn 8, second speech sample) *j'aurais passé en quatrième – I would have passed the fourth level* (talking about previous school performance). In this utterance, the auxiliary *be* should have been used instead of the auxiliary *have* according to normative French grammar – but this type of mistake is a common one in current (particularly popular) practice since the normative rules specifying the use of auxiliaries *être* (*be*) and *avoir* (*have*) are somewhat flexible and since other intransitive verbs indicating movement [e.g., *marcher – to walk, changer – to change* (physically)] are accompanied with the auxiliary *have*, therefore allowing for erroneous generalization by analogy with other movement verbs.

Attributive groups, adverbial groups, conjunction groups and phrases, and preposition groups and phrases are used and correctly formed except in three minor cases: In utterance 34, the adverb *drôlement* (*in a funny way*) is twice formulated *drôl'dement*, which is not uncommon in colloquial French; in utterance 35, the adverbial group *toute façon* should be *de toute façon* (*in any way*); and, in utterance 39, the conjunction phrase qualifying *habillé* (*dressed*) should be *à l'as de pique* (see Note 3 following the English translation of the speech turns in Appendix 2) and not *comme l'as de pique*; but again, the latter preposition is not unheard of in regional French.

Above the clause level, Halliday distinguishes clause complexes that he proposes to analyze in terms of types of interdependency and in terms of logicosemantic relationships between clauses. Françoise's correct use of parataxis and hypotaxis attests to her mastery over the clause complex dimension. The only clear insufficiency observed in this respect is in utterance 58, where Françoise initiates a dependent clause introduced by the causal conjunction *parce que* (*because*) that should have been finite but was not, since she produced one embedded clause followed by another dependent clause before apparently losing sight of the fact that the causal dependent clause needed completion before starting up a new utterance (*parce que maintenant toutes les tous les chemises qu'il a vraiment sur son estomac qu'elle dit ma soeur – because now all the all the shirts that he really has on his belly that she says my sister*). Given the nature of the text recorded, the logicosemantic relations holding between primary and secondary members of clause complexes typically are of the expansion kind. Within this type, secondary elaborations, enhancements, and extensions of primary clauses are correctly realized.

Regarding *the information structure of the language* produced (*beside-the-clause analysis*), Françoise's clauses are correctly organized according to the given-new contrast. The typical sequence, that is, given followed by new, is used everywhere. This demonstrates Françoise's sensitivity to the interlocutor's knowledge regarding the information being exchanged in the conversation, as the given-new contrast is considered to be listener oriented, and her capacity to constantly monitor her speech according to the ongoing modification of this knowledge. There are a few cases in

Françoise's production in which tonic prominence is not located over the last word of the portion of the clause containing the new information, as should be the case (e.g., utterances 3, 12 , 32, and 39). In these cases, the outside elements are conversational fillers (e.g., *comme ça – like that, enfin – in the end*) with no real function in the information structure of the language exchanged. In one additional case, however, it could be considered that the given-new contrast is violated: In utterance 59, third clause, the given element (or what should have been the given element), that is, *ma mère – my mother*, is not clearly given, since, from the first two clauses in the same utterances as well as from preceding utterances, starting with utterance 48, one would expect the mentioned "punishment" to be for Françoise's sister rather than for her mother.

Finally, as to *textual cohesion (around-the-clause analysis)*, the four means distinguished by Halliday, that is, reference, ellipsis, conjunction, and lexical cohesion, are all used by Françoise. Yet the impression left by most of her large speech turns is that they are somewhat lacking in cohesion. A part of this impression no doubt is not specific to Françoise but has to do with the fact that this is spontaneous speech transcribed verbatim. (If you are not convinced, record yourself in a familiar unprepared conversation, transcribe your speech verbatim, and see how less verbally cohesive you are than you may think.) But another portion of this impression is probably correct and corresponds to the limited but real difficulty encountered by Françoise in some aspects of textual organization. As it appears in the speech excerpts analyzed, it is particularly the conjunction process that is (partially) defective (as in many normal immature speakers, i.e., children). Françoise uses a number of conjunction forms (e.g., *et – and, alors – then, mais – but, donc – therefore*), often positioned at the beginning of the utterances. However, these forms do not really supply a true coordinating network for inserting utterances. They rather seem to be conversational fillers and/or loose sequential connectors. Many utterances contain repetitions of the same words, locutions, or phrases. Stereotyped idiomatic expressions are placed here and there in the utterances [e.g., *comme vous voyez – as you see, si j'peux l'dire platement – if I may say it flatly, pour vous l'dire honnêtement – to tell (it to) you honestly*]. This seems to go by speech turn. Once Françoise has begun producing one such stereotyped expression, she tends to continue using it in the rest of the speech turn, as if the first production had a priming effect. Also Françoise appears to have a tendency to alternate ideas in a pairwise fashion, that is, to express one idea, turn to a related one, return to the first idea, and then go on with the second one, all with a somewhat limited explicit marking of the semantic relationships holding between the two ideas. In one case (utterance 59), two alternative statements are "announced" by the use of *soit (either)*, but the second branch of the alternative is found missing. In a few other utterances, there is a minor semantic discontinuity with the preceding one(s). For example, in utterance 27, Françoise specifies that she rarely goes out when the weather is hot. This comment is not directly related to the preceding utterances, which describe what takes place at the women's meeting every Thurday in Françoise's home. The unexpressed link may be hinted at in utterance 25, where Françoise mentions "sitting." She may have had in mind "sitting outside." This would explain, in utterance 27, why she specifies that she rarely does it when it is too hot. In the unanalyzed speech turns that follow analyzed speech turn 5 (first speech sample) – see Appendices 1 and 2 – Françoise is mixed up in trying to estimate J.F.B.'s height by comparison with her brother-in-law. She computes "three heads" as being equal to the difference between 1.75 and 1.92 m. (Other reflections on Françoise's low physical and mathematical ability are available in Section 5.8.2.)

These characteristics attest to a difficulty in (microlevel) text planning. In this respect, the stereotyped fillers that Françoise uses may be the verbal equivalent of the hesitation pauses studied by Goldman-Eisler (1968,1972) and others (e.g., Hawkins, 1971; Holmes, 1988), assumed to correspond to moments of planning the discourse ahead (but see also Butterworth, 1980, and Piolat, 1983).

Despite these apparent difficulties in text planning and organization, there are several examples in the corpus demonstrating Françoise's sensitivity to the necessity of making herself clear for the interlocutor's sake. This may be observed in utterance 27, where she repeats *moi – me* on each side of an embedded clause (*tandis que moi quand il fait des chaleurs comme ça moi – whereas me when it is hot like that me*); in utterance 32, where she repeats the first two elements of an independent clause interrupted by a conditional one (*c'est si j'peux l'dire c'est un peu comme ici enfin – that is if I may say it that is a bit like here in the end*), and again in utterance 39 (*habillé si je peux l'dire tout platement aussi habillé comme l'as de pique enfin – dressed if I may say it bluntly also dressed like "l'as de pique" in the end*).

Discursive coherence (in the sense defined in Section 5.4.1.2.1) was not assessed specifically. Upon casual examination of the whole conversational corpus between Françoise and J.F.B., it would appear that overall conversational connectedness was quite satisfactory (acknowledging the fact that J.F.B. did his best to let Françoise express herself as "comfortably" as possible).

Finally, very few lexical errors are observed in Françoise's utterances. She occasionally uses incomplete locutions (e.g., *y a, y avait*) instead of the correct forms (*il y a – there is, il y avait – there was*) (again, this is not unusual in familiar French), incorrect word forms [e.g., *décrapitude* instead of the correct *décrépitude* (the state of something falling apart)], and incorrect expressions such as *il m'faut déjà toutes les plumes pour voler* instead of the correct *il m'faut déjà toutes mes plumes pour voler – I already need all my feathers to fly*. This last error is quite interesting. It relates to the linguistic expression of so-called inalienable possession in French (see Fillmore, 1967; Hatcher, 1944a, 1944b; Rondal, 1977b; for developmental data attesting to its late acquisition in normal children, see Rondal, 1977c). The standard (idiomatic) expression with the possessive pronominal determiner violates the pattern of inalienable possession for stylistic reason (i.e., stressing the fact that the person referred to needs all his *own* "feathers" to function correctly from a given point of view). Françoise appears to have treated ("regularized") this idiom phrase as a "novel," componentially analyzed phrase, in which the article would be the correct determiner. The subtleties of inalienable possession in French usually are not mastered before 7 or 8 years of age (depending on the particular subform) and show social class and regional variation. *Voluntary* violation of the regular pattern for stylistic reason is probably an even later achievement, but no developmental data are available on this specific point to the best of my knowledge.

Nowhere does Françoise seem to have difficulty in retrieving words that she knows and regularly uses in spontaneous speech. It would appear that her lexical access (see Levelt, 1989, 1992) is mostly preserved. However, no specific investigation was undertaken on this part of Françoise's language organization.

5.4.1.3 Additional expressive language data

Some additional comments are in order to complete the report on Françoise's expressive language. First, as to *articulation,* Françoise's speech is perfectly articulated. In two hours of recorded conversation and numerous other contacts with her, no one in my research team has detected the slightest articulatory problem. She speaks with the clear regional accent characteristic of the people living in her part of the (Francophone) country. Her utterances are properly intoned and the tonic stress is correctly distributed on the last pronounced syllable of the word group (as is the case in French). Moreover, Françoise uses emphatic stress relatively often, making her speech quite expressive. On a coarticulation test (devised by Borel-Maisonny, 1953; see Rondal, 1979a; list of items supplied in Appendix 7.1), Françoise proved capable of correctly repeating nonwords (so-called logatomes), embodying the possible phonological sequences of French and containing up to four syllables, without error. On the last sublist, containing nonwords of five syllables (such as "zoltiduseltor" or "pulblagoritel"), she missed five items out of eight, committing errors of omission, substitution, and inversion of vowels or consonants. Few normal people perform errorlessly on the last list of this test.

Second, according to Levelt (1989), one may define the "canonical setting for speech" (p. 30) – of which conversation supplies the best illustration – as one in which speakers interact for some purpose in a shared spatiotemporal environment. Prominent aspects of the interactional character of conversational speech center around issues of cooperation and turn taking. Speakers' dependence on the spatiotemporal context is illustrated in the deictic character of speech. The purposeful character of conversational speech is correctly captured in the notions of communicative intentions and speech acts (Austin, 1962; Grice, 1975; Searle, 1979). Françoise's correct use of the major types of deixis distinguished in the literature (see, e.g., Lyons, 1977) has been documented in the preceding section and includes *person deixis* (personal pronouns in conversational exchange), *social deixis* [she always uses the polite plural *vous, votre,* etc., and the concordant plural verb forms, when addressing J.F.B. or referring to him in conversation (J.F.B. addresses her using the familiar second-person singular pronouns, *tu*, *ton*, etc., at the beginning of the first encounter, and, then, switches to the "polite" forms after which Françoise remarked – purposefully (?) – that the "you-forms" were casually used among members of her family)], *place and space deixis* (e.g., the proximal-distal contrast), *time deixis* (use of adverbial and verbal forms referring to time), and *discourse deixis* (pronominal coreference).

As to interlocutors' cooperation, Grice (1975) specifies two sorts of rules: those for the allocation of speech turns and those governing the character of the contributions. Françoise's turn-taking behavior is quite appropriate, as can be judged by reading the transcription of the conversational exchanges with J.F.B. and from listening to the tapes (only one speaker talking at a time, virtually no vocal clashes, few observed lapses, i.e., extended silence between conversation units). Also Françoise clearly signals the approaching end of her speech turn (transition-relevant places according to the classical analysis of Sack, Schegloff, & Jefferson, 1974; but see also O'Connell, Kowal, & Kaltenbacher, 1990) using several means, most often in conjunction. (The ending of the paragraph and/or of the sentence can be roughly predicted on semantic and/or formal grounds; she clearly lowers the intonation and the vocal intensity over the intended last segments of her speech turn; at times, she herself assigns the next turn to her interlocutor by directing a question to him.) Cooperativeness also applies to what parties have to say with respect to each other when at turn. Although no systematic analysis was made, it seems clear that Françoise's contribution to dialogue is appropriate, intelligible, and clear within the textual cohesive limitations mentioned in the preceding section. Referring to the well-known Gricean four sets of so-called maxims (Grice, 1975), it can be said that Françoise's contribution to the conversational exchange with J.F.B. satisfactorily conforms to the maxims of *quantity* ("Make your contribution as informative as required for the current purpose of the exchange"), *quality* ("Do not say what you believe to be false"), *relation* ("Be relevant," i.e., "Make your contribution relate to the ongoing exchange of talk"), and *manner* ("Avoid obscurity of expression and be orderly"), even acknowledging the fact, as has been noted many times in the literature (e.g., Levinson, 1983; Sperber & Wilson, 1986), that these maxims lack specific operational definitions or may be difficult it not impossible to check for sure, at least for some of them (e.g., maxim of quality).

Of course, J.F.B.'s assigned task ("Let her talk and stimulate her talking") as well as his natural good will and kindness certainly made things easier for Françoise in the conversational exchange. It could be questioned whether she would display such good command over interactive mechanisms in less protected interpersonal exchanges. However, judging from other contacts with Françoise and from informal reports from the staff of La Fermette on Françoise's use of descriptive and narrative speech, for example, our observations seem to have general validity. Françoise may be credited with a good control over the general pragmatic aspects of speech.

As to the purposeful character of speech, it may be useful to recall the four major classes of illocutionary force among the speech acts (leaving aside so-called declarations) according to Searle's taxonomy (1979): *assertives* (the purpose of which is to commit a speaker to something being the case), *directives* (getting the addressee to do something), *commissives* (the speaker committing himself to some future course of action, feeling, or thinking), and *expressives* (the speaker making his feelings known with respect to some state of affairs). Sentential forms are assumed to correspond to speech-act types although the correspondence is not one to one. In Françoise's speech, declarative clauses are characteristically employed to assert. They are dominant in her conversational and mostly descriptive corpus, which was both expected and normal. Imperative as well as interrogative clauses are characteristically used to direct the interlocutor's behavior, feeling, or thinking, or, in some cases, to commit oneself explicitly to some course of action, way of thinking, or feeling. Such clauses rarely appear in the corpus recorded given the type of interpersonal exchange and the situation, but there is no doubt that communicative intentions of that kind belong to Françoise's mental apparatus. Finally, there is no major characteristic clause type for either commissives or expressives in normal speech. Rather, any clause type may be used to convey these two types of communicative intentions. This is certainly true of Françoise's corpus regarding expressive illocutionary force. Predictably, again, given the type of speech exchange and situational context, no clear commissive communicative intention was formulated within the corpus.

Third, as for productive lexicon, no systematic procedure for assessing productive lexicon from spontaneous speech that would have a reasonable amount of theoretical validity exists to the best of my knowledge. A modest indication of quantitative diversity of the lexical elements available to the subject at one moment in time is supplied by the type-token ratio (TTR). It is usually computed in reporting the number of different words – from all grammatical categories – identified in a randomly selected portion of the corpus (usually a section containing one hundred consecutive words) to the total number of words (Siegel & Harkins, 1963). TTRs were computed on the first hundred consecutive words of four randomly selected speech turns within the first and the second speech excerpts, respectively (speech turns 2, 4, 7, and 10). The resultant TTRs are .53, .48, .53, and .56, respectively. The average computed TTR is .525 with a narrow variation interval (.08). Tables for interpreting TTR are lacking, unfortunately. According to the data compiled by Rondal for English-speaking mother-child dyads, the same TTR values as those for Françoise are observed in mothers addressing their normally developing offsprings around 36 months and their MR children when they have reached approximatively MLU 3.00 (see Rondal, 1978b, 1978c, 1985b). Additional comparative English data on TTRs may be found in Siegel (1963) and in Siegel and Harkins (1963). These authors had NR adults assembled with institutionalized MR subjects (aged between 9 and 17 years; IQ not reported) in free conversation, interview, and tutoring conditions (i.e., instructing the child how to assemble a form board). The average TTRs obtained in these data varied between .41 and .47, varying slightly depending on the condition and on the language level of the subjects addressed (relatively higher TTRs in the tutoring than in the free-conversational and interview conditions; relatively higher TTRs when addressing more language-advanced subjects). As for French, the only data available refer to the so-called "corrected TTR." For reasons discussed in detail in Rondal (1985b), the TTR index as usually computed may be relatively lacking in sensitivity, particularly development-wise. This is because it merges two different sorts of data in the same count: a small class of frequently occurring grammatical terms (the function words) and a large class of less frequently occurring terms (the content words) (see frequency tables, e.g., the Thorndike-Lorge frequency list for American-English and the frequency tables prepared by Gougenheim, Rivenc, Michéa, & Sauvageot, 1964, for French). The former terms are often repeated from utterance to utterance out of grammatical necessity; the latter ones are not necessarily repeated across utterances, depending on the meaning conveyed and on the productive lexical sophistication of the speaker (also depending on the language comprehension level of the interlocutor). A more sensitive index of lexical diversity of use (or corrected TTR) should count only the different content words (i.e., the members of the formal classes of adverbs, adjectives, verbs, and nouns), leaving aside functors, and report their number to the total number of content words in the sample of speech analyzed. Gregoire (1980; see Rondal, Bachelet, & Perée, 1986, for a detailed summary of her data) conducted this type of compilation with samples of conversational speech obtained in free play between mothers and children at home with a group of 72 normally developing French-speaking children (half boys, half girls) aged from 2 to 4 years and 11 months. She reported along with children's ages corrected TTRs increasing from .44 to .57 in average values with standard deviations comprised between .05 and .10. In comparison, Françoise's corrected TTRs are .71, .62, .65, and .77, for speech turns 2, 4, 7, and 10, respectively (average TTR value .688, variation interval .15). It should be clear from this data and comparisons (no matter how imperfect they are) and from reading the conversational transcriptions that Françoise's productive lexical diversity is not markedly restricted. And yet this is accomplished by relying on a productive lexicon that seems to be limited (another indication that casual conversation may be carried on normally with limited vocabulary). Indeed, on a picture-naming task designed at the University of Liège (Neuropsychology Unit) for the linguistic evaluation of aphasic patients, Françoise was unable to label 8 items (out of a total of 54), and she approximated the correct answer, but without producing it, for 10 other items – on the whole, a performance suggesting limited productive lexical development. On a lexical association task (devised in the same Neuropsychology Unit), she obtained low scores in the phonemic and semantic induction conditions, again suggesting limited productive lexical capacity. From this discussion, it follows that lexical diversity of use (as measured by the TTR) of one sampling is not to be confused with overall productive lexical ability.

5.4.2 Receptive lexical capacity

Several tests were administered to Françoise to assess her receptive lexical capacity: the Test de Vocabulaire Actif et Passif (TVAP; Deltour & Hupkens, 1980) for ages 5 to 8 years, the Test des Relations Topologiques (TRT; Deltour, 1982), the Test of Basic Concepts (Boehm, 1969), the Vocabulary Subtest of the Wechsler Adult Intelligence Scale (WAIS; adapted and standardized in France for subjects aged 13 to 75 years; Wechsler, 1968), and the Lexical Subtests of the Epreuves Différentielles d'Efficience Intellectuelle (Perron-Borelli & Misés, 1974).

The TVAP is an all-purpose vocabulary test. It was standardized with a balanced sample of 300 normally developing French-speaking children aged 5 to 8 years. Thirty target vocabulary items (common nouns and infinitive verbs) are tested through a verbal definition task (always coming first) and a picture-pointing task [black-and-white drawings displayed on a (30 × 10)-cm cardboard in groups of 6 – 1 correct representation and 5 distractors]. The items are said to be sequentially organized in order of increasing difficulty. They were selected from the French version of the Wechsler Preschool and Primary Scale of Intelligence (WPPSI; Wechsler, 1972), from the French version of the Wechsler Scale of Intelligence for Children (WISC; Weschler, 1957), and from picture books for children, according to criteria that are not supplied in the test manual. Some of these items belongs to the list of 1,063 frequently used terms established by Gougenheim et al. (1964) for French.

On the TVAP, with words such as *jonquille (jonquil)*, *vautour (vulture)*, and *diligence (diligence)*, Françoise gave 12 so-called primitive verbal definitions (i.e., definitions that were imprecise, anecdotal, tautological, or based on examples) out of a total of 30 items. Two additional words were clearly misdefined: *coquillage (empty shell)*, which she seemed to confuse with *coquille* (in the sense of *eggshell*), and *clou (nail)*, which she defined as a hand *tool* of the carpenter. Françoise correctly pointed to the pictures corresponding to 28 of the 30 words tested. In a few cases, she chose a close distractor to the correct referent (e.g., *screw* instead of *nail-clou*; *bottle* instead of *flask – flacon*). Her pointing was clearly incorrect in two cases: For *coquillage (empty shell)*, and consistent with her wrong definition given before, she pointed to the eggshell on the cardboard rather than to the correct empty shell; for *éclabousser*, she pointed to the picture representing a water tap rather than to the scene of a car splashing a pedestrian. In the latter case, the response is less incorrect than it may appear at first glance. Indeed, in her verbal definition of the same word, Françoise had employed the example of a water pipe, and her subsequent pointing is consistent with her first response. Françoise's standard scores on the TVAP correspond to the predicted population means for 8-year-old children.

On the vocabulary subtest of the WAIS (a verbal definitional task covering 40 items), Françoise achieved a standard score of 7 (population mean 10, SD 3), that is, she figures among the 34% of people who would be predicted to score one SD below the population mean. On this test, the following items receive imprecise definitions:

grouper (*to group*), *réparer* (*to repair*), *portion* (*portion*), *clôture* (*fence*), *empoigner* (*to grasp*), *aumône* (*alms*), *tanière* (*den*), *édifice* (*building*), and *bienfait* (*kindness, service*). The following words are incorrectly defined: *instruire* (*to instruct*), *fade* (*tasteless*), *couperet* (*chopper*), *persévérant* (*persevering*), *incinérer* (*to incinerate*), *falsifier* (*to falsify*), and *monopole* (*monopoly*), which she confuses with *acropolis*.

Similar results were obtained with the Epreuves Différentielles d'Efficience Intellectuelles, which need not be reported in detail. This test contains a verbal definition task and a picture-pointing vocabulary task.

The TRT is a picture test aimed at the receptive evaluation of a spatial lexicon. It was standardized with a balanced sample of 240 normally developing French-speaking children aged 3 to 6 years. Twenty-five spatial terms (prepositions and adverbs) are presented (reportedly) in order of increasing difficulty. They are tested in a pointing-to-picture task [black-and-white drawings displayed on a (30 × 10)-cm cardboard in groups of two, three, or more – correct item and distractors]. On this test, Françoise scored 48 (out of a maximum of 50 points). She missed item 19: preposition *sous* (*under*) for which she pointed to the representation of *à côté de* (*next to*). Item 16, however, the preposition *à côté de*, was correctly responded to. It is unlikely that the responses to items 16 and 19 really indicate that Françoise overextends the meaning of the preposition *à côté de* to refer to that of the preposition *sous*. The error most probably is a performance one (attentional?). There are three arguments in support of this interpretation. First, it is an isolated mistake within the spatial test. Second, correctly understanding the meaning of *sous* (*under*) is a relatively early accomplishment in development according to the specialized literature [see, e.g., Rondal, 1986, for a summary of the Francophone developmental literature on this question; for English, see Olson & Bialystok, 1983; additionally, these latter authors logically posit and empirically support the more consistent use and developmental prevalence in descriptive speech and memory tasks (mental representations) of so-called vertical (ego-environment-related) spatial functors such as *top*, *bottom*, *over*, *under*]. It is surprising in this respect to find *sous* – *under* located in 19th position on a scale of increasing difficulty in the TRT test, since the test constructors claim to have based their ordering of the items on findings (not specified) from the developmental psycholinguistic literature. Given other aspects of Françoise's spatial lexical knowledge, it would be astonishing if she had a "referential hole" regarding the preposition *sous*. Third, Françoise uses the preposition *sous* with apparent correct denotative meaning in her productive speech. It is unlikely that contextual facilitation would be strong enough to cover completely an otherwise consistent lexical deficiency.

Boehm's Test of Basic Concepts is also a picture test. It contains 50 items assessing the understanding of spatial terms (19 items, prepositions and adverbs), quantitative expressions (14 items), temporal terms (1 item), and other diverse elementary lexicalized notions and concepts. On this test, Françoise scored 47 (out of a maximum of 50 points). She failed 3 items: 2 quantitative ones, that is, *a pair of*, and the notion of *intermediate size* (with three stimuli of unequal sizes), and one spatial one, that is, *in between* (possibly a performance error in the latter case, as she did succeed on the same lexical item in the TRT test, and the pictural display for this item is somewhat ambiguous).

In summary, it would appear that Françoise's lexical referential comprehension is at the level of normally developing children aged 5 to 8 years. Regarding word definition, Françoise's capability appears to be markedly more limited. This limitation is not due to a difficulty in verbally expressing herself. It is partially a cognitive one reflecting, more than lexical use, her general cognitive limitations (to be fully documented in Section 5.8 on nonlinguistic data). One should also keep in mind that verbal definition is an exercise in metalinguistics (i.e., using language to talk about language). Giving good definitions requires controlling not only word meaning but also definitional form. It has been shown to be strongly affected by opportunities to practice the required definitional form (Snow, 1990). Metalinguistic development takes place markedly later than linguistic (functional) development,[6] the exact chronology depending on the specific component considered (metaphonology, metalexicon, metasemantics, metasyntax, metapragmatics – see Brédart & Rondal, 1982, and Gombert, 1990, on these topics; for English, see, e.g., Hakes, 1980, and Bialystok & Ryan, 1985). It has been recognized at least since the seventeenth century that language acquisition and language functioning are distinct and independent from advanced linguistic awareness, which largely appears to be the result of express linguistic instruction (see, e.g., de Cordemoy, 1666/1968, a disciple of Descartes). But linguistic awareness also depends on general cognitive capacity. If the latter turns out to be seriously limited, so will the former. I will return to Françoise's linguistic awareness with additional data in Section 5.5.

5.4.3 Receptive morphosyntactic capacity

It is clear from the analysis of Françoise's speech in preceding sections that she must have at least a minimal comprehension (and probably much more) of the grammatical structures of French. This assumption is consistent with the opinion in current linguistic and psycholinguistic work according to which language production and language comprehension up to a certain extent entail the same formal mechanisms and implicit grammatical knowledge in the subjects.[7] However, discourse comprehension in ordinary speech exchanges (i.e., outside ad hoc experimental constraints) may be greatly facilitated by contextual cues and information (both linguistic and extralinguistic). To assess properly Françoise's receptive morphosyntactic ability, it was therefore necessary to submit her to experimentally controlled receptive tasks. For basic receptive grammatical functioning, we turned to two all-purpose tests, the Epreuve de Compréhension 0.52 (Khomsi, 1985) and the French adaptation of the Northwestern Syntax Screening Test – Lee, 1969 – the Evaluation des Aptitudes Syntaxiques chez l'Enfant (Weil-Halpern & Chevrie-Muller, 1974). The results were straightforward, as expected. Françoise proved able to understand correctly the masculine/feminine contrast on the third-person personal pronoun (*elle* – *she*; *il* – *he*), concord in number between subject and verb (e.g., *Un oiseau vole* – *One bird flies*; *Des oiseaux volent* – *Birds fly*), the singular-plural contrast on the definite article (*le*, *la* – *les*), and on the third-person possessive pronoun (*sa*, *son* – *ses*), verb-expressed temporal contrasts such as immediate past and so-called periphrastic future (e.g., *Le monsieur est parti* – *The man is gone*; *Le monsieur va partir* – *The man will go*), comparative structures (e.g., *La fille est plus grande que le garçon* – *The girl is bigger than the boy*; *La fille est moins grande que le garçon* – *The girl is less big than the boy*), and the like.

Beyond this basic stage, I chose to concentrate in a more controlled way on five specific tasks involving advanced receptive linguistic ability. The selected tasks examined understanding of reversible and nonreversible relative clauses introduced by the relative pronouns *qui*, (*who*) or *que* (*whom*, *that*, *which*); the understanding of causative subordinate clauses introduced by *parce que* (*because*), either preceding or following the main clause; temporal subordinate clauses with the order of events matching the order in which these events are referred to in the clause, or not; the understanding of declarative affirmative active and passive sentences systematically varying according to transitivity features; and the understanding of the mechanism of coreference in the case of personal pronouns (third person) in nonambiguous and ambiguous paragraphs (in the latter case, what was under investigation was not the correct application of the coreference rule, since there were two plausible coreference relations – see later – but rather the subject's coreferential strategies in a situation of forced interpretive choice).

5.4.3.1 Understanding affirmative active and passive sentences

Sixty-four grammatical sentences (containing only one clause) were given – half actives, half full verbal passives. Full verbal passives were chosen since it appears that truncated verbal passives (e.g., *The bank was robbed*) and adjectival passives (e.g., *John was interested in Mary*) are easier to process ceteris paribus (see Hayhurst, 1967; Grodzinsky, 1990). The sentences were borrowed from a developmental study with 5-year-old French-speaking children conducted by Rondal et al. (1990) – see this reference for a full report on the specific methodology used, the detailed way in which the sentence types were selected, the actual sentence tokens constructed, and the results obtained with the normally developing children studied. The sentences varied systematically as to voice, plausibility ("realis" or "irrealis"), "kinesis," and punctuality, while being similar along other transitivity features (e.g., "telicity," affirmation; see Hopper & Thompson, 1980, for a presentation and a discussion of the role of transitivity features in grammar and discourse). These features were selected because they have been demonstrated to play a role in passive sentence comprehension (Sudhalter & Braine, 1985; Maratsos, et al., 1985; Rondal et al., 1990) and in passive sentence production (e.g., Pinker, Lebeaux, & Frost, 1987), although their theoretical status in the process of language comprehension is not entirely clear at the present time (Rondal & Thibaut, 1992). All the words used in the sentences had a relatively high frequency of occurrence in French according to the frequency tables compiled by Gougenheim et al. (1964). All the verbs were conjugated in the present tense. All the sentences employed the definite article in the noun phrases to avoid cueing the subject on the identity of the theme-rheme elements, therefore affecting the choice of the underlying grammatical subject and/or underlying grammatical object (Hupet & Le Bouedec, 1975). All the noun phrases were singular, since there seems to exist a preference for singular-plural sequences in clause organization (Hupet & Costermans, 1976). The 64 experimental sentences are supplied in Appendix 3 (presented in two blocks). They were presented to Françoise in random order within each block. Four transitivity categories were constituted resulting from the crossing of the variables kinesis and punctuality: (1) action-punctual (*frapper – hit, mordre – bite*); (2) action-nonpunctual (*soigner – care, porter – carry*); (3) nonaction-punctual (*apercevoir – see,*[8] *oublier – forget*); and (4) nonaction-nonpunctual (*détester – hate, imaginer – imagine*). Scales of relative verb kinesis and punctuality (considered separately) were available for 25 verbs, established by Rondal et al. (1990) with a group of 150 first-year university students with no background in linguistics. Four types of sentences varying in plausibility were constructed: (1) plausible and plausibly reversible sentences, (2) implausible but plausibly reversible sentences, (3) plausible but not plausibly reversible sentences, and (4) implausible and not plausibly reversible sentences. See Appendix 3 for examples of these various types of verbs and categories of sentences. The thematic (or event) reversibility feature was introduced because it has been known to influence sentence comprehension and particularly passive sentence comprehension at least since the work of Slobin (1966), Bever (1970), and Sinclair and Ferreiro (1970). However, considering reversibility independently of plausibility is not satisfactory and may be misleading, since sentences once reversed may or may not be plausible.

The sentences were orally produced by the experimenter, one by one, at a normal articulatory pace with as neutral an intonation as possible. Each sentence was followed by a request to specify a particular one of the two participants, either the underlying grammatical subject or the underlying grammatical object. The request was either an active interrogative sentence "Qui (verbe)?" ["Who (verbs)?"] or a passive interrogative sentence "Qui (est verbé)?" ["Who (is verbed)?"],[9] randomly but equally distributed over the 64 experimental sentences and the two voice categories. The necessity of varying the voice of the request in tasks of this sort was shown in the experiment reported by Rondal et al. (1990) conducted with NR children.

Françoise correctly interpreted 61 out of the 64 sentences. The 3 sentences incorrectly responded to are sentences 8, 14, and 28. As may be seen in Appendix 3, sentence 8 is active action nonpunctual implausible and not plausibly reversible; sentence 14 is active nonaction (built around the so-called mental verb *détester – to hate*) nonpunctual plausible but not plausibly reversible; sentence 28 (in block 2) is passive nonaction (mental verb *oublier – to forget*) punctual implausible and not plausibly reversible. Sentences 8 and 28 were followed by passive interrogative requests. Sentence 14 was followed by an active interrogative request. The most parsimonious explanation for the three errors observed probably is a mild lapse of attention. This is fairly plausible if one recalls that sentence presentation was made orally (only one repetition of the experimental sentence and of the interpretive request was provided; no additional repetition was requested by Françoise). Françoise's performance therefore may be considered to be virtually, if not fully, normal in the comprehension of active and passive monopropositional declarative sentences. Most remarkably, she could therefore correctly identify the underlying logical subject or the underlying logical object in irrealis (implausible) sentences with low-transitivity verbs (see Hopper & Thompson, 1980 – e.g., block 2, sentence 32, *Le livre est imaginé par la boîte – The book is imagined by the box*) with no semantic and pragmatic help, even in irrealis sentences that would turn realis were they reversed (e.g., sentence 31, *Le monsieur est imaginé par le livre – The man is imagined by the book*), therefore going against pragmatic interpretive tendency. This performance attests to a truly linguistic processing of the sentences and an extensive mastery over sophisticated sentential structures. This by no means represents a trivial achievement. In the same task, the normally developing 5-year-olds studied by Rondal et al. (1990) scored .60 correct responses on the average for all types of verbs and categories of sentences confounded. They were presented with two pictures for each sentence. The pictures represented the arguments of the verb. An oral repetition of the tested sentence by the experimenter followed the request, which was a designating request since the children's responses consisted in pointing to the picture chosen. It is usually considered, in the English-speaking developmental psycholinguistic literature, that linguistic mastery over full passive forms is not established before 9 or 10 years. The same is true for French (Rondal & Brédart, 1985). The French language has passive rules similar to those of English and close speaking habits in this respect, since passives are much rarer than actives in French as well as in English [perhaps even less frequent in French than in English, because of the prevalence, in ordinary speech, of the active construction with the impersonal pronoun *on* (*one*) over the passive construction (e.g., *On a dévalisé la banque – One has robbed the bank*) – but comparative frequency statistics are missing]. Even in adults, sentence transitivity features such as verb kinesis may affect decision time in sentence interpretation. This was shown in an unpublished work by Rondal & Thibaut (1990) using tasks in which subjects had to read silently declarative prototype sentences varying in voice, actionality, and plausibility (e.g., *Garçon voit fille – Boy sees girl*; *Garçon porte divan – Boy carries coach*; *Table est portée par fille – Table is carried by girl*; *Divan admire garçon – Coach admires boy*) and to answer questions bearing on the identity of the arguments of the verbs in the same way as in Rondal et al.'s experiment (1990). As a rule, action verb sequences, whether active or passive, plausible or implausible, were responded to (correctly in almost all cases) significantly faster than were nonaction ones.

5.4.3.2 Understanding relative clauses introduced by *qui* (*who*) or *que* (*whom, that, which*)

The syntactic problems related to the production and the comprehension of relative clauses (particularly relatives modifying subject and object noun phrases and relatives involving subject or object extraction) – including the developmental aspects – are relatively well known. They have been empirically documented and theoretically discussed in numerous publications in English and in French (e.g., Deyts & Noizet, 1973; Amy & Vion, 1976; Ferreiro, Othenin Girard, Chipman, & Sinclair, 1976; Hakes, Evans, & Brannon, 1976; Sheldon, 1977; Antinucci, Duranti, & Gebert, 1979; Goodluck & Tavakolian, 1982; Amy, 1983a, 1983b).

Four major points to be considered in the processing of relative clauses are as follows: (1) sequential structural dependencies: relative clauses may occur within the main clause (center embedded) or at the edge of the clause (right or left branched, depending on the language) – (juxtaposition); (2) lexical form of the relative pronoun: the form is determined by the grammatical role of the pronoun within its own clause (in French, the relative pronoun *qui* has the function of grammatical subject; the relative pronoun *que*, the function of grammatical object); (3) [following from (2)] order of constituents in the relative clause: The relative clauses introduced by *qui* (so-called subject relatives) follow an SVO (subject-verb-object) word order, whereas the relative clauses introduced by *que* (object relatives) follow an OSV word order, that is, the relativized constituent always occurs at the beginning of its clause; (4) the identity/nonidentity of grammatical functions in the main and in the relative clause: in the embedded subject relatives, the coreferential nominal element and the relative pronoun have the same grammatical function of subject (SS type); in the juxtaposed object relatives, the coreferential nominal element and the relative pronoun have the same grammatical function of object (OO type); in the two remaining cases (embedded object relatives and juxtaposed subject relatives), there is a crossing of grammatical functions between coreferential nominal element and relative pronoun from the main to the relative clause (SO and OS types). One additional feature (pragmatic– and semantic-syntactic) is also interesting to take into consideration: thematic reversibility. It has been observed that thematic reversibility (actually plausible thematic reversibility) affects the understanding of relative clauses in children as well as in adults (see e.g., Amy, 1983a, 1983b), generally rendering it more difficult.

Concretely, we gave to Françoise 64 sentences containing a relative clause introduced by *qui* or by *que*, embedded or juxtaposed, either plausible and plausibly reversible, or plausible but not plausibly reversible, and with parallel or nonparallel grammatical functions between main and relative clauses. The sentences were borrowed (with a few minor modifications) from a preceding test conducted by Monseur (1988) in my laboratory on relative clause comprehension in normally developing children aged 5 to 10 years. The sentences are supplied in Appendix 4 (there are 32 relative clauses introduced by *qui*, 32 introduced by *que*; in each of these two groups, 16 relative clauses are embedded, 16 are juxtaposed; in each of these groups, 8 sentences are plausible and plausibly reversible, and 8 are plausible but not plausibly reversible; on the whole, 16 sentences are of the SS type, 16 of the SO type, 16 of the OO type, and 16 of the OS type). As said, in French, the lexical form of the relative pronoun contains information on its grammatical function (*qui* has the function of grammatical subject, *que* the function of grammatical object). This is not the case in English with the grammatically more neutral pronouns *who* and *that* (most developmental studies in English have made use of the relative complementizer *that*). It should be added, however, that in a number of dialects of English, a differentiation of pronouns by grammatical function, parallel to that existing in French with *qui* and *que*, is made in *who* versus *whom*. As French developmental data show, the lexical cue is not sufficient for identifying the grammatical function of the relative pronoun. If it were the case, there would be no strategy of not changing the grammatical role from noun to coreferential pronoun observed in the SO and in the OS relatives (see Amy, 1983b, for a discussion). All the noun phrases in the sentences are singular (except one in sentence 16: *les graines – the seeds*). All the verbs are conjugated in the present tense. And all noun phrases, the heads of which are not a proper noun, include a definite article.

The sentences were presented orally by the experimenter, one by one, randomly taken from the list but keeping a balanced order of presentation among the eight categories identified in Appendix 4. They were read clearly twice with an intonation as neutral as possible. Each sentence was followed by a question of the type "Qui 'verbe' syntagme nominal objet?" ("Who 'verbs' object noun phrase?") raised about the main clause and then about the relative clause, or conversely (randomized order), in the case of the main clause or the *qui*-relative; and by an interrogative of the type "syntagme nominal sujet 'verbe' qui?" ("Subject noun phrase 'verbs' who?") in the case of the *que*-relative. A double interrogative was employed to avoid leading the subject to concentrate exclusively on the relative clause when listening to the test sentences. Its possible additional effects may have been to facilitate the comprehension of the embedded relatives in those cases where the interrogative request was first directed to the relative, since the first noun-verb-noun sequence is concerned with the relative clause, and, conversely, to facilitate the understanding of the juxtaposed relatives in those cases where the interrogative was first directed to the main clause.

Françoise correctly answered 122 out of the 128 questions. No errors were observed in the interpretation of the main clauses, even in those cases where the main clause was interrupted by an embedded relative clause (sentences 17–32 and 49–64) or where the two verbs (the verb of the relative clause and that of the main clause) directly followed each other (sentences 49–64). This suggests a well-functioning parser and the existence of a sufficient amount of mental computational space devoted to that function. No errors were made in the interpretation of the plausible but not plausibly reversible relatives clauses. A marked superiority of the thematically nonreversible relative clauses over the reversible ones has generally been found with children and is still clearly observable in adults (Amy, 1983a). It obviously attests to the multiple strategies (including, in this case, relying on pragmatic and lexical cues) that can be used by the subjects in sentence interpretation. The six errors concerned sentences 20, 37, 38, 54, 55, and 56. Sentence 20 has an embedded *qui*-relative SVO clause with no change in grammatical role from the main clause. Since its interpretation does not entail more complexity, its misinterpretation is probably accidental. This also is the only error concerning the *qui*-relatives. A receptive superiority of the *qui*-relatives over the *que*-relatives ceteris paribus has generally been documented in the literature (Amy, 1983b). Sentences 37 and 38 use juxtaposed *que*-relatives (OVS) with no change in grammatical role from the main clause. Since there were 8 reversible sentences of this type proposed, Françoise's score is 75% correct. Given the way the test probes were formulated (as previously described), it is likely that chance-level performance could have reached 50%. Françoise's score corresponds to (is slightly below) the average correct interpretive score obtained by Monseur (1988) with her older subjects, aged 9 to 9 years 11 months (85% correct responses; $N = 20$). Relatives 54, 55, and 56 are embedded *que*-relative clauses (OVS) with change in grammatical role from the main clause. This type of relative clause is known to be the most difficult one to process with respect to sentences containing a single level of embedding. Françoise's score was 60% correct, that is, only slightly above chance (50%). Her score again corresponds closely to the average correct score obtained by Monseur (1988) with her older group of children, aged 9 to 9 years and 11 months (57% correct responses; $N = 20$). It is not the change of grammatical role from main to relative clause, nor the embedding, or OVS word order, or thematic reversibility, each by itself, that causes difficulties for Françoise,[10] as well as for normally developing 9-year-olds and adults (see Amy, 1983b). It is probably the conjunction of these formal characteristics in a task experimentally devoid of extrasentential linguistic and situational cues.

Françoise's receptive performance with relative clauses, as it appears, is quite satisfactory and is fairly comparable to that of normally developing children aged 9 years, as already indicated. Françoise's performance with relative clauses introduced by *qui* or *que* is even superior to that of French-speaking normal adults tested by Amy (1983b). Amy reported similar response patterns to those already reported vis-à-vis subtype of relatives, changing of grammatical roles, location of embedding, and thematic reversibility, but the level of correct answers was lower (ranging from 25 to 50%). There were, however, two important methodological differences between Amy's research and that reported here (as well as that of Monseur, 1988). First, Amy had his subjects act out the sentences. This had the consequence of allowing the subject a choice between three nominal possibilities against our two, therefore rendering the task more difficult. Second, the double questioning used in the present evaluation may have facilitated the interpretive task and consequently raised the scores somewhat.

5.4.3.3 Understanding causative and temporal subordinate clauses

Causation and time are often conceptually confounded (e.g. the well-known Latin axiom, Post hoc ergo propter hoc). Also the use of coordinating conjunctions as well as temporal adverbial structures may suggest temporocausal relations between events that may or may not correspond to reality. It is well known that complex cognitive notions such as those relating to cause-effect and time relationships between events take a long time to develop in children (see Piaget, 1925, 1928, 1930, 1937, 1946, 1955). The various steps in this evolution are well documented in the specialized literature and need not be summarized here. However, even when the conceptual notions are mastered, or being mastered, the difficult task of correctly mapping the causative and temporal vocabulary of one's language onto these notions and understanding and possibly using the formal freedom allowed by the language in these matters remains. For example, in French as well as in English, it is grammatically acceptable to express statements containing causal relations in two ways: The causative clause may precede or follow the clause containing the determined event [e.g., *L'homme s'est enfui parce quelqu'un a tiré sur lui – The man ran away because someone shot at him*; *(C'est) parce que quelqu'un a tiré sur lui (que) l'homme s'est enfui – Because someone shot at him the man ran away*]; in the same way, temporally related events may be referred to linguistically either with clause order matching the order in which the events happened, are happening, or will happen, or not. The specialized literature contains reports indicating that this conceptual-linguistic mapping is not a simple matter and that it takes some time to develop. For example, Bullock and Gelman (1979), Emerson (1979), and Bebout, Segalowitz, and White (1980) report congruent experimental data showing that until about 8 years of age, children tend to consider the first event presented in a verbal sequence as constituting the cause of the following event(s). They seem to operate from an axiomatic hypothesis stating that utterances are always ordered in a unidirectional causative way, corresponding to the "Post hoc ergo propter hoc" interpretation. At that stage, no real comprehension of the conjunction *parce que* (*because*) is guaranteed. It is only after age 8 typically that children begin to understand that order of statements and order of events are independent in principle and that languages supply formal means that can be used in this matter to prevent referential ambiguity.

Concerning the linguistic expression of the temporal relationships, there is an abundant literature showing that several formal and pragmatic means are used by the child to express temporal references. It seems that these means may be classified developmentally according to the following sequence: (1) order of utterances directly reflecting sequential order of events; (2) inappropriate and then appropriate use of temporal conjunctions, prepositions, and adverbs; (3) incorrect and then correct use of verbal forms (aspect generally preceding tense) (see Ferreiro, 1971; Ferreiro & Sinclair, 1971; Hatch, 1971; Bronckart, 1976; Coker, 1978; Ehri & Galanis, 1980; and Trosborg, 1981). Generally, it is not before 9 or 10 years that the formal means available in the language for expressing time relationships are properly understood independent of the sequential characteristics of the physical events and are integrated into a coherent system of verbal-temporal reference.

Of course, additional variables may influence the comprehension of causative and/or temporal clauses, such as thematic reversibility and plausibility (see Kuhn & Phelps, 1976), the implicit directional causative organization of the verb-argument structure of some verbs (e.g., verbs such as *kill, congratulate, sell,* and *telephone*) that may facilitate mental representation and sentence interpretation (Chafe, 1970; Garvey & Caramazza, 1974), temporoaspectual characteristics of the verbs such as simultaneity, continuity, resultativity, or finiteness of the one event referred to with respect to the other(s), and verb punctuality (punctual events may be easier to represent mentally, which may facilitate sentence processing; see Rondal et al., 1990; Rondal & Thibaut, 1992).

It was particularly interesting to test Françoise for linguistic comprehension of temporal and causative characteristics of sentences, since she showed relative weaknesses or at least imprecision in related aspects of her productive discourse (false causatives introduced by *parce que – because* or followed by an utterance or a segment of an utterance containing the "should be" resultative *donc – therefore,* loose temporal connections between related or apparently unrelated clauses with frequent use of markers such as *et – and, alors – then, enfin – in the end,* etc.; see the analysis of her conversational speech).

Françoise was given 80 sentences to interpret. They were subdivided into 32 with causative subordinate clauses introduced by the conjunction *parce que – because,* 32 with temporal subordinate clauses introduced by the conjunction *quand – when,* and 16 with temporal subordinate clauses introduced by the conjunction *après que – after that* (the complete liste of sentences is presented in Appendix 5). The subordinate clauses therein were controlled for the following features: relative plausibility of the causal link, implicit causality in verbs (the implicit causative verbs used were *frapper – hit* and *soigner – nurse*; the nonimplicitly causative verbs used were *goûter – taste* and *écouter – listen to*), and verb punctuality. The two following features pertaining to the whole sentences were also controlled: sequential order of the main clause and the subordinate causative or temporal clause; temporoaspectual characteristics of the verbs in the main and in the subordinate clause (contrast between perfect and present tense of the indicative mood for marking anteriority, except following the conjunction *après que – after that*, which, in French, obligatorily calls for the use of the present of the subjunctive; use of present indicative in the main and subordinate clause for marking simultaneity). All the heads of the noun phrases were singular, and all the noun phrases the heads of which were not proper nouns employed the definite article, except in the stereotyped phrase (*soigner) ses petits* – (care for) *his young ones*. The sentences were read one by one by the experimenter in a random order and repeated once. They were pronounced with as neutral an intonation as possible. The sentences containing a causative subordinate were followed by the interrogative request "*Peux-tu dire pourquoi X fait ça?*" – *Can you tell why X does that ?*" (*X* being the grammatical subject of the main clause).[11] The sentences containing a temporal subordinate were followed by the disjunctive interrogative request "*Est-ce que les deux choses se passent en même temps ou est-ce qu'il y en a une qui se passe avant l'autre?*" – "*Do the two things happen at the same time or does one happen before the other?*" either in that order or in the reversed order (alternated).

Françoise correctly interpreted all 32 sentences containing a causative subordinate clause. She at times substituted the proper name or modified the common noun within one of the noun phrases of the subordinate clause, but that had no bearing on the interpretation of the semantic-grammatical relations involved. For example, in sentences 4 and 8, she replaced *l'instituteur* [*the (primary school) teacher*] by *le professeur* (*the professor*). Françoise correctly interpreted 46 out of the 48 sentences containing a temporal subordinate clause. She missed sentences 43 and 47 (two simultaneous *quand*-sentences). There were a few trivial lexical substitutions and modifications (e.g., in sentence 65, she replaced *Philippe* by *Nathalie* in the two clauses, and *Nathalie* by *Philippe* in the main clause; in sentence 78, she replaced *Pierre* by *Philippe*). Upon careful examination, however, sentences 43 and 47 (meant to imply simultaneity of the events described in the main and in the subordinate clauses – since the present tense was used in both cases) actually are fairly logically interpretable as implying an anteriority relationship, that is, the punishment of the dog following his touching the meat. The conjunction *quand* (*when*) having, in these two cases, the general temporal (or conditional) meaning of *each time (that)* (each time the dog touches the meat, he receives a punishment from Johan).

It therefore appears that Françoise's comprehension of advanced causative and temporal subordinates is mostly accurate. This is the case whether the subordinate clauses precede or follow the main clauses, whether the indicated causal link between clauses is plausible, neutral, or irrelevant (going against or at least leaving aside pragmatic tendencies in interpreting the sentence according to the somewhat meaningless or "crazy" request of the experimenter), whether there is implicit causality in the lexical meaning of the verb or not, whether the verb is semantically punctual or not, and even disregarding temporoaspectual characteristics of the verbs to concentrate on the strict interpretation of the temporal conjunction (in those cases where the *quand* conjunction ties two clauses describing events expressed in the present tense), again attesting to a fairly impressive capacity with the formal grammatical aspect of the language.

Given this indication, and looking back on Françoise's relatively loose use of causal conjunctions and of temporal prepositions, conjunctions, and adverbs in her spontaneous conversational speech, it is likely that the observed looseness in production does not reflect true competence limitations but rather the effect of extra-grammatical factors and, perhaps most of all, the relative logicosemantic looseness of familiar conversational productions.

5.4.3.4 Understanding personal pronominal coreference

As observed in her productive speech, Françoise's control over the grammatical mechanisms of personal pronoun coreference seems to be appropriate. It was judged relevant, however, to evaluate her capacity in this area for two reasons: First, to obtain confirmation of the naturalistic observations already mentioned; second, to investigate the nature of her interpretive strategies when confronted with paragraphs that were ambiguous with respect to particular pronominal anaphora.

In French, a lexical rule dominates the identification process in the case of the anaphoric personal pronouns: Pronouns must correspond in number and grammatical gender with their nominal coreferent. It is not before 7 years usually that normally developing children come to master this rule and that they apply it correctly in their productive and receptive language performance (see M. Kail, 1976, 1983; Kail & Léveillé, 1977; Chipman & Gérard, 1983). A similar situation prevails in English, where the relevant identification rules for the assignment of pronoun antecedents are not basically different from the French (Garvey, Caramazza, & Yates, 1975; Caramazza, Grober, Garvey, & Yates, 1977).

A number of factors may influence anaphoric pronoun assignment, as indicated in the specialized literature. Most important are contrastive stress (Maratsos, 1976; Solan, 1983), surface structure distance between pronoun and possible nominal coreferent (M. Kail, 1976), sequential order of nouns (M. Kail, 1976), voice of clause or sentence (tendency for assignment of the coreferent of the pronoun to be made vis-à-vis the grammatical subject; Garvey et al., 1975), grammatical function and semantic characteristics of nominal antecedents (parallel function strategies; Grober, Beardsley, & Caramazza, 1978; M. Kail, 1983; Solan, 1983), structural relation (C-command; Chomsky, 1981) between the pronoun and its potential coreferent (there is clear evidence that young children are sensitive to this structural relation in comprehension), syntactic relationship between clauses in complex sentences or between sentences in a paragraph (e.g., if a clause or a sentence is introduced by the oppositive conjunction *mais*, there is a strong tendency to assign the grammatical subject of the first clause or sentence as coreferent to the pronoun (Grober et al.,

1975), semantic characteristics of the verbs (e.g., implicit directional causality in verb meaning; Garvey et al., 1975), social status of the persons mentioned in the noun phrases that are possible antecedents for the pronoun (Garvey et al., 1975), and inferences and reality-based or imaginary referential constructions by the subjects (Wykes, 1981). (See the two volumes edited by Lust, 1986, particularly the extensive introductory section to Vol. 1, for a thorough review of this literature and a discussion.)

Françoise was given 24 paragraphs composed of two sentences each, with the second one containing a third-person anaphoric personal pronoun, the possible nominal antecedents of which figured in the first sentence. The paragraphs are presented in Appendix 6. They were borrowed from Rondal, Leyen, Brédart, and Perée (1984). The sentences were in the indicative or imperative, all in active voice. There were always two possible nominal antecedents for each anaphoric personal pronoun. The pronouns were singular and had the grammatical functions of subject and object, respectively. In half of the paragraphs, the anaphoric pronoun had the function of grammatical subject, in the other half, grammatical object. Half of the paragraphs allowed for a clear assignment of anaphoric pronoun antecedent. In these paragraphs, the two nominal antecedents were of a different grammatical gender, and only one of them corresponded in gender to the anaphoric personal pronoun. In the other half of the paragraphs, the two nominal antecedents were of the same grammatical gender (either masculine or feminine). This type of paragraph does not allow for unambiguous assignment of pronoun antecedent. Since no further questions were accepted from the subject, and since the response choice was forced, these paragraphs were used to investigate the subject's spontaneous strategies as to pronoun assignment. The verbs in the sentences were chosen to be as neutral as possible with respect to their implicit "causal valence" (Garvey & Caramazza, 1974), in a way so as not to systematically induce a particular choice of antecedents as coreferent for the anaphoric pronoun. However, since no definitive criteria exist in this respect, selection was made on an intuitive basis.

The experimenter presented Françoise with the paragraphs read one by one (two times), with completely neutral intonation, in random order, but with the following constraints: The series had to begin with a nonambiguous paragraph; it could not have two ambiguous paragraphs immediately succeeding each other. The whole task was presented to Françoise as a "detective-story" communication game. Each paragraph was followed by an interrogative request of the type "*Qui* + phrase?" – "*Who* + clause?" (the clause being the totality or the central part of the second sentence in the paragraph). For example, as to paragraph 4 (*Le docteur examine Madame Dufer demain après-midi. Tout de suite après, vous la mettrez au courant de notre plan* – The doctor will examine Mrs. Dufer tomorrow afternoon. Immediately after you will let her know about our plan). The interpretive request was "*Qui mettrez-vous au courant de notre plan?*" – "*Who will you let know about our plan?*"

The results were straightforward. The 12 nonambiguous paragraphs were correctly interpreted according to the lexical rule for anaphoric pronoun assignment. A few lexical substitutions or modifications took place that had no influence whatsoever on the experimental task (e.g., in paragraph 9, she substituted *Madame Lebon* for *Madame Sulon*). Regarding the ambiguous paragraphs, the analysis of Françoise's responses is as follows. She seems in most cases to resort to a minimal distance principle to ground reference, selecting among the two possible ones the nominal element nearer to the anaphoric pronoun in the paragraph sequential structure, disregarding grammatical parallelism whenever this was necessary. It may be questioned whether the minimal distance principle is the most natural strategy. Grober et al. (1978) and Solan (1983) claim that a parallel function strategy corresponds to a higher order heuristic, but they do not provide clear explicit arguments supporting their position. The parallel function strategy consists of assuming that the thematicogrammatical organization prevailing in the first sentence will be relevant to the interpretation of the second sentence. If the pronoun functions as grammatical subject in the second sentence, it will likely refer to the noun-subject in the first sentence, and similarly for the object function. However, in a large-scale study conducted with French-speaking children, adolescents, and adults (Rondal et al., 1984), it was shown that the dominant heuristic in ambiguous cases (only active sentences were used) was "Select the topical theme or grammatical subject of the first sentence as coreferent for the anaphoric personal pronoun of the second sentence whether this pronoun functions as grammatical subject or as grammatical object." The tendency to "choose subject" or topical dominance (in otherwise unmarked sentences with respect to thematic organization) actually increased with the age of the subjects (from 10 to 14 years and onto early adulthood). Françoise does not appear to use either parallel function or dominant topical strategy. Rather she relies in ambiguous cases on a purely sequential heuristic, one that is characteristic of the interpretation strategies preferred by normally developing children around 3 years and that they release (but not totally) in favor of the parallel function strategy around 5 years, according to the data experimentally obtained by Kail (1976). It is to be noted, however, that in further work with normally developing children aged 7 to 14 years, M. Kail and Léveillé (1977) also reported a tendency to choose grammatical subject in ambiguous anaphoric cases, a tendency that increased with age.

It is quite clear that, in nonambiguous cases, Françoise is perfectly able to correctly assign anaphoric personal pronoun antecedents using the rules available in her language. This receptive capacity is perfectly in line with her apparent excellent control over anaphora as observed in her spontaneous speech – again, a nontrivial linguistic achievement considering the ages at which these capacities are fully demonstrated in the development of NR children.

In conclusion, Francoise's functioning with respect to the psycholinguistic processing of such complex material as thematically reversible passive sentences, *qui-*

and *que*-embedded and juxtaposed relatives, reversed-order causative and temporal subordinate clauses, and anaphoric pronoun coreference assignment are essentially normal. Particularly impressive and important is the fact that she is able to disregard pragmatic cues when placed in an (experimental) situation where these cues are put in conflict with the formal grammatical cues. This certainly attests to an advanced grammatical ability.

5.5 Metalinguistic ability

Françoise's metalexical capacity has already been touched upon in the section on receptive lexical capability with specific regard to word definition. Of course, the notion of linguistic awareness is much larger and it deserves a more systematic investigation, which we have partially done. This notion, as currently referred to in the literature, is not completely or satisfactorily specified. It covers different types of skills and knowledge (whether verbally explicit or implicit in language judgments and other metalinguistic activities). I will not enter much here into some of the (subtle) distinctions proposed in the field – for example between "epilinguistic" and metalinguistic activities, as instances of metacognitive processes. Briefly stated (for more detail, the interested reader is referred to sources in the specialized literature, e.g., Culioli, 1968; Flavell, 1977; Hakes, 1980; Brédard & Rondal, 1982; Gombert, 1990), *epilinguistic activities* refer to unconscious metalinguistic activities of the type that are needed in language functioning. The expression is also used to label aspects of linguistic performance that seem to belong to the metalinguistic domain but do not entail a "truly conscious" monitoring, such as self-corrections and "behavioral" judgments that may be obtained or provoked in children as early as 3 or 4 years of age (e.g., Slobin, 1978). The terms *metalanguage* or *metalinguistic activities* usually refer to conscious reflective activities on language, its organization, and its uses. In this respect, depending on the specific language subdomain considered, terms such as metaphonology, metasyntax, metasemantics, and metapragmatics are employed. A partial evaluation of some aspects of Françoise's metalinguistic abilities follows.

First, Françoise was given a *metaphonological task* consisting of 10 subtests orally presented and administered in the order indicated. In subtest 1, she was requested to produce a word rhyming with the target word supplied by the examiner. She proved able to do it readily for the 10 words proposed: *camion – truck; chou – cabbage; soleil – sun; chanson – song; couteau – knife; poupée – doll; éléphant – elephant; trois – three; fourchette – fork; fleur – flower;* to which she replied, respectively: *mignon – darling; bijou – gem; oseille – sorrel; floraison – flowering; marteau – hammer; loupée – missed; entend – hears; noix – nut; bichette – young doe;* and *peur – fear.* She proceeded in decomposing each target word into its syllables (in whispering) before giving her response out loud. For the word *elephant,* she first tried to find a response word ending in *fan,* could not, and resorted to *entend* (*hears*), a word ending in the same vowel sound *ã*. In subtest 2, she was to choose among 3 proposed words (e.g., *pont – bridge*; *rose – rose*; *chaise – seat*) the one that rhymed with a target word provided first (in this case, *citron – lime*). She could do the 10 items given with no mistakes, again proceeding in decomposing the target word into syllables before giving her answer. The whole operation was very slow, however (between 1 and 2 minutes per item). In subtest 3, she was asked to choose among 3 words (e.g., *roue – wheel*; *pantalon – trousers*; *banane – banana*) the one that began with the same sound (consonant) as the target word (in this case, *pou – louse*). She could do it correctly for 8 of the 10 items. (For the 2 mistaken items, she let herself be influenced by the ending of the words; e.g., in the preceding case, she wrongly selected *roue* as the corresponding answer for *pou*.) It is important to note, however, that Françoise was doing the task each time (whispering evidence) by comparing the first syllables of the 3 proposed words to the first syllable of the target word. In subtest 4, Françoise was requested to choose among 3 words (e.g., *soupe – soup*; *chambre – room*; *moule – mussel*) the one whose final sound or syllable was similar to the final sound or syllable of the target word (in this case *lampe – lamp*). She correctly answered 6 of 10 items, again proceeding through comparisons of syllables. She gave incorrect answers on those items for which the corresponding cue was not a syllable but a (consonant) sound [e.g., target word: *coq – cock*; stimulus words: *sac – bag*, *chatte – cat* (feminine form), *mot – word*]. In subtest 5, she was to remove the first sound (consonant) of the word proposed (e.g., *boeuf – ox*) and pronounce the remaining part of the stimulus, which in each case formed a meaningful word (phonolexical facilitation) (e.g., in this case, *oeuf – egg*). With several repetitions of the words and some help from the examiner, Françoise could do the task properly only for the first 2 of the 10 items proposed (i.e., *boeuf – oeuf*; and *brève – brief*; *rève – dream*). Metalinguistically manipulating two levels of structure simultaneously, for example, phonological and lexical, proved exceedingly difficult for her. In subtest 6, she was requested to remove the first sound (consonant) of a given word (e.g., *chat – cat*) and replace it with another one in such a way as to produce a word rhyming with the original one (e.g., in this case, *tas – pile*). Françoise could not treat any item properly in this subtest. She tried and succeeded in identifying the first syllable of each target word (but not the first sound) and (mistakenly) produced a new word beginning with the identified syllable (e.g., *village – village* for the target word *ville – town*). In subtest 7, Françoise was asked to compare two words phonologically (e.g., *drame – drama* and *rame – tow*) and to produce the (consonant) sound that was missing in the second word (in this case, *d*). She proved able to execute the task correctly for the 10 items proposed. In subtest 8, Françoise was to construct a (meaningful) word by fusing the first syllable of 2 target words (e.g., target words: *lacet – lace*, *peinture – painting*; fused word: *lapin – rabbit*). She did it correctly in 4 cases (out of 10) and approximately correctly for the rest (e.g., target words: *poteau – pole*, *chemin – way*; correct answer: *poche – pocket*; Françoise's answer: *pochette – pouch*). In subtest 9, Françoise was requested to subtract the first, second, or third syllable from the target word (depending on the item) and to produce what was left from the word, that is, a nonword (e.g., target word: *telephone* – *telephone*; first syllable to be removed: *té*; answer: *léphone*). She could correctly perform the requested operation in 5 cases (out of 15); she missed 5 other items and gave incorrect answers (but not far from being correct) in the remaining 5 cases (e.g., target word: *avocat* – *barrister*; second syllable to be removed: *vo*; correct answer: *acat*; Françoise's answer: *vocat*). This type of error occurred most often when the median syllable in the word had to be removed. Finally, in subtest 10, Françoise was requested to spell 5 common words (i.e., *chat* – *cat*; *reine* – *queen*; *plage* – *beach*; *balance* – *balance*; and *papier* – *paper*). She completely failed despite additional requests and encouragement from the examiner. Instead, she did the "spelling" in syllables with some degree of overlapping between neighboring syllables and in omitting some phonemes.

These results show that Françoise is able to consciously segment common French words into syllables (but very slowly and at times with some degree of overlapping between juxtaposed syllables, particularly the ones located in the middle section of the word). However, she usually is not able to push the analysis of the "word-envelope" much further. She cannot regularly identify the separate phonemes combining to form words. A beginning of phonological awareness seems to be present, however. In subtests 3 and 4, Françoise, comparing syllables, ended up producing a number of correct responses. This strategy fails, however, as could be expected, whenever the task requires a comparison of individual segments only (some items in subtest 4). A comparison of her performance on subtests 5 and 7 is similarly revealing. In subtest 5, Françoise proved largely unable to strip the first consonant from a given word and to pronounce the part of the word remaining, in each case, itself constituting a word common in the language (of which fact Françoise was informed beforehand). It is worth noting that this result confirms and may at least partially explain Françoise's inefficiency in phonemic induction reported in Section 5.4.1.3 regarding lexical matters. In subtest 7, Françoise could perfectly compare 2 words similar except for the first phoneme (vowel or consonant) and produce that phoneme, therefore demonstrating at least some ability to manipulate segmental as well as syllabic structure. The "phoneme stripping" task in subtest 7 was arguably easier than in the other subtests, since each item presented 2 words that were identical except for one phoneme, the initial phoneme in the word.

In her performance, Françoise appears to be comparable to most NR children aged 5 or 6 years, according to the relevant literature, that is, children with some experience in the oral language but no systematic exposure or learning experience with the written language. As a rule, these children can consciously segment words into syllables but not into phonemes (which, of course, they correctly use in speech perception and production). Fox and Routh (1975) presented children with syllables composed of two or three phonemes. They asked them to repeat "just a little bit of what I say." Results indicate 28%, on average, of correct phoneme extraction at 3 years, 70% at 4 years, 86% at 5 years, and 93% at 6 and 7 years. However, this work has been criticized on methodological grounds (e.g., Gombert, 1990), and it may yield developmental indications that are too optimistic. Zhurova (1973) reports that less than 50% of the children prior to 5 and 6 years are able to isolate the first phoneme of their first name, even when the experimenter places particular stress on that phoneme. In more controlled studies where the children were requested to remove the initial, the final, or the middle phoneme in meaningful words and to produce the remaining (meaningless) verbal material aloud (e.g., Bruce, 1964; Rosner & Simon, 1971), it was observed that the correct conscious phonological analysis could not be made by most children before 7 to 12 years, depending on the specific nature of the task (initial phonemes easier than final ones, final phonemes easier than median ones, and double consonants more difficult than simple ones). Other studies with Anglophone children confirm that awareness of syllables develops prior to awareness of phonemes. Many 4-year-olds and the majority of 5-year-olds are indeed able to manipulate syllables, but most children master the ability to manipulate phonemes only after the ages of 6 or 7 years (Fox & Routh, 1980; Treiman & Baron, 1981). Such relatively late ages for the development of metalinguistic skills (particularly phonological awareness) have been put in question by Chaney (1992), who reported that most normal 3-year-olds can make metalinguistic judgments and productions (at the phonological, word, and structural levels) in structured tasks. She further claimed that the so-called autonomy hypothesis – viewing metalinguistic awareness as a distinct type of linguistic acquisition developing later than, and mostly independently from, say, ordinary linguistic functioning (i.e., language expression and comprehension) – is not the correct one. More correct is the conception that metalinguistic skills emerge at a young age and interact positively with the acquisition of basic comprehension and expression processes (i.e., Chaney's so-called interaction hypothesis). It should be observed, however, that Chaney's tests of metaphonological awareness did not include any one of the "hard" tasks (i.e., phoneme deletion and spelling); they did include phoneme synthesis, though. Therefore, she may have witnessed, through the use of an appropriate informal methodology, the early steps in the development of phonological awareness.

Indeed, one study has recently documented the existence of an intermediate step in the development toward phonological awareness, that is, awareness of a sublexical level composed of the onset (consonant or cluster of consonants preceding the vowel) and rime (vowel and any ensuing consonant). For example, the word *brisk* is composed of the (complex) onset /br/ and the rime /isk/. Developmental studies seem to show that onset and rime units are more difficult to manipulate than syllables, but that they are easier than phonemes (e.g., Treiman, 1985; Bruck & Treiman, 1990). Expectedly, languages containing a greater variety and frequency of complex syllabic onsets (e.g., Czech) favor higher levels of awareness for complex onsets in children prior to formal schooling, as opposed to languages with more frequent simple onsets (such as English) (see Caravolas and Bruck, 1993).

It is unlikely that Françoise has even reached this intermediate level in the development of phonological awareness consisting in an increased sensitivity and awareness of onset and rimes sublexical units (see earlier evidence from the analysis of her performance on metaphonological tasks 5 and 6).

The fact that Françoise learned to read and write to a considerable extent (she was taught according to an analytical method, therefore with code-emphasis instruction; see Section 5.6) with limited metaphonological ability is intriguing. According to the specialized literature (e.g., Alegria & Morais, 1979; Morais, Cary, Alegria & Bertelson, 1979; Alegria, Pignot, & Morais, 1982; Content, 1984, 1985; Morais, 1987a, 1987b; Bertelson & de Gelder, 1991; Wimmer, Landerl, Linortner, & Hummer, 1991), it would seem that learning to read in an alphabetical orthographic language renders necessary the activation of some sort of metaphonological competence, probably already present in the subjects for some time but mostly useless until alphabetic literacy begins. Françoise seems to have acquired her nontrivial reading ability without well-developed metaphonological competence; moreover, she does not seem to have developed much phonological awareness as a consequence of her learning to read (years ago) and subsequent reading practice. Her case certainly demonstrates that it is possible to learn to read (and write) and to have considerable reading and writing practice for a long time without being able to consciously (or fully) segment words into phonemes. Such an indication is bound to pose problems for those theorists who argue that metaphonological competence in general, or the ability to manipulate single phonemes in particular, is prerequisite (e.g., Bradley & Bryant, 1983), necessary sequitur (e.g., Morais et al., 1979), or both (e.g., Morais, Alegria, & Content, 1987) for learning to read (see Gombert, 1990, and Goswami & Bryant, 1990, for reviews of this literature). Could Françoise's general mental retardation be causally related to this problem? Research on the ability of persons with moderate and severe mental retardation to analyze spoken words into their syllable and phoneme segments is mostly lacking [it is true that (some of) these persons have only been systematically taught to read and write in the past few years]. One exception to the preceding statement is a work by Cossu, Rossini, & Marshall (1993) with 10 Italian DS children, CA between 8 and 15 years 8 months (mean MA 5 years) matched for reading ability with a group of 10 chronologically younger NR children (CA between 6 and 7 years). Results indicate that adequate reading of words at a level characteristic of normal 7-year-olds can be achieved by DS children despite a clear failure on tests of phonological awareness (which caused little difficulty to NR children). Particularly interesting is the fact that DS children are as good as the NR controls at reading nonwords. Therefore, they seem to use "normal" implicit segmentation skills. What they are not able to do, apparently, is access those abilities metalinguistically. It may thus well be that phonological awareness is not causally tied to the acquisition of reading. The association between the two in NR subjects might be a manifestation of some kind of intellectual maturation (Liberman, Shankweiler, Liberman, Fowler, & Fisher, 1977). However, a relatively important degree of phonological awareness could exist in some MR subjects according to the results of a study by Gottardo and Rubin (1991), who documented the ability of a group of 17 MR children and adolescents, aged 10 to 15 years, to analyze words into syllables and phonemes. The subjects were grouped by method of learning to read (code-emphasis reading instruction vs. so-called whole-word reading instruction). The mean of correct responses on a syllable deletion task was 83% for both method-ological subgroups of subjects. The same index drastically differed on a phoneme deletion task (75% mean correct responses for the code-emphasis instruction group vs. 25% for the whole-word instruction one). For phoneme counting, it was 84% in the former group versus 41% in the latter. Judging from these results, it would seem that mental retardation per se is no prevention for conscious phonemic analysis. This certainly contradicts suggestions of the type of those by Marsh, Friedman, Welch, and Desberg (1980) linking the development of the capacity to analyze words into phonemes and to use grapheme-phoneme correspondences to decode new words, to the child's reaching Piaget's concrete operations period, since it is known that most moderately and severely MR subjects never really attain that stage of cognitive development (see Section 5.8.1). Gottardo and Rubin's data (1991) also are in con-tradiction with these of Cossu et al. (1993), unless Cossu et al.'s subjects were all trained to read using a whole-word reading instruction, in which case it could be argued that they were somewhat similar to Gottardo and Rubin's second group of subjects (those trained to read in that same way; but even this comparison is imperfect since Cossu et al.'s subjects obtained only 8% correct responses in mean value on the phoneme deletion task; for phoneme counting, Cossu et al.'s subjects and Gottardo and Rubin's whole-word instruction subjects are closer, with means of 32% and 41% correct, respectively). No information is given by Cossu et al. on the reading instruction given their subjects. However, as their DS subjects proved able to read nonwords as well as (actually slightly better than) NR children – despite the additional fact that the DS children's MA was 5 years on the average versus 8 years for the NR children – it would seem that those DS subjects had developed a fair ana-lytical ability in reading. As previously reported, Françoise exhibits only minimal phonetic awareness despite a long period of reading practice and having received code-emphasis reading instruction. This is in clear contradiction with Gottardo and Rubin's empirical indication. Quite clearly, a good deal of additional research is needed on the question of the exact relationship between reading ability and instruc-tion, and phonological awareness in NR as well as in MR subjects.

Next, Françoise was given a sentence judgment task that assessed the grammati-cality (well-formedness) and semantic acceptability (Gleitman & Gleitman, 1970) of monopropositional, active, declarative, affirmative sentences (word strings) orally presented by the examiner. The sentences (or word strings) were (1) grammatical and semantically acceptable, (2) ungrammatical but semantically acceptable (incor-rect word ordering, e.g., *Les enfants le regardent film – *The children the watch film*; incorrect case marking on pronouns or lack of number agreement between subject and verb, e.g., *Les élèves finit de copier la phrase* – *The students finishes copying the sentence*), or (3) grammatical but semantically abnormal (violation of lexical selection rules, e.g., *La carotte mange l'âne* – *The carrot eats the donkey*; conflict between tense of the verb and time marked adverbially, e.g., *Demain j'avais mangé un morceau de tarte* – *Tomorrow I had eaten a piece of cake*). The three types of sentences were randomly presented in such a way so as not to have sequences of several sentences either correct or exhibiting the same type of grammatical or semantic problem following each other in a row. After presentation and one repetition of the experimental sentence, Françoise was asked whether the stimulus was correct ("Is it correct language?" "Is it the way people normally talk?"). Whenever she answered negatively, she was invited to correct the expression. Additionally, she was requested to "explain" her correction. Results indicate that Françoise is able to detect and correct word order errors appearing in grammatically incorrect but semantically appropriate utterances. She gave appropriate justifications for her corrections. She could also detect and mend the grammatically correct but semantically abnormal sentences. The justifications that she gave were inappropriate in some cases (e.g., for the sentence *Demain j'avais mangé un morceau de tarte* – *Tomorrow I had eaten a piece of cake*, she rightly corrected *Demain je mangerai un morceau de tarte* – *Tomorrow I will eat a piece of cake*, but insisted *On mange le morceau de tarte le jour même* – *One eats the piece of cake on the very same day*). However, Françoise did not detect any morphological mistakes (pronominal or verbal). She confidently declared that the sentences containing these irregularities were correct.

Although the literature on the evolution of metasyntactic abilities in children is far from being congruent (due, for one reason, to methodological problems and, also to the still insufficient operationalization of the notion of metasyntax and metasyntactic activities), it is possible to make a few comparisons with Françoise's performance. It would seem that most NR 5-year-old children learning strict word-order languages tend to reject (as ungrammatical) utterances that are incorrectly patterned as to word order. However, it may take them a few more years before they can correct such utterances and propose coherent justifications for their corrections (Hakes, 1980; Gombert, 1990). Françoise, in this respect, certainly compares with NR primary school children. From the developmental studies concerned with the detection of violations of features of lexical selection (e.g., Gleitman, Gleitman, & Shipley, 1972; Hakes, 1980), it would appear that it is not before 7 or 8 years, as a rule, that NR children reject sentences violating rules of lexical selection for that reason (and not for personal, experiential, or other irrelevant reasons). Again, Françoise compares well with normal children at these developmental levels. Curiously, as previously reported, she failed to detect the grammatical morphological errors that were incorporated in some of the proposed sentences (which, it should be noted, did not have a bearing on the semantic interpretation of the sentences). Such a detection is not attested to before 7 or 8 years in NR children (Ryan & Ledger, 1979). Proper correction of ungrammatical morphological forms may be even more delayed in development (Gombert, 1990).

Third, Françoise was given an elementary task of grammatical analysis of 20 monopropositional, active, declarative, affirmative sentences presented in written form. She was requested (in the following order, and when applicable) to underline in different colors the verb of the sentence, the grammatical subject of the verb, the direct object, the indirect object, and the time and place complements. She proved able to correctly execute the task. Typically, Françoise would read the sentence, quickly find the verb (actional as well as nonactional verbs were used in the sentences), then ask herself (aloud) the usual school-type questions: *qui* (*who*), for the grammatical subject (including cases in which the grammatical subject was inanimate or was a locative entity); *quoi* (*what*) for the direct object of the verb; *à qui* (*to whom*) or *à quoi* (*to what*) for the indirect object; *quand* (*when*) for the time circumstantial complement; and *où* (*when*) for the locative circumstantial complement. Formally more complex sentences (i.e., active, declarative, affirmative sentences with object relatives) were also given to Françoise for grammatical analysis. In such cases (e.g., *Un oiseau picore les graines que nous avons jetées dans le jardin – A bird is picking the seeds that we have thrown in the garden*), she would correctly identify the main clause, analyze it in the just described way, and leave the subordinate clause unanalyzed. When urged by the examiner to analyze the subordinate clause, Françoise would do it correctly except for the relative pronoun, to which she appeared unable to assign a grammatical function. Interestingly, this problem exists only at the conscious (meta-) level. As documented in Sections 5.4.1.2.2 and 5.4.3.2, Françoise has no particular productive or receptive functional difficulties with the various types of relative clauses.

In conclusion, Françoise's metalinguistic ability, assessed in the aforementioned (limited) way, appears to be something of a patchwork. It corresponds to a number of isolated bits of knowledge; the type of conscious knowledge that may be expected (or, perhaps, slightly ahead of what might be expected) from someone with the type of general cognitive limitations that she has. Metalexically, as documented in Section 5.4.2, Françoise is seriously limited. Her phonological awareness is limited. She has only clear syllabic awareness. Françoise's performance proved better in metagrammatical and metasemantic ability. In this respect, she seems to function not unlike NR children around 7 or 8 years. Finally, her grammatical analysis performed on written sentences reflects a beginning (and somewhat artificial) knowledge of a small number of basic formal notions learned and practiced at school. Regarding grammaticality and semantic acceptability judgments, Françoise's performance appears to match those reported by Bellugi et al. (1988) for their Williams syndrome subjects as well as those of Yamada (1990) concerning Laura. In any case, however, Françoise's metalinguistic skills far from match her functional expressive and receptive linguistic abilities. Particularly interesting in this respect are the two dissociations documented in our data: First, Françoise's apparent insensitivity at the conscious level to incorrect grammatical morphology contrasts with her well-developed expressive and receptive functional-grammatical-morphological capacity; and, second, Françoise's apparent inability to attribute a grammatical label to relative pronouns contrasts with her expressive and receptive capacity with relative subordinate clauses. The preceding observations are additional indications (if needed) that linguistic awareness and actual linguistic expressive and receptive functioning constitute distinct entities.

5.6 Written language assessment

Françoise's capacity for productive and receptive written language was also examined.

5.6.1 Reading and comprehension of written language

Françoise was given the list of logatomes and isolated conventional words from Borel-Maisonny (see Rondal, 1979a). This list (supplied in Figure A7–1) also contains a few common sentences. The logatomes are artificial and meaningless "words" comprised of one up to five syllables presenting the various phonemes of the French language in a systematic and balanced way. The list is usually employed for assessing co-articulation (see Section 5.4.1.3), but it was used here for evaluating deciphering and reading capabilities. Françoise could read the Borel-Maisonny list without difficulty. It was necessary to tell her twice that the logatomes had no meaning because she kept asking for an indication about meaning or reflecting aloud that she did not know the meaning of "that one." Only one error appeared in her reading: item 1 in sublist 5, *mandurnalo*, was read *mandrumalo*.

She then was presented with two texts: one entitled *Le printemps* (*Springtime*) (see Figure A7–2) was borrowed from an ordinary second-grade reading book; the other entitled *Le printemps est là* (*Springtime is there*) came from an ordinary third-grade reading book. It is more complex than the first one due to its somewhat more "poetic" tone and character, the peculiar text display, the systematic lack of capital letters on the first word of the utterances, the lack of some regular punctuation marks, and the presence of possible distractors (printed drawings) on the sheet (see Figure A7–3). As it appeared, the reading is normal with correct intonation and segmentation according to the punctuation marks. No reading error was observed except in text 2, line 6, where she pronounced the final *s* of the word *quels* (*rayons*) that is not to be pronounced. In one instance (text 2, line 9), after noticing that she had failed to stop at the punctuation mark signaling the end of the sentence, Françoise spontaneously recast the whole sentence properly marking the final stop. The 124 words of text 2 were read in 95 seconds (no speed instruction had been given), which is slow (a couple of normal adult controls read the same text aloud in about 50 seconds).

For assessing written language comprehension, two tasks were used. In the first one (borrowed from the Epreuve pour l'Examen du Langage – Chevrie-Muller, 1975), five written sentences are presented together with each one written on a separate piece of cardboard. Together with the written sentences, the subject is shown five drawings. Sentences and drawings are displayed in a random order in front of the subject. The instruction is to match each sentence with the corresponding drawing. The sentences are as follows:

1. Un petit garçon, Bernard, se promène avec son chien Patapouf.
   (A small boy, Bernard, is walking his dog Patapouf.)
2. Mais Patapouf court trop vite et Bernard tombe dans la boue.
   (But Patapouf runs too fast and Bernard falls into the mud.)
3. Bernard est tellement couvert de boue qu'il a envie de pleurer.
   (Bernard is so dirty with mud that he wants to cry.)
4. Bernard prend un bain et maman va laver les vêtements sales.
   (Bernard takes a bath and mummy is going to wash the dirty clothes.)
5. Bernard sourit en se regardant dans le miroir car il est propre.
   (Bernard smiles as he looks at himself in the mirror because he is clean.)

Françoise could correctly read the proposed sentences and had no difficulty in matching each sentence with the corresponding drawing.

In a second task, Françoise was requested to recall orally the major information from a text that she was first to read. This task (also borrowed from the Epreuve pour l'Examen du Langage – Chevrie-Muller, 1975) is questionable as a test of written language comprehension since it mixes in the same dependent variable the product of three different capacities, that is, reading, remembering, and orally expressing oneself. However, given Françoise's well-established oral language capacity, it was decided that this task could be used since it would yield interpretable results. The text administered was as follows:

– Françoise a reçu une poupée. C'était une belle poupée de porcelaine. La poupée avait les yeux bleus et une robe jaune. Mais le jour même où Françoise avait reçu cette poupée, la poupée est tombée et s'est cassée. Françoise a beaucoup pleuré parce qu'elle aimait bien sa poupée.
– (Françoise received a doll. It was a beautiful China doll. The doll had beautiful eyes and a yellow dress. But on that very day that she received the doll, the doll fell down and broke. Françoise cried a lot because she was very fond of her doll.)

Françoise's immediate recall (transcribed according to the same principles and convention rules as in Section 5.4.1) follows:

– /[1]la petite fille a reçu une belle poupée/[2]la poupée est en porcelaine/[3]c'est une poupée de porcelaine/[4]elle a les yeux bleus comme elle et peut être aussi la même robe jaune/[5]puis comme ça arrive souvent elle dormait tous les jours avec elle/[6]elle a laissé tombé la poupée et elle s'est cassée/[7]la petite fille a pleuré beaucoup parce qu'elle aimait beaucoup sa poupée/

– (/[1]the little girl received a beautiful doll/[2]the doll is made of China/[3]it is a China doll/[4]she has blue eyes like her and perhaps also the same yellow dress/[5]then as that happens often she was sleeping every day with her/[6]she dropped the doll and she broke/[7]the little girl cried a lot because she was very fond of her doll/)

As can be seen, Françoise provides a correct recall of the story that avoids using the first name of the little girl in the story, which happens to be the same as hers (probably wanting to avoid any too close identification with herself in a story patently too childish for her level of development and autonomy). Françoise actually supplied an account richer than the text proposed (she allows the girl to sleep and to play with her doll for some time before the breaking episode takes place), perhaps finding the original story too simplistic to her liking or having somewhat misunderstood the instruction as a request to upgrade or to freely reconstruct the text given. Formally, there are only two (minor) problems with the recall: First, in recalled utterance 4, it is not clear what she means by *comme elle* (*like her*), talking about the doll's eye color, and by *même* (*same*), talking about the doll's yellow dress; second, in recalled utterances 5 and 6, Françoise confusingly twice uses the third-person feminine pronoun *elle* (*she*), once to refer to the little girl in the story and once to refer to the doll. This expression is a little surprising given Françoise's good demonstrated command of pronominal anaphora in spontaneous speech. It could be that trying to avoid using "Françoise" as a name for the little girl, she got herself into (relative) referential trouble, from which she could have escaped by using paraphrasal expressions such as "the girl" or "the little girl" but did not have the cognitive or the momentary attentional resources to do so.

In summary, Françoise's reading ability is well established although she is slow. This contrasts with her fully speed-appropriate oral verbal ability. Her written language comprehension is about that of the third grade with specific limitations, either lexical or conceptual, that are reminiscent of her general intellectual shortcomings.

5.6.2 Written language expression

Françoise was invited to submit a short written text on whatever topic would please her. She chose to write about one of her days at La Fermette – a special day in fact, since it followed her 34th birthday. Her text is reproduced without modification in Figure A8–1 (except for the more personal information, which was withdrawn). A literal English translation is also supplied with her text. Françoise's spontaneous text, although revealing a basic ability to express herself and to communicate through the written medium, is clearly deficient in several respects: punctuation marking, narrative microstructures, grammatical marking, and conventional orthography, particularly in its grammatical aspects. Let me describe these problems in more detail. First, Françoise fails almost completely to use punctuation marks, as well as capital letters at the beginning of sentences (and inappropriately uses capitals in other contexts). This contrasts with her oral language, where she clearly marks the beginning and the end of utterances and speech turns with the proper conventional means. Second, she has difficulties with the narrative style of her discourse; the tenses used are not always appropriate and most of all, she appears to be trying to present the episode of her being offered flowers for her birthday as well as other parts of the report in an impersonal manner that is inadequate and, in fact, clumsy [in saying "nous tous dit que c'était l'anniversaire de Melle___ nous l'avons appelé avec tous les cris" – "we all say that it was the birthday of Ms.___ we have called her with all the shouting," she actually means that once the table had been set with the glasses, her friends said that it was her birthday and called her by shouting at her to have her come to the little party organized in honor of her birthday; in saying "une activité au choix qui s'aime et qui passe leur après-midi" – "an activity freely chosen which one likes and that goes on for the afternoon," she actually means that one is free to choose one activity that one likes and that the activity is supposed to last for the whole afternoon]. Third, she poorly negotiates the tense marking and the tense agreement between related clauses and sentences. Fourth, the orthography is deficient in several respects. A number of words are incorrectly written (e.g., *Fernette* instead of *Fermette* – *little farm*; *madi* instead of *mardi* – *Tuesday*; *comme d'Habitude* instead of *comme d'habitude* (with a lower-case letter beginning *habitude* and not a capital letter) – *as usual*; *a peu avant* instead of *un peu avant* – *shortly before*; *verres* instead of *Verres* (no capital letter at the beginning) – *glasses*; even *Françoise* is written *françoise*, which must be a performance error). But there are also many grammatical-orthographical mistakes, relating mostly to homophonous forms [e.g., *j'ai (eu) passer* instead of *j'ai passé* – *I have had*; *tous le monde* instead of *tout le monde* – *everybody*; *nous sommes tous remonter* instead of *nous sommes tous remontés* – *we have all gone up*; *choissi* instead of *choisit* – *chooses*; *viens* instead of *vient* – *comes*; *nous tous dit* instead of *nous tous disons* – *we all say*; *nous l'avons appellé* – instead of *nous l'avons appelée* – *we have called her*; *sont* (*éducatrice* – *educator*) instead of *son* (confusion between the third-person plural present indicative of the verb *être* – *to be* and the third-person possessive pronoun *son* – *her*; the "masculine form" of the pronoun is used here instead of the feminine form because the following word – *educatrice* – begins with a vowel)]. Notice, however, that there are a number of correctly used grammatical markings [e.g., *je suis venue* (feminine past participle of the verb *venir*) – *I have come*; *j'ai pris mon bain* (masculine past participle of the verb *prendre*) – *I have taken my bath*; *nous avons repris notre activité* (masculine past participle of the verb *reprendre*) – *we have resumed our activity*; *le repas qui se fait* (third-person singular of the reflexive verb *se faire*) – *the meal that takes place*; *lui a offert* (masculine past participle of the verb *offrir*) – *has offered her*; *je suis retournée* (feminine past participle of the verb *retourner*) – *I have (returned)*].

Françoise's orthographic difficulties (lexical as well as grammatical) were confirmed in a subsequent evaluation. The text of *Le printemps* (*Springtime*), which she was given before in the course of the reading assessment (see Figure A7–2), was dictated to her. The resulting text (with the errors underlined) is displayed in Figure A8–

2). As can be seen from the text, Françoise used capital letters at the beginning of each sentence except on two occasions (sentences 4 and 5). She also used punctuation marks (except for two commas in sentence 5) but these were given as part of dictation. The text contains 36 content words. She incorrectly wrote 6 of these. The errors are minor ones, however (*temp* instead of *temps*, *solleil* instead of *soleil*, *pés* instead of *prés*, *paquerette* instead of *pâquerette*, *colerette* instead of *collerette*, *fètes* instead of *fête*). Eight other errors are grammatical errors [*gambade* should be *gambadent*, since the subject is plural; *au tous parfums* should be *au doux parfum* – here Françoise wrongly identified the intended referential quality *doux* (soft) for the collective personal pronoun *tous* (*all*), and she then somewhat logically added the plural grapheme *s* to the word *parfum* (*perfume*); *se caches* should be *se cache*, since the subject is singular; *tous revit* should be *tout revit* (collective impersonal pronoun *tout* confounded with collective personal pronoun *tous*); *tous* in the following sequence should be *tout*, for the same reason; *et* should be *est* (third-person singular of the present of the indicative of verb *être* – *to be*); and *fètes* should be *fête* (singular form instead of plural, probably induced by the preceding incorrect plural *tous*)].

When specifically requested to write the plural form of short singular statements, one by one, Françoise appears able to do it correctly – for example, *Le chat dort* (*The cat sleeps – is sleeping*); but *Le chat et le chien dorment* (*The cat and the dog sleep – are sleeping*); *La jolie rose est dans le vase* (*The pretty rose is in the vase*), *Les jolies roses sont dans le vase* (*The pretty roses are in the vase*); *Je suis une fille* (*I am a girl*), *Nous sommes des filles* (*We are girls*). In the same way, she is able to contrastively mark lexical forms for gender in short sentences – for example, *Le petit garçon boit du lait* (*The little boy drinks milk*), *La petite fille boit du lait* (*The little girl drinks milk*).

In summary, Françoise appears to be quite able to express herself through the written medium, albeit at a somewhat primitive level, with persistent (but nonspecific) difficulties including the use of the conventional punctuation system. When the writing task is simplified, however (e.g., when short sentences are presented in isolation), she proves able to apply the basic rules of the writing system. In her spontaneous written expression as well as in text dictation, she seems to be overwhelmed by the number of operations to perform within short periods of time, the obvious consequence being a release of control over some of these operations (the ones that are less centrally concerned with the transfer of meaning activity). These limitations in writing markedly contrast with the ease of functioning that Françoise displays in the verbal-oral sphere, as demonstrated before.

5.7 Cerebral hemispheric specialization

An assessment was made of cerebral hemispheric specialization for speech stimuli in Françoise as well as in a group of other DS adults attending La Fermette. Receptive functioning was tested using a dichotic-listening paradigm. Cerebral dominance for speech production was assessed with a dual-task paradigm (see Chapter 2 for background information).

5.7.1 Dichotic-listening study

In addition to Françoise, the subjects were 24 DS adults (15 males, 9 females) aged from 21 to 36 years. It is known that a relatively large proportion of DS subjects have hearing difficulties, mostly of the conductive type (see Chapter 2). We selected the DS adults in this study in such a way as to minimize this possible confounding variable. Judging from their medical records, the DS subjects retained for the study had no more than 30 decibels of loss in either ear over the major speech frequencies (many of them had less and seemed, in fact, to enjoy normal hearing). As indicated earlier (Section 5.1), Françoise is free of auditory deficiency. Manual laterality was established in having the subjects perform five tasks (writing their first names, drawing a circle, cutting a piece of paper with a pair of scissors, opening a box, and throwing a ball with one hand only) and computing the dominant laterality pattern. This way of establishing handedness, currently used in the cerebral specialization literature, was borrowed from the Edinburgh Handedness Inventory (Oldfield, 1971). Individuals who write with their right hand and use their right hand for at least three other activities are considered right-handed. Five men (one-third of the group) were left-handed and 10 right-handed. All the women were right-handed.

A recorder REVOX A77 (four tracks) was used to present the dichotic message to the subjects, through earphones, at a volume comfortable for each subject (but not lower than 70 decibels in output intensity level, given the possibility of a mild functional hearing loss in some subjects). The experimenter also had a pair of earphones through which she could establish that the tape was proceeding smoothly. The speech stimuli were six syllables (*ba, da, ga, bi, di, gi,*) presented in such a way that they arrived in pairs simultaneously at the two ears. The pairs of syllables were presented regularly at 5-second intervals. A total of 60 experimental trials was presented to each subject. The original tape had been designed for the neuropsychological assessment of patients with cerebral damage. We felt that it was appropriate for our purpose since it presented successive stimuli separated by a relatively large interval of time and since it made minimal demand on short-term memory in presenting only one stimulus per ear at a time. Testing took place in one session for each subject. The experimenter spent approximatively two days at La Fermette getting to know the DS subjects, and they, her. The testing sessions were conducted in a separate, quiet room in one of La Fermette's buildings.

The procedure used was a "directed attention procedure" (Bryden, Munhall, & Allard, 1983). Subjects were told to attend to one ear for a block of trials and to report only the items presented to that ear. Accuracy in the right ear when told to attend to it was compared with accuracy in the left ear when told to attend to it. This procedure was chosen because it is known to reduce attentional biases[12] (a welcome perspective with a group of MR subjects) (see, e.g., Tannock, Kershner, & Oliver, 1984), because the right-ear-advantage (REA) paradigm is considered to be a robust one, and because it reduces the variance among subjects (see Bryden, 1988, for a technical discussion and a review of the relevant literature). Seven of the male subjects and five of the female subjects – randomly chosen – started the experimental trials with the instruction to report from the right ear, and the others, including Françoise, with the instruction to report from the left ear – this as a further control for possible attentional biases or the effect of other variables unrelated to cerebral specialization such as stimulus bias, unintentional priming, or other listening strategies (see Section 2.4.1). Also the experimenter kept pointing one finger in the direction of the body side from where the hearing report had to be done, to prevent or at least to minimize the effect of possible confusions or instruction forgetting in the subjects. Of course, particular caution was exercised to make sure that the DS subjects had correctly understood the task. The task was explained conversationally with a number of repetitions. Several preparatory trials were performed. The experimental trials in themselves did not start before one could be sure that the subjects had grasped the exact nature of the task to be performed.

One score was computed expressing the proportion of *intrusion* errors, that is, the number of times the subject reported in one ear the syllable that was actually presented to the other ear on that trial out of the total number of speech stimuli presented. This measure is the preferred one in the literature on dichotic listening. It avoids confounding the commission errors in each ear, potentially resulting from a variety of factors (attentional deficit, hearing difficulty, pro– or retroactive inhibition in the series of syllables presented, etc.), with the truly intrusive influence of one ear over the other one, which is the major variable of interest in a dichotic-listening task (see Tannock et al., 1984, for further technical details and for a discussion). The following formula was computed for each ear:

$$\text{dichotic-listening score} = \frac{(30 - E\,1) \times 100}{30},$$

where 30 is the number of syllables presented to each ear and $E1$ the number of intrusion errors from the other ear. From there an REA, an LEA (left-ear advantage), or a null difference (no ear advantage) could be calculated.

Taking a percentage difference of at least 10 points to indicate ear advantage (Hartley, 1985), it was found that among DS women three exhibited an REA (from 30 to 77%), four exhibited an LEA (from 16 to 64%), and two no ear advantage. Françoise exhibited a clear REA (63%). Among the DS men, six exhibited an REA (from 10 to 63%) and nine exhibited an LEA (from 10 to 77%). It did not make any difference whether the subjects were instructed to report from the right ear or from the left ear to begin with.

It therefore appears that the general tendency for DS subjects to exhibit more of an LEA (right-hemispheric dominance) for speech perception than an REA (left-hemispheric dominance), usually reported in the specialized literature (see Chapter 2), was found again in our data collected with (young) DS adults. However, in the sample studied, there also were several subjects, including Françoise, exhibiting an important REA and therefore a clear left-hemisphere dominance for speech perception of the type usually reported for normally developing or normally developed subjects.

5.7.2 Dual-task study

In addition to Françoise, the subjects for this study were 19 DS adults (9 females, 10 males) – all right-handed (see later) – taken from the same sample from La Fermette as earlier. The study took place in La Fermette approximatively 1 week after the completion of the dichotic-listening study. The dual-task procedure consisted of a finger-tapping task combined with a sound-shadowing task.

A standard IBM personal computer was used together with a homemade processing program to record the subjects' tapping responses during the tapping task and to compute the usual descriptive statistical analyses on these data. Three series of 10 words each were used in the sound-shadowing task. The words were selected from the word frequency tables established by Gougenheim et al. (1964) for French. Each word list was composed of frequent and concrete monosyllabic words having the same average frequency of occurrence in the language – list 1: *temps* (*time*), *chant* (*song*), *beau* (*beautiful*), *pain* (*bread*), *eau* (*water*), *jeu* (*game*), *point* (*point*), *lit* (*bed*), *nom* (*name*), *fond* (*bottom*); list 2: *fois* (*time*), *lait* (*milk*), *mois* (*month*), *camp* (*camp*), *coup* (*stroke*), *fou* (*mad*), *bois* (*wood*), *vin* (*wine*), *pied* (*foot*), *nuit* (*night*); list 3: *bon* (*good*), *nez* (*nose*), *gens* (*people*), *faim* (*hunger*), *mot* (*word*), *voix* (*voice*), *bout* (*end*), *bas* (*low part*), *main* (*hand*), *long* (*long*). These lists were recorded on a standard Panasonic tape recorder at the frequency of 1 word every 2 seconds.

The experimental procedure entailed the following five steps. *Step 1*: The subject is requested to repeat the words on list 1 one by one; this provides a sound-shadowing baseline for each subject. *Step 2*: The subject now faces the computer; his task is to tap repeatedly with the index finger of the right hand on a given key facing him right in the body axis as fast as possible; this supplies a baseline for finger tapping with the right hand for each subject. *Step 3*: Same as step 2, but the tapping is now performed with the index finger of the left hand; this supplies a baseline for finger tapping with the left hand for each subject. *Step 4*: Same as step 2, but in addition the subject is now requested to repeat one by one the list of words (list 2) presented by the experimenter on the tape recording. *Step 5*: Same as step 3, but in addition the subject is requested to repeat one by one the list of words (list 3) presented by the experimenter on the tape recording. Each tapping period lasted for 20 seconds. Half of the male subjects and half of the female subjects including Françoise – randomly chosen – received step 1, step 2, step 3, step 4, and step 5, in that order. The other half received step 1, step 3, step 2, step 5, and step 4, in that order.

The dependent variables are two (times two levels for each one): (1) the proportion of words omitted by each subject in comparison with his baseline while finger tapping with the right hand and with the left hand, considered separately; (2) the proportion of discrete taps produced by each subject for each hand with and without concurrent sound shadowing.

As indicated in Chapter 2, the interpretation of dual-task studies of this type is as such: When right-handed individuals are required to speak while performing a demanding unimanual task, the concurrent speech is expected to interfere more with right-hand movements than with left-hand movements (theoretically the disturbing influence may go both ways since the hand movement could also perturb the concurrent speech); this is due to interference between brain centers controlling the verbal and the manual tasks. Normally there is more interference with right-hand movements than with left-hand ones because the former are controlled by the left hemisphere, which is also in control of speech production (Kinsbourne & Hiscock, 1983). Conversely, if this is not the case or if the interference is more between speech and left-hand movements, this is suggestive of a right-hemispheric dominance for speech production.

Two male subjects and 2 female subjects had to be rejected because instead of producing repetitive tapping on the computer key, they pressed for several seconds before releasing the key. No additional instruction or training could lead them to act otherwise. For the 15 remaining subjects, the results indicate such large interindividual variation for both the male and the female subjects' finger tapping as to render any group statistics virtually meaningless. Among the male subjects, the frequencies of finger tapping compared for the right hand and for the left hand with and without concurrent speech production reveal the expected interference between verbalization and right-hand finger tapping in 6 out of the 8 available subjects. The relative amount of interference (RAI) averaged per second may be evaluated with the formula:

$$RAI = \frac{(\text{Tapping step 2} - \text{Tapping step 4}) - (\text{Tapping step 3} - \text{Tapping step 5})}{20}$$

The RAI index is positive for six subjects out of eight varying from 4.05 to 9, and it is negative for the two remaining subjects (−1.40 and −1.90, respectively). Regarding speech production, the relative losses were minor (maximum one word not repeated during finger tapping with either the right or the left hand). Among the female subjects, the expected interference between verbalization and right-hand finger tapping is observed in only three of the seven available cases with lower RAI than that in men (the RAI index being 3.20, 3.05, and 4.10, respectively); in two cases, there were few differences in the effects of verbalization on right-hand and left-hand finger tapping (RAI values at or close to null); in the two remaining cases, the RAI index was negative (−3.90 and −4.50, respectively). As was the case for the men, the relative losses in speech production in DS women did not go beyond one word during finger tapping except in one case where it reached three words during right-hand as well as left-hand finger tapping. Françoise exhibited an interference between verbalization and finger tapping clearly more marked for the right hand than for the left hand (positive RAI of 4.05).

It would appear, therefore, that despite a great deal of interindividual variation, a number of the male and the female DS adults studied, including Françoise, exhibited a noticeable interference between verbalization and right-hand movements compatible with the hypothesis of a left-hemispheric dominance for speech production in these subjects. Things are less marked with the female DS subjects than with the males, and the degrees of interference observed are lower in the former (including the case of Françoise) than in the latter. This finding is consistent with the observations of Elliott, Edwards, Weeks, Lindley, & Carnahan (1987) according to which women, whether NR or DS, may be less lateralized for speech production than males [a hypothesis itself compatible with the well-known fact that language disorders, particularly of the productive type, are more prevalent – about four times so – at all ages in men than in women (Rondal & Seron, 1989)].

5.7.3 Discussion

From these observations, it would seem that Françoise's hemispheric dominance for speech functions is not basically different from what is reported to be the case in most normal people. However, one should keep in mind a number of caveats rendering somewhat tentative the interpretation of the performances in tasks assumed to uncover cerebral specialization for speech, such as dichotic-listening and dual verbal-motor tasks, particularly in the case of MR individuals. First, MR subjects of other etiologies than DS but of comparable MAs are reported to exhibit the expected right-ear/left-hemispheric superiority in dichotic-listening tasks (Hartley, 1981).

Second, as reported in the literature and as also observed in our data, there exists relatively large interindividual variability (assuming intraindividual stability) in the performances of the MR persons in the tasks used for assessing cerebral dominance for speech. A certain amount of interindividual variability has been demonstrated in NR people as well. In this respect, even disregarding age in NR people (and also in MR people, where, however, the effect of age has not been systematically studied to my knowledge), it is not fully clear what levels of REA in speech perception and RAI in speech production correspond to "complete" or "sufficiently complete" brain specialization for speech. There has been little attempt to relate the degree of observed right-ear/left-hemispheric superiority in dichotic listening or the level of right-hand interference in dual tasks to the language capacities of MR subjects. One exception is a study by Sommers and Starkey (1977), who, using a dichotic task (with words), contrasted the speech-perceptual functioning of two groups of DS children with markedly different speech and language skills to that of MA-matched NR children. They observed an average 23% REA in the NR children but not in the DS children, for whom, regardless of level of speech and language functioning, the average ear effect was essentially zero. Another exception is the work of Hartley (1985). She tested a group of DS children and a group of MR children of other etiologies on part 5 of the Token Test for Children (DiSimoni, 1978) and on a dichotic-listening test (using digits). The DS and the other MR children were matched for CA and for their scores on the PPVT. Hartley found that the DS children showed a significantly greater left-ear advantage on the dichotic-listening test than did the group with other mental retardation, and also that the DS children performed more poorly than the non-DS children on those tasks requiring an understanding of complex syntactic structures (such as temporal subordinates), whereas they showed no such deficit in performing verbal-spatial tasks. Hartley (1985) divided her subjects into groups comprised of those showing an REA, an LEA, or no ear advantage, disregarding etiology of retardation. Little difference was found in the language performance of the LEA and the no-ear-advantage children. However, the REA group proved superior to the other two groups on the syntactic tasks, but not on the spatial tasks. In discussing her results, Hartley (1985) suggests the existence, in neurologically intact children, of a *direct* link between ear advantage and receptive language abilities. It is not clear, however, what she means by "neurologically intact" in the context of her study, as she tested only MR children who are, or may all be rightly suspected of not being, intact from a neurological point of view. Moreover, it seems to me that one should be cautious in proposing such a direct relationship between hemispheric brain dominance and language functioning in the present state of knowledge.

Third, and returning to our own data, it is interesting to compare the language abilities of Françoise with those of the other adults from the La Fermette group exhibiting similar degrees of REA or important degrees of LEA in the dichotic-listening test, and similar or higher degrees of RAI in the dual verbalization/finger-tapping task, as well as to inquire into the homogeneity of left-hemispheric dominance for speech perception and speech production among the DS adults exhibiting a clear cerebral asymmetry. The results are straightforward. In addition to Françoise, three DS females exhibited an REA (from 30 to 77%). Six DS males also exhibited an REA (from 10 to 63%). Retaining those individuals for whom the REA is equal to or exceeds 50%, one has, again in addition to Françoise, two female and one male DS subjects. These three subjects all have positive RAI values in the dual-task study. Therefore, according to the criteria as set (and used in the specialized literature), they may be considered as being relatively homogeneously left-hemispheric dominant for speech perception and speech production. However, upon meeting them and according to the information contained in their files at La Fermette (coming from standard speech and language examinations conducted by certified speech pathologists), it is quite clear that their receptive and expressive language abilities are standard for DS persons. Such is also the case of the other adults in the La Fermette group, taking into account the usual variability between DS subjects, but apparently irrespective of the indications obtained from the dichotic-listening and the dual-task studies.

In conclusion, considering these data and problems, it would seem that no solid prediction can be made directly linking what people usually take to be appropriate indications of hemispheric dominance for speech and actual speech and language performance in DS individuals. Some DS adults studied (including Françoise) appear to process speech stimuli with their left cerebral hemisphere. However, it seems that there is little ground for a conception of DS as *necessarily* leading to the transfer of whole or parts of the speech cerebral organization from the left to the right hemisphere (as witnessed in cases of congenital localized brain lesions in the left hemisphere; see Levy, Amir, & Shalev, 1992; Woods, 1991).

5.8 Relevant nonlinguistic data

Additional information concerning Françoise was gathered on general intellectual functioning and Piagetian development, computational capacity, visual perception, left-right discrimination, instrumental functions, attention-concentration, episodic memory, semantic memory, and working memory.

5.8.1 General intelligence and Piagetian development

One will recall that, for technical reasons discussed earlier, Françoise was given the WAIS (Wechsler, 1968) twice – once in May 1988 and once in late 1991. On the first administration of the WAIS, the standard scores for the verbal subscale were as follows: information, 5; comprehension (i.e., actually comments on a set of proposed lexical terms, idiomatic expressions, or proverbs), 3; arithmetic operations (performed mentally, the results of which were reported orally), 4; similarities, 7; immediate memory for digits, 7 (Françoise's longest series repeated without error forward and backward contained four digits); and vocabulary, 7. This comprised the basis for a (so-called) verbal IQ of 71. On the performance (nonverbal) subscale of the WAIS, the standard scores were as follows: cubes (spatial structuration), 4; object assembly, 1; image completion, 4; sequential and logical arrangement of images, 5 (she could correctly do most of the proposed sequences but slowly, hence the relatively low subscore obtained); and code, 4 (she did not commit mistakes but performed slowly – 21 signs in 90 seconds). This constituted a performance IQ of 60. Global IQ was 64. Françoise's slow pace of responding (in nonverbal tasks only) is in line with the typical low processing speed (non-task specific) of MR persons (see R. Kail, 1992).

On the second administration of the WAIS, the standard scores for the verbal subscale were as follows: information, 3; comprehension, 4; arithmetical operations, 3; similarities, 8; immediate memory for digits, 7 (Françoise's longest series repeated without error forward and backward was again four digits); and vocabulary, 5. Verbal IQ was 70. On the performance subscale, the standard scores were as follows: cubes, 5; object assembly, 1; image completion, 3; sequential and logical arrangement of images, 5; and code, 4. Performance IQ was 64. Global IQ was 65. As it appears then, there are no grounds for suspecting a possible age-related general cognitive decline in Françoise over the 4-year evaluation period. Nor were there behavioral or other indications that would have led us and/or the personnel of La Fermette (where Françoise spends 2 days a week) to develop any such suspicion.

Françoise was also given the Epreuves Différencielles d'Efficience Intellectuelle (EDEI; Perron-Borelli & Misés, 1974), a composite test of "intellectual efficiency" composed of a series of eight subtests, verbal or nonverbal. On these subtests, the standard scores were as follows: vocabulary, 7; word definition, 10.6; general information, 9.6; social adaptation (questionnaire), 9; practical knowledge, 5.3; conceptualization, 10.3; object classification, 7.6; and categorial analysis, 4.3. This yielded a verbal MA of 9 years and 10 months, a nonverbal MA of 5 years and 8 months, which made up a composite MA of 7 years and 4 months.

Françoise was tested for the Piagetian tasks of seriation, classification, and conservation to assess her level of intellectual-operational development according to Piaget's terminology (see Flavell, 1963, and Piaget & Inhelder, 1969, for indications on the definition of these tasks, their measurements, and their places in the assessment of mental development). Partially corresponding data were available for a group of young adults (males and females) attending La Fermette (Jarbinet, 1991). They are used here as reference control indications.

Françoise is able to correctly classify 18 tokens (varying as to shape – squares, circles, and triangles – color, and size) and 27 pictures of familiar objects (varying as to nature – cups, flowers, etc. – color, and size) according to one criterion at a time. She can juxtapose two classifications, each organized according to a given criterion (e.g., grouping together, on the one side, all the cups and subdividing them according to color, then placing on the other side all the flowers and subdividing them according to color); but she appears unable to organize integrated or related classifications (i.e., double-entry tables or matrices – e.g., classifying yellow and green squares and circles in four compartments arranged according to two dimensions). This is the capacity for more elaborate schemes that marks the achievement of a genuine operatory (or operational)[13] classification, according to Piaget. This stage is reached at about 8 years in normal development.

Françoise was also given a seriation task with 5 and, then, 10 sticks of different colors. She was requested to arrange the sticks according to increasing or decreasing size. She could do it without particular difficulty, seeking first the smallest (largest) element, then the smallest (largest) of those left over, what Piaget considers to be the "operatory method." This substage is reached by NR children at 7 or 8 years. Another mark of operativity in the seriation task is the ability to insert a stick upon request and place it immediately in the correct position in the series. Françoise could do this operation correctly as well.

A set of conservation tasks was given to Françoise: conservation of number and term-to-term correspondence, conservation of length (comparison of a straight line with another line of the same length that was first straight, then broken), conservation of surface (by displacement of elements), conservation of liquid (in which task the contents of glass A are poured into a narrower glass B or a wider glass C), conservation of solid (and continuous) substance (judging the changes in shape of a lump of clay) and of discontinuous quantities, and conservation of weight (weighing lumps of clay or Plasticine on a scale, then judging of the weight following changes in shape). The NR child attains these conservations between 7 and 9 or 10 years. Françoise could correctly solve all the conservation problems presented. However, she used only one argument to justify her conservation judgments, that is, the so-called simple or additive identities argument (e.g., as to conservation of liquids, "It is the same water," "It has only been poured," and "Nothing has been taken away or added, therefore it is still the same"). She never made use of the other two operatory arguments – surer indications of operationality, according to Piaget, particularly if they are produced together – that is, reversibility by inversion (e.g., "You can put the water in B back into A where it was before") and compensation or reversibility by reciprocal relationship (e.g., "The water is high, but the glass is narrower, so it is still the same amount"). Interestingly, during the execution of the conservation tasks, Françoise spontaneously acknowledged that years ago she had been trained by her father (a mathematics professor, aware of some of Piaget's works) to disregard the physical appearance of objects following transformation and to remember that it was always the same quantity that remained, because nothing actually had been added or taken away. It is not clear whether Françoise's cognitive functioning really demonstrates "decentration" from action or physical appearance and a capacity to subordinate concrete states to reversible transformations, or whether she has learned stereotyped answers and, therefore, exhibits only pseudo-operational cognitive structuration.

Recapitulating the above data, Françoise seems to have reached operational seriation. She is close to operational classification, but fails to understand and use spontaneously matrixlike arrangements of elements. On conservation tasks, she is no longer functioning at the preoperational level (fully preoperational children usually refuse the adult suggestion according to which transformations do not falsify the initial equality). Françoise properly uses the identity argument to nullify the adverse effect of the physical appearances, and she is able to successfully resist countersuggestions by the examiner. But she does not seem to be fully operational, because she is limited to one (the most elementary one) of the conservation arguments and because she ignores reversibility. On the whole, and keeping in mind that for Piaget this is the grouping or the systemic aspect of the psychological operations that counts most (i.e., the "structures de groupement"), I would be tempted to diagnose Françoise as being cognitively somewhere between preoperational and full concrete operational levels, but closer to the latter one. This level is compatible with her MA as evaluated with the EDEI Test (see earlier).

The "control" group of young DS adult subjects from La Fermette was tested using the tasks of classification, seriation, and conservation of number, length, and surface. The majority of subjects proved able to classify 18 tokens, according to one criterion (shape, color, or size) at a time, but none demonstrated any ability for operational matrixlike arrangements. Eleven subjects (out of a total of 28, i.e., approximatively 40% of the sample) could seriate in an operational or operational-like manner (no stick-insertion test was applied, unfortunately). Twenty-one subjects (out of a total of 32, this time, approximatively 66% of the sample) seemed to produce conservation judgments regarding number, 22 subjects (out of 32, i.e., 69% of the sample) produced conservation judgments concerning length, and 8 subjects (out of 32, i.e., 25% of the sample) produced conservation judgments regarding surface. But these results have to be taken with caution because the report (Jarbinet, 1991) does not contain an analysis of the conservation arguments supplied by the subjects and because no "countersuggesting" was attempted by the examiner. It might be the case, then, that a number or all of these alleged conservation judgments testify to the existence of only pseudoconservation structures. Additionally, we ourselves tested 2 DS adult subjects (1 male and 1 female) from La Fermette on the same Piagetian tasks as those administered to Françoise. They both demonstrated preoperational classification and seriation, nonconservation of number, length, surface, liquids, continuous as well as discontinuous quantity, and weight. Overall, they had significant difficulties in understanding the instructions, to the extent that a part of their operational limitations, as they appeared, could have to do with this lack of understanding. In an independent investigation, Stassart (1991) reported only 1 adolescent with moderate mental retardation (non-DS) out of a group of 27 subjects examined, who had reached the level of using reversibility arguments in the task of conservation of liquids. Of course, one will recall Inhelder's classical contribution (1969) showing that, in general, moderately and severely MR subjects do not reach the grouping structures characteristic of the Piagetian concrete operational stage of mental development, whereas mildly MR subjects reach that stage but are prevented from developing into the formal operational stage attained only by NR subjects in the course of early adolescence.

In summary, it would seem that Françoise's level of cognitive development according to Piaget's scheme is somewhat intermediate between the preoperational and genuine concrete operational. Although being quite weak by NR standards, Françoise's level of operational development may be slightly more advanced than that exhibited by most other (regular) moderately and severely MR subjects, with DS or with other etiologies.

5.8.2 Computational capacity

Françoise's computational capacity was assessed using various means in addition to the arithmetic subtest of the Wechsler scale. She can correctly read and write the first 1,000 numbers and beyond. She knows the first 10 multiplication tables and can correctly perform multiplication and division operations on numbers contained in the tables, albeit slowly for the upper tables (except table 10) and often counting with her fingers. Beyond table 10, any mental operation of multiplication or division is very slow, difficult, and often yields an incorrect result. Written operations of adding and substracting are realized up to 4-digit numbers, with difficulties in correctly positioning the numbers with respect to one another, particularly when they do not contain the same number of digits, and in correctly reporting intermediate units. The written operations of multiplying and dividing pose problems with frequent forgetting of intermediate operations.

5.8.3 Visual perception

Françoise was given the test of the "Figures Enchevêtrées" of Poppelreuter (1985) (a task in which the subject is requested to discriminate and label a series of familiar objects represented embedded into one another in a picture). Her performance was normal.

5.8.4 Left-right discrimination

On the test of Head (Head & Holmes, 1911), where the subject is requested to execute complex cross-lateral gestures upon verbal instruction, Françoise's performance was also considered to be within normal limits.

5.8.5 Instrumental functions

Visuographic ability was assessed using several tests. One of the two complex figures of Rey (1964, 1966) was administered (the more difficult one; see Figure A9–1). Françoise exhibited difficulties in interpreting the macrostructure of the drawing to be reproduced. She proceeded by juxtaposition of small parts; sometimes wasting time on the proper setting of insignificant details of the structure. But she proved able to spontaneously correct a number of her mistakes with the consequence that the final global product was coherent with respect to the model that she had first to copy, and then, after a 3-minute delay, to reproduce from memory (as expected, performance was much better in the former case) (see Figures A9–2 and A9–3). Françoise was also requested to copy one cube and one house from both their left and right perspectives (see Figures A9–4 and A9–5). She proved unable to draw according to perspective (drawings were slightly more accurate in the left perspective than in the right one). The faces of the model items were left unintegrated into the whole, and the bases were flattened accordingly. On the Bender-Gestalt test – revised and abbreviated form – (Santucci & Galifret-Granjon, 1960), Françoise received a total score of 27 (for six items), which corresponds to the median score for 6-year-old children.

Expressive gesturing was assessed through immediate imitation of finger and hand gestures – from simple to complex configurations (Bergès & Lézine, 1978). Fifteen out of the 16 configurations in the test could be correctly reproduced. Symbolic gesturing was assessed using Galifret-Granjon's instrument for the developmental study of ideomotor praxis (Galifret-Granjon, 1979). This test consists of mimicking 10 meaningful gestural sequences upon verbal instruction (e.g., closing a door with a key, lighting a candle with a match). Françoise scored within the 12-year-old range (upper limit) in the test for 9 out of 10 gestural sequences, and within the 10-year-old range for the remaining 1 (angling with rod and line, and pretending to catch a fish, an activity for which she probably lacked precise models and practice).

In summary, Françoise's expressive and symbolic gesturing proved well developed and probably not far from normal. In contrast, her visuographic ability is poorly developed and compatible with her MA. These limitations are not to be ascribed to deficiencies in the areas of visual perception or basic lateral discrimination, as indicated by the results of the specific tests performed. Rather, they probably attest to the incompleteness of Françoise's development in the visuospatial domain.

5.8.6 Attention-concentration

On a task of concentrated attention, the Barrage Subtest of the KLT Scale (Kettler, Laurent, & Thireau, 1964), where eight types of small drawings, varying in shape and alternating along rows in an irregular manner, had to be discriminated, Françoise made no mistakes but forgot a number of stimuli; being very slow, she could not finish the task within the 4-minute period of time allocated. She received a score of 22 of a maximum possible of 90. This score places her within the lower quartile of the normal population.

On a more difficult task of attention-concentration involving two visually closed letters (*p* and *b*) equipped with quotation marks and apostrophes in varying spatial combinations – Test D2 of Hogrefe, 1962/1966 – Françoise scored within the bottom 2 percentiles of the reference population.

5.8.7 Memory

5.8.7.1 Episodic memory

On a classical task of learning paired-associate conventional (French) words auditorily presented, Françoise exhibited little ability. She could correctly associate only two words with their respective stimulus word in eight pairs [i.e., the first pair in the order of presentation *poupée – marteau* (*doll – hammer*), and the third pair *tabac – journal* (*tobacco – newspaper*)] after four presentations of the series, and only one word (the first pair) within the first three presentations. On a corresponding task in which the second elements in the pairs were nonwords (e.g., *gribu, piva, oustal*), she proved unable to learn a single association over four presentations of the series. It must be added that, on this latter task, her motivation quickly deteriorated, since she started repeating "drôle de nom" (funny name). Three young DS adult control subjects from La Fermette (one male, two females, with IQs between 30 and 40 on the WAIS, and "regular" language levels for DS persons) could not learn a single association between words and nonwords, either. With conventional words, only one of them could form one association from the first presentation of the list onto the fourth one [it concerned the first pair of words in the order of presentation, i.e., *poupée – marteau (doll – hammer)*]. These data indicate that in simple associative lexical learning, Françoise does not seem to be much better than other (regular) DS adult subjects.

Françoise was administered the "Test of the Fifteen Words" – Taylor's forms A and B (Test des 15 mots, Rey, 1964, 1967). In this Test, a List A of 15 common words related to the country is presented five times in succession interspersed with five (free) recalls. Then List B composed of 15 common words having to do with nature in general (but not with the country in particular) is presented followed by a free recall. Recall of List A is then requested from the subject without prior re-presentation of the list. Thirty minutes later, a free recall of List A is again requested. Françoise's results are more or less one standard deviation lower than those of the population of normal adults. However, the scores obtained in the recall following learning of a concurrent list (i.e., List B) as well as in the delayed recall (30 minutes) indicate that learning is relatively stable.

Françoise was also given a modified version (Gilon, 1988) of the cued recall and selective reminding task of Buschke (1973, 1984). As the procedure in this task is somewhat complex, it will be explained in some detail. The subject is presented with a set of 10 cards displayed according to a 2×5 matrix. On each card, the name of a familiar object, animal, flower, or vegetable is written. The first part of the task consists in encoding the items. The subject is requested to point to and label the items one by one upon verbal presentation of a functional cue by the examiner (e.g., "There is something to drink; show it to me; what is it?"). Part 2 consists in a free recall of the items. Part 3 is a cued recall (the examiner prompts the possibly missing items by reiterating the verbal cue used before; e.g., "There was something to drink; it is . . . "). In part 4, the examiner re-presents the cards with the items that may still be missing and has the subject reencoding these items in the same way as in part 1. The same sequence of free recall, cued recall, and selective reminding, may be repeated three times. If the subject correctly evokes all the items in the free recall, one proceeds directly to a new free recall, until all the items have been correctly recalled twice. Twenty minutes later, the examiner proceeds to a new free recall of the items and, the case being the same, has it followed by a cued recall. Buschke's procedure allows in principle to distinguish between possible encoding and retrieval problems in memory learning. Françoise proved able to recall correctly the 10 items after three trials. In the first free recall, she remembered 7 items and could complete the list on the following cued recall. The delayed recall 20 minutes later showed a perfect remembering of the item list. Control data on the modified version of Buschke's task are available for regular adult DS subjects (13 subjects, males and females, aged 21 to 40 years) and for normal adults (15 subjects, males and females, aged 20 to 40 years) in the report by Gilon (1988). The normal adults remember an average of 9.47 items on the first free recall and receive maximum scores on the second free recall as well as on the delayed free recall (which suggests the existence of a ceiling effect). DS subjects, as a group, remember 5.54 items on the first free recall, up to 6.62 items on the third and the fourth free recalls, and 5.92 items on the delayed free recall. Françoise's performance on the modified version of Buschke's task is clearly better than that of the regular DS adults, and it falls near the normal range of functioning.

Six months later, Françoise was administered the complete cued recall and selective reminding task of Buschke (1984) with 15 items. She could correctly remember 9 items on the first free recall, up to 13 items on the fourth free recall, and 14 items in the delayed free recall, the missing items being retrieved each time in the cued recall. This performance again is close to that of young normal adults according to the experimental reference data available in the Neuropsychology Unit of the University of Liège (Buschke's published work does not itself contain reference data).

As is clear from this data, the difference between Françoise and the normal adults, on the one hand, and Françoise and the regular DS adults, on the other, both concern the encoding and the retrieval of the material to be recalled. The free recalls yielded markedly lower results in the regular DS adults, and the cued recalls proved also less efficient with these subjects. Interestingly, Françoise, as well as the normal adults, made a large spontaneous use of spatial cues in free recall, that is, they took advantage of the way the card items were displayed in front of them during initial presentation, a retrieval strategy apparently completely lacking in the regular DS adults. Whenever cues are available or are supplied by the experimenter, with respect to encoding and/or retrieval of the items, Françoise's episodic memory learning is markedly better than that of regular DS subjects, and it falls short only of the corresponding performance of normal adults.

Another episodic memory-learning task was proposed to Françoise: a paired-associate name/face-learning task designed by Gilon (1988). The test material consists of one standard black-and-white photograph of the faces of each of five adult persons unknown to the test subjects. The procedure is similar to the one employed in traditional paired-associate word learning. A delayed recall is performed 20 minutes after completion of the first part (learning recall) of the test. Françoise correctly associated the five names with the five photographs following the second encoding. She missed two names on the first immediate recall. On the delayed recall (20 minutes), she could correctly associate four names with four photographs. Françoise's performance on this task is slightly better than that of a control group of 10 adult DS subjects (mean number of correct associations on the first immediate recall was 2.69, on the delayed recall, 3.65) and is lower than that of a group of young normal adults (mean number of correct associations on the first immediate recall was 4.80, on the delayed recall, 4.60), according to the data gathered by Gilon (1988).

In summary, Françoise's episodic memory capacity generally appears to be reduced in comparison with normal adults but superior to that of other MR subjects. It varies according to the type of test administered, and therefore depends on the type of task presented. She can recall lists of words related to particular semantic domains, even to levels only slightly lower than those of normal adults when functional semantic cues are provided. But she appears little able to associate pairs of meaningful or meaningless words, and she becomes quickly discouraged in tasks of that sort. Delayed recall (tested up to 30 minutes from what precedes) is no problem for Françoise, indicating correct trace consolidation in longer term memory.

5.8.7.2 Semantic memory

Two tasks were given to Françoise, as well as to three regular DS adults from La Fermette serving as controls (two females, one male; aged 28, 30, and 27 years, respectively, with IQs between 30 and 40 on the WAIS, and standard language abilities for DS persons), to obtain some preliminary indications on their semantic memory capacity and basic organization: a free-word-association task and a lexical prototype task.

Free associations were obtained from Françoise and the three regular DS adults for 54 concrete words common in the French language [e.g., *arbre – tree, bateau – boat, boire – (to) drink, cheval – horse, train – train, voiture – car*]. They were selected among 122 French words for which association norms were available (Lieury, Iff, & Duris, 1976). These norms were established with 297 native French-speaking psychology students from the Paris area. Only for 6 target words did Françoise supply an associated word that was relatively close to the ones currently given by the normal adults. These words were *feuille – leaf* in response to the target word *arbre* (a response given by 7% of the normative sample – the most frequent associate in the normal adults being *forêt – forest*, 10% association), *eau – water* in response to *bateau – boat* (6% normative association – most frequent associate *mer – sea*, 15% association), *football – soccer* (20% normative association – most frequent associate *ballon – ball*, 25% association), *eau – water* in response to *mer – sea* (6% normative association – most frequent associate *bleue – blue*, 10% association), *fruit – fruit* in response to *pomme – apple* (12% normative association – most frequent associate *poire – pear*, 21% association), and *lumière – light* in response to *soleil – sun* (9% normative association – most frequent associate *chaleur – heat*,

12% association). Françoise failed to associate a word to the target stimulus in 7 cases. For the 41 remaining target words, Françoise supplied rare associates, the normative frequency of which varied from 0% (14 items) to 4%. A number of these associations clearly were of the syntagmatic type (e.g., *du bon sens – some good sense* in response to the target word *vouloir – (to) want*, or *par terre – on the ground* in response to the word *jambe – leg*). Corresponding results, but even more discrepant with respect to normative data, were obtained from the three DS adult control subjects. In these subjects, a larger number of rare associative responses than with Françoise (up to 35) – many being of the syntagmatic type – were observed. It is known that a shift from predominantly syntagmatic to predominantly paradigmatic free word associations takes place between approximatively 7 and 10 or 11 years in NR children (the ages varying with the studies and the word classes studied) (see Brown & Berko, 1960; Entwistle, Forsyth, & Muuss, 1964; and Entwistle, 1966; for the French language, see Noizet & Pichevin, 1966, and Pichevin & Noizet, 1968). Various explanations (not mutually exclusive) have been proposed for the observed syntagmatic-paradigmatic shift. According to Brown and Berko (1960) as well as to Erwin (1961), the reasons for the shift are mainly syntactic. It signals the gradual reorganization of semantic memory according to syntactic principles. McNeil (1966) on the contrary suggests a purely semantic explanation for the syntagmatic-paradigmatic shift. According to him, the shift results from the gradual enrichment of word meaning into semantic features. When a given level (not specified) of enrichment in semantic features is reached, the probability for the minimal contrast between two words to take place within the same formal class dramatically increases. Francis (1972) stresses the role of operational development (in particular, the development of the classificatory structures) in the syntagmatic-paradigmatic transition. This transition corresponds to a better organization of the mental lexicon allowed by access to more efficient cognitive operations of comparison and class inclusion. Several studies have assessed the syntagmatic-paradigmatic shift in mildly MR subjects (e.g., Keilman & Moran 1967; Semmel, Barritt, Bennett, & Perfetti, 1968; Seitz, Goulding, & Conrad, 1969). Between 10 and 15 years, the MR subjects supply significantly fewer paradigmatic associative responses than do CA-matched NR peers. However, when the comparisons are made between MA-matched NR and MR subjects, no difference appears in the proportions of paradigmatic associations obtained, which, indeed, seems to attest to the intervention of a general cognitive factor in this development. I do not know of any published study on syntagmatic/paradigmatic associations in moderately and severely MR subjects.

Returning to my data regarding word associations with Françoise and the three DS adult control subjects, it may seem that a syntactic explanation for the syntagmatic and the idiosyncratic character of many of their word associations can be ruled out, at least for Françoise, given her attested grammatical ability. The likely explanation lies in the relative poverty of her lexicon with respect to semantic features and their organization – this relative poverty, perhaps, itself being related to cognitive difficulties in conceptual matters such as concept comparison and class inclusion.

A lexical prototypic task was also given to Françoise as well as to the same three regular DS adult subjects from La Fermette. The task consisted of orally producing, in 1-minute, basic-level words (see later) belonging to a superordinate semantic category identified beforehand. With this type of task, the interpretive assumption is that the composition of the lists of words supplied by the subject tells something nontrivial about the content and the organization of the semantic categories. There are many kinds of lexical relations that can exist between the meanings of different words, including synonymy, antonymy, and hyponymy. The only lexical relation to have received any explicit attention in studies of MR subjects, to the best of my knowledge, is hyponymy, that is, the subordinate-superordinate relationship. From a review of this literature conducted by Barrett and Diniz (1989), it appears that MR subjects sometimes acquire a knowledge of superordinate and subordinate words, although this knowledge is not as advanced as their knowledge of basic-level words (i.e., the most general categories in a categorical hierarchy to contain objects sharing many attributes – Rosch, 1978; e.g., *table, chair, wardrobe*; superordinate category, *furniture*; subordinate categories, e.g., *kitchen table, armchair*). But these matters are far from being fully clear (see Barrett & Diniz, 1989, for a discussion). The studies, however, have used only mildly MR subjects. We have no knowledge on this and related semantic issues as far as moderately and severely MR subjects are concerned. Superordinate semantic categories also are organized "horizontally," that is, in each category, there exist elements that are more representative of the category than others (e.g., *eagles* are better representatives of the category *bird* than *ducks* or *hens*). The former elements are labeled prototypes. According to Rosch and Mervis (1975), prototypes are defined as those items having the most attributes in common with other members of the same category and the fewest attributes in common with members of other categories. In a number of experiments, Rosch and associates (see Rosch, 1975; Rosch, Simpson, & Miller, 1976) have documented a number of psychological characteristics of lexical prototypes, that is, shorter reaction time, earlier acquisition in children, speed of learning, reduced interindividual variation in classification tasks, and most important for what follows, a high positive correlation between order of pronunciation in tasks of lexical production and estimated prototypicality (prototypes corresponding to the lexical items first pronounced in free lists).

Seven semantic categories were proposed to Françoise and to the three regular DS adult subjects: animals, fruits, vegetables, flowers, furniture, clothes, and means of transportation. Expressive norms (i.e., mean frequency values) obtained from 75 native French-speaking NR adults (university students) are available in a study by Dubois (1982). They were used for the purpose of comparison. In the animal category, Françoise produced 14 words in the time allotted (1 minute). Only 8 were truly different (she repeated herself twice and produced 4 diminutive synonyms for 4 words already produced, that is, *âne – ânon* (*donkey – little donkey*), *cochon – porcelet* (*pig – piggy*), *chat – chaton* (*cat – little cat*), and *chien – chiot* (*dog – doggie*). In the fruit category, she produced 12 different words. In the vegetable category, she produced 10 words (9 different words, 1 repetition). In the flower category, she produced 9 words (8 different words, 1 repetition). Françoise produced 13 words in the furniture category (9 different words, 2 repetitions, 2 synonyms). She produced 15 words in the clothes category [10 different words, 1 repetition, 3 synonyms, and 1 "syntagmatic synonym," i.e., *noeud* (*tie*) directly following *cravate* (necktie) in the sequence]. Finally, in the means-of-transportation category, Françoise produced 12 words (9 different words, 3 synonyms). All the words produced, it is to be noted, belong to the requested superordinate semantic categories. However, when it comes to the assumed relation between the first words produced per category and the prototypic nature of these words for the category, things are different. The first words produced by Françoise for each category and, more generally, the sequential order in which she pronounced her words within each category do not correspond to the frequency norms supplied by Dubois (1982). Similar data were obtained with the three DS adult controls. These subjects, however, produced fewer basic-level words than did Françoise in most superordinate semantic categories. This was particularly true for one of the two female subjects, who supplied only 3, 3, 5, 4, 6, 3, and 2 items, in 1 minute, for the categories animals, fruits, vegetables, flowers, furniture, clothes, and means of transportation, respectively.

Summarizing Françoise's semantic organization, it would appear that she can produce a number of lexical forms apparently correctly classified into major usual semantic categories. This, of course, does not mean that her lexical forms are always comparable to those of normal adults in terms of extension and intension. Actually, the indications obtained through the administration of lexical tests (see Section 5.4.2) point to the existence of differences between Françoise's lexicon and that of NR adults in these respects. The results of the semantic tasks described in this section seem to go in the same direction. Françoise's free word associations are largely idiosyncratic. A major proportion of these associations are of the syntagmatic type, which may attest to a relative poverty of a number of lexical domains defined in semantic features. Also, there is no clear indication that Françoise's superordinate categories are organized along lines similar to those of NR adults, especially in terms of the particular representativeness of some items within the categories (i.e., prototypicality) – assuming, of course, that the tasks employed are valid indicators of this organization, particularly with MR subjects. Françoise seems to have no particular problem with the production of lexical items (as "significants"), but she has difficulties with the exact meaning of some words and their mental organization – difficulties that are commensurate with her general level of cognitive development, as corresponding observations from regular DS adults indicate.

5.8.7.3 Working memory

In assessing Françoise's working memory as well as the working memory capacity and processes of a number of other DS subjects, used as controls, I have relied mainly on Baddeley's model of working memory (e.g., Baddeley, 1990). This model together with some complementary and alternative indications is comprehensively presented in Section 6.5.2.

5.8.7.3.1 Auditory-verbal short-term memory

The first component of working memory to be assessed in Baddeley's model is the so-called *phonological loop*. This component is made of two subsidiary systems: a *phonological store* and an *articulatory control process* based on inner speech. The Immediate-Memory-For-Digits Subtest of the WAIS gave us an indication of Françoise's phonological store capacity, as already indicated. She can repeat up to four digits in the correct or in the reverse order. This result locates her approximatively two standard deviations below the estimated normal population mean. Control data obtained with a group of 31 young DS adults from La Fermette, using the Immediate-Memory-For-Digits Subtest of the WAIS, show that none of them, but one, has a span for digits in excess of two (some cannot even repeat sequences of two digits; when presented with such sequences, they repeat only one digit, usually the last one). A few individuals attempt repeating sequences of three and four digits. They sometimes correctly recall the digits but not the order. The one DS adult subject with a four-digit span turns out to have a level of language development (both productively and receptively) that is standard for a DS individual, except for articulation, which is better than that in other regular DS subjects. It is likely that the digit span does not evolve much in DS subjects between 8 years or so and adulthood, as further data collected with a group of younger DS individuals tend to indicate. Twenty-seven DS children and adolescents (boys and girls, aged between 8 and 16 years, with IQs between 32 and 76) were given the Intelligence Test of Terman-Merrill, Form L (French adaptation by Cesselin, 1968), as part of the assessment of intellectual functions routinely performed by the Early Intervention Team of the APEM (Association de Parents d'Enfants Mongoliens, based in Verviers, a town near Liège). Only three subjects (among those with the highest IQs except in one case) exhibited a digit span of three items. The other subjects were limited to spans of two items.

To test Françoise's auditory-verbal short-term memory (AV-STM) further, she was given six series of 12 unrelated common words (2–3 syllables long) to recall freely and immediately, series by series. The first condition was oral presentation at a rate of one word every 2 seconds. The second condition was visual presentation of the words individually written on (12 × 7)-cm cardboards, also at a rate of one word every 2 seconds. Françoise was given 1½ minutes following list presentation to recall the words listed. She recalled between 3 and 5 items per list in the auditorily presented lists and between 2 and 5 items in the visually presented ones. Virtually no items from the first half of the series of words were recalled (i.e., no prerecency effect was demonstrated). In the two conditions, she regularly recalled the last 2 or 3 words of the lists, demonstrating the well-known (short-term) recency effect considered to represent the immediate output of those items currently held in STM to which appropriate retrieval strategies are applied (Baddeley, 1990).

Consider the functioning of Françoise's phonological loop in more detail now. In Baddeley's model (1990), the phonological store is considered to be based on a phonological code. Hence, items having similar codes will be more difficult to recall immediately in the correct order than will items that are dissimilar in sound or in articulatory characteristics. This is the phonological (or acoustic) similarity effect. Its presence attests to the phonological nature of the AV-STM. Françoise was requested to serially recall lists of items composed from two to seven letters (in increasing order) taken from the alphabet, either presented auditorily or visually [written in capital letters on individual cards (5 × 10)-cm]. Rate of presentation was one letter per second (read by the examiner) in the auditory modality, and one letter every 2 seconds in the visual modality. Some of the lists were made of auditorily dissimilar (distant) phonemes (e.g., K-R; R-K-M);[14] other lists were made of auditorily close phonemes (e.g., B-V; G-T-D) or visually dissimilar graphemes (e.g., A-X; R-X-O); yet other lists were made of visually close graphemes (e.g., E-H; F-H-L). The order of presentation of the letters had to be respected in the recall. Testing was discontinued whenever Françoise missed all the five items in a given list. The same lists – in the auditory modality only – were presented to three DS adult control subjects from La Fermette with standard language abilities for DS persons (the same subjects as in Section 5.8.7.2 on semantic memory). No visual modality presentation was possible with these subjects since they (as well as the other DS adults from La Fermette) are not able to read or identify letters.

The existence of a phonological similarity effect can be demonstrated in Françoise for the auditory and the visual modalities. As a rule, phonologically similar material leads to lower levels of recall with her (in the auditory modality, she correctly recalls five series of three phonologically dissimilar letters, and three of four letters; three series of three phonologically close letters, and none of four; in the visual modality, she correctly recalls four series of three graphically dissimilar letters, four of four letters, and none of five letters; two series of three graphically close letters, two series of four letters, and none of five letters). Although being present, the difference in processing between phonologically similar and phonologically dissimilar material is not large, probably due to the fact that the proposed tasks lack sensitivity in the case of Françoise, since she is not able to recall much of the longer series. The three regular DS adult control subjects could recall little of the series of letters presented in the auditory modality, and they showed no difference between phonologically close and phonologically dissimilar material.

Corresponding results were obtained for Françoise with meaningful monosyllabic words instead of letters. Phonologically similar words led to lower levels of recall (in the auditory modality, she correctly recalled five series of two phonologically dissimilar words, four series of three words, and none of four; five series of two phonologically close words, one of three words, and none of four; in the visual modality, she correctly recalled five series of two graphically dissimilar words, four series of three words, three of four, and none of five; five series of two graphically close words, four series of three words, and none of four).

An important determinant of immediate memory span is the spoken duration of the words (see Section 6.5.2 for more detail). Since memory span for words is inversely related to their spoken duration, the span for shorter words (i.e., words containing fewer syllables) should be larger than that for longer words. Conversely, the existence of a word-length effect implies some form of subvocal rehearsal. Françoise was presented with lists of (meaningful) words in increasing number (from two to eight), which she was requested to recall immediately in the exact form and in the correct order. Testing was discontinued when she missed all the series (i.e., five) in a given list of words. Two sets of lists were prepared (one containing shorter words, i.e., words made of one or two syllables, and one with longer words, i.e., words containing three to five syllables) in each one of two modalities, auditory and visual [words written in standard typewritten characters with no capital letters on individual cards (5×10)-cm]. The rate of presentation was one word every second (read by the examiner) in the auditory modality, and one word every two seconds in the visual modality. The words were the same in the auditory and in the visual presentation, but they were grouped and ordered differently to minimize the possibility of a learning effect from one part of the assessment to the other. The shorter and longer words were matched for frequency of use in the language according to the frequency tables compiled by Gougenheim et al. (1964) for the French language. The same tasks were also administered to the three DS adult control subjects from La Fermette already identified, but only in the auditory modality. Françoise demonstrated a word-length effect in her immediate recall performance. In the auditory modality, she was able to recall correctly the five series of three shorter words, but only two series of two longer words. In the visual modality, overall performance was slightly depressed (perhaps due to Françoise's relative slowness in reading), but the same trend appears in the results. She can correctly recall four series of three shorter words, but only two series of two longer words. Regarding the three DS adult control subjects tested, one subject was unable to recall more than one of the series of two shorter words and even of the series of longer words; one other subject could recall correctly two series of two shorter words but none of the series of three shorter words (she could not recall correctly any of the series of longer words); the third subject correctly recalled the five series of two and three shorter words, and four series of two longer words. Despite the relative lack of sensitivity of this task for a subject such as Françoise (she does not go beyond series of three words, even with short words), the results suggest that subvocal rehearsal is used in her processing of auditorily presented words. Results also indicate that her articulatory control process is capable of converting written material into a phonological code and registering it in the phonological store, since the word-length effect was also observed in the visual modality.

Actually, Françoise's behavior during testing already clearly attested to the existence of spontaneous and active rehearsal. She would usually rehearse in whispers, and sometimes mezza voce, during the time between the end of stimulus presentation and the beginning of her out-loud response. Even when asked to do the task silently, she could not refrain completely from whispering. Her whispering activity obviously is directly related to the immediately passed stimulus and to the incoming response. Nothing of the kind was observed with the three regular DS adult subjects. They showed no evidence of "external" rehearsal in the way Françoise did or in any other way. If one applies Vygotsky's developmental sketch of inner speech, he would say that Françoise has developed a form of private speech that seems to have the major functional and formal properties of inner speech (i.e., simplified morpho-syntax, condensation, and lexical reduction; see Vygotsky, 1929/1962), but not (quite) the mechanical characteristics (i.e., marked reduction or removal of peripheral muscular activity). The latter is a relatively late achievement in (normal) child development [rough estimates may be 7 years for a barely detectable voice level when rehearsing, 10 years, and often later, for completely internalized, i.e., really covert private speech (Flavell, Beach, & Chinsky, 1966) – although even in those cases, most subjects including adults usually exhibit some latent "speech" activity in the articulatory and lower face muscles that can be detected through the use of finer observational techniques, such as electromyography; see Sokolov, 1972; Rondal, 1976]. Similarly, in the visual modality, Françoise apparently felt compelled to read mezza voce. She resisted all suggestions to read "purely" visually.

Having established the existence and use of subvocal (vocal) rehearsal in Françoise during memory activities, we proceeded to articulatory suppression. It could be assumed that the operation of the phonological loop would be disturbed if articulation of irrelevant items is required during the execution of a memory task. Actually, in normal subjects, forgetting will occur only if the memory task is rendered sufficiently difficult (e.g., when longer delays take place between stimulus presentation and recall) or if the interfering task is sufficiently demanding in terms of attentional resources (e.g., suppressed articulation by continuously uttering the word "the" and expressions such as "bla bla bla," or repeating digits usually causes no or only little forgetting; similarly, finger tapping even at a sustained rate does not affect short-term memorizing; but counting backward in threes usually does to a marked extent) (Baddeley, Lewis, & Vallar, 1984). The controlling attentional system that supervises the two working memory subsidiary systems (i.e., the phonological loop and the visuospatial sketch pad; see later) in Baddeley's model (1990) is called the *central executive* (see Section 6.5.2).

A version of the Brown-Peterson task (J. Brown, 1958; Peterson & Peterson, 1959; Van der Linden, 1989) was used with Françoise. She was presented with (5 × 10)-cm cards on which were printed trigrams of consonants (e.g., M Q C) randomly chosen from a stock of visually dissimilar and monosyllabically sounding French consonants. As an additional precaution, no selected trigram could be readily associated with a well-known acronym. Françoise was requested to read the three consonants on the trigram in a loud voice. Then the card bearing the trigram was withdrawn, and she was invited to concentrate on retaining the trigram for a specified amount of time (0, 5, 10, or 20 seconds) without repeating it orally. This was followed by an ordinary recall of the trigram in the correct order. This condition is known as the "empty interval" condition, since there is no interfering task set between stimulus presentation and recall. There was another condition, called the "full interval" condition, in which Françoise was requested to repeat, in the reverse order, series of two digits orally supplied by the examiner, during the interval of time between stimulus presentation and recall. Time interval varied from 2, 5, 10, to 20 seconds. The rate of presentation by the examiner of the digits to be repeated in the interfering task was one digit per second. In a variant of this task also executed, Françoise was requested to finger tap on the table at a rate of approximatively one tap per second (instead of repeating pairs of digits) during the interval of time between stimulus presentation and recall.

In the empty interval condition, Françoise correctly reproduced 16 trigrams of consonants out of 24 (66% correct performance). The errors were evenly spread over the task, did not present particular characteristics in terms of their nature, and equally concerned the four intervals of time between stimulus presentation and overt recall. Despite the explicit instruction not to repeat the trigrams orally during the interval following stimulus presentation, Françoise was continuously observed moving her lips, clearly silently articulating the consonants presented. In the full interval condition with reverse repetition of pairs of digits, Françoise was able to recall correctly only 4 trigrams out of 24 (17% correct performance). The number of incorrect recalls increased with the duration of the interval: 3 errors after 2-second intervals, 5 errors after 5-second intervals, and 6 errors (i.e., maximum ratio) after either 10- or 20-second intervals. Inversions of pairs of digits were correctly done, except on one occasion, the fourth pair in a 20-second interval of time between stimulus presentation and overt recall. Françoise's strategies for coping with the Brown-Peterson task are worth reporting. She was repeating the pairs of digits, sotto voce, in the direct order, then in the reverse order, before producing them out loud. Also, before overtly recalling the trigrams, she would try them sotto voce. In the full interval condition with finger tapping, Françoise correctly recalled 6 trigrams in 12 before refusing to go on with the task, protesting that it was too difficult. Before deciding to stop, she demonstrated some reluctance to apply the instruction strictly, slowing down or trying to avoid finger tapping altogether. Clearly, articulatory suppression disturbed the operation of Françoise's phonological loop, which, in a reverse way, confirms the functional value of her articulatory loop. However, these results also indicate the existence of drastic limitations in Françoise's controlling attentional system, that is, the central executive component of working memory, since Brown-Peterson's types of task are considered to supply a (gross) assessment of the functional capacity of this component.

Françoise was also given a modified version (Vallar, Papagno, & Baddeley, 1991) of a paradigm originally devised by Baddeley and Hitch (1977) to investigate long-term recency phenomena. This is an incidental memory task. She was presented with a list of 16 five-letter anagrams, preceded by 1 practice item. Each anagram was written in uppercase letters on a (12 × 7)-cm piece of cardboard. The instruction was to find a real word from each five-letter string, being allowed a maximum of 60 seconds for each anagram. In case of failure, the solution was auditorily provided by the examiner. Each anagram was followed by a paper-and-pencil arithmetic task, requiring the addition of two 2-digit numbers (e.g., 28 + 19), which were written in a column. Following the last addition (after the 16th anagram), the (delayed) free recall of all the solutions – both those proposed by the subject and those (possibly) supplied by the examiner – was requested. Françoise was not informed in advance that there would be a final recall of the anagrams. In this paradigm, STM components are considered likely to be suppressed by the interpolated arithmetic task (Vallar et al., 1991). Françoise was fully accurate in the arithmetic task. She could also solve the 16 anagrams proposed (confirming her ability in activities of the kind, e.g., the "Scrabble game," as independently reported by her father). She recalled 8 of the 16 items, 3 from the first half of the series (prerecency effect) and 5 from the second half, including the last 2 items (recency effect). Comparative data for 14 normal adults (Italian-speaking) are provided by Vallar et al. (1991). The average total recall score of control subjects was 4.50 (range 3–7). The prerecency and recency average recall scores was 1.15 (range 0–4) and 3.35 (range 2–5), respectively. Françoise's excellent ability in solving anagrams is another indication of the correct functioning of her phonological STM store.[15] The activity, consisting of constructing a word from a series of letters, requires segmentation and combination (and recombination) of individual letters until a meaningful word is built up. The processes may require temporary storage in phonological memory, as suggested by Vallar et al. (1991). Françoise's recall performance (actually superior to the one of Vallar et al.'s normal subjects) and the long-term recency effect that she demonstrated probably represent the unimpaired involvement of long-term memory components as well as the use of appropriate retrieval procedures.

In conclusion, it would seem that although Françoise's immediate span for isolated items is markedly reduced in comparison with normal subjects – which significantly hampers her in learning lists and the like, particularly if the material to recall is meaningless – the functioning of her phonological loop is basically normal, with correct phonological coding as attested to by the presence of the phonological similarity effect and correct operation of the articulatory control process as indicated by the demonstration of the word-length effect and the articulatory suppression effect. Additionally, since her overt speech rate is normal (see Section 6.5.2 for the report of a specific measurement on this point), it may be hypothesized that her rehearsal rate is not too unlike the normal rate with the proviso that as her spontaneous "inner" speech appears to be dependent on peripheral muscular activity, this rehearsal rate must be somewhat slower than that of mature normal people, equipped with "true" inner speech or completely centralized motor programs. Françoise is also able to phonologically transcode verbal-visual information, registering it in her phonological store. Her phonological loop also appears to function basically correctly in this respect despite seemingly functional limitations probably due to her insufficient automatization of the reading activity. In a nutshell, and perhaps a bit schematically, Françoise's AV-STM appears to be limited in scope but normally functioning in its major component processes. There is no guarantee that the same is true for other moderately and severely MR subjects. Our limited control data on regular DS adults seem to suggest that besides drastically reduced spans, these subjects present phonological loops that are little used and probably inefficient for several (at least partially related) reasons (e.g., imprecision of the phonological stock, slowness of speech and rehearsal rates). As these subjects did not know the correspondence between graphemes and phonemes, it was not possible to assess the functional character of their articulatory loop in terms of transcoding from the written to the phonological code followed by phonological short-term storing. Other data reported and discussed in Section 6.5.2 concerning other regular moderately and severely MR subjects also implicate low speech and rehearsal rates in the limited STM capacity of these subjects. However, Françoise's drastically limited attentional resources at the level of the central executive component of working memory, as attested to by her performance on the Brown-Peterson task, should be stressed. Finally, Françoise's demonstrated astonishing ability in anagram construction suggests appropriate long-term memory functioning and retrieval in this respect.

5.8.7.3.2 Visuospatial short-term memory

The second major component of Baddeley's model of working memory is the visuospatial sketch pad (Baddeley, 1990). This system is assumed to be responsible for setting up and manipulating visuospatial images. Current data and discussions suggest separate (and interacting) visual and spatial components of imagery (with different anatomical locations within the brain). But I did not attempt to separate them here. In order to assess her visuospatial (VS-)STM span, Françoise was given the Block-Tapping Test (Smirni, Villardita, & Zappalia, 1983), in which blocks displayed in front of the subject are hit in a given sequence to be reproduced immediately following demonstration. Françoise demonstrated a span of four. This is surpassed by 92% of the normal population according to reference data supplied by Smirni et al. (1983).

Françoise was also administered the Delayed Recognition Span Test (DRST) adapted from Moss, Albert, Butters, and Payne (1986) by Gilon (1988). The material of the test is composed of a board (46×61 cm) with five rows including six squares, marked 9 cm apart, in each row, 25 white game pieces 6 cm high, 25 colored game pieces of the same height, and 25 game pieces of similar dimensions with each one supporting a black-and-white photograph of an unfamiliar human face (the faces only varied in their physical characters – no glasses, etc.). The subject is first invited to watch the examiner setting one white game piece on a given location of the board (observation time 10 seconds). The board is then removed from the subject's sight and a second white piece is added. The subject is shown the board (observation time again 10 seconds) and verbally requested to point to the newly disposed piece. A third game piece is added out of sight of the subject, who is then shown the board again and requested to point to the new element, and so on. The same basic procedure is used with the colored game pieces and with the face pieces later on. As this description indicates, DRST is a visuospatial recognition task that does not evaluate the order component in the subjects' responses (since they are not requested to specify the order in which the pieces are set).

In the first part of the test (white game pieces), Françoise was credited with a span of 5.20. This is close to the mean span computed by Gilon (1988) in the same task with a group of 12 normally developing children (7 females, 5 males, aged 3 to 8 years, mean age 5 years and 5 months), that is, 5.17, but markedly lower than the estimated average span of a group of 15 normal adults (8 females, 7 males, aged 20 to 40 years), which is 12.08. Gilon's report (1988) also supplies data obtained in the same task with a group of 28 regular DS adults (12 females, 16 males, aged 21 to 40 years). Their mean span is 3.86. In the second part of the DRST (colored game pieces), Françoise was attributed a span of 6.40 (vs. 6.77 for the normally developing children, 10.07 for the normal adults, and 2.83 for the regular DS adults). Finally, in the third part of the test (face pieces), Françoise received a span of 6.60 (vs. 6.00 for the normally developing children, 15.63 for the normal adults, and 2.99 for the regular DS adults). On these three tasks, Françoise very likely could have done better if it were not for her relative slowness in visually sampling and analyzing the positions of the pieces on the board. Particularly when the board was covered with more than 7 or 8 game pieces, she needed more than the 10 seconds allowed to analyze the situation fully.

Although Françoise's performance on the DRST is by no means comparable to those of normal adults, she functions markedly better than the regular DS adult subjects. The differences between Françoise and this control group increase from task 1 to task 3, that is, with the addition of color and faces. These elements may serve as additional cues in the recognition situation to the extent that they are properly used, which does not seem to be the case with the regular DS adult subjects. These subjects, as their scores indicate, are more confused than helped by the increased discriminability of the stimuli.

Another visual recognition task (borrowed from Defleur, 1989) was given to Françoise. In this task, one picture of a familiar object (e.g., pencil, trousers, fork) is presented every 2 seconds and then hidden from the subject's sight. Series containing from 2 to 6 pictures were prepared. Following presentation of the series, the subject is requested to identify the pictures previously seen, *in the exact order of presentation*, in a display of 12 containing the ones presented. Françoise could correctly recall the five series of 2 pictures and three of the five series of 3 pictures in the exact order. She could not recall exactly the order of the series of 4 items, but the identification of the items previously seen was properly done. Beyond 4 items (i.e., the series containing 5 and 6 pictures), neither the order nor the identification of the items were correct. The normal adults (13 subjects between 20 to 50 years of age) studied by Defleur (1989) obtained a mean span of 4.75. Françoise's VS-STM span in this task is markedly lower than the one obtained in the DRST, presented before, probably because of the additional necessity to retain in memory not only the identity of the pictures, but also their exact order of presentation.

Françoise was also administered the visual reproduction task from the "Clinical Scale" of Wechsler (Wechsler, 1974). In this paper-and-pencil task, the subject is requested to reproduce three relatively simple abstract drawings from immediate memory after a 10-second exposure for each drawing. Françoise's global score on this task was 4. This locates her in the very low portion of the normal adult distribution on this test, as the population mean is estimated to be 11.42, SD 2.76.

In conclusion, Françoise presents a VS-STM span and functioning compatible with what is demonstrated by younger normally developing children around 5 years of age. Although being shorter than that of normal adults, Françoise's visuospatial span is longer than those of other (regular) DS adult subjects. She also proved capable of integrating the additional cues made available to her by the examiner into her immediate visuospatial memory activity and to use these cues to improve her recognition performance – a capacity lacking in regular DS adult subjects, who, on the contrary, appear to be hampered when additional visual cues are supplied. Only a superficial analysis of VS-STM processes was possible here because of a relative lack of specification of these processes in Baddeley's working memory model,[16] as well as in the current relevant literature. As assessed, Françoise's VS-STM seems to have a capacity of approximately three items (in order), which is slightly less than her AV-STM (i.e., four items in order). In that, she conforms to the normal pattern (in direction, at least, if not in magnitude), as has been documented for some time in normal adults, that immediate memory span is larger for auditory than for visual input (the so-called modality effect; see Section 6.5.2). Regular DS subjects have been reported not to present the same modality pattern, having either similarly reduced AV- and VS-STM spans or VS-STM spans that are actually larger than their AV-STM spans (Marcell & Armstrong, 1982; Marcell & Weeks, 1988). According to

Marcell and Weeks' report (1988), non-DS MR subjects, on the contrary, exhibit a reliable modality effect (in the same sense as do NR subjects, albeit inferior in magnitude due to lower auditory scores).

Notes

1. Actually, Halliday's system encompasses one additional category: "beyond the clause" (i.e., metaphorical modes of expression). It was left out of the analysis as no (true) expressive metaphorical capacity was demonstrated in Françoise's conversational data (no evaluation of potential receptive metaphorical ability was undertaken).
2. What follows actually concerns major clauses. So-called minor clauses are clauses without mood (see later in text). They have no thematic structure either. They typically function as calls, greetings, and exclamations (e.g., *Good morning, Well done*). Minor clauses are not always distinguishable from elliptical clauses (see later in text).
3. This statement should be specified, however. According to Hagège (1985), epithets following things tend to have purely relational meanings. In the preceding example, *un homme grand*, the man is said to be *tall* as a man (he may still be short if the standards were those of the species brontosaurus). Epithets preceding things may qualify in a less or nonrelational way, (*un grand homme* is not necessarily *un homme grand – a tall man*; in the same way, *un sale type – a morally very dubious person –* is not necessarily *un type sale*, i.e., *a person who is physically dirty*; or *un heureux poète – a happy poet*, i.e., someone who skillfully writes poetry, may actually be a very unhappy person).
4. It should be added that groups and phrases can form complexes in the same way as words and clauses do (see later in text). Only elements having the same function can be linked in this way. The interdependency realized by the linkage is of the same paratactic or hypotactic type as for the clauses (see later in text).
5. Non-WH-exclamatives have the same grammatical structure as corresponding declaratives (the only difference having to do with intonation). In what follows, no attempt was made to sort out true exclamatives from regular declaratives, since this distinction is of little interest in the context of the present work.
6. Some beginning "awareness" of language constraints, formal regularities, and/or mechanisms is, of course, possible in the younger child and has been observed (e.g., Slobin, 1978; for a review of what he calls epilinguistic awareness, i.e., early or premetalinguistic awareness, see Gombert, 1990).
7. This statement, of course, is a massive oversimplification. There are many theoretical sketches or models of language parsing and interpretation in existence today, some of them postulating the possibility of the parser employing as many resources as possible, grammar being only one of them and in many cases constituting only a "minimal power" (see, e.g., Johnson-Laird, 1983, from whom the latter expression is borrowed). Among the prominent advocates of the similarity hypothesis regarding the basic processes involved in language production and perception (except, of course, that they do not apply in the same "direction"), one may quote Chomsky (e.g., 1968, 1987) and Winograd (1983).
8. The French verb *apercevoir* is punctual, whereas its English counterpart *see* is not.
9. Unlike its English counterpart, the French pronoun *qui* (*who*) may have an animate or an inanimate noun as its coreferent.
10. Change of grammatical role in itself should be no major problem for Françoise, as suggested by her mostly correct interpretation of passive sentences.

11. The use of the verb *faire* (*to do*) in the interpretive requests may be questioned, since all the main clauses are not actional-factitive ones. However, it did not cause any problems in the experimental task, probably given the somewhat "flexible" denotative meaning of this verb.

12. From a theoretical point of view, it is clear, however, that attentional and structural factors are both relevant to the production of dichotic laterality effects (Bryden, 1988).

13. The two terms, *operatory* (e.g., Piaget & Inhelder, 1969) and *operational* (e.g., Flavell, 1963), are used interchangeably in the English-speaking literature as translations for the French adjective *opératoire*.

14. To the English-speaking reader: Please recall that the testing was conducted in French; therefore, auditory phonological distance or proximity was judged according to French standards.

15. It is interesting to contrast Françoise's phonological ability with anagrams to her limited phonological awareness, as documented in Section 5.5. The implication is that Françoise's ability in anagram construction does not involve much awareness at the purely phonological level. In the same way, a comparison of Françoise's capacity for anagrams with her apparent organizational limitations in semantic memory suggests that the former mostly is a formal skill.

16. According to Baddeley (1990), there are reasons to believe that the visuospatial sketch pad is organized along lines corresponding to those of the phonological loop, but he acknowledges that, at the present time, the exact processes of the former subsystem are less well documented.

6   Theoretical discussion

As reviewed in Chapter 3, there is a small number of documented cases of mentally handicapped individuals with exceptional language capacities despite otherwise severe cognitive limitations. The case of Françoise is particularly striking among these cases, and so far it is undoubtedly one of the most thoroughly studied. This case, as do the others, begs for an explanation. How is such a state of affairs possible? Before trying to approach this difficult question, let me review the extent to which linguistic development of the type exhibited by Françoise is truly exceptional in comparison with other (typical) mentally handicapped persons.

6.1 Exceptional and nonexceptional language development in mental handicap

As I have demonstrated in what precedes, Françoise's nonlinguistic cognitive abilities in general are only moderately better than what is known of most Down syndrome persons. Her performance IQ on the WAIS is 60 (64 at the second administration), and she is credited with a nonverbal MA of 5 years and 8 months on the EDEI scale. This performance IQ is higher than the reported mode of 45–50 for the typical trisomy 21 DS population (Moor, 1967; Gibson, 1981). However, her nonverbal MA is almost compatible with the average MA of the DS population, which is about 5 years (again according to Gibson, 1981). Although cursorily presented as nonverbal, the performance section of the Wechsler Scales actually is saturated with speech (e.g., the instructions in each subtest are given verbally), which, of course, may favor those subjects with a good receptive command of the language. This may account, at least partially, for the difference between Françoise's nonverbal IQ and the population modal IQ for typical trisomy 21 DS. Most noticeable are Françoise's limitations in general intellectual and operational functioning, general information and knowledge, computational capacity, and visuographic ability. Her immediate memory spans are limited, as are her attentional resources and episodic memory capacity.

Françoise's reading and writing abilities may be considered to be superior to that usually exhibited by DS persons. She seems to have benefitted from the early training that she received in this respect, at a time when most educators and parents believed that such training was useless for DS children and that written (if not oral) language was beyond their capacities. However, compared with the written language achievements of DS children educated today, Françoise's level is probably still above average. It is difficult to be more specific in the absence of available large-scale reports on written language development in DS children and adolescents (see Buckley, 1985, and Buckley & Bird, 1993, however) and the exact efficacy of educational and remedial procedures applied to these subjects nowadays (see Snyder-McLean & McLean, 1987). In any case, it seems clear that Françoise's achievements in this respect remain moderate in absolute value, particularly compared with her significant oral language ability. Her capacities in reading, writing, and text comprehension are far from being normal or quasi-normal. As for text writing, she does not appear to quite measure up to the exceptional case documented by Seagoe (1965), although comparison is difficult given the sketchy nature of Seagoe's report.

In contrast, Françoise's oral language is truly exceptional for a DS person, at least in some (important) respects. Her phonological ability and her receptive as well as her productive grammatical abilities are extremely developed, as I have shown, to the point of being normal or near normal, as far as it is possible to tell and as far as the notion of language normality – or for that matter grammatical normality – has a specifiable intension. Françoise's truly remarkable phonological and grammatical capacities are in sharp contrast with what is known of the same capacities in typical moderately and severely MR persons, including DS subjects. The incidence of speech deficits in moderately and severely MR people is close to 95% (Schlanger & Gottsleben, 1957). It varies moderately depending on the specific criteria used and the particular groups tested (see Rondal, 1975b). The DS population is particularly prone to disordered phonology (Schlanger & Gottsleben, 1957; Zisk & Bialer, 1967). DS subjects usually exhibit more numerous and variable articulation errors than do MA-matched MR subjects of other etiologies (Rondal, Lambert, & Sohier, 1980). Grammatical development is also markedly reduced in moderately and severely MR subjects, including DS persons (see Chapter 2; also Rondal, 1985a, 1988a, 1988b, for reviews of this abundant literature).

Françoise's lexical and pragmatic abilities are much less impressive. Her productive and receptive lexical abilities, although evaluated as being below average or weak according to general psychometric standards, are still above average for a DS person, but clearly only moderately so compared with her phonology and morphosyntax. Considering pragmatic functioning, it is difficult to make a general statement, for the elements entering into the field of pragmatics are diverse. The basic cooperative and purposeful aspects of the speech exchange are not problems for Françoise. When it comes to planning and sequentially organizing a series of "paragraphs" into a whole text (textual cohesion), however, she exhibits signs of processing difficulties. Her pragmatic functioning, although being better than that of typical moderately and severely MR individuals (who, as a rule, are markedly limited in terms of discursive ability; see Chapter 2; also Rondal & Lambert, 1983), remains below average in comparison with the general population, but it is hard to tell exactly to what extent because of the lack of general performance standards in this arena. What kind of explanation is one to propose for Françoise's exceptional phonological and grammatical abilities?

6.2 Rejecting a simple teaching-learning explanation

As indicated before, a severe language delay (with almost complete lack of productive speech) is attested to in Françoise until 4½ years after birth (parental information and first report from the Speech Clinic of the University of Liège). But by the time she was 8 years old, Françoise seemed to have a well-developed language. At 8 years or so, her language is globally described by her teachers and speech therapists as advanced and as being markedly more developed than is usually the case with DS and other moderately and severely mentally handicapped children. Unfortunately, no systematic investigation of Françoise's language was made at the time. It is therefore quite possible that she continued to make language progress between 8 years and the time when we started to study her (she was 32 years old at the beginning of the study). But from what we know, it is likely that her phonological and grammatical functioning before puberty were about what they were when we started studying the case.

A first general explanatory hypothesis one could propose is gradual learning, between approximately 5 and at least, say, 10 years of age, of the basic and advanced structures of French, prompted by Françoise's speech pathologists, schoolteachers, and parents. According to such a hypothesis, Françoise as well as the other exceptional cases of language development reported in the mental retardation literature would be subjects exposed to highly efficient language remediation programs who responded most appropriately to such programs. This explanatory hypothesis must be rejected for the following reasons.

It is not known whether remediation programs applied to moderately and severely MR children have met with outstanding success in teaching phonology and grammar. At the end of a thorough review of the literature on intervention for children with severe language and communication disorders, noted specialists such as Snyder-McLean and McLean (1987) acknowledged that language intervention can be moderately effective in modifying the impact and the course of those disorders, but that it remains fairly difficult to go beyond this global conclusion because there are so many unresolved methodological and evaluative problems in remediation work and because few of the published intervention studies provide data regarding the maintenance and/or the generalization of treatment effects to real-world communicative contents in which purportedly acquired skills must ultimately be used (for corresponding opinions, see Cunningham, 1983, 1990; Guralnick & Bricker, 1987; Price, 1989; and Hauser-Cram, 1989). In the case of Françoise, the logopedic intervention took place more than 25 years ago, when few specifics were known on the psychology of DS,[1] on developmental language disorders, and on the early intervention techniques applicable in such cases. From the information that we were able to obtain, the educative intervention concerning Françoise, although remarkable for the time, did not contain anything special. In the case of Paul, the DS person whose written language was studied by Seagoe (1965), any systematic intervention that could have taken place (Seagoe's report is silent on this point) would have occurred at least 60 years ago. Curtiss (1988 and elsewhere) and Yamada (1990), as well as Bellugi et al. (1988) do not report information on the possible language intervention conducted with their exceptional subjects. It would seem that none of these subjects had any language intervention before they were studied.

Even assuming, just for the sake of the discussion, that language intervention can to some degree teach advanced phonology and grammar, it would still need to be explained how and why the cases reviewed and analyzed in this book are exceptional. If teaching-learning were a valid explanation for these cases, there ought to be thousands of exceptional cases of language development in the mental retardation population, as numerous MR children are now receiving systematic language remediation on an early intervention basis in the developed countries (see Guralnick & Bennett, 1987, for a large-scale review of these intervention programs). Clearly, this is not the prevailing situation. At best, it could be considered that the learning experience[2] may be fully effective with some (unfortunately rare) children because these children are exceptional among their MR peers to begin with.

This conclusion should come as no surprise given the fact that no learning or teaching-learning theory of language acquisition has succeeded so far. As it is known, the conditioning theories of language learning (e.g., Skinner, 1957; Staats, 1968, 1971a, 1971b, 1975, 1976) have largely failed in their attempts to "explain" language functioning and development. The inadequacy of these theories was clearly exposed by Chomsky in his deadly attack against Skinner's formulations (Chomsky, 1957b). Chomsky's criticisms were directed to Skinner's proposals, but they apply equally to Staats's more elaborated but basically similar theoretical suggestions. Bandura (e.g., 1976; also see I. Brown, 1979) proposed that language acquisition was but a particular case of observational learning. This approach acknowledges that language differs from other forms of human behavior but only in degree of complexity. Bandura and followers claim that "abstract modeling" may account for the learning of intricate sets of rule-governed "behaviors" like those incorporated into language systems. Abstract modeling is a paradigm in which subjects observe models and perform different behaviors embodying the same principles or rules. Observers must discern the common features in seemingly diverse behaviors to formulate an abstract rule for generating new behaviors (the properties of the rules, and how they are discerned, are not described or explained, however). After learning, an observer's behavior may be unique in that he may exhibit particular behaviors that were not demonstrated by the model but that are governed by the same or similar rules (i.e., rule generalization). In my opinion, this theory has yielded no interesting product either. It is reminiscent of the previous imitation accounts of language acquisition in this century (dating back at least to Guillaume, 1925, and Piaget, 1923, 1945, including the notion of structural imitation). Imitation may serve diverse communicative functions in language development (see, e.g., the contributions described by Speidel & Nelson, 1989; also see Rondal, 1983). It has been known for some time, however, that imitation cannot constitute a major determinant of language development for at least four reasons: (1) the poverty of stimulus argument and the creative nature of language (presented in Chapter 4); (2) the existence of important interindividual differences in children's propensity to imitate (to the extent that some children imitate very little or simply do not imitate other people's language productions) (see Bloom, Hood, & Lightbown, 1974; Ramer, 1976; Masur, 1989; Snow, 1989); (3) the fact that for those children who do imitate adult speech, there is a sharp rapid decrease in frequencies of spontaneous imitation in development (in Rondal's 1978b data, for example, one passes from an average value of 28.17% exact and partial repetitions of immediately preceding maternal utterances at children's MLU 1.00–1.50 to a value of 3.17% at MLU 2.50–3.00; a similar decrease in the frequency of imitation of maternal speech with language growth in children has been reported by Seitz & Stewart, 1975 (the percentages in Rondal's imitation frequency data may be spuriously high, particularly at MLU 1.00–1.50, since partial repetitions by the children of their mothers' utterances were included in the counts; because these children were producing only one or two words at a time, the probability for these words to immediately follow maternal production would always be relatively high); and (4) the fact that those children who do imitate mainly repeat the last part of the immediately preceding adult utterance (in Rondal's 1980a data, NR children 20–32 months old had a mean length of the portion of mother's utterances that followed the part imitated by the child varying between .19 and .49 morphemes with no significant difference between language levels). Considering MR and DS children, it is known that at comparable CAs and general development ages, they tend to imitate less than do NR children (Rondal, 1980a; Rondal, Lambert & Sohier, 1980b, 1981; Mahoney, Glover, & Finger, 1981). However, at corresponding MLU levels, DS children imitate their mothers' utterances in the same quantitative and qualitative ways as do NR children (see Rondal, 1980a, for a comparative analysis). This suggests that it is the level of language development that determines children's imitation and not the reverse (see Slobin & Welsh, 1973, for an earlier indication along the same lines from a study of elicited imitations).

The most interesting teaching-learning approach certainly is that of Moerk (1983, 1989a, 1991, 1992), who claims that there is no need for innate linguistic predispositions and structures since the parents actually teach language in specific ways to their children through daily interactions for several years. As a result, children, drawing on regular (nonlinguistic) cognitive processes, are able to gradually learn their mother tongue. Moerk bases his theoretical suggestions on extensive microanalyses of the verbal interactions between three "Harvard" children and their mothers (transcripts originally established by Roger Brown at Harvard University; see R. Brown,

1973), particularly those between one child, Eve, and her mother. Moerk's contributions as well as those of many others in the specialized literature (see Rondal, 1985b, for a review and extensive discussions) attest to the existence of formal and content simplifications in the adult language transmitted to young children (however, it could be questioned, with Newport, Gleitman, & Gleitman, 1977, e.g., whether some features of "motherese" – e.g., the high proportions of yes-no questions and WH-questions – do not actually render some aspects of this speech more complex to process and may, in some instances, through "simplifications" of motherese, produce ungrammaticality, e.g., by virtue of stripping away or otherwise omitting obligatory grammatical morphemes and inflections). These simplifications also appear in the speech of fathers (e.g., Rondal, 1980c), and they have been reported to exist in various social classes and ethnic environments despite some variation (see Rondal, 1985b, for a comprehensive review and analysis). Such simplifications may facilitate the child's task in analyzing the formal structure of his community language, since he is presented with language that is considerably simpler than the one usually used between adults and is tuned to his momentary level of development (see Marshall, 1987, for an opposite point of view). No firm demonstration has been supplied so far that this is indeed the case, however. But no empirical refutation of the facilitating hypothesis has been provided, either. Bickerton (1981, 1984) has suggested, in relation to his language bioprogram hypothesis (see Chapter 4), that Creole grammars are (historical) genuine inventions on the part of the first generation of children having started with a Pidgin as their linguistic input. If confirmed, this fact would be the first radical evidence against any possible active role of the linguistic environment and the adult-child verbal interactions in language acquisition (particularly grammatical acquisition). However, Bickerton's hypothetical reconstruction of the birth and early evolution of Creole languages has been criticized by some creolists (e.g., Muysken, 1988; Youssef, 1988). One therefore must remain cautious. But Moerk's theoretical position (1983, 1992) goes much beyond the (simple) recognition of a possible facilitating role of linguistic input. As already indicated, he insists that language is fully taught by adults to the children through daily verbal interactions. This position is not supported by solid facts. It is true that motherese is child-sensitive, but *child*-controlled. I have shown elsewhere (Rondal, 1978b, 1978c, 1979b), in comparing mothers' speech with their respective DS and NR children, that this speech predictively varies in relation to the language development level of the child (and not the age level, the intellectual capability, or the level of physical development, per se) and that many mothers have a reasonable knowledge of the global levels of development reached by their children concerning the phonetic, lexical, and superficially morphosyntactic aspects of language. However, nowhere, in my opinion, is there a clear demonstration that the major language structures are gradually exemplified and trained in the sense advocated by Moerk. It would seem that rather than teaching language to children (even assuming that they have the conceptual means to do so, not to speak of the motivation), the parents' main objective is to maximize the efficiency of their verbal interactions with their children (Snow's so-called conversational hyopothesis, 1977). In so doing, and led by pragmatic and referential objectives, the parents use a series of specific strategies. For example, they discuss simple topics with contents adapted to the children's cognitive capacities. They make their messages explicit and use appropriate paraverbal means. They speak clearly and intelligibly, stimulate the children by means of various types of questions and requests, and the like. The simplification of the topics and contents in parental speech helps to induce the formal simplifications found in their language to young children.

Moreover, Moerk's (1983, 1992) so-called demonstration of parental language teaching involves only one child (Eve) and a limited number of language aspects (e.g., the present progressive, the linear expansion of prepositional phrases, and particulars of the English system of temporal morphemes) for which input and frequency effects are to be expected, almost by definition. It is precisely the core and the more abstract features of the grammatical system, the acquisition of which Moerk largely ignores, that have motivated other theorists to consider it impossible to construct an acquisition theory without a complex innate component. Notice that it is epistemologically false to oppose innateness and learning strictly. Leibniz (1765/1927) had already rejected the suggestion that everything one learns is not innate, out of necessity. We may have truth principles in us as human beings and yet be obliged to learn or develop them in the sense that we do not display them at birth (e.g., mathematics, music, language, and visual perception). The learning approach in psycholinguistics is certainly mistaken, however, in excluding, a priori, possible innate determinants of language development and, in particular, grammatical development.

Another serious problem for the teaching-learning approach to language acquisition is the *feedback problem*. According to learnability theorists (e.g., Culicover & Wexler, 1977; Wexler & Culicover, 1980), a certain class of transformational grammars is learnable (from a corpus of structures no more embedded than sentences that contain sentences that contain sentences) given assumptions about three sets of entities: the nature of the input data, the mechanism that selects the appropriate grammar, and the notion of correctness. Accordingly, the datum that is presented to a potential learner at any point in time must be either a positive or a negative instance (i.e., a grammatical or an ungrammatical utterance or sentence) of the target language (for updated learnability proposals, which need not be discussed here, see, e.g., Lightfoot, 1989). Related to the positive evidence question is the poverty of stimulus argument, already discussed. Related to negative evidence is the question of whether *all* "language-learning" children are actually provided with negative information about the grammatical status of strings in their language (or, more exactly, about the ungrammatical status of those strings that do not correspond to the formal specifications of the target language). Several authors (e.g., Atkinson, 1982; Wexler, 1982; Pinker, 1984) – on the basis of very limited information at the time on the existence of negative information in children's input – have stated that parents usually do not correct children, in a way that is contingent and relevant, as to the syntactic well-formedness of the children's prior utterances. Moerk (1983, 1991, 1992), in opposition, claims to have identified numerous instances of grammatical feedback in Eve's mother. But his analyses remain anecdotal and concern only a single mother-child dyad within a limited period of time (9 months; from 18 to 27 months of age; MLU 1.50–4.25). It is doubtful whether Moerk's findings on this point may be generalized to developing language in *all* children.

I have reviewed and analyzed elsewhere (Rondal, 1988c) the results of two empirical studies on the subject – the only ones available at the time (i.e., Hirsh-Pasek, Treiman, & Schneiderman, 1984; Demetras, Post, & Snow, 1986). Penner's (1987) and Bohannon and Stanowicz's (1988) more recent research yields data that are in agreement with the previous studies. Adding the results of these studies to those of the well-known Brown and Hanlon study (1970), one may conclude: (1) Little explicit feedback contingent upon children's preceding utterances is produced by the parents, and when it is, it relates mostly to the truth-value and referential aspects of children's productions; (2) it is not the case that demonstrated comprehension failure by the parents (i.e., parental "non sequiturs") relates only to children's ill-formed utterances or to utterances categorized as grammatically primitive; (3) as parental feedback seems to be motivated mainly by contentive and referential characteristics of children's utterances, it is typically the case that grammatically incorrect but communicatively and referentially appropriate children's utterances are approved of and that grammatically correct but referentially inadequate utterances are disapproved by the parents; (4) *implicit* parental feedback contingent upon preceding children's utterances (i.e., repetitions, expansions, corrections, pursuits, and no comments) is more frequent than *explicit* feedback and could in principle be used by children to evaluate the grammaticality of their uttterances (e.g., *statistically*, the majority of adult follow-up utterances and exact repetitions of children's utterances seem to follow utterances that are grammatically well formed; the majority of adult clarification requests, expansions, and extensions of children's utterances seem to follow grammatically ill-formed productions); (5) it is doubtful that this kind of tailored feedback is the case, however, because such an operation – amounting to establishing and to keeping in mind a gigantic multi-level matrix of conditional probabilities relating to the grammatical status of thousands and thousands of utterances produced – would be quickly and overwhelmingly taxing on the child's memory; (6) even assuming that such enormous computations could somehow be executed by children, it still remains the additional observed fact that in a large number of cases, it is difficult if not impossible to determine exactly the element(s) of the child's utterance to which the implicit adult feedback that follows applies. Pinker (1989a) also refutes the hypothesis that "subtle" negative evidence could exist in parental feedbacks (i.e., slight differences in parents' repetitions, questions, etc., and following up on children's well-formed vs. ill-formed sentences) and be used by the children for grammar-learning purposes. He states that (1) this type of "negative evidence" is not related to all of the ungrammatical sentences of all children but only to some productions of some children some of the time; (2) much of the parental feedback that has been reported in the literature is not feedback about grammaticality; (3) feedback rates sharply decline after the age of 2 while there is obviously a lot of the language (particularly grammar) left to be developed at that age; (4) parental feedback is "noisy" (i.e., grammatical as well as ungrammatical sentences tend to be repeated by parents); (5) there is no proof that negative evidence, if it exists, is useful or required for grammatical development; (6) there is no proof that negative evidence, if useful, is used by the child or, if used, that it is instrumental in bringing about grammatical development. Also analyzing the available literature on the negative evidence issue, Marcus (1993) confirms that noisy feedback is unlikely to be necessary for language development because (1) it is too weak to be a plausible way of eliminating errors (Marcus has computed that even under statistically optimal conditions, a child would have to repeat a given sentence verbatim more than 85 times to eliminate an error from his grammar), and (2) no kind of noisy feedback is provided to all children at all ages for all types of errors. Marcus (1993) adds that noisy feedback may even largely be an artifact of defining parental reply categories relative to the child's utterance. For instance, the observation that the majority of adult exact repetitions of children's utterances follow children's grammatical utterances more than their ungrammatical utterances is guaranteed by the fact that nearly all parental speech is grammatical. Given this, it is most unlikely that adult feedback – even noisy feedback – would play a specific or important role in grammatical development (it could play a role in referential and communicative development, however). Consequently, it seems wiser to consider only acquisition mechanisms that do not depend crucially on negative evidence (Pinker, 1984) and to accept the idea that internal mechanisms are necessary to account for the unlearning of ungrammatical utterances (Marcus, 1993).

Keeping with the input problem, but turning to MR and DS children, it has been demonstrated (Buckhalt, Rutherford, & Goldberg, 1978; Rondal, 1978b; Gutmann & Rondal, 1979) that at corresponding MLU levels, MR children are exposed to language environments and receive language input (including verbal feedback contingent upon their language productions) that do not differ quantitatively or qualitatively in major respects from those of NR children. Yet, as is known, MR children by far do not develop language at the same rate or to the same extent as do their NR peers, with the exception of the very few language-exceptional cases documented. This should suffice to prove that environmental factors in themselves are not major determinants of language development. If this were the case, MR subjects would develop linguistically much more fully than they actually do. As it seems, linguistic determinism is largely intrinsic.

6.3 Rejecting a global developmental cognitive explanation

It could, perhaps, be argued that because Françoise has a nonverbal MA of about 6 years and an almost concrete operational Piagetian cognitive level, her language "after all" is compatible with these levels of cognitive development (Moerk, 1989b). Along the same line of reasoning, one could add that the language achievements of the nonexceptional MR subjects are compatible with the 4 or 5 years MA and Piagetian preoperational levels of development that constitute the upper limits of mental development in most of these persons (Gibson, 1981, for DS; also Inhelder, 1969). It could be the case then that the linguistic development of Françoise and that of the regular DS individuals "simply follows" from their spared cognitive capacities.

I believe that this is not a convincing explanation. As was demonstrated in preceding sections, Francoise's productive and receptive grammatical functioning is well beyond the 5- or 6-year-old level of normal language development. It is true that Françoise's IQ, MA, and Piagetian level are above those of most language-typical MR subjects, but only moderately so, and certainly not in proportion with the language gap existing between them. For some other language-exceptional MR subjects (particularly the ones studied by Curtiss and Yamada; see Chapter 3), the discrepancy between MA, or level of operational intelligence, and language functioning is even more significant than is the case with Françoise. Françoise's lexical and semantic development is more compatible with her general level of mental development. The dissociation between Françoise's and other exceptional subjects' phonological and grammatical capacities, on the one hand, and their lexical and semantic limitations, on the other hand, demands an explanation, for it cannot be accounted for by MA or Piagetian indices. As for nonexceptional MR subjects, the data I have summarized in preceding chapters show that their phonological and grammatical performance often falls short of their mental developmental levels as evaluated by MA measures or the like, whereas their lexical, semantic, and basic pragmatic capacities are better predicted by their MA. As indicated before, these data suggest that global cognitive developmental measures such as MA, IQ scores, or Piagetian operational variables are not valid predictors of phonological or grammatical development.

This conclusion, of course, does not mean that specific cognitive mechanisms (e.g., working memory) could not play a significant role in phonological and grammatical development. The question is an empirical one and still largely open at the present time (see later). The relative polysemy of the terms *cognition* and *cognitive* is something of an embarrassment in this context, for they refer to central processors responsible either globally (e.g., Fodor, 1983) or in modular ways (e.g., Chomsky, 1988) for "general" knowledge, as well as to specialized mechanisms located somewhere between the sensory modalities and the output systems (e.g., memory, supervisory attentional system).

6.4 Modularity and dissociations

6.4.1 Neuropsychological evidence for language modularity

To better evaluate the dissociations documented in Francoise's language system as well as in the language systems of other exceptional MR subjects, it may be useful to take a further look at the literature on modularity, particularly language modularity. As indicated in Chapter 4, Fodorian modules are predicted to be domain specific, innately specified, hardwired, and autonomous. They are also said to be informationally encapsulated, their processes mandatory and rapid, and their output shallow. Intermediate-level representations are considered to be largely inaccessible to central processors. Modules follow a characteristic pattern of development and deterioration. Fodor does not distinguish between these properties with respect to relative weight. He has stated that to him the major property is informational encapsulation (e.g., Fodor, 1991). Moscovitch and Umilta (1990), however, propose that only some among the listed properties are essential in order to distinguish between modular and nonmodular systems. These features are (1) domain specificity (whether modality or material), (2) informational encapsulation, (3) shallow output, and (4) inaccessibility of intermediate-level representations. Garfield (1987a, 1987b) suggests as major criteria (1) domain specificity, (2) mandatoriness, (3) informational encapsulation, and (4) speed. There is a 50% overlap between Garfield's and Moscovitch and Umilta's selections. I will stay with the latter as it seems to me that Garfield's four properties are less independent than Moscovitch and Umilta's.

With regard to *domain specificity,* each module operates only in a restricted domain and/or typically deals with a specific material. The information a module processes and the output it generates are highly circumscribed. It cannot process information about anything outside its domain. *Informational encapsulation* refers to the impermeability of modular processes with respect to top-down cognitive influences. General knowledge about the world and beliefs of the functioning organism cannot affect the operations or the outputs of modules (Fodor, 1985). The best examples of informational encapsulation are probably visual illusions. They persist despite any attempt to have them conform with rational expectations (see, e.g., Kanizsa, 1979). As for *shallow output,* the output of a module is said to be shallow if it is not already semantically interpreted but instead is confined to its domain-specific features. A good case in point would be people who can read but with no or little understanding of the meaning of what they read (as reported, e.g., in some demented patients – Schwartz, Saffran, & Marin, 1980; Saffran, 1982 – or in some deep dyslexics and some hyperlexic children – e.g., Aram & Healy, 1988; Laine, Niemi, Niemi, & Koivuselkä-Sallinen, 1990). Finally, *inaccessibility of intermediate-level representations* refers to the fact that although there may be several intermediate steps in generating the final output of a module, steps that result in different representations at each level, only the final output can be fully accessible to consciousness.

Most importantly, Moscovitch and Umilta (1990) believe that basic modules may be assembled to form a collection that, once assembled, functions as an indissoluble unit (except, in pathological cases). So-called type-II and type-III modules (presenting some characteristics of Fodorian modules but not all, plus additional features) are of that sort. Type-II or *innately assembled modules* "consist of a collection of modules whose organization is innately given and whose output is integrated or synthesized by a devoted but nonmodular processor" (Moscovitch & Umilta, 1990, p. 15). By "devoted" processor, they mean a processor that is able to deal with information coming only from a particular group of modules, and so is module specific in a less restrictive sense. Type-II modules are considered to be capable of modification by learning (not just maturation). Type-III or *experientially assembled modules* "are similar to type-II modules except that central processes are involved in assembling the basic components that, once integrated, carry out functions that become modular with practice" (p. 17). Examples of nonlanguage systems potentially qualifying as basic or Fodorian modules include devices that process information about sensory features (among them acoustic frequency and sound location), face perception, each of which can be impaired (individually) while all other functions remain normal. Object recognition modules are of the type-II sort. The neuropsychological evidence here comes from complex types of agnosia, for example, visual object agnosia (see, e.g., Bauer & Rubens, 1985). Type-III or experientially assembled modules are exemplified by such organizations as those supporting skilled motor performances (e.g., riding a bicycle).

The modularity issue in language is still undecided at this time. In psycholinguistics, modularists as well as antimodularists draw most of their theoretical arguments from observations and speculations concerning natural language perception and understanding. Modularists usually insist on the modular properties of speech perception, word recognition, and syntactic parsing. Some neuropsychological evidence for the plausible modular status of spoken and written word recognition, as well as of syntactic parsing, is summarized later. For speech perception, according to Liberman and Mattingly (1985, 1989; also see the contributions gathered by Mattingly & Studdert-Kennedy, 1991), the domain of a speech module is a speech gesture (not a set of acoustic features), actually "the intended phonetic gestures of the speaker, represented in the brain as invariant motor commands that call for movements of the articulators through certain linguistically significant configurations" (Liberman & Mattingly, 1985, p. 2). It follows that speech perception and speech production are intimately linked since they share the same set of motor invariants. The link between the two is not a learned association (as Liberman considered some years ago). Rather, it is innately specified, requiring only epigenetic development (including speech exposure) to be brought into play. It is known, however, that people who are congenitally incapable of controlling their articulatory organs are nonetheless able to perceive speech normally (see, e.g., MacNeilage, Rootes, & Chase, 1967). Liberman and Mattingly (1985) consistently indicate that the characteristic invariant properties of the gestures that the motor theory requires must not be seen as peripheral movements but rather as the "more remote structures that control the movement" (p. 23). Only radical modularists dare to venture much beyond speech perception, word recognition, and syntactic parsing (e.g., Roeper, 1987b, suggesting that meaning itself has modular origins).[3] Antimodularists point to the apparent important involvement of general knowledge and expectations in sentence and discourse understanding (see the contributions gathered by Garfield, 1987a, for a good example and many more details). Russel (1987), for example, argues from a general point of view that "true language modularity" is implausible (actually impossible), since Chomsky's computational conception of the mind, with its view that mental processes are radically independent of mental contents, is untenable because it leads to plain circularity. For example, theoretical linguistics in the Chomskyan style is not intelligible without "the deployment of the very intuitions that are supposed to test it" (p. 229). Marslen-Wilson and Komisarjersky Tyler (1987) insist that the modularity hypothesis is misleading since it gives the wrong kind of account of the organization of the language system. Such a remark is based, first, on a series of empirical contributions (e.g., Tyler & Marslen-Wilson, 1977; Marslen-Wilson & Tyler, 1980; Marslen-Wilson, Brown, & Komisarjersky Tyler, 1988; see also Marslen-Wilson, 1989) and, second, on a reanalysis of Fodor's suggestions about the modular characteristics of language organization. On the empirical side, Marslen-Wilson, using diverse experimental techniques (lexical identification or decision tasks, shadowing tasks, interpretation of ambiguous sentences, etc.), claims to demonstrate the basically interactive nature of the several speech and language-processing levels. Lexical access, for example, depends on a word recognition process (a bottom-up procedure based on the analysis of the acoustic signal for the spoken word), but it is influenced in important ways by top-down information originating in the semantic and syntactic analyses of the incoming message. The same is true at the level of syntactic analysis (syntactic parsing). The incoming sentence structures are computed on the basis of syntactic knowledge and information interacting in important ways with the available semantic and contextual information. Marslen-Wilson rejects the "usual" counterindication according to which the effect of the background information is actually not modular but postmodular (Swinney, 1979; Fodor, 1983, 1985, 1987). He insists that the interactions between analyzers is constitutive of the process of language treatment and starts very early in the analytical process.

On the theoretical side, Marslen-Wilson and Komisarjersky Tyler (1987) argue that Fodor has largely "misidentified the basic phenomena that need to be explained" (p. 37). They examine the "diagnostic features" for modularity one by one and find them wanting on a number of grounds (not only conceptually but also with respect to a number of empirically documented points) and unable to define a type of subsystem distinguishing either modular from central processes (as defined by Fodor), or linguistic from nonlinguistic processes. More fundamentally, Marslen-Wilson and Komisarjersky Tyler question the type of psycholinguistic ontology incorporated in Fodor's modularity point of view, that is, the general assumption that there is a level of symbolic representation (e.g., a purely syntactic-analytic level) mediating between lexical representations and mental models. Instead, they suggest that there are procedures for directly mapping the former onto the latter, and it is these procedures that differ from language to language. Syntax is a description of this general process of constructing a semantic interpretation. On this line of theorizing, it becomes uninteresting, and even perhaps meaningless, to try documenting or rejecting interactions in the strict sense between various levels of a putative hierarchically organized system. What one has are multiple sources of cues for mapping lexical representations onto semantic ones that may or may not be used punctually depending on the relative transparency of the language stimuli (and, of course, the individual's ability to do so). (For a closely related general point of view, see the "competition model" of language acquisition, developed in Bates & MacWhinney, 1987, and MacWhinney, 1987.)

Despite these important negative considerations, Moscovitch and Umilta (1990) suggest that language may be a type-II module, that is, a collection of modules – some of which are Fodorian or close to Fodorian-type modules – each with its own function, which are structured to form an intricate sytem.

There indeed seem to be nontrivial indications along that line from the study of the aphasias and degenerative and dementing diseases, such as Alzheimer's disease, Pick's disease, and so-called progressive aphasia (Mesulam, 1982, 1987).[4] In agrammatic aphasia (also labeled Broca's aphasia), subjects are unable (to a variety of degrees depending on particular cases) to organize their verbal productions grammatically or to assign grammatical and thematic roles to lexical items in sentences. Agrammatism of the constructional type is characterized by minimal phrase structure but preserved syntactic – often called grammatical – morphology (Tissot, Mounin, & Lhermitte, 1973). (Standard) expressive agrammatism is defined as a disorder of speech planning in which syntactic structures are reduced in number as well as complexity, and function words and inflectional morphemes are frequently omitted (much more frequently than are major lexical class items), and there is a predominance of verbs in the infinitive form (Hecaen & Anglelergues, 1965; Berndt & Caramazza, 1980). However, in these forms of aphasia, lexical use and interpretation may be spared to an important degree. There is even evidence that agrammatic speech may occur without comprehension disorders (Miceli, Mazzucchi, Menn, & Goodglass, 1983). In contrast, in some forms of aphasia (e.g., those called Wernicke's aphasia or acoustic aphasia), a kind of converse situation prevails. The subjects may be able to speak grammatically (although one may often observe the existence of jargon – jargonaphasia – and more or less subtle forms of "dyssyntaxie" – Hecaen & Anglelergues, 1965 – i.e., inappropriate use of some syntactic structures), but they have marked difficulties in consciously (or automatically) assigning meaning to lexical items. It would seem, judging from these dissociations, that on-line syntactic processing (i.e., syntactic parsing and sentence-meaning recovery) and receptive lexical analysis are effectuated by separate entities that may be selectively impaired in agrammatic aphasia and receptive aphasia, respectively. Of course, it might not be the syntactic module or the lexical module that are damaged in such aphasias (or in some such cases), but rather either the (devoted?) central processor or the interface between the module and the central processor (e.g., something wrong with the shallow output of the module). There is indeed evidence in the literature that aphasics may be capable of making on-line grammaticality judgments, therefore retaining an implicit access to syntactic knowledge (Linebarger, Schwartz, & Saffran, 1983a; Shankweiler, Crain, Garrell, & Tuller, 1989).[5] Linebarger et al. (1983a), extended in Schwartz, Linebarger, Saffran, and Pate (1987), propose that the deficit in agrammatic aphasics should be characterized as an inability to map syntactic functions onto correct thematic roles.[6] Shankweiler et al. (1989) also suggest that agrammatic aphasics have difficulties not with the system that represents grammatical knowledge, but with the reduced capability of the central processor when it comes to construct a syntactic structure for an input string. [See Grodzinsky, 1990, however, for criticisms regarding the claims that agrammatics have no real syntactic deficit (syntactic loss) but exhibit failure of other cognitive (processing) systems; see also Mauner, Fromkin, & Cornell, 1993, and Hickok, 1992, for grammatical-representational rather than mapping explanations.] Concerning receptive aphasia, there are also indications in the literature that subjects demonstrate semantic-priming effects for words that they appear not to understand "explicitly" (e.g., Millberg & Blumstein, 1981; Millberg, Blumstein, & Dworetzky, 1987). These observations, likely to be fatal (or at least extremely embarrassing) if correct to a basic-module theory, can be accommodated in a looser assembled-module conception such as the one proposed by Moscovitch and Umilta (1990).

The study of the primary degenerative diseases also offers interesting hints as to the existence of possible modular entities in the organization of the higher mental functions. Primary degenerative diseases – such as progressive aphasias, Pick's disease, or Alzheimer's disease – seem to have a "predilection" for particular sites of the brain and often result in isolating functional subsystems. In particular, observations by Schwartz and Chawluk (1990) support the conclusion that perceptual systems, including those that treat language material, indeed yield shallow outputs, that is, outputs that are not or only very partially semantically elaborated. One patient, carefully studied by Schwartz and Chawluk (1990) over a period of 4 years, progressively lost her expressive spoken and written abilities, as well as her knowledge of word meaning. For example, over a 14-month period of time (about in the middle of the study period), her receptive vocabulary, as measured by the PPVT, dropped from 82 (MA 11 years)[7] to 49 (MA 5 years). Other tests (homemade) were given to assess more finely the subject's lexical comprehension. One test alternated concrete with abstract terms, matched for frequency of use in the language according to the Thorndike-Lorge count. As frequency declined, the subject became more inappropriate in her responses. Concreteness of the item, by contrast, did not seem to have a detectable influence on her performance. A subsequent test of superordinate matching (e.g., musical instruments with the picture of an orchestra) attested to a significant imprecision in the meaning representations recoverable from spoken names. Of interest is the report that the patient's semantic performance was not influenced by performance modality: The same words tended to be misunderstood or misclassified in the same way in spoken and in written presentations. It is likely, therefore, that the processing problem responsible for the observed state of affairs had to be located in the meaning representations shared by spoken and written input modalities rather than in the mechanisms of access to this store (see Shallice, 1987, for relevant discussion). Regarding syntactic competence, judging from sentence repetition and grammaticality judgment tasks (the same battery as that used by Linebarger et al., 1983a, with Broca's aphasics – see the earlier discussion – was employed), the same subject seemed to have kept only some degree of sensitivity to basic phrasal organization as realized in word order.[8] Yet, despite these serious impairments in the semantics, syntax, and phonology of the subject's language, it could be proved through appropriate additional testing that the progressive aphasia had spared some aspects of the language system, particularly in relationship to the input subsystems that deal with auditory and visual material in order to assign them linguistic description, principally lexical status and grammatical category. The patient studied by Schwartz and Chawluk (1990) indeed was able to reliably identify auditory or visual stimuli as being words or pseudowords in her language. In the same way, she could indicate mostly correctly in a phrase or sentence decision test whether phrases or sentences (e.g., *the first person*, *It's a treat*) and corresponding pseudophrases (i.e., strings of lexemes scrambled with respect to canonical word order, e.g., **to person it,* it's treat not*) belonged to her language. As Schwartz and Chawluk (1990) remark, the results of this decision task stand in marked contrast with the subject's previously documented inability to extract meaning from simple phrases. It seems likely, in summary, that Schwartz and Chawluk's subject benefitted from a relative sparing of her lexical and phrasal "input systems" in the face of devastating phonologic, syntactic, and semantic impairments.

Deriving some conclusions from this evidence and speculation, one could probably say, if in favor of a modular conception, that major language subfunctions present a number of characteristics making them reasonable candidates for the status of basic modular entities. They are speech perception, spoken and written word recognition (with basic similarities but also noteworthy differences in the mechanisms involved in the two modalities; see Marslen-Wilson, 1990), phrase and, perhaps, sentence recognition, and primary syntactic parsing. Current interpretations do not favor the modularity thesis as to lexical meaning, structural meaning, pragmatic aspects, or discourse analysis. Also, Moscovitch and Umilta's (1990) proposal to consider the language system as a type-II module – that is, innately given but capable of modification by learning, and incorporating nonmodular entities – appears to be a reasonable hypothesis. Most obscure, however, remains the debate over the relationship between the receptive and the productive aspects of language organization in the modularity context. Some Fodorian modularity seems to exist in several of the language-receptive subsystems. But what about the production subsystems? Liberman and Mattingly (1985, 1989) claim that there must be only one module for speech perception and speech production. They speculatively add that this must be true for language perception and language production in general. Most authors, however, are not that assertive and avoid committing themselves, at this time, regarding the specific modularity status of language production entities.

6.4.2 Dissociations in language-exceptional mentally handicapped people

The dissociations observed in the language organization of exceptional mentally handicapped subjects other than Françoise have been presented in detail in Chapter 3. They are in fair agreement with those documented in the case of Françoise in a number of aspects. But there are also differences. Françoise as well as Van, Crystal, and Ben, the three subjects studied by Bellugi et al., and Antony, Rick, and Laura, the three subjects studied by Curtiss and associates, and Yamada, have normal articulatory and auditory skills. They all have advanced grammatical skills, morphological as well as syntactic, varying from one individual to the other; the most advanced one, both in terms of productive and receptive performance, probably is Françoise. Lexically, the picture is less clear. The Williams syndrome subjects seemed to have well-developed lexicons, sometimes with the ability to appropriately use rare lexical items, but not quite at CA levels. As for Françoise, her vocabulary skills have developed to a satisfactory degree, but she remains below population standards on lexical testing; and it is perfectly clear that her lexical ability does not match her grammatical ability. In contrast with Françoise and with the Williams syndrome subjects, the subjects studied by Curtiss and Yamada were semantically deficient, lexically and propositionally, to the extent of being seriously limited in language use and conversation. The MR hydrocephalic individuals studied by Hadenius, Swisher, and Pinsker, Anderson, and Tew also seemed to present (together with normal articulation and advanced grammatical skills) the characteristics of tending to use unusual vocabulary items; their lexical and propositional comprehension, however, is markedly impaired, pointing to an important dissociation between language production and language comprehension. Of course, it is important to keep in mind that because of the additional attentional, memory, and other loads embodied in formal tests, performance on comprehension *tests* may seriously underestimate a person's comprehension abilities and linguistic competence more generally. Such a dissociation between expression and comprehension apparently was not the case with D.H., the

MR hydrocephalic adolescent studied by Cromer. Contrary to other MR hydrocephalic subjects, D.H. seemed to have a correct understanding of what she said and what others were saying to her. Bellugi et al.'s report contains little information on the pragmatic dimension of Van's, Ben's, and Crystal's language, but judging from the fact that these subjects were loquacious, skilled at conversing, and eager to do so, it may be hypothesized that their basic pragmatic skills were satisfactorily developed. In contrast, the three subjects studied by Curtiss-Yamada seemed to have difficulties with this aspect of language, particularly with conversational and discursive monitoring activities such as topic maintenance, relevancy, and informativeness. As to Françoise, she is quite able to maintain a topic for a large number of utterances and to accommodate to the listener's expressed interests. She also is relevant and reasonably informative. But she has some difficulty with textual cohesion.

Cromer (1988) suggested the possibility of a dissociation between grammatical morphology and syntax in language-exceptional MR subjects (preserved syntax but deficient grammatical morphology). He seems to have based his hypothesis on the sole case of Curtiss's Rick. It is true that Curtiss-Yamada have reported occasional morphosemantic difficulties (e.g., gender-marking errors with pronouns), not only for Rick, but also for Laura and Antony). But these problems were not major ones for Curtiss-Yamada's subjects and they do not qualify as being general for the other exceptional MR subjects studied.[9] Such a dissociation between grammatical morphological and syntactic aspects of language has been documented in the aphasia literature, however. In some cases of agrammatic aphasia (e.g., constructional agrammatism), phrase structure is considerably altered but grammatical morphology is preserved (Tissot et al., 1973). In other types of agrammatic aphasia, grammatical morphology is seriously impaired or largely missing but basic word order is preserved (in simple constructions) (see Grodzinsky, 1990).

The dissociations documented in the language organization of the exceptional MR subjects are more encompassing and less extreme than the ones reported in the aphasia and in the dementia literature. But they seem to attest to some minimal domain specificity of the functional entities involved. Also it seems clear that a good degree of informational encapsulation holds true for phonological and grammatical functioning (particularly productive grammatical organization in several of the cases studied), since the severe limitations of other cognitive systems have little negative effect on them. The data from MR subjects therefore may be considered as globally supporting the language modularity hypothesis.[10]

Finally, as noted previously, Françoise's skills in written language (reading and writing), although far from being negligible, do not match her oral language abilities, making, therefore, for a marked difference between oral and written language. As indicated also, this discrepancy cannot be attributed to differential learning since Françoise was "taught" to speak, write, and read at the same time. There unfortunately is little to discuss in this regard for Paul, the DS subject studied by Seagoe (1965), because of the lack of a systematic comparison between Paul's oral and written language abilities. However, there is a relevant report in the literature of a case of trilingual hyperlexia alongside severely reduced oral language in a moderately MR microcephalic adolescent named Isabelle (Lebrun, Van Endert, & Szliwowski, 1988; also see Lebrun & Van Borsel, 1991). This case illustrates a clearer case of dissociation between oral and written language organization. Isabelle's IQ was estimated to be 55 on the Terman-Merrill. She is able to read aloud in three languages: Dutch, French, and English. But her reading ability in a given language is not higher than that of chronological age-mates (it is, therefore, a case of relative hyperlexia). Contrary to a number of (NR) hyperlexics (see Aram & Healy, 1988), Isabelle did not show any "precocious" reading skill (although it may have been precocious compared with her other linguistic abilities). Her special talent was not discovered until she was 5 years old and proved able to read the titles of the daily newspapers. Lebrun et al. (1988) supply evidence as to Isabelle's minimal semantic comprehension of what she reads (e.g., as assessed through the use of matching-sentence-to-picture tasks). The evaluation, however, was complicated by the fact that Isabelle is often not able to plan nonverbal behavior of any degree of complexity in relation to the information expressed in written form. Her exact reading comprehension level, therefore, could not be ascertained. Isabelle cannot, however, be taught to write a whole word by herself. She is able only to provide a missing letter for a word she is familiar with. Remembering the alphabet is much beyond her capacity. Isabelle speaks Dutch only. Her oral language is highly defective with delayed echolalia, ritualized phrases and sentences, fillers, reduced lexicon, and morphosyntactic difficulties. Her articulation is deviant. She makes frequent consonant substitutions and deletions. Her final consonants are often protracted or repeated (stutteringlike phenomenon). Isabelle's study illustrates the existence, in pathological cases (also see the literature on alexia, e.g., Albert, Yamadori, Gardner, & Howes, 1973), of dissociations between oral and written language abilities, within written language between reading and writing, and between reading and comprehension. (For a review of a number of cases of "nonretarded hyperlexia" demonstrating similar types of dissociation, see Aram & Healy, 1988.)

6.5 Explaining exceptional language development in persons with mental retardation

We still need to explain and discuss the major observation of the present study together with corresponding observations in a series of related cases, that is, the fact that advanced or normallike phonological and grammatical development is possible in spite of severe deficits in general cognitive resources.

6.5.1 Phonological development

Except for Ingram (1976), I do not know of anyone who has tried to closely tie phonological development and cognitive development.[11] Ingram explicitly links Piaget's

stages of preoperational and operational development with so-called stages of phonological development: prelinguistic vocalization and phonology of the first 50
words within Piaget's sensorimotor period (0 to 18 months), phonology of single
morphemes (child gradually expanding inventory of speech sounds) within the
period of concrete operations (18 months to 12 years), completion of phonetic inventory (including "troublesome" sounds) within the so-called intuitional subperiod (4
to 7 years, approximately), morphophonemic development (acquisition of the morphophonemic rules of language) within the concrete operations subperiod (7 to 12
years), and spelling ability within the period of formal operations (12 to 16 years).
Ingram's objective evidently was not simply to order phonological development
with reference to cognitive evolution. Rather, he favorably envisaged the hypothesis
according to which phonological development could be explained by specific
aspects of cognitive development considered within Piaget's conceptual framework.
Ingram (1976), however, did not specify further which aspects of cognitive development are causally related to phonological evolution, nor did he supply empirical data
supporting his theoretical claim. It would seem that phonological data in Françoise
as well as in the other exceptional MR individuals studied so far are sufficient to ruin
any hypothesis causally tying phonological and cognitive developments.

The autonomy of phonological development is further asserted in Liberman's theory of speech perception and production as a Fodorian module. According to
Liberman's proposal (Liberman & Mattingly, 1985) the speech module, central to
speech perception as well as to speech production, is concerned with motor invariants or inner structures controlling phonetic gestures. These gestures are considered
to be innately specified. It is of importance to stress that for Liberman and Mattingly
(1985) speech perception and production are biologically linked. This makes the perception of speech a special sort of perception quite unlike general auditory perception in that speech perception would have automatic access to phonetic gestures
without translation from the auditory form that the sounds have on psychoacoustic
grounds. Not surprisingly, not everyone is sympathetic to the developmental
implications of Liberman and Mattingly's theoretical suggestions. For example,
Boysson-Bardies, Halle, Sagart, and Durand (1989; also see Boysson-Bardies, 1991)
advocate a position in which each infant is seen as having to rediscover the relevant
phonetic gestures through particular attention to the speech of other persons. Vihman
(1991) proposes a variant of such a constructivist position. She claims that each child
must work out the speech gestures and their relation to acoustic patterns anew. This
epigenetic development is based primarily on feedback from the child's own production practice during the babbling stage and secondarily on perception of the speech
of others.[12]

Although there is considerable evidence that speech is perceived by a specialized
device in adults, perhaps a module in Fodor's sense, it is still unclear whether young
infants show a similar specialization, as Liberman and Mattingly (1985) posit. The
cross-language research reveals that young infants are capable of discriminating

contrasts in speech sounds including those that do not occur or are not used contrastively in their language environment (Mehler & Dupoux, 1990; Bertoncini, 1991; Werker, 1991). Older children and adults have more difficulty in discriminating nonnative contrasts, particularly those that correspond to a single phoneme category in their native language. This developmental transition between infants' and adults' discriminating capacities is evident by the end of the first year (Boysson-Bardies et al., 1989; Werker, 1991). It suggests that some important reorganization has occurred in the child by this time.

Whatever the exact relationship between speech production and speech perception, and the specific nature of the phonetic gestures that are conferred by such a central status in the motor theory, it remains clear that the speech component of language must be accorded a special status and a marked autonomy with respect to other components of the linguistic system. Such an autonomy is obvious in the language of normal people. Some persons gifted with excellent lexicogrammatical ability may have important articulatory difficulties for a variety of reasons or exhibit stuttering. Conversely, people with adequate articulatory skills may demonstrate limited language ability. (Also see Section 3.6 for other empirical indications along the same line.) A marked autonomy between phonetic gestures and the rest of the linguistic system is further attested to (in a sort of reverse way from the preceding argument) by the profound similarities between sign language grammars and spoken language grammars, including striking phonological (but clearly not phonetic) parallels (see Stokoe, 1972; Klima & Bellugi, 1979; Rondal, Henrot, & Charlier, 1986; Poizner et al., 1987). This autonomy is also demonstrated in the cases of "wild children," such as Kaspar Hauser or Genie (Curtiss, 1988) – see Section 6.5.3 – who could develop lexically, semantically, and phonologically but not, or only a little, grammatically, after years of total isolation during the normal period of language development. If Liberman is right in postulating the existence of a purely phonetic module, then there are two possibilities. Either the innately defined information normally contained in the module is preserved in MR subjects (including the MR individuals affected with genetic syndromes) and is prevented from being expressed phenotypically by the organic infelicities of epigenetic development or this information is totally or partially absent in regular MR subjects, rendering phonetic development totally or partially impossible or very difficult, and in this latter case always atypical (as it would not proceed along the normal path). A large series of syndromes leading to various degrees of mental retardation (more than a hundred; see Grossman, 1983) exists. A number of these have *no* genetic basis. They are caused by ongoing or punctual pathological processes or conditions in the course of pregnancy (e.g., syphilis or rubella in the mother). In such cases, at least, it can be assumed that the genetically coded phonetic information is available. The situation is less clear when it comes to the genetic syndromes directly causing the problems that lead to mental retardation (e.g., DS or trisomy 21,[13] Edwards syndrome or trisomy 18, Pateau syndrome or trisomy 13). In such cases, it can be argued either that the genetic anomalies leading to these syndromes also cause the total or partial destruction of the genetically coded phonetic information or that they do not. If the first alternative is correct, speech problems are to be viewed as intrisinc to the syndrome and not as a secondary consequence of nonlinguistic deficiencies. If the second alternative is correct, one finds oneself in the same theoretical situation as with nongenetic mental retardation syndromes. The fact is that phonetic and phonological development do not appear to differ substantially and qualitatively in MR infants and children whether their mental handicap has a genetic origin or not. As indicated earlier, one differentiating observation regularly made in this respect concerns speech production in DS subjects. But this difference may be accounted for by the frequent presence in those subjects of additional organic problems (motor and/or auditory; see Chapter 2). It could, therefore, be hypothesized that the genetically coded phonetic information is present in the genetic syndromes constitutive of mental retardation as it is in the nongenetic syndromes. In regular MR subjects, this information may be prevented from being expressed by epigenetic factors (see Section 6.5.3). Such prevention would not exist in MR language-exceptional subjects (more exactly, phonologically exceptional MR subjects) for reasons that have remained mysterious so far.

The alleged independence of phonetics from other language components implies that the observation that all the language-exceptional mentally handicapped individuals studied so far have normal articulatory skills is coincidental. There could be language-exceptional MR persons with impaired articulatory skills. Actually, Lebrun and Van Borsel (1990; also Van Borsel, 1991) have described the case of a DS adolescent with marked articulatory deficiencies (e.g., slurred articulation, phoneme substitutions and deletions) and stuttering symptoms (e.g., prolongations of sounds, blocks, phrases, words, syllables, and sound repetitions with both initial and final sounds; dysfluency index 15.5%). This subject exhibited a nontrivial degree of grammatical competence as demonstrated in her spontaneous speech (i.e., correct use of inflectional affixes on nouns and verbs; function words; grammatically correct declarative, interrogrative, and imperative sentences; and mostly simple sentences with occasional compound sentences).

6.5.2 Working memory and language processing

As a possible type-II module (Moscovitch & Umilta, 1990), language may enjoy specific relations with specialized cognitive processors such as memory, particularly working memory. Could it be the case that auditory-verbal short-term memory (AV-STM), for example, plays a significant role in the exceptional language functioning documented, and if so, how? Before examining this possibility, it is necessary to look into the psychological and the neuropsychological literature on STM and its possible role in language functioning and development.

Since the late sixties, memory models in which a number of distinct memory stores are postulated have become increasingly popular among researchers (see Norman, 1970, for a review). The multistore views did not go unchallenged, however (e.g., Craik & Lockhart, 1972; Crowder, 1982). Recently, it has become clear that they are incomplete and that earlier theories of STM, for example, cannot account for a large number of facts uncovered in experimental psychology and neuropsychology. Probably, the fullest model to date is the one proposed by Baddeley (1990; see also 1983, 1986, in press). According to Baddeley, a model of working memory[14] corresponding reasonably well to the available evidence is the one in which a controlling-attentional and resource-coordinating system (labeled "central executive"), also of limited capacity – supervises two "slave" systems able to retain limited amounts of information at a time: *the articulatory or phonological loop* responsible for the manipulation of speech-based information, and *the visuospatial sketch pad or scratch pad* responsible for setting up and manipulating visual images. It is true that, at times, in the "working memory literature," the central executive has been assigned a storage as well as a control function. But the parameters characteristic of this possible storage function have not been specified. It has been considered, for example, that the residual component of recall left when subjects are performing articulatory suppression should be attributed to the storage function of the central executive (e.g., Baddeley & Hitch, 1974, although it is fair to mention that more recently Baddeley himself seems to have had reservations about the idea – personal communication with Charles Hulme, quoted in Hulme & Mackenzie, 1992, p. 37). Following Hulme and Mackenzie (1992), I will restrict the central executive to an attentional, controlling, and organizational role (i.e., retrieving relevant information from other parts of the memory system, and forming associations and relationships between items). (See Hulme & Mackenzie, 1992, for a full discussion.)

The first major slave system, the phonological loop, is assumed to comprise two subcomponents : *a phonological store*, capable of holding speech-based information, and *an articulatory control process* based on inner speech. Because the phonological loop is subject to passive loss of information over time, rehearsal is necessary to refresh the decaying traces of items held on the loop. The term "phonological" used by Baddeley (1990), in this context, is meant to be neutral, for the precise nature of the store is not fully clear at the present time, nor is it entirely clear whether this store contains sound, phoneme, or articulatory information (Shallice & Vallar, 1990). What is clear, however, is that the store has a strong temporal-ordering component and that it is based on some sort of phonological coding. This is proved by the phonological similarity effect, that is, the fact that phonologically similar items have codes that may easily be confounded, leading to impaired memory performance. The phonological store will hold the incoming information for about 2 seconds. The articulatory control process refreshes items in the store by means of subvocal rehearsal, allowing the rehearsed items to be retained in STM for a longer period of time and/or possibly to be processed into long-term memory (LTM). The articulatory loop is also capable of subvocally recoding visual material (phonological recoding), leading to its registration in the phonological store. Very likely, however, the spoken material has direct access to the phonological store without a need for the articulatory control process. Based on neuropsychological indications (e.g., Vallar & Cappa, 1987), it would seem that the input phonological STM store, articulatory rehearsal loop, and phonological recoding process are separable components of the system. Baddeley (1990) contends that the phonological store does not contain semantic information.[15] It should also be indicated that the articulatory control process does not depend upon peripheral speech musculature for its operation. Anarthric patients, for instance, who are unable to produce any sound, may demonstrate normal use of the phonological store. This observation suggests that some form of motor program can be run at a central level in spite of the absence of peripheral muscular participation (Baddeley, 1983; Baddeley & Wilson, 1988; Vallar & Cappa, 1987). However, although overt articulation is not necessary for inner speech to operate, the functioning of the phonological loop is disturbed if overt or covert articulation of an irrelevant item is required (providing the task is made difficult enough to put the functioning of the attentional central executive system in jeopardy). This effect, referred to as articulatory suppression, is assumed to occur because the articulation of an irrelevant item prevents the articulatory control process from being used to rehearse the relevant material in order to maintain it in the phonological store, or to code visual material in such a way as to register it into the phonological code. Articulatory suppression may have the additional drawback of feeding the irrelevant spoken material into the phonological store.

An important determinant of immediate memory span is the spoken duration of the words treated. Immediately recalling series of monosyllabic words such as *bag*, *top*, *sun*, *rug* may be a relatively easy task. Most subjects, however, have difficulty in recalling series of polysyllabic words such as *university*, *constitutional*, *aluminium*. From a set of studies examining the relationships between word length, speaking or reading rate[16] (depending on mode of presentation of the material to be recalled), and probability of recall for words varying in number of syllables, Baddeley (1990; also see Cowan, 1992) concludes that immediate memory span represents "the number of items of whatever length that can be uttered in about two seconds" (p. 74), according to a formula such as "words held on the loop = length of the loop × speech rate," where the length of the loop is estimated to be about 2 seconds. This gives a linear relationship between correct recall and articulatory or reading rate. I do not take "uttered," in the preceding statement, literally, since it is known that words in inner speech may be extremely reduced in form and time of realization (see McGuigan, 1966; Sokolov, 1967, 1971, 1972; Rondal, 1976, for theoretical and experimental discussions of inner speech and its role in mental processes), and as Baddeley himself acknowledges, rehearsal may be operated centrally by some form of motor program even in the absence of peripheral muscular activity. Most importantly, Baddeley's estimation of the length of time the phonological store can retain memory traces is correct only for unrelated items, that is, when semantic and/or associative factors play no part in the retentive process, what Craik (1971) called primary memory; for, when such factors come into play, memory decay may be delayed by several seconds. For example, Ehrlich (1972) showed that the average number of both unrelated words or unrelated sentences that subjects can correctly recall vary from about 6.2 to 6.8 (the lists were composed of 10 elements), depending on the number of syllables composing the words or the number of words composing the sentences, respectively. In the case of 4-word sentences, the correct recalling of 6.2 sentences means approximatively 24 words, which, assuming a rate of overt or covert articulation as high as 4 words per second – see later – corresponds to approximately 6 seconds of STM retention.

As indicated in what precedes, the number of related items recalled is not simply a function of the amount of time that they require for articulation. This is in line with Miller's classical data (G. A. Miller, 1956) according to which memory span corresponds to a constant number of "chunks" (in the mature individual) – seven, more or less – regardless of the characteristics and contents of those chunks. A chunk is a meaningfully coded unit of STM. The chunking process ("located" in the central executive in Baddeley's working memory model) and capacity may be one of the most important features of human information-processing systems (Simon, 1974). Chunks may be relatively large – for example, when words make up larger constituents, as is the case in phrases and sentences. This suggests that constituents and chunking determinants (semantic, syntactic, pragmatic, and at times, textual knowledge, in the case of words of the language) play a central role even in immediate verbatim recall. In a series of experiments, Zhang and Simon (1985) and Yu, Zhang, Jing, Peng, Zhang, and Simon (1985) have explored the relationship between the articulatory loop and the chunking process. They support an integration of the two mechanisms in the functioning of working memory. The span is indeed determined by rehearsal rate, but the rate itself depends on the three factors listed in Equations 1 and 2. These factors are (1) the time (a, in milliseconds) necessary to bring each chunk into the articulatory mechanism; (2) the time (b, in milliseconds) required to articulate each syllable in the chunk; (3) the average size of a chunk in syllables (s). Thus, the related Equations 1 and 2 express either the duration of the storage parameter T, or the STM capacity expressed in chunks (C):

$$T = C\,[a + b(s - 1)]; \tag{1}$$

$$C = \frac{T}{[a + b(s - 1)]}. \tag{2}$$

Zhang and Simon (1985) and Yu et al. (1985) claim that these equations fit a wide range of experimental data collected in Chinese and in English.[17]

The second major slave system in Baddeley's scheme (1990) is the visuospatial sketch pad (VS-STM). It is assumed to be responsible for manipulating visuospatial images. The VS-STM span seems to have a capacity of four or five unrelated visual items in normal subjects (Defleur, 1989). The exact developmental path to this level is not known. The span is usually greater for auditory (see later) than for visual input.

This is known as the "modality effect" (Conrad, 1964; Penney, 1975). It would seem that the visuospatial system has important organizational analogies with the phonological loop. Like the phonological loop, the visuospatial system can be fed either directly through visual or spatial perception or indirectly through the generation of a visual and/or a spatial-mental image. Access to the store by visual information seems to be obligatory. Construction of a visual image is optional. Additionally, there is evidence from animal research and human neuropsychology (summarized in Baddeley, 1990) according to which mental imagery may have two separable components or be made of two separate subsystems: the so-called *what*-subsystem, concerned with pattern detecting and processing; and the *where*-subsystem, devoted to location in space. These components appear to have different anatomical locations within the brain (very likely the occipital lobes for the *what*-component and the parietal lobes for the *where*-component). Finally, it should be specified that if the visuospatial sketch pad has been shown to participate centrally in visual imagery mnemonics, it does not seem to be responsible for the demonstrated best memorability of highly imageable words (an LTM phenomenon). This is likely why Baddeley labels the visuospatial STM system, sketch pad (or, at times, scratch pad).

There are a number of studies available on the development of verbal STM. One clear feature of memory development is the increase in digit or word span with age. An average mature normal span for digits or unrelated words contains six items (Baddeley, 1990, p. 86). Wechsler (1968) gives a smaller estimate for digit span (about five digits) for the normal adult mean. Chi (1976) reports an auditory span of seven or eight digits at 16 years. These numbers do not represent fixed quantities, it should be kept in mind. They vary across material type: Span for digits is typically greater than span for familiar words, which in turn is usually greater than span for nonword materials (Saffran & Martin, 1990). Such differences likely refer to differences in rehearsal time for the various materials and to lexical influences (e.g., the typical difference in span between word and nonword materials). Lexicality is quite clearly a sustaining factor in the functioning of STM. STM shows few, if any, losses with age. Most studies, for example, have found no significant age difference in digit span forward (Kriauciunas, 1968; Drachman & Leavitt, 1972), in word span (Talland, 1965), or in letter span (Botwinick & Storandt, 1974). The digit span (and possibly the spans for other separate materials) may tend to decrease slightly (about 1 unit) beyond 50 years (until 70 years according to data obtained by Lafontaine, 1988), but it could also be that older subjects have somewhat decreasing attentional resources available, as suggested by Craik and Byrd (1982) and as indicated by data collected by Van der Linden and Brédart (1993), and/or that they show evidence for an encoding deficit (spontaneously using encoding strategies less frequently than younger people) (Craik, 1984). Development toward full span takes a long time. It goes on until and, actually, beyond 10 years of age according to studies by Hulme, Thomson, Muir, and Lawrence (1984). Mackenzie and Hulme (1987) document AV-STM development in a longitudinal study conducted with a group of 28 children over a period of 5 years. They assessed digit span using the Auditory Sequential Memory Subtest from the Illinois Test of Psycholinguistic Abilities (ITPA; revised version, Paraskevopoulos & Kirk, 1969). Digit span increases from an average of 3.8 (SD 0.6) around 5 years CA to 4.6 (SD 0.79) around 7 years, and 5.5 (SD 0.84) around 10 years. As expected, high and significant correlations hold between memory span and CA as well as MA. Wechsler's data (1957, 1968, 1972) are from about three items at 5 years to about five items at 8 years and 3 months, to about eight items at 13 years and 3 months. This developmental time frame may be at least in part tied to the maturation of the posterior parietal region of the left cerebral hemisphere that seems to be neurologically responsible for the immediate recall of words, letters, or digits (see the contributions gathered by Vallar and Shallice, 1990, in this respect). One thing that is clear, however, is that the rate of trace decay is the same in children and in adults (Belmont, 1972).

It has been suggested also (e.g., Nicolson, 1981; Hulme & Muir, 1985) – consistent with the working memory model – that the increase in word or digit span with age is due to the ability of older subjects to rehearse faster. Data collected by Nicolson (1981), subsequently replicated and extended in other studies (e.g., Hulme et al., 1984), appear to confirm this hypothesis. Accordingly, younger children (4-year-olds) articulating one to two words per second can recall an average of one to two words per list. Seven-year-olds are able to articulate two words per second and recall an average of two to three words per list. Ten-year-olds articulate two to three words per second and recall an average of two to four words per list. Adults can articulate up to four words per second and recall up to five or six words per list (see Hulme et al., 1984, for more details). Of course, if the words are longer, the recall performance drops in proportion. The word-length effect, however, is restricted to spoken material at least until 10 years of age, suggesting that if the tendency to rehearse spoken items appears relatively early in development (around 4 to 5 years, Conrad, 1971; R. Kail, 1984; or as young as 4 years, Hulme et al., 1984), the conversion of a visual item into a phonologically coded element that can then be rehearsed is a later achievement. These developmental data confirm the previous findings as to the importance of covert (or overt) articulation in the rehearsal process refreshing memory traces and momentarily preventing decay. They also suggest that at any given age (data for very young children are missing, however), genuine immediate memory capacity might be roughly constant (Hitch, 1990). What actually increases with age is speech rate, which in turn, may be interpreted as an index of the speed with which spoken material can be rehearsed within the articulatory loop. This development itself is dependent on the process of privatization and internalization of non-communicative speech taking place in the NR child between approximately 4 and 10 years (or more).

These findings concern memory span for unrelated digits, letters, words, or pseudowords. As soon as semantic and associative factors (lexical, syntactic, or otherwise) are involved – for example, when sentences are to be recalled – the immediate span (labeled sentence span, in that case) may, and usually does, extend considerably. In adults, sentence span may be around 20 words (see later). The exact developmental course of sentence span extension is not known, but it is obvious that it must follow linguistic development. The Wechsler Preschool and Primary Scale of Intelligence (WIPPSI; Wechsler, 1972, for the French version) contains some useful information in this respect. On the subtest consisting of repeating verbatim grammatical and meaningful sentences (all monopropositional except for the longest one), the modal values exemplify a linear progression from 4 to 7 years (upper limit of the test). Children from 4 years on appear able to repeat sentences composed of 4 to 8 words, sometimes more, correctly.

Sentence span development obviously is linked to chunking and STM processing capacity, which in turn depend on the use in working memory of specific information stored in LTM and recalled for dealing with incoming data of a given type. The exact functional relationships between STM and LTM are far from clear at the present time. Different viewpoints have been proposed as to the possible role of AV-STM in long-term learning, mainly (1) short-term storage is an essential stage in long-term retention (e.g., Atkinson & Shiffrin, 1968), (2) long-term learning and STM involve separate and parallel subsystems (e.g., Shallice & Warrington, 1970), and (3) long-term learning involves deeper and semantically richer encoding of the material than the superficial coding in STM (e.g., Craik & Lockhart, 1972).

Current evidence favors the first and the third alternatives. AV-STM appears to be necessary as an intermediate stage, the function of which is to hold information and in so doing allow it to be gradually transferred to LTM (see Baddeley, Papagno, & Vallar, 1988). More details are beginning to be available on the exact role of AV-STM, coming from neuropsychological studies of patients with impaired short-term verbal memory functions. For example, it is necessary to distinguish between tasks consisting in learning unfamiliar verbal material, in which AV-STM is important, and those consisting in forming associations between meaningful items that are already known, in which AV-STM plays no essential role (Baddeley et al., 1988). Not inconsistently, Waters, Caplan, and Hildebrandt (1991) claim – and empirically document through the study of one subject (B.O.) diagnosed as having a primary disturbance of the articulatory rehearsal process of STM and, possibly, some impairment of the phonological store – that articulatory rehearsal is not needed for the assignment of syntactic structures and its utilization to specify aspects of propositional semantics (e.g., thematic roles and coindexation of noun phrases, using Chomsky's, 1981, terminology). Articulatory rehearsal seems needed in sentence comprehension, however, to maintain items for the time necessary (1) to construct an interpretive semantic structure on the basis of the syntactic structure characterizing the incoming sentence and (2) to transfer the interpreted semantic structure into long-term store after which the exact lexical items (or a part of them, at least) may be left to decay producing the well-known Sachs's observation (1967) – that is, usually only semantic interpretation is retained in LTM. The results of an experiment conducted by Martin and Feher (1990) with aphasic patients with restricted memory spans point in the same direction. They showed that the processing of syntactically simple (i.e., imperative) sentences with many content words draws on the STM capacity as assessed by memory span (visual as well as phonological), while the processing of sentences matched in content words but varying in syntactic complexity does not. If it is indeed the case that AV-STM is essential for at least some aspects of long-term verbal learning, significant problems in language tasks are to be expected in those cases where deficits of STM can be demonstrated.

As for the third alternative, that is, the level-of-processing interpretation, there is agreement (see Baddeley, 1990, for a discussion) that semantic processing will typically produce richer memory traces than occur with the phonological and/or the visual coding of verbal material. Such richer traces subsequently will significantly enhance recall and recognition, probably because they set up memory traces that are more discriminable in the memory store than are items that have been encoded in a more superficial way (e.g., on a purely phonological basis). In addition, compatible with the level-of-processing interpretation is the indication that active rehearsal, besides maintaining information over a limited period of time, allows for the elaboration of new information and its incorporation into the old providing there are structures in LTM able to "receive" and organize the incoming information. No detailed explanation of these processes is available to date, but a number of suggestions have been made in connection both with semantic coding and with maintenance rehearsal and elaboration[18] (see Baddeley, 1990, for a review of the current relevant literature).

In the transition from STM to LTM, semantic enrichment and elaborative processes may be considered important dimensions along which incoming information is treated. When envisaged in the reverse direction, that is, from LTM to STM, semantic enrichment corresponds to the associative or chunking process in STM referred to earlier. It implies processing incoming material by applying to it a number of lexical, semantic, and/or syntactic operations stored in LTM and called upon in STM working space. Whether this relationship between STM and LTM is the same (two-way) process or whether there exist different mechanisms (one "going" from STM to LTM and ensuring semantic deepening and elaboration of incoming material in order to place it efficiently in the long-term store, and the other from LTM to STM supplying the categorical basis for the chunking process) remains to be established. But clearly these mechanisms are important components of the STM-LTM "interface."

Young children (up to 6 years or so) are less adept than older children, adolescents, and adults at organizing incoming information. They can recognize simple objects effectively but perform at chance level when it comes to recognizing scenes and complex situations (McShane, 1990). The same is true in the auditory domain. Treatment of complex stimuli requires the scanning and extraction of information that, once extracted, can be stored as separate sets of features or be clustered into meaningful chunks. Younger children are not especially good at such tasks (see, e.g.,

A. Brown, 1976; Flavell, 1977; Mandler, 1978; Esperet, 1984; and Schneider & Pressley, 1989, for more details and for a number of findings on the development of encoding and retrieval strategies, and on awareness and knowledge about memory, i.e., metamemory, from infancy onto early adulthood). The younger child is in the peculiar situation of having a sharply limited STM span or a sharply limited ability to rehearse fast enough – assuming, as remarked earlier, that immediate memory capacity could be roughly constant across ages – or both, together with immature encoding, chunking, and retrieval strategies (and, of course, little or no schematic or metamnemonic ability), which renders all the more difficult his task of analyzing complex language stimuli. (This, incidentally, makes even more impressive the fact that a good deal of language acquisition occurs before 6 years CA.) It is only progressively that these limitations are removed: STM span may increase as a result of neurological maturation, rehearsing gets faster, and encoding and retrieval strategies become more appropriate; span and processes interact to make the STM system a more efficient cognitive tool.

Considering STM capacity and development in MR subjects, now, the idea that learning-disabled and particularly MR subjects have weakness of STM is a relatively old one (e.g., O'Connor & Hermelin, 1963), including its relevancy for sentence processing (Graham, 1968). Spitz (1973) experimentally specified the auditory digit span for groups of mildly MR children (mean CA 11 years and 5 months) as encompassing ±4 items. Bilovski and Share (1965) and Marinosson (1974), using the ITPA in cross-sectional studies, reported poor digit span performance in MR subjects, including DS subjects, between approximatively 10 and 16 years CA.

Mackenzie and Hulme (1987) supply longitudinal data on memory span development for a group of 10 DS children (MA 5 to 7 years, CA 11 years at the beginning of the study), and a group of 8 severely subnormal subjects of mixed etiologies (MA 5 to 7 years, CA 11 years at the beginning of the study). Digit span was assessed using the Auditory Sequential Memory Subtest from the ITPA. The AV-STM span for digits increased little over a 5-year period of time for the DS group: from 3.1 (SD 0.57) at 11 years CA to 3.6 (SD 0.71) at 16 years. It did affect most subjects in the group, however, since the age difference in digit span proved statistically significant ($p < .01$). Similar results (slightly better) were observed with a group of severely subnormal children from etiologies other than DS: from 3.5 (SD 0.76) at 11 years to 4.1 (SD 1.13) at 16 years (significant at the $p < .01$ level). According to Mackenzie and Hulme's data, AV-STM span development is late, slow, and remains limited in moderately and severely MR subjects, including DS subjects, at least until 16 years CA. Maranto, Decuir, and Humphrey (1984) did not find any significant statistical association between digit span scores (nor rhythm span scores) and CA in a group of 25 moderately and severely MR subjects aged 12 to 22 years. There was a significant correlation (Pearson's $r = .55$, $p < .01$), however, between digit span scores and MA. AV-STM probably remains quite limited beyond these ages, as our control data with a group of young DS adult subjects suggest (see Section 5.8.7.3). In a more recent cross-sectional work with a 5-year follow up, conducted with 55 DS and 55 non-DS MR subjects, Hulme and Mackenzie (1992) confirm that there is indeed little improvement in the retarded subjects' STM capacities between 9 and 38 years. AV-STM performance remains poor in MR subjects despite noticeable gains over time in MA. In older DS subjects, some data (e.g., Haxby, 1992) suggest a reasonable parallel between age-related memory change in normal aging and in DS. But the generalizability of these findings in unclear, since it is not easy to find older DS adults in whom detailed testing can be performed. Other investigators (e.g., Caltagirone & Nocentini, 1990) claim that there are smaller age-related declines in memory in DS adults relative to other abilities. Clearly, additional data are needed to solve the matter.

Our data, as exposed in Section 5.8.7.3, indicate lower digit span estimates in DS subjects in comparison with Mackenzie and Hulme's data (1987) (approximately one digit lower in our DS adult subjects as well as in our DS children). This may have to do with the specific tasks used in the studies for assessing digit span. As indicated, Mackenzie and Hulme used the Auditory Sequential Memory Subtest of the ITPA. In this test, the lists are read by the examiner at a rate of two digits per second as opposed to a rate of one digit per second in the digit span subtests of the WAIS and the Terman-Merrill that were employed in our studies. Given that there is trace decay in the phonological store, faster presentation rates should be expected to lead to better recall performance. However, slower rates will allow more time for rehearsal, which could balance any effects of decay. In normal adults (Baddeley, Lewis, & Vallar, 1984) and in older children (Hitch, 1990), faster rates of presentation indeed seem to be advantageous. The same effect was not observed with younger children (Hitch, 1990), who do not spontaneously rehearse or do less so. Since most moderately and severely MR children and adolescents, and a fair proportion of the retarded adults, may be considered not to rehearse actively and spontaneously, or only little (not to speak of the dubious quality, slow rate, and limited efficiency of their rehearsal when they perform it), it could be hypothesized that faster presentation rates (within reasonable perceptual limits) would lead to relatively better recall in these subjects. This may be the explanation for the differences in span estimates observed between Mackenzie and Hulme's study (1987) and our studies.

It is not easy to explain the data on immediate memory span in mentally handicapped subjects because an indication of limited span may result from several factors acting separately or in interaction – for example, reduced speed of item identification, incomplete acquisition or incomplete automatization of phonological items, rehearsal difficulties and/or slowness of speech rate, specific limitations in short-term storage capacity, and possibly motivational variables. Few studies have addressed these questions with MR subjects. Marcell and Armstrong (1982) studied a group of DS and non-DS children and adolescents with respect to the WISC digit span task and the Auditory (and Visual) Sequential Memory Subtest(s) of the ITPA. They suggest that the limited span is due to a weakness of the memory of these subjects to retain long enough an appropriate "echoic image" of the stimuli. This is hardly an explanation, and is most likely false since it is largely reminiscent of Ellis's earliest explanation of STM deficits in MR subjects in terms of a greater fragility and quicker fading of the "traces" of stimuli left in memory stores (N. Ellis, 1963). No evidence (including neurological) has been found to support the idea of poor stimulus trace in MR subjects. N. Ellis himself (1978) has revised his opinion on the matter. He now sees the STM deficits of MR subjects more in terms of inadequate use of memory strategies and control processes. Das (1985) and Varnhagen, Das, and Varnhagen (1987) claim that the major problems with AV-STM in MR subjects (mildly MR children in Das, young adults with DS and young adults with moderate and severe mental retardation from other etiologies in Varnhagen et al.) are located, so to speak, within the articulatory loop. We have obtained data seemingly interpretable along the same line with our control DS adults (with standard language abilities for moderately and severely MR persons) – see Section 5.8.7.3. It could be the case that one of the major difficulties of the regular MR individuals, when it comes to AV-STM, is with the articulatory control process. A similar conclusion is reached by Hulme and Mackenzie (1992). They favor an interpretation in terms of a failure to employ rehearsal, or efficient rehearsal, in moderately and severely MR subjects, which leads to deficits in the operation of the articulatory loop. In this respect, if those with mental retardation largely failed to utilize rehearsal to maintain information in the phonological store, then even if their articulatory skills improved with age, no sensible change in span would be expected. Even assuming for the sake of the discussion that regular moderately and severely MR subjects rehearse sometimes and somehow, it would still be the case that their speech rate is slow due to difficulties in phonetic realization and motor programming. According to a quick and rough estimate of speech rate made by us with a few DS adult subjects, their overt speech rate varies from 37 to 79 words per minute (i.e., 1 word – 4 to 5 phonemes – per second and less) versus around 200 words per minute (i.e., approximately 3.3 words – 12 to 15 phonemes – per second) for Françoise and for normal adults (males and females) of corresponding ages (which is about the normal rate for continuous speech, according to Caron, 1989). Incidentally, Kaneko (1989) also found recited sentence duration time in Japanese to be significantly longer in MR than in NR subjects (the difference between the two groups of subjects, 7 and 14 years of age, increasing from slightly less than 200 to slightly more than 500 milliseconds for sentences containing 7 words). Additional mechanical difficulties with phoneme realization, as they are known to exist in DS, may explain the observation sometimes made (e.g., Rempel, 1974; Marcell & Armstrong, 1982; but not in Hulme & Mackenzie's 1992 well-controlled study with 55 DS and 55 non-DS MR subjects, however) that DS subjects exhibit poorer digit span performance than do non-DS MR subjects of similar MAs. Indeed, additional articulatory difficulties may complicate and contribute to slow down further the rate of rehearsal in DS subjects, wherever rehearsal does exist.

Returning to Zhang and Simon's (1985) formula for estimating the STM capacity (see earlier), it could be that regular MR subjects (1) need more time (than normals) to bring each chunk into the articulatory mechanism, *whenever they do it*, if they do it, and (2) require more time to produce each articulated syllable in the chunk, *whenever they do it*. These limitations probably are compounded by more central deficits (including at the level of the central executive component of working memory) and by the related fact that in many tasks the average size of the chunks in the MR person's STM system is probably smaller than that in normals. Judging from this evidence, it is not too difficult to understand why moderately and severely MR subjects suffer and keep suffering from drastic AV-STM limitations. This certainly warrants attempts at teaching MR children STM skills (Hulme & Mackenzie, 1992; Broadley & MacDonald, 1993).

What about language-exceptional MR individuals? Unfortunately, STM data are not reported by Bellugi et al. (1988) apropos of their three exceptional Williams syndrome adolescents. This is also the case in the several reports (including the one by Cromer, 1991) on exceptional hydrocephalic MR children and adolescents. Curtiss (1988) and Yamada (1990) have supplied some information on the STM capacity of their exceptional subjects. Antony is reported as having an auditory STM (ITPA Auditory Sequential Memory Subtest) at the 7-year-old level. This corresponds approximately to a digit span of 4.6, according to the data supplied by Mackenzie and Hulme (1987). A similar span is supplied by Curtiss (1988) for Rick's AV-STM. No information is supplied on Antony's visual STM. For Rick, it is estimated to be below 2 years (ITPA Visual Sequential Memory Subtest), a noticeable dissociation with regard to his auditory STM. Curtiss (1988) conservatively estimated Laura's AV-STM to be at the 3-year-old level. Yamada (1990) reports a digit span of three on the Auditory Sequential Memory Subtest of the ITPA, and a word span of three on the Auditory Memory Span Test (Wepman & Morency, 1973). On a nonstandardized test of word span designed by Yamada (1990), consisting of some of her favorite words (e.g., *Beatles, cake, fat*), Laura exhibited a similar capacity of three items. As to visual STM, Laura was able to reproduce sequences of up to three elements on the Visual Sequential Memory Subtest of the ITPA, obtaining an age score of 4 years and 1 month.

Concerning Françoise, data and processing analyses regarding working memory have been supplied in Section 5.8.7.3. She has an AV-STM span of four and a VS-STM span of three. Françoise demonstrated a phonological similarity effect, a word-length effect, and problems with articulatory suppression, these effects attesting to the existence of phonological coding and active and spontaneous rehearsal during memory tasks. These observations seem to warrant a diagnosis of an AV-STM that is limited in scope and power, but basically functionally normal, together with the existence of important limitations at the level of the central executive component of working memory. This component may be selectively impaired in some traumatic brain pathologies (see Van der Linden, Coyette, & Seron, 1992). In the case of

Françoise, however, the impairment probably goes along with her more general cognitive shortcomings.

Now, what relationships may be established between the functioning of working memory in the language-exceptional MR subjects and their exceptional language abilities? Before indulging in this exercise, it is necessary to summarize minimally the current complex and sometimes conflicting literature on the relationship between working memory and language processing, including developmental aspects.

A number of claims have been made in the recent literature regarding the relationship between working memory, or particular components of it, and several aspects of oral language receptive functioning and development. The evidence comes from studies on language development in normal children and on the performance of patients suffering from impaired STM following brain damage (see Baddeley, 1990, for summaries of these works). Working memory is claimed to support language processing in two basic ways. First, it provides temporary storage for information as language is being processed. Second, working memory supports information processing in supplying a working space for the treatment operations of the material stored. More concretely, it is contemplated that working memory may play a role in the acquisition of vocabulary and in the comprehension of language.

In *vocabulary acquisition*, STM may support phonological learning. Gathercole and Baddeley (1989, 1990a) supply evidence demonstrating a significant correlation between nonword repetition ability (an ability known to depend on the proper functioning of the articulatory loop) and size of receptive vocabulary (British Picture Vocabulary Test, Dunn & Dunn, 1982). They followed longitudinally children aged 4 and 6 years at the beginning of the study. A mechanism possibly accounting for this relationship is that the longer the new word is held in short-term storage, the greater is its chance of being learned. If proved correct, this interpretation might help explain the difficulty of some language-disordered children in learning new words despite normal or normallike conceptual development (Gathercole & Baddeley, 1990b). These children could have poor short-term phonological storage capacities, which would render learning new words more difficult. Acquiring a new word involves both (long-term) semantic construction of the underlying concept and association of it to a particular phonological sequence that is a possible word in the language ("wordlikeness"). It is this latter step that is presumed to depend more particularly on the articulatory loop component of working memory. The same reasoning may be applied to MR individuals. As indicated earlier, regular moderately and severely MR subjects typically have markedly reduced AV immediate memory spans. Since there is a relationship between nonword or new word repetition and phonological memory at least until approximately 8 years in NR children (beyond that stage, repetition tasks become too easy and are no longer a sensitive measure of phonological memory) (Gathercole & Baddeley, 1990b), it may be hypothesized that limitations in phonological memory are responsible, in part, for the difficulties and delays in vocabulary learning in MR subjects. Presumably, limitations in phonological memory and a possibly noisier functioning of the phonological loop in these subjects render difficult and unstable the organization of temporary phonological representations of new words in STM, which then prevents or delays the construction of corresponding LTM representations. In the MR subjects, these peripheral difficulties (so to speak) may add to conceptual deficits to make vocabulary development problematic. Regarding the language-exceptional children studied, it is not clear whether the same phonological memory limitations may be advocated to explain, even partially, their lexical limitations (recalling that these are milder than those of regular mentally retarded persons). Curtiss's Antony and Rick (Curtiss, 1988) have auditory STMs estimated at the 6- to 7-year-old level (digit span four to five). Yet they demonstrate severe and persisting receptive and productive lexical difficulties. This was also the case of Yamada's Laura, but Laura's AV-STM span, as reported, does not exceed three items. Part of her lexical difficulties therefore could have to do with limitations in phonological memory. As for Françoise, her AV-STM span is four items. She is able to repeat nonwords containing up to four syllables without error, as documented in the articulatory testing reported in Chapter 5. It is unlikely, therefore, that much of the relative underdevelopment of Françoise's lexicon could be explained in terms of phonological memory limitations. Presumably, the lexical difficulties exhibited by Curtiss's subjects, as well as the milder deficit of Françoise in the same respect, must be traced primarily to their conceptual limitations. As to Laura, the possibility that she has in addition to her conceptual difficulties, a marked deficit of phonological memory, cannot be ruled out; but it is difficult to be more specific since apparently no nonword repetition test was performed with her. Turning to the difference between Françoise's expressive and receptive lexical capacities and those of typical DS subjects, it is conceivable that her better functioning with respect to the phonological loop – itself very likely a reflection of her better speech and speech rate – could explain at least a part of this difference. There could be a sort of general bidirectional effect: from speech to the phonological loop and from a better phonological loop to further vocabulary acquisition. Of course, this is not the only possible explanation. Françoise's general cognitive capacities are moderately better than those of most typical standard trisomy 21 subjects (see Chapters 3 and 5 for quantitative indications on this point). As acknowledged, referential and conceptual aspects of lexical development are sensitive to general cognitive development, which may also contribute to explaining this difference.

Working memory has also been claimed to play an important role in *language comprehension*. Language comprehension depends on a number of capacities and knowledge: knowledge of vocabulary, knowledge of propositional semantics and of the morphosyntactic rules of the language, and strategy selection, as well as the capacity to coordinate these various phenomena. Regarding working memory, it could be that comprehension of oral language is related to the proper functioning of the articulatory loop and the central executive, but to what extent for each component?

It has been suggested (e.g., Baddeley, 1990, and in press) that the phonological store plays an important buffering role in retaining strings of incoming words for a short period of time pending the construction of a more durable representation of the structure and meaning of the sentence. This function may be particularly useful with certain sentence types, whereas others may be treated more automatically (because their components are easier to parse and/or because such sentences or parts of it are overlearned). Sentence types for which the momentary preservation of the incoming surface information may be necessary because the internal representation is more difficult to build include longer sentences, particularly those with redundant verbiage confusing canonical sentential relationships. However, the current evidence for the importance of AV-STM in language comprehension is far from overwhelming. The most interesting data in this respect come from neuropsychological studies. For example, Saffran and Marin (1975), Caramazza, Basili, Koller, and Berndt (1981), Vallar and Baddeley (1984a, 1984b, 1987), and Baddeley and Wilson (1988) have presented individual cases of patients with relatively pure STM deficits and correlated language comprehension problems. The results were generally interpreted as showing that a gross impairment in the functioning of the AV-STM store is likely to lead to comprehension difficulties with oral language and, to a lesser extent, with written language. A sentence span of 7 words is sufficient, according to the studies of Vallar and Baddeley, to allow normal comprehension except with particularly long and complex sentences, where maintenance of the surface characteristics of the linguistic material is necessary for performing a given task (e.g., detecting long-distance syntactic anomalies occurring in long sentences thus separated by several intervening words). Baddeley and Wilson (1988) suggest that shorter sentence spans are likely to have a dramatic effect on language comprehension. The patient they studied had a sentence span reduced to three words. He showed no difficulty in comprehending short sentences but demonstrated increasing problems in comprehension as sentence length increased and, most particularly, in processing sentences that were long and plausibly reversible. However, this type of interpretation – that the crucial factor determining comprehension problems is indeed STM limitation and overload – has been questioned. Butterworth, Campbell, and Howard (1986) and Butterworth, Shallice, and Watson (1990) have argued that in the cases studied the possible existence of specific syntactic processing problems had not been ruled out. They also presented "countercases" of patients with limited STM spans and normal comprehension, suggesting, on that basis, that AV-STM is not necessary or of only a limited utility for auditory comprehension (see Baddeley & Wilson's 1988 as well as Vallar & Baddeley's 1989 replies and counteranalyses, however). Butterworth et al. (1990) carry the theoretical discussion one step further. They argue, taking into account additional clinical and experimental data of their own, that since a reduced immediate span of, say, three words can be proved to be sufficient for normal sentence comprehension, it may be assumed that the AV-STM contribution to sentence comprehension is only three words or so. Therefore, with messages "yielding adequate representations" (p. 210), there is no important role for phonological memory in comprehension. Nonphonological stores or working spaces containing the additional information for dealing with the semantic and syntactic information must be assumed to play the major role, and comprehension difficulties, when present, with such messages have to be attributed to a deficit with these latter systems. (For a corresponding theoretical proposal and converging empirical data from comprehension studies with brain-damaged subjects, see Caplan & Hildebrandt, 1988.)

It would seem that the observations concerning Françoise are congruent with Butterworth et al.'s (1990) interpretation. Françoise's digit span is 4, it may be recalled. Her word span is about 4. We also measured her sentence span. It is approximatively 14 words. At times, she is able to repeat correctly sentences containing up to 19 and 20 words. This may be considered near-normal functioning according to data reported by Miller and Selfridge (1950) and by Craik and Massani (1969). Butterworth et al. (1986) presented university undergraduate students with 40 sentences 15–21 words long for immediate recall. They recalled 25 of them perfectly. Most of the errors were omissions and word substitutions; very few word order errors were observed. Such was also the case with Françoise for most of the sentences containing more than 14 words. In contrast, two regular DS adult subjects from La Fermette (one female, one male), used as controls, could not repeat correctly sentences containing more than 7 or 8 words. One other DS adult subject (female), also from La Fermette, could not correctly repeat sentences with 5 words. Additionally, it will be recalled that Françoise had little problem in correctly interpreting (center-) embedded subject and object relatives (see Chapter 5) when the relative pronouns and their coreferring nouns were separated by several incoming words. Nor did she have particular difficulties in correctly establishing pronominal coreference across sentences in nonambiguous paragraph interpretation, or with personal pronouns and coreferring nouns separated by several incoming words. It seems reasonably clear that the contribution of Françoise's immediate phonological memory to sentence treatment is minimal. Her demonstrated capacity with the comprehension of sentential material may be postulated to depend mainly on linguistic operations and (implicit) linguistic knowledge recalled from LTM and momentarily stored in nonphonological working memory. These data seem to be compatible with Potter and Lombardi's so-called regeneration hypothesis (1990). According to this conception, the accuracy in immediate recall of a sentence is not due to a surface (i.e., verbatim) representation of the string of words but to the regeneration of the sentence from a conceptual representation, using activated lexical entries. Lombardi and Potter (1992) further suggest that in regenerating a sentence from its conceptual representation, the selection of the verb determines the syntactic structure of the sentence. When more than one syntactic structure is compatible with the conceptual representation and with the chosen verb, a structure that has been recently activated is likely to be reused.

Basically, the same reasoning could be applied to Curtiss's Antony and Rick, if only one had more detailed information on their memory capabilities. Like Françoise, Antony and Rick have limited immediate memory spans. There is, however, one important difference between Françoise, on the one hand, and Antony and Rick, on the other. In contrast with Françoise, the latter subjects have significant comprehension problems. From the reports, it appears that the bulk of these problems is semantic and pragmatic (plus attentional). They do not seem to entail specific difficulties with the grammatical organization of receptive language. If this is indeed the case, then the interpretation suggested earlier with regard to the necessity of postulating a major role of nonphonological working memories in syntactic processing for Françoise may hold true for Antony and Rick as well. The case of Laura is different, since she has limited digit and word spans but presents genuine grammatical difficulties in comprehension.

All in all, there does not appear to be solid empirical support for the idea that phonological memory plays an important role in explaining particulars of language understanding in the language-exceptional mentally handicapped subjects and, especially, the astonishing capacity of Françoise in the syntactic treatment of long complex sentences.

Before leaving the memory domain, let me point to and discuss the most remarkable aspect of the exceptional MR subjects' language organization, that is, their language production skills, particularly from a grammatical point of view. Indeed, what best distinguishes the linguistic capacity of these subjects, beginning with Françoise, is the excellent quality of the grammatical patterning of their productive language. We know that, for Françoise, it is normal or normallike. Language production, it is known, implies a number of steps, mechanisms, linguistic knowledge concerning productive rules, and the like (see Levelt, 1989, for an extensive analysis). Several knowledge stores as well as a number of processing components need to be postulated. Levelt (1989; see also 1992), for example, posits the necessity for the language-producing subject to dispose of a *conceptualizer* yielding a preverbal message. The preverbal message consists of conceptual information whose expression is the means for realizing the speaker's intention. It serves as an input to the next processing component in the system, which Levelt labels the *formulator*. A formulator is supposed to consist of two subcomponents: a grammatical encoder and a phonological encoder. The grammatical encoder retrieves so-called lemmas (i.e., nonphonological representations of an item's lexical information) from the lexicon (lexical selection) and generates grammatical relations reflecting conceptual relations in the message. The phonological encoder, acting on the basis of the preceding (grammatically encoded) structure, produces a "phonetic plan," which Levelt assimilates to internal speech, that also contains the information for generating the prosody of the future utterance. This serves as output to a third component, the *articulator*, which is responsible for the execution of the phonetic plan as a series of neuromuscular routines. The resulting movements yield overt speech. However, it would be erroneous to think that the language productive system always works in a strictly serial way. Message encoding, formulating, and articulating can run somewhat in parallel, but on different "pieces and bits" of the utterance in construction. Levelt (1989) labels this characteristic "incremental processing." As a rule, "a processing component will be triggered by any *fragment* [Levelt's emphasis] of characteristic input" (p. 24).

Functionally related to the productive system is a self-monitoring subsystem. Of course, the speaker has access to his overt speech through an auditory processing component. However, the speaker can also access his own internal speech and in so doing detect problems in it and correct them before he has completed the articulation of the message. That the planning, linearization, and monitoring processes are not infallible is attested to by the hesitations, false starts, pauses, fillers, dysfluencies, faulty triggering, and combinatory speech errors typically observed in casual speech. These phenomena have been estimated to comprise an average of 40–50% of speaking time in ordinary speech (Goldman-Eisler, 1968). Actually, a major source of differentiation between slow and fast speakers is in the amount of hesitations between words (more than in the rate of articulation itself), according to Maclay and Osgood (1959).

Levelt (1989) makes the reasonable assumption that the components of speech production act relatively autonomously in transforming their respective characteristic input into their characteristic output and that the procedures involved apply without much interference from other components in the system. Most importantly, it is assumed that intermediate representations such as preverbal messages, grammatical structure, and phonetic plan have their own kinds of units and that there must exist storage facilities and working spaces for these representations as they become available and need to be organized (or reorganized). A preverbal buffer can store preverbal messages. A grammatical buffer can store bits of grammatical structures. An articulatory buffer can store phonetic structures. These stores are open to inspection by the self-monitoring system(s). While Levelt's model is still largely hypothetical and, at this stage, only partially supported by empirical data concerning the detailed architecture of the system, it clearly assigns an important role to the storage mechanisms in speech production. Levelt (1989) uses the expression "working memory" and explicitly refers to Baddeley's work in presenting his model, particularly the storage of the information (procedural knowledge) necessary for message-generating procedures and/or for monitoring devices. This is assimilating some of the contents and the mechanisms for speech production and speech reception under the same "polyvalent" working memory function – an assimilation that is not explicitly made by Baddeley,[19] and that, strictly speaking, must be considered as Levelt's own additional hypothesis. Baddeley (1990) links his model of AV-STM to the reception of speech and language. But it is true that he somewhat "leaves the door open" with respect to speech and language production. In his 1991 paper, he writes, "In the case of the slave systems, it seems probable for example that the phonological loop represents an evolution of the basic speech perception and production systems to a point at which they can be used for active memory. Any adequate model of the phonological loop is thus likely to overlap substantially with an adequate model of speech perception and speech production" (p. 19). Actually, it is one thing to ask whether the phonological loop overlaps with mechanisms of speech perception and speech production, and another to ask whether it plays an important role in language output. On this latter point, Baddeley is much reserved. He indicates that the (clinical) evidence seems to be against the view and that he, on the whole, tends to assume that the phonological store is concerned with input rather than speech production (Baddeley, 1992). Clearly the matter is not resolved, and the exact relationship (or absence of relationship) between receptive and productive working memory needs to be specified further. Shallice (1988) indicates, from a neuropsychological standpoint, that very likely the (receptive) immediate auditory-verbal memory span is not a sub-component of the speech production system. He goes on, asserting that "evidence from the normal literature is now leading to the same conclusion" (p. 59). Evidence seems to exist, however, implicating a response buffer in errors in both spontaneous speech and STM. It comes from speech errors, particularly so-called Spoonerisms (i.e., speech errors in which phonological segments of words are misordered) – see A. Ellis (1980), for a review. Theoretical models also exist that combine aspects of the functional architecture of single word-processing and immediate memory (e.g., Caramazza, Miceli, & Villa, 1986). Such models identify a phonological output buffer within the STM system and conceive of it as a working memory space where phonological segments are temporarily stored prior to the application of various output processes (Burani, Vallar, & Bottini, 1991). In addition to its role in speech output, the phonological output buffer is also considered to be involved in the rehearsal process of the acoustic-vocal input momentarily stored in AV-STM and in the phonological recoding of visually presented verbal material into the AV-STM store (Vallar & Cappa, 1987; Shallice & Vallar, 1990). But, again, other authors (e.g., Klapp, Grein, & Marshburn, 1981, quoted by Burani et al., 1991, Note 3) caution that the articulatory programming of external speech and the silent rehearsal process might reflect the activity of distinct components.

Detailed experimental investigations on the nature, content, and architecture of the output buffers, as well as their possible relationship with the input buffers are mostly lacking, to the best of my knowledge. Burani et al. (1991) asked Italian adult subjects to make phonological judgments regarding initial sound similarity and stress assignment on pairs of both written words and pictures. Several experiments were carried out to assess separately the effects of concurrent articulatory suppression, chewing (i.e., nonspeech articulatory mobilization), and unattended auditory speech on phonological judgments. Results showed that articulatory suppression had a significant disrupting effect in all four conditions tested, whereas neither articulatory nonspeech (chewing) or unattended speech had any effect on the subjects' performance. These results can be interpreted as supplying an argument for the existence of a multicomponent phonological store that would have a role both in immediate verbal memory and in lexical processing.

Daneman and Green (1986) and Daneman (1991) have reported experiments purporting to demonstrate that working memory is an important source of individual differences in verbal fluency. They rightly contend that speakers must maintain their semanticosyntactic frameworks active in working memory for constant reference and self-monitoring while they select, retrieve, and activate the lemmas (to keep up with Levelt's terminology – Levelt, 1989) from the appropriate part of the lexicon and insert them into the grammatical structure, prior to issuing this input to the articulator. According to Daneman (1991), the facility with which a speaker can produce and coordinate appropriate lexical items on line is directly related to the processing and temporary storage functions of working memory. Along this theoretical line, Daneman and Green (1986) have devised a so-called speaking span test, designed to measure working memory capacity for language production, in which the subject is presented increasingly larger sets of unrelated words individually for 1 second each. At the end of the set, the task is to use each word to produce aloud a grammatical sentence containing that word. Daneman (1991) administered the speaking span test to university students whose performance was also assessed on measures of verbal fluency (i.e., a speech generation task requiring subjects to produce a 1-minute speech about a picture they were looking at; a technique used for eliciting Spoonerisms, and consisting in having the subject read potentially phonologically interfering word pairs on a computer screen at a rate of one word pair per second). Results indicate that speaking span is related to speaking activity. Individuals with smaller speaking spans are less fluent and prove more prone to making speech errors. In her contributions, Daneman (see 1991) seems to envisage a sort of multipurpose working memory system varying as a function of how efficient the subject is at the specific task proposed (e.g., language comprehension or language production). This, to me, is a very unclear proposal. Additionally, Daneman's speaking span test may probably be questioned on the ground of methodological validity as a measure of sentence production. I wonder whether retaining in immediate memory increasingly larger sets of words and using each word to generate a sentence containing that word can really tell us anything interesting on the functioning of the working space in sentence production. We applied Daneman's speaking span test to Françoise. Consistent with her word span, it yielded a span of 3. As demonstrated, her productive language proves normal or close to normal in terms of utterance construction and lexical insertion. Her MLU is 12.24 with an SD of 9.65 and a range from 1 to 58 words plus bound grammatical morphemes. Under these conditions, it is difficult to recognize much validity to Daneman's speaking span as an index of productive memory capacity. It is doubtful whether this index measures anything more than word span in "linguistically noisy" conditions (i.e., in this case, sentence production). Lacking a better alternative, I would be tempted to trust MLU more in this respect. MLU relates to overt speech and not directly to the formulating stage and related working space(s), to use Levelt's terminology. It is a (final) product and not an index of containing capacity. What is produced within the same utterance boundaries (sometimes sets of complex sentences) must have been planned in close temporal proximity and structural connection, maintaining the semantic-syntactic framework(s) active in the working space while searching for appropriate lemmas, and performing the necessary grammatical rules on the message being assembled. In this respect MLU probably gives a relevant rough estimate of working space capacity at the level of Levelt's formulator component of language production.

Curtiss and Yamada's Antony, Rick, and Laura were not measured for MLU, nor was Cromer's D.H. But judging from the published reports, it is certain that their language productive capabilities were most remarkable, particularly from a morphosyntactic point of view. Bellugi et al. (1988) report MLUs varying from 8.6. to 13.1 for their three Williams syndrome subjects, which is also impressive and normal or close to normal productive language characteristics. In contrast, regular MR adolescents and adults (DS or otherwise) demonstrate MLUs from approximatively 3 to 6 morphemes (see Chapter 2). Very likely, these latter subjects do not possess appropriate working space for language formulation.

In conclusions concerning the language production issue, the language-exceptional MR subjects studied all have noteworthy capabilities for producing structurally complex language and uttering long grammatical sentences. It seems likely that such competence cannot be possible without mostly intact functioning of working spaces devoted to organizing the language production. Those working spaces are not well understood at the present time, which, in turn, does not allow their empirical investigation to be more specific. Judging from the exceptional cases reviewed, it would seem that the productive working spaces in the exceptional subjects do not present the same limitations as do their receptive auditory-verbal immediate memory stores and may not depend on the latter.

6.5.3 Linguistic knowledge and operations

The major differences between language-exceptional and regular MR subjects are in the former's capacity for complex productive and receptive syntactic operations, with the possible help in the case of language production of well-developed productive working memory spaces. The double question is, Where does the procedural language knowledge come from in exceptional MR subjects, and why is it not available to regular MR individuals?

As argued previously, it is very unlikely that this knowledge could have come about as the gradual product of teaching-learning interactions between the MR children and their parents or other normal adults. Some scholars (particularly those working in the Piagetian tradition) believe that language development basically follows from general cognitive development or from operational development. This may be at least partially true for such components as lexicon, semantic structures, and pragmatic rules, but certainly not for phonology and grammar, as the developmental psycholinguistic literature indicates for the NR child and as data on language-exceptional MR subjects clearly confirm. Could these latter subjects have worked their way through the grammatical system by taking advantage of extraordinary capacities at the level of receptive AV-STM (assuming just for the sake of argument that this alone could be sufficient for securing advanced grammatical development)? The answer is no. The language-exceptional MR subjects studied all had AV-STM spans shorter than normal (Curtiss's Antony, however, had a AV-STM corresponding to his CA). Moreover, judging from Mackenzie and Hulme's (1987) longitudinal data in NR and MR children and adolescents, their AV-STM spans probably were even shorter at the time of their language development, which reinforces the preceding negative conclusion.

Let us assume that, for language production, one has three major subcomponents linearly connected – a simplification – that is, the conceptualizer, the formulator, and the articulator (following Levelt's 1989 taxonomy and presentation), and that for oral language reception and comprehension, there are also three linearly connected subcomponents, that is, an auditory analyzer, a language comprehension system (responsible for decoding grammatical relations and retrieving the meaning of the lexical units in the incoming messages), and a conceptualizer (the same as for the language production system or one that shares a great deal of information with the former).[20] Only the first two subcomponents in the former case and the last two in the latter case matter for the following discussion. It may be suggested that the semantic basis of language (at the level of the conceptualizer) develops in relation with general cognitive development, ordinary world knowledge (entities and relationships), and lexical knowledge. It would seem that limited cognitive development is sufficient to warrant correct receptive and productive use of semantic relationships in rudimentary linguistic messages. As reported in Chapters 2 and 3, regular MR subjects do not have particular difficulties with the basic semantic structures of language, either productively or receptively. Things are different when it comes to the functioning of the grammatical encoder of the formulator and its receptive counterpart. Regular MR subjects are not able to go much beyond simple linear chaining of a few words and simple phrases usually correctly organized as to word order, embodying minimal and often ungrammatical morphosyntactic gender and number concord between elements of the utterance. Correct word ordering and minimal morphosyntactic marking with these subjects are not to be seen as the product of the application of truly grammatical rules. They are the product of simple associative learning applied to chains of lexical elements corresponding to elementary argument structures. These subjects understand sentences only to the extent that they can resort to lexical, pragmatic, and situational information and/or simple heuristics based on word order. In contrast, language-exceptional MR individuals function (at least expressively for some of them) in many ways like normals. I do not see any convincing explanation for these facts except (1) the existence of implicit grammatical knowledge derived from innate predispositions in language-exceptional MR subjects and (2) the absence (or, better, the nonexpression) of such predispositions in regular MR individuals. The same reasoning is applicable here as with the genetically coded phonetic information postulated by Liberman (see Section 6.5.1). If Chomsky and others are right in postulating the existence of genetically coded grammatical information in humans,[21] the same information must be recognized in all MR subjects with nongenetic syndromes because these subjects are genetically intact. For the genetic syndromes, one could consider either that the genetically coded grammatical information is totally or partially destroyed as a direct consequence of the genetic anomalies causing the syndromes or that it is spared, in which case one finds oneself in the same theoretical situation as with the nongenetic syndromes.

One strong reason to favor the latter explanation is that, as already noted, genes in genetic syndromes such as DS are normal (Epstein, 1991). Additionally, and just as for phonology, grammatical development and functioning are not qualitatively different in genetic syndromes (e.g., DS) from what they are in nongenetic syndromes leading to moderate and severe mental retardation. As for phonology, this observation is supportive of the hypothesis according to which genetically coded grammatical information is also available in the genetic syndromes constitutive of mental retardation. Also supporting this hypothesis is the fact that mosaic DS subjects do not exhibit grammatical abilities that are qualitatively different from those of non-mosaic DS subjects. It seems to me that if the genetic problems causing DS destroyed the genetically coded grammatical information in the standard and translocation DS cases, there should be important qualitative differences between those and the mosaic DS subjects, as well as between mosaic DS subjects themselves, depending on the proportion of cells affected with trisomy 21. Such observations have not been reported. The exact reasons for the nonexpression of genetically coded grammatical information in the case of the regular MR persons cannot be defined at the present time, nor can the exact reasons for the expression of genetically coded grammatical information in the case of the language-exceptional MR subjects. One reason that genetic grammatical predispositions are not expressed phenotypically is the lack of speech exposure during the first years, as shown by the dramatic stories of the "wild" children (see later). This reason does not apply to MR children. But there may be other reasons linked to organic problems involved in mental retardation that may result in blocking the expression of intrinsic grammatical propensities.[22] In suggesting the second explanation regarding language-exceptional MR subjects, I am rejoining Curtiss (1988), Cromer (1991), and Yamada (1990). These authors have all concluded that their study cases marshaled evidence in favor of domain-specific and innate principles in grammatical development. These principles may be those of universal grammar as presented by Chomsky or some other sets, yet to be discovered. Of course, at the present time, we can only speculate on the nature of the genetic structures involved in language growth. Concerning the, perhaps, 100,000 human genes, less than 1% have been roughly defined as to their position (Kimberling, 1983). It will obviously take some time before this knowledge is sufficiently extended so as to allow molecular biology to provide direct evidence on the question of the innateness of language. However, current informed speculations on this point are no more daring than corresponding speculations regarding other (nonlanguage) structural or functional organizations (as Lenneberg, 1967, remarked). For example, we know that the development of the heart or the liver is genetically coded, but we do not know which of the 10^7 DNA sequences are specifically responsible for that development.

Bickerton (1990) has proposed that the human languages known today evolved in two steps. What first emerged in some particular species of the hominid line (perhaps *Homo erectus*, about 1 million years ago) was a protolinguistic mode – a protolanguage – lacking most if not all of the formal properties that characterize modern languages. Such a protolanguage, it may be supposed, consisted of a referential lexicon with a set of protogrammatical items that did not refer directly but either referred indirectly or allowed for the performance of communicative functions requiring abstract elements (i.e., negators, question words, pronouns, space and time markers, quantifiers, and modals). These elements permitted the expression of elementary thematic structures. But no syntax was involved (no regularities of word order, no systematic expansion of structure in phrases and clauses, no obligatory expression of subcategorized arguments, etc.). As to expression, Bickerton assumes that such a protolanguage used the vocal channel from the very beginning but that the unanalyzable wholes produced were more like grunts or gurgles than like speech. Indeed, it would seem from paleoanthropology and evolutionary biology that no species (including Neanderthals) prior to ours was really equipped for fully articulate speech (see Lieberman, 1984; Bresson, 1991). One could probably not develop large vocabularies in that way, but there is no reason to believe that original vocabularies were very large. As vocabulary grew, however, it could have exerted a selective pressure. Those hominids who were able to produce (articulate) and comprehend a larger number of words probably were more likely to occupy leadership roles in their groups, to be mates more sought after, and to leave more numerous progeny than less able hominids. Vocabulary and articulation may have evolved gradually under natural selection following sequences of mutations. Another series of mutations at some point in time during the post-*erectus* period (i.e., *Homo neanderthalensis* and overall *sapiens* – originating in Africa or nearby; Cavalli-Sforza, 1991 – in the last 75,000 years) would have brought about "true language," characterized by the existence of grammatical (morphosyntactic) principles.[23] Bickerton (1990) assimilates the formal protolanguage organization to NR children's language under age 2 to the utterances of signing chimpanzees elicited by specific training, to the structure of historical pidgins, and to the case of Genie, the "modern-day" wild child studied by Curtiss and associates (Curtiss, Fromkin, Krashen, Rigler, & Rigler, 1974; Curtiss, 1977). Genie had been completely isolated from the age of 20 months until 13 years and 7 months.

When she was discovered, she could barely walk, could not chew or bite, understood only a few individual words, and did not speak at all. From the time of her discovery on, she developed relatively rapidly despite the fact that aside from sign language instruction, she had very little overt language training. Four years later, she had demonstrated most aspects of concrete operational intelligence, in the sense of Piaget. Her language progressed relatively rapidly in terms of the acquisition and enrichment of referential lexical skills and relational semantics. However, the acquisition of grammatical rules and their use in progressively more complex utterances never followed. Her speech remained grammatically much underdeveloped (word order was globally appropriate, but language productions were devoid of almost all bound and free grammatical morphemes and syntactic devices). In addition to her semantic knowledge, Genie demonstrated knowledge of some lexicosyntactic subcategorization facts. For example, she could answer WH-questions by producing the correct constituent category. Genie's failure to develop appropriate morpho-syntax was attributed to her having passed the estimated boundary of the assumed critical period for grammar acquisition (see Lenneberg, 1967).[24] Her case also demonstrates that operational intellectual development is not sufficient for promoting grammatical development. A corresponding (but not similar) case to that of Genie, Chelsea, is mentioned by Curtiss (1988). Chelsea is a hearing-impaired adult in her 30s at the time of the study. She attempted first-language (oral) acquisition only in her thirties on the basis of successful auditory amplification. Although the evidence on Chelsea's case remains fairly unsystematic, it would seem that she presents many of the same dissociations (e.g. conceptual-grammatical) as Genie, probably for the same reasons.[25]

Along the same Bickertonian line, regular MR subjects could be said to exhibit mostly protolanguage. The correspondence between Bickerton's description of protolanguage and my characterization of the language organization of the regular MR individuals is striking indeed. It could be, therefore, that in these MR subjects only the evolutionary older genetic predisposition corresponding to protolinguistic organization proves robust enough to express itself phenotypically in spite of the concomitant organic vicissitudes due to mental retardation.

Another interesting point is the delay observed in the language development of some of the language-exceptional MR subjects studied. Françoise's onset of language development was about 4½ years. Laura is reported by Yamada (1990) as having been developmentally delayed from birth on, including in language. But no further information is given, except that around 4 or 5 years, Laura had already developed her language substantially. No information is available regarding Rick, the hyperlinguistic MR hydrocephalic children, or the Williams syndrome adolescents. However, Antony is reported by Curtiss (1988) as having had onset of speech at 1 year and producing full sentences at 3 years.

It is known that the onset of speech is usually markedly delayed in DS (Lenneberg, 1967; Fowler, 1988). Regular DS children most often do not produce much speech before 3½ or 4 years (Rondal, 1985a, 1988b). Françoise conformed to this usual early developmental picture for a DS individual. As already indicated, architectonic analysis of the brain of DS persons reveals an important quantitative reduction of neurons. As said also, such a drastic reduction in neurons may place a limiting condition on the expression of grammatical capacity. One could speculate further that given the reduction of the neuronal substratum, onset of language development is delayed in DS because it takes a longer time for sufficiently articulated neuronal networks to emerge (Kean, 1989). The delays in the onset of grammatical development in Françoise and Laura may be related to the additional time that may be necessary for MR subjects to build the cognitive and semantic bases from which triggering of the grammatical system may take place (when there is something to be triggered, which is probably not the case of the regular MR subjects). Perhaps one should reach some baseline in cognitive and semantic abilities roughly equivalent to that of a normal child of about 2 years for the grammatical module to really start functioning. If this is correct, then the case of Curtiss's Antony is all the more astonishing. Antony is severely mentally retarded and yet he seems to have developed language and grammar within the normal time boundaries.

A last word is in order on epigenetic grammatical development in the language-exceptional MR subjects. Pinker (1987) remarks:

Innate constraints dictate that there exist noun phrases, that they are subject to parametric variation (e.g., position within verb phrase), and that they have certain universal properties (e.g., NPs [noun phrases] function as bounding nodes). But the child still must *find* noun tokens in the input so that their observed language-specific behavior can be used to fix parameters or to apply universal principles (e.g., to determine whether the language orders its verbs before its nouns or vice-versa or to determine whether a given phrase in the language functions as a bounding node). (p. 400)

This is the important (so-called bootstrapping) problem of how the child gets a proper start in forming the correct types of rules for his language. No definitive answer to this problem has been arrived at yet, but there are interesting theoretical proposals. Pinker (1987) first rejects two proposed solutions to the bootstrapping problem that cannot work according to him: Correlational bootstrapping (e.g., Maratsos & Chalkley, 1981; Braine, 1987) assumes that the child analyzes distributional properties of the input, such as serial positions, inflections, and so on, and in so doing constructs his grammatical categories (counterarguments are several: e.g., impracticability and existence of many linguistically relevant properties that are not perceptually marked in the input – e.g., phrase structure configuration, binding). "Prosodic bootstrapping" (e.g., Morgan & Newport, 1981) posits that the child records the intonation contours, stress patterns, and pause distribution in input sentences and, on this basis, infers the phrase structure trees of the sentences (no explicit model has been proposed yet as to how the children would actually effectuate such analyses). Pinker then proposes a semantic bootstrapping hypothesis (already outlined in Pinker, 1984, and suggested in MacNamara, 1972) considerably reworked from previous formulations. The basic claim of the semantic bootstrapping hypothesis is that the child initally uses semantic notions ("flags") as evidence for the presence of grammatical entities. For example, the names of persons and things may be taken as indicating nouns. Actions may be taken as indicating verbs, attributes as adjectives, and spatial relations or directions as prepositions. Pinker (1989a, 1989b) insists that the syntactically relevant semantic notions are not simple copies of pre-existing corresponding conceptual categories. They must be constructed (we have already encountered this problem in Chapter 3). As far as grammatical functions are concerned, agents of actions and causes of events may be related to subjects; sources, locations, and instruments to oblique objects; and patients and themes to objects. Phrase structure rules are learned with the help of lexical entries plus syntactic-semantic correlations pertaining to phrase structure (e.g., grammatical subject precedes verb phrase). Once this is accomplished, the child's search for other rules of grammar (e.g., does subject agree with verb?) can be more constrained than would be the case otherwise, and the universal principles that are couched in the same abstract vocabulary as the rules learned can apply automatically (e.g., leading to the grammatical acceptance of sentences such as *Who did you read a book about?* and to the automatic rejection of ungrammatical sentences such as **Who did a book about please you?*, because it violates the universal principle stating that one cannot extract a WH-phrase out of a complex noun phrase).

But the child can only get so far with semantic bootstrapping since many nouns do not refer to objects (e.g., *the landing of the plane*), many verbs do not denote action (e.g., *to desire*), and many subjects do not denote agent of action (e.g., *John received a gift*). The theory states that once a basic organization of semantic-syntactic correspondence is in order, the child may learn how to categorize "semantically opaque" (i.e., nonprototypical) language entities by observing their distribution within the known structures. With reference to such a hypothesis, it is necessary that the early input to children exhibit good semantic-syntactic correspondence. For example, in English (as well as French) full passives, agents are oblique objects and patients are grammatical subjects. One should not have the young child draw conclusions about grammatical relations from such sentences. The child might filter them out of the input using linguistic or nonlinguistic signals. Or the adults may filter verbal passives out of their speech to the young child (this is indeed what seems to happen, since verbal passives are extremely rare in the speech to young children; Maratsos, Fox, Becker, & Chalkley, 1985; Rondal & Cession, 1990). Hochberg and Pinker (1985; see also Pinker, 1985) and Rondal and Cession (1990) have supplied empirical data showing that the semantic-syntactic correspondence is quite robust in parents' input to young children.

However, even if it is plausible with regard to input characteristics, the semantic bootstrapping hypothesis has a number of problems lucidly analyzed by Pinker (1987). They all relate to whether semantic notions serve as a unique and sufficient condition for the positing of syntactic rules (not to mention whether children ever, in fact, construct semantically based rules). I will not enter into this discussion. These difficulties have led Pinker to modify partially his previous assumptions into another type of acquisition mechanism, labeled "constraint acquisition model." This new model accommodates the possibility of multidirectional and more opportunistic learning. The semantic information continues to be considered as the most important source to get the learning model started, but other sources of evidence (e.g., those advocated by the correlational bootstrapping account) are no longer rejected. They may play a role (particularly later) in development (i.e., once a certain amount of learning has already taken place). Briefly sketched, the model works like this. The *constraints* to be satisfied and that markedly restrict the number of possible solutions to the problem are those of universal grammar (e.g., notions that subjects have certain properties in their relation with word order rules). They are *boundary conditions* specified by the input that permit the network to get started. This information must be extracted from the input sentences. To that extent, the child is considered to be equipped with a sentence parser attempting (as the adult parser) to assign words to their formal categories, to group sequences of adjacent formal categories into phrases and phrases into clauses, to check on the affixes, to construct a representation of the predicate-argument structures of the sentence, and so on. Finally, there is a *pattern-matching process* working to match configurations of symbols in an input representation to rule prototypes and "already-acquired language-specific rules," and the converse. By rule prototype, Pinker means, by partial analogy with the literature on categorization, a rule that is easier for the child to identify (e.g., phrases referring to agents are easier to identify as subjects for the child during learning than are phrases referring to abstract arguments).[26] No matter how sketchy and incomplete this summary of Pinker's model is (see the original sources for more informed discussion and details), it makes clear the large extent to which the epigenesis of grammar, conceptualized in that way, is dependent on remarkable cognitive capacities such as cue detection, prototype and category construction, inference making, hypothesis testing, generalization, and autocorrection. It is hard to believe that moderately and severely MR subjects with drastically limited cognitive abilities could develop exceptional grammatical abilities in that way. On this point, one may seem to be sent back again to the innate constraints and predispositions as a palliative to missing cognitive capacities. It is not that proposals such as Pinker's do not make sense; for the normal child, they probably do. But when it comes to MR individuals, I do not see any possibility given their cognitive handicap that these individuals could behave in the manner indicated. Lasnik (1989) insists that children developing language are subject to so many innate constraints that a "small amount" of distributional analysis – distributional data being available all along – will be sufficient to yield the correct categorizations of grammatical elements. ["The more structure that the language acquisition device has, the less data (of any sort) is needed" (p. 102).] Equipped in that way, exceptional MR subjects could develop grammar to a normal or close-to-normal extent. It would seem that this is the only way that they could. Regular MR subjects, on the contrary, do not stand a chance that their grammar would develop, since its genesis is blocked and its epigenesis is out of cognitive reach.[27]

Notes

1. Or even the medical aspects. Although DS conditions were first described by Esquirol, in 1838, and second by Langdon Down, in 1887, the genetic basis was ascertained only in the late fifties (Lejeune, Turpin, & Gautier, 1959).

2. It is probably better, terminologically speaking, to say that the exceptional MR subjects have developed language to a large extent (or that they exhibited significant language growth) rather than to say that they have learned it. There is no question that language development entails diverse sorts of "internal" learning, i.e., learning that the subject makes himself on the basis of his inner propensities and knowledge in relationship with the available input, but this type of learning is not what is usually meant by the term "learning" within the theoretical framework of so-called (instructional) learning psychology. See Piattelli-Palmarini (1989) for a neat opposition between traditional "instructive" learning (assuming a transfer of structure from the environment to the organism) and learning by internal selection – together with the documented indication that there has been a general and uncontroversial demise of learning in the traditional sense in the biological sciences, and the somewhat extreme thesis that there may be no such thing as true instructional learning in reality. Also see Fodor (1983, 1985) for considerations along the same line.

3. For example, Roeper (1987) argues that the definition of an agent must originally be linked to at least two different parts of the mind: an inference system and a syntactic system, both modular.

4. In the limited review that follows, I deal only with the question of the existence of convincing neuropsychological data attesting the plausible modular nature of the language system. Many important related questions are not dealt with, e.g., what is the modus operandi of the modular entities, how are their ouputs represented, to what type of neural architecture do they correspond, and what are the characteristics of their interfaces with devoted and nondevoted central processors?

5. Some authors (e.g., Zurif & Grodzinsky, 1983) have questioned the appropriateness of the grammaticality (or acceptability) judgments for evaluating remaining syntactic knowledge in aphasics on the grounds of a "lack of naturalness" – allowing agrammatic subjects to use exotic processing routes (see the reply by Linebarger, Schwartz, & Saffran, 1983b, however) and further refinements of these abilities (Hickok, 1992; Mauner, et al., 1993).

6. This has to do with central processing or with the interface between the syntactic module and a central processor only if Roeper's suggestion of a (structural) semantic module is not accepted (Roeper, 1987); otherwise, the deficit would have to be interpreted as a problem in module interaction.

7. Although there is a good relationship between MA and lexical development, as documented before, the PPVT does not really yield an MA indication, even if it is sometimes used that way.

8. The picture in this case is at variance with the literature on dementia (not only primary degenerative diseases), where a classical observation is the preservation of most if not all syntactic competence concurrently with the existence of significant impairments in semantic processing (see Irigaray, 1973; Whitaker, 1976; Schwartz, Marin, & Saffran, 1979; Kempler, 1984; Kempler, Curtiss, & Jackson, 1987).

9. Children with SLI (specific language impairment) most often exhibit selective impairments in the use of grammatical morphemes, particularly verb inflections and function words such as auxiliaries and articles (see Johnston, 1988, for a review). This could be because their grammars lack certain morphosyntactic features, such as person and number (Gopnik, 1990), or because they do not have access to rules of regular inflection (Gopnik & Crago, 1991). Leonard, Bortolini, Caselli, McGregor, and Sabbadini (1992), however, hold that SLI children have processing problems, in particular with those surface segments that are more difficult to perceive (e.g., the unstressed syllables). Frome Loeb and Leonard (1988) also claim that SLI children regularly show moderate deficits in a range of other language areas, including syntax. In partial opposition, Clahsen (1989) maintains that dysphasic children have particular problems with the morphological categorization of verbal elements as well as with building up agreement paradigms, but not so much with the acquisition and use of syntactic rules. Along this line, some reported syntactic difficulties in SLI children (e.g., problems with verb-placement patterns in German) could perhaps be regarded as secondary to these children's problems with morphological categorization. If this hypothesis were to be proved correct, one would have an additional case of demonstrated dissociation between grammatical morphology (or, at least, aspects of it) and syntax.

10. The question of what exactly proves or does not prove the existence of functional dissociations (linked to focal lesions, degenerative pathologies, or cases of diffuse neuropathological states, as in mental deficiency) is still hotly debated at the present time (see, e.g., Shallice, 1988, for an in-depth discussion from a neuropsychological point of view). A valuable notion seems to be the "double dissociation." Accordingly, a double dissociation empirically documented between two functions across two or several syndromes constitutes a strong argument in favor of the relative autonomy of the two functions with respect to each other. This indeed seems to be the case for some mental functions and particularly some language subfunctions considered in preceding pages and sections. For example, a double dissociation of language and cognition, and of cognition and language, seems to hold developmentally, if one takes into consideration, on the one hand, the exceptional cases of language development in MR subjects, as documented, and, on the other hand, the cases of SLI children (cognitively normal) documented in the specialized literature. It has been argued, however (e.g., Ganis & Chater, 1991, cited in Gopnik, 1992), that fully distributed systems with no modularity can generate double dissociations. Therefore, the mere fact that a double dissociation exists between two functions does not in itself guarantee that these functions are governed by two autonomous modular systems. Other indications may be necessary – for example, evolutionary constraints, as suggested by Ganis and Chater (1991). Actually, it could be the case that a single dominant gene is implicated in at least some cases of SLI (see Note 21 for more detail). Such genetic evidence would illustrate a direct mechanism by means of which some aspects of language could have evolved independent of other cognitive functions. The pattern of double dissociation just mentioned coupled with this genetic evidence would satisfy a more stringent criterion for modularity. It is unlikely that the dissociative data from Françoise's case could be considered to supply additional genetic indication in the sense of Gopnik's argument. Trisomy 21 obviously modifies the individual's genotype but consists in an alteration of the number (or dosage) of an important number of otherwise normal genes (Epstein, 1991).

11. The title of a book by Jonathan Kaye, *Phonology: A cognitive view* (1989), is totally misleading in that the author does not supply any analysis as to possible cognitive influences on phonological functioning. It is true, however, that so-called constructivist or functional theorists in developmental phonology (e.g., Macken & Ferguson, 1983; Menn, 1983) have sometimes referred to their positions as being cognitivist, meaning that they oppose innate specifications. But the term *cognitive* or *cognitivist* used with this type of intension is not appropriate.

12. Interesting recent evidence (additional to the traditional evidence from congenitally deaf infants) on the importance of hearing one's own babbling for speech development has been supplied by Locke and Pearson (1990) with the longitudinal study (from 5 to 20 months) of a tracheostomized infant (also see Locke, 1983).

13. It is currently held that chromosome 21 comprises approximately 1.7% of the human genome, of which about 40 million base pairs are within the long arm of the chromosome (according to Patterson, 1987, 10–20% of chromosome 21, the 21q22 band on the long arm, is involved in DS). This seems to constitute sufficient DNA to contain from 500 to 1,000 genes. A number of them may be presumed to contribute to the DS phenotype. Unfortunately, our lack of knowledge as to the individual and interactive effects of gene expression prevents the identification of those organic and functional systems that are directly affected by the consequences of excess gene product and those that are only indirectly affected.

14. In what follows, the terms *working memory*, *immediate memory*, and *short-term memory* are used interchangeably to refer to a limited-capacity system (i.e., a system that can be improved by the use of organizing strategies but cannot be extended beyond its limits) for temporary storage of information during the effectuation of cognitive tasks, this is the case in most of the specialized literature. (For additional terminological considerations, see Baddeley, 1990, and in press.)

15. This view does not go unchallenged. For instance, Saffran and Martin (1990) insist that the role of lexical structures in STM performance has been neglected. Martin, Yaffee, and Shelton (1992) and Shelton, Martin, and Yaffee (1992) supply neuropsychological data purporting to demonstrate that there is a nonphonological component to memory span that is lexical and/or semantic in nature. I will not enter into this discussion. The interested reader is referred to the rapidly expanding literature on these questions. Much of the controversy revolves around the issues of specifying the nature and the number of subcomponents in the working memory system, as well as the content units and modus operandi of these subcomponents.

16. Including articulatory and/or reading rates in languages as diverse as English, Welsh, Spanish, Hebrew, Arabic, and Chinese (Cantonese). Hoosain and Salili (1988), for example, report a mean articulation rate of 265 milliseconds per digit for Cantonese, compared with data from Ellis and Hennelly (1980) indicating 321 milliseconds per digit for English and 385 milliseconds for Welsh. Correspondingly, the mean digit span is 9.9 for Chinese subjects, 6.6 for English subjects, and 5.8 for Welsh subjects.

17. The use of the Chinese language is justified by the interesting characteristics offered by this type of writing system from an STM and chunking point of view. Chinese has about 200 radicals or basic written forms entering into the composition of its characters (letters) and words, which have no commonly used oral names.

18. Maintenance rehearsal and elaboration, although related, should be kept distinct as working memory processes. According to Baddeley (1990), maintenance rehearsal typically will have the effect of reinforcing the priming of already existing material and structures within memory. Elaborative rehearsal, in contrast, favoring associative learning, is an instance of reorganizing the incoming material to fit in with known structures. It is more likely to lead to substantial long-term learning than will maintenance rehearsal since the latter merely maintains the status quo in the information.

19. Of course, the articulatory control process of the phonological loop in Baddeley's model is motor in nature. The question is to know whether the programming of external speech and the articulatory control process of input STM are one and the same component, two separate but intimately related components, or two independent subsystems. Morton (1970) suggested that units in his so-called logogen system (a coding system for the words or morphemes that a person knows) subserve both language perception and production (also see Crowder & Morton, 1969). In more recent work (e.g., Morton, 1979), he postulated separate but linked logo-gen systems for language recognition and production.

20. I am not proposing, which would be difficult to prove correct, that language comprehension is an exact reversal of language production, or vice versa. This sketch is only intended to sustain the discussion that follows.

21. Recent studies with SLI subjects supply evidence that some aspects of grammar usage have a genetic basis (see Tallal, Ross, & Curtiss, 1989; Tomblin, 1989; Gopnik, 1990; Hurst, Baraitser, Anger, Graham, & Norell, 1990; and Gopnik & Crago, 1991). Language impairments have been found in 3% of first-degree family members of normal probands but 23% of language-impaired probands (Tomblin, 1989), a fair distance from random distribution in the second case. The impairment has been found to be 80% concordant in monozygotic twins and 35% concordant in dizygotic twins (Tomblin, unpublished data, quoted by Pinker, 1991). Gopnik (1990) and Gopnik and Crago (1991) have investigated a three-generation 30-member family, 16 of whom had SLI. The impairment follows the pattern of a dominant fully penetrant autosomal gene. These are cases with impairment in abstract morphology (Gopnik & Crago, 1991), "feature blindness" (Gopnik, 1990), or grammatical agreement (i.e., syntactic-semantic features such as the marking and significance of number, gender, tense, aspect, case, subject-verb agreement, and the use of determiners, articles, auxiliaries, and copulas; Clahsen, 1989). Such a "single-gene theory" (not the genetic determinism in itself) has been criticized by Studdert-Kennedy (1992), who points out that most probably "many other genes are likely to be no less crucial for the development of normal sensitivity to features than the one . . . isolated" (p. 524). Plomin and Thompson (1993) also argue that major genes will not be found for behavioral organization, either in the general population or in a family. "Rather, for each individual, many genes make small contributions to variability and vulnerability" (p. 75). Incidentally, a line of research that could be of value in the preceding general respect would be to study the genotype-phenotype relations from a language point of view *comparatively* in trisomies 21, 13 and 18, in partial trisomies (e.g., 13–15, 17–18), as well as in other genetic conditions such as 8q trisomy (Chitham, Gibson, Loesch, & Rundle, 1977), or subjects with "fragile X chromosome." In this last respect, suggestive work was recently conducted by Wolf-Schein et al. (1987) and by Sudhalter, Cohen, Silverman, and Wolf-Schein (1990). These researchers claim to have identified areas of deviant conversational language in males with fragile X chromosome (e.g., when answering questions, initiating conversations, and maintaining conversational topics) that are distinct from males with DS.

22. One can only speculate about these reasons in the present state of knowledge about human genetics and brain development. For example, some of the very serious problems affecting brain growth in DS have begun to be better known. With respect to neurobiological development (see Ross, Galaburda, & Kemper, 1984; Epstein, 1986, 1987; Nadel, 1986; Lot, 1986; Wisniewski, Laure-Kamionowska, Connell, & Wen, 1986; Kemper, 1988; Becker, Mito, Takashima, & Onodera, 1991), several important findings have been reported that may be directly related to mental retardation. In particular, within DS there exists a severe neuronal reduction focused on granule cells in several cortical areas (e.g., temporal, parietal, and occipital lobes; cerebellum; hippocampal formation). Brain weight is significantly reduced particularly in the cerebellum and brain stem (Crome & Stern, 1967), two structures involved in the control of movements and muscular tonus. [The early hypotonia characteristic of DS, and so detrimental to articulatory development, could be due to a disruption in cerebellar function.] There is a reduction in neuron density in a number of brain areas affecting particularly layers 2 and 4, rich in short-circuit (associational) neurons. Neurotransmitter abnormalities (e.g., serotonin, noradrenaline) have been noted (see McCoy & Enns, 1986, for a review of the literature on this question), although their early developmental course is not clear at the present time (see Becker et al., 1991). Early structural alterations caused by biochemical imbalances at critical periods of brain maturation, associated with the over expression of some genes in the band 21p22 of chromosome 21 and, therefore, excess gene product have been noted (e.g., S-100 protein, a calcium-binding protein, with particular respect to the temporal lobe).

A convincing suggestion is that DS results in arrested maturation of neurons and synapses sometime around birth. The specific reason(s) for this arrest are not known. If one adopts a modular approach to mind, one will predict that a premature arrest or a marked slowing-down of brain development will affect more those neural systems that are at a peak in the process of maturing or that would have matured after the arrest in development (Nadel, 1986). Major psychobiological problems in DS could primarily reflect the distortions in relatively "late" developing mental systems, due to the premature arrest in neuron and synapse formation, the overall neural reduction, and the structural alterations and biological imbalances determined by excess gene product. At this stage, it could be suggested that genetically coded phonological and grammatical information, corresponding to late developing mental systems (according to the time scale envisaged in this discussion), will not be realized phenotypically in typical MR cases because of early developmental anomalies in some brain areas (possibly the posterior perisylvian sector of the left cerebral hemisphere, including the basal ganglia, with particular respect to the processing of speech sounds, the assembly of phonemes into words, and the selection of entire word forms, and the anterior perisylvian sector of the left hemisphere, including the basal ganglia, with respect to receptive and expressive morpho-syntax; this speculation is based on recent neuroanatomical suggestions by Damasio & Damasio, 1989, 1992).

Nadel (1986), most interestingly, speculates that there may also be inappropriate hippocampal development (the hippocampus is an inner cortical structure connected with the limbic system) in DS related to the premature arrest in neuron and synapse formation, responsible, in particular, for an improper maturation of the dentate gyrus of the hippocampus, which is rich in late maturing granule cells. Among other functions, the hippocampal formation is thought to be of great importance in serving as an index to neocortical storage sites, providing a basis for the integration of information dispersed throughout the neocortex (see O'Keefe & Nadel, 1978; Squire, 1992). Such a hippocampal pathology in DS would render conceptual learning quite difficult. It could also prevent the establishment of necessary associations between a priori phonological and grammatical information, possibly stored in several sites of the cortex, and the language analyzers, therefore impeding the guidance, constraint, and control of language development according to this information.

23. Actually, Bickerton (1990) suggests that a single mutation may have given rise to the changes characteristic of human species, including languages equipped with syntax. This is doubtful as it seems that (by far) the most likely way for complex designs to evolve is through sequences of mutations with small cumulative effects (so-called gradualism) (see Dawkins, 1986; Pinker & Bloom, 1990) – not to mention the "punctuationist" version of Gould and Eldredge (1977) and others. See Studdert-Kennedy (1992) for other criticisms regarding Bickerton's genetic conceptions. Curiously, in his earlier book (*Roots of language*, 1981), Bickerton was an advocate of gradualism. He does not explain why he now has adopted a saltationist account of language origins.

24. Lenneberg (1967) proposed several neurological mechanisms, which have not received support in subsequent work, to explain the critical period. Also, his tying the end of the critical period for grammatical development to puberty is probably questionable and gives a "closing date" that seems somewhat late judging from a number of indications in the child aphasia and developmental neurolinguistic fields (see Van Hout & Seron, 1983, for a review of this literature).

25. Curtiss (1988) also mentions the case of Kaspar Hauser (in the nineteenth century – Feuerbach, 1832), totally isolated from the age of 3 or 4 years until he was about 16. Reportedly, Kaspar never mastered the morphology and syntax of his maternal language (i.e., German). However, he developed most remarkably in other areas including the semantic aspects of language and intellectual abilities (e.g., mathematics). Incidentally, other studies further attest to the existence of maturational constraints on language development (also see Borer & Wexler, 1987). For example, Newport (1990) reviews evidence from deaf children and adolescents learning American sign language. Learners who begin this task in childhood reach more systematic grammatical levels of language functioning than those who begin in adulthood. These data are compatible with the hypothesis that maturational change occurs in the specific constraints needed for the acquisition of language structures, leading the older learner to less success in inducing the linguistic system to which he is exposed. Johnson and Newport (1989, 1991; see also Newport, 1992) confirm that the specific endowment allowing humans to develop languages undergoes a broad deterioration as learners become increasingly mature, in showing with a group of native Chinese speakers learning English as a second language that their correct application of the universal principle of subjacency (Chomsky, 1981) continuously declines over age of beginning of exposure to English from childhood to adulthood. (Johnson & Newport's interpretation has been criticized, however, as having failed to rule out possible effects of interference in second-language learning, i.e., the fact that second-language learning is inhibited to some extent by prior attainment in a first language – see Hurford, 1991, for a discussion.)

26. Bates and MacWhinney (1982, 1987) and MacWhinney (1987), in their competition model (see Chapter 4), also appeal to a notion of syntactic prototype close to that of Pinker but with some differences (discussed in Pinker, 1987, e.g., regarding the relative goodness of some instances of formal classes in languages as compared with others).

27. It does not seem that connectionist approaches to language learning (e.g., Rumelhart & McClelland, 1986, 1987; Elman, 1990a, 1990b) would yield a more optimistic picture with respect to grammatical development in MR subjects. So-called parallel-distributed-processing (PDP) connectionism (to make it short because there are distinct brands of connectionism; see Quinlan, 1991) holds that mental functions, such as learning and cognition, are rooted in the way neurons interconnect and communicate in the brain. Neural networks do not use linguistic rules. In learning verb forms, for example, their connections are "simply" weighted according to the correlations they detect between input and output verbs (e.g., *throw* becomes *threw*, *blow* becomes *blew, grow* becomes *grew*). Extrapolating from preliminary work, PDP connectionists tend to posit that children learn the correct grammar of their language from scratch and do so by unconsciously adjusting connections within networks of neurons. Pinker and Prince (1988) have analyzed the linguistic and the developmental assumptions of the model put forward by Rumelhart and McClelland. The model fails on a number of important aspects of language acquisition (e.g., it cannot learn many rules; it can learn rules not found in human language, such as mirror-reversing the order of phonemes in a string to form the past tense; it fails to learn mappings found in all human languages, such as preserving or copying the stem as part of the past-tense form; it cannot explain morphological and phonological regularities; it cannot explain the difference between irregular and regular forms). Pinker and Prince (1988) conclude that the connectionists' claim about the dispensability of rules in explaining facts of language acquisition must be rejected.

In more recent publications, however (see Pinker, 1991, 1993; Pinker & Prince, 1991), Pinker concedes that connectionist models may represent interesting implementations of the associative memory component of language, helping people to store information about word forms (e.g., irregular verbs), but he insists that they are very unrealistic as models of grammar and grammatical development. It is not known that MR subjects exhibit a better control over irregular patterns than over regular patterns in languages, or that they are particularly clever at associating word forms in memory, remembering them, and analogizing them to similar forms. It would seem, therefore, that whatever help language learning might receive from associative networks, it could be as problematic for typical MR subjects as the proper functioning of their rule-governed processing systems. Studies of overregularization in language acquisition of MR children (with comparison to the studies of Marcus et al., 1992, and Clahsen, Rothweiler, Woest, & Marcus, 1992, conducted with NR English-speaking and German-speaking children) would be most interesting to carry out in this respect.

According to Pinker's so-called rule-associative-memory hybrid theory (1991; also see Prasada & Pinker, 1993), regular grammatical morphology is handled by a system that is independent of real-world meaning, nonassociative (e.g., unaffected by frequency and similarity), sensitive to abstract formal distinctions (e.g., noun vs. verb), developed on a schedule not timed by environmental input, organized by principles that could not have been learned, and possibly with a distinct neural substrate and genetic basis. Irregular grammatical morphology (in contrast) is handled by a distinct subsystem that is part of associative memory. Consequently, preserved grammatical abilities and deviant retrieval of high-frequency words are preconditions for overregularization. As soon as NR children develop grammatical structure, overregularization of morphological forms appears (from 2 years of age or so on). They are probably due to the child applying the morphological rule that he possesses (e.g., past marking) to irregular forms for which he fails to retrieve an appropriate form from memory. Later, with consolidation of the irregular form in memory, the overregularization phenomenon disappears (in late school ages, according to the developmental data gathered by Marcus et al., 1992). Corresponding data from German obtained by Clahsen et al. (1992) allow us to confirm that the processing difference between regular and irregular morphological forms is not simply a question of input frequency. German children avoid overregularizing most of the irregular noun plurals despite their high frequency in the German language (a situation different from English, where morphological regularity and higher frequency are confounded). German children also overregularize the regular participle ending despite its lack of input domination.

Turning to language pathology, Pinker (1991) recalls observations showing that, in agrammatic aphasia, irregular plural and past forms are read with much greater accuracy – controlling for frequency and pronounceability – than are regularly inflected forms, which should be predicted if associative memory is less affected than the grammatical system by the pathological factors. In the same way, and probably for the same reasons, SLI children exhibit more difficulty with regular verbs than with irregulars in experimental tasks in which they are requested to convert present-tense sentences into past ones. Also, regular past-tense forms are virtually absent from the children's spontaneous speech, whereas irregulars often appear. Correspondingly, Clahsen et al. (1992) report that the use of noun plurals in German, which is not determined by grammatical agreement, is not specifically impaired in German-speaking SLI children.

Regular MR subjects have serious limitations in their grammatical abilities, and they also have problematic retrievals of words from memory. They consequently have little reason to demonstrate overregularization of irregular morphological forms. Specific data are mostly lacking, however. The only published reference that I could find on this question concerns a study by Ryan (1975). She mentions that, at corresponding MLUs, DS as well as non-DS MR children, aged 5 to 10 years CA, produce ratios of incorrect generalizations of grammatical inflections in free conversational speech similar to those of NR children aged between 2 and 3½ years. Unfortunately, Ryan is no more precise except for reporting that the range of individual variation was very great. It is not possible, therefore, to establish whether her observation concerns true overregularizations of irregular forms or whether they should be more parsimoniously attributed to some MR subjects incorrectly analogizing some word forms to similar forms. Regarding language-exceptional MR subjects, Curtiss and Yamada's reports do not contain any indication concerning possible overregularizations of word forms in their subjects. Bellugi et al. (1988) and Klima and Bellugi (unpublished data, quoted by Pinker and

Prince, 1991) mention that their William syndrome subjects overregularized at high rates (16%), one of their few noticeable grammatical errors (irregular past-tense form). Over-regularization of grammatical forms may be expected particularly in young exceptional MR subjects since these subjects have mostly preserved grammatical abilities together with cognitive and memory limitations. No instance of morphological overregularization was recorded with Françoise in free conversational speech, and no specific testing was attempted with her on this point. French is roughly similar to English in this respect, with a limited number of high-frequency irregular verb forms. No information is available on possible overregularization in Françoise's speech when she was younger and developing her grammatical system.

7   General conclusions

The productive and receptive language functioning of Françoise, our DS subject, was thoroughly examined and found to be normal or close to normal in its phonological and grammatical aspects. It proved more compatible with what can reasonably be expected from a moderately MR person with regard to other language subsystems, such as lexicon, semantics, and pragmatics. Françoise's awareness of aspects of her receptive and productive language (including phonological and grammatical aspects) were extremely limited. Corresponding data available from studies conducted by Curtiss, Yamada, Cromer, Bellugi, and others, were also examined. The empirical evidence clearly supports Chomsky's (1981) proposal according to which computational aspects of language, that is, phonology and syntax, are autonomous components, largely independent from general cognitive abilities, whereas conceptual aspects of language, that is, lexicon, semantics, and pragmatics, are more dependent on cognitive functioning. As established, converging evidence exists in the so-called delay-difference literature on language development in regular mentally handicapped subjects when various aspects of language development are systematically compared with respect to mental age.

The data reported and analyzed concerning language-exceptional MR individuals are strong counterindications for any theory attempting to causally relate advanced phonological and grammatical development to general cognitive variables. In particular, the theoretical suggestions coming from the work of Piaget as to the existence of specific ties between operational development and grammatical development were found wanting in many respects. Another cardinal indication to be dismissed on the basis of the present work is the idea that children, particularly MR children, develop linguistically to the extent that they have been trained and taught. Françoise's language training over the years appears to have been appropriate but not overextensive, nor did it contain particular treatments that could be considered to have had outstanding effects.

Confronted with the most difficult task of trying to explain Françoise's phonological and grammatical exceptionality, I have followed several avenues so to speak, gathering additional data and testing them against theoretical considerations. The search has yielded mixed results. Françoise's hemispheric cerebral specialization for speech stimuli was examined using dichotic and dual-task techniques. Although she demonstrated receptive and productive speech functions homogeneously lateralized in the left hemisphere, this indication alone was not sufficient to distinguish her from other moderately and severely MR subjects. Contrary to previous reports in the specialized literature, a number of DS control subjects with regular language capacities also exhibited left-hemispheric dominance for speech stimuli. The *specific* tie postulated by Curtiss (1988) – on the basis of her neurolinguistic assessment of Genie (demonstrating right-hemispheric language processing), data on childhood hemispherectomy and hemidecortication, and of course, data on adult acquired aphasias – between specialized grammar development mechanisms and the left cerebral hemisphere was not confirmed in the present investigation. Left-hemispheric dominance is no more a sufficient condition for normal or normallike grammatical development in MR than in NR people. It may not be a necessary condition either. Françoise's working memory was carefully examined. It was found to be basically normal in terms of the processes postulated in Baddeley's model (except for central attentional resources) but not in receptive span capacities which were markedly reduced in comparison with those of normal adults. A much better capacity in productive language storage was suspected but could not be demonstrated for lack of specific validated assessment techniques available for this purpose. The discrepancy between Françoise's word span, on the one hand, and sentence span, as well as general productive and receptive language abilities, on the other, is most striking. It seemingly cannot be explained without taking into account the remarkable implicit grammatical knowledge that she demonstrates. This amazing knowledge, informationally encapsulated with respect to Françoise's major cognitive deficiencies, and the grammatical functioning that it permits and sustains have some interesting characteristics of the linguistic modules currently discussed in the specialized literature. There does not appear to be any clear way that this knowledge could have been learned or cognitively developed in the usual senses of the terms. A reasonable explanation is that this procedural knowledge is the product of a specific predisposition of the type postulated by Chomsky and others under the name of universal principles of core grammar interacting with minimal epigenetic learning, plus, of course, like anybody else, the casual learning of the peripheral aspects of French syntax.

Language-regular MR subjects appear to be restricted mainly to a kind of protolinguistic organization, to use Bickerton's bold descriptive formula. This type of organization may be more robust in terms of its genetic substratum, for speculative reasons that have been discussed. It could be argued that these subjects' true linguistic capacities are strictly limited, or even nil – in the strict sense – because of a probable lack of adequate expression of the genetically coded phonological and grammatical information. In my opinion, fundamental research should be directed toward understanding why the phenotypic expression of this a priori information is regularly blocked as a result of the early developmental misfits of mental retardation, with the hope that in the not-too-distant future, something decisively positive could be done about it.

Appendixes

Appendix 1 Speech excerpts

Notation: The framed paragraphs (numbered 1–10) were those selected for grammatical analysis. The slashes indicate utterance separation. There are no punctuation marks and no capital letters on the transcripts except those signaling questions and proper nouns, respectively. Bold italics indicate the words in which (major) tonic prominence or stress was located (in the first speech sample only); and numbers with asterisks denote the (major) clauses that were analyzed according to the levels of clause structuring defined in Chapter 5. (F., Françoise; J.F.B., interrogator.)

First speech sample

F: /et alors de la route justement il y a une pancarte /et en montant encore un peu plus haut on arrive à Banneux/

J.F.B: ah oui c'est vrai

---

1. F: /¹comme ça directement/²*et mon frère il habite sur les **roches** /³*quand vous venez donc de la vallée entre Verviers et **Liège** comme ça mon frère habite juste au-dessus dans un chalet juste sur les **roches**/⁴une grande un grand morceau d'route comme ça/⁵*il faut faire très attention **là** parce que il y a un grand **tournant** et alors pour tourner il faut bien tout **ça**/⁶au parce que des fois il fait rencontrer/

J.F.B: oui des collisions

F: /pas une collision mais/là c'est un laid coin là/moi je n'vais jamais là/

J.F.B: ah vous habitez à Fraipont?

F: /oui/ben moi je n'suis pas née à Fraipont/j'suis née à Verviers/

J.F.B: ah moi aussi je suis né à Verviers

F: /tiens/pas le pas le même hôpital quand même j'espère/c'est rue Masson moi qu'je suis née à Verviers/

J.F.B: à l'hôpital civil?

J.F.B: et bien le monde est petit et vous habitez dans la vallée à Fraipont ou bien plus sur le dessus?

269

2.   F: /⁷ben c'est-à-dire que Fraipont/⁸* j'ai une ***amie*** qui habite juste sur la place de Fraipont la place de ***l'église*/⁹* c'est bien ***simple*/¹⁰* il y a une église juste dans **l'*fond*** et alors vous montez un peu plus haut comme ça en traversant le un grand ***pont*** parce qu'il y a un petit et un grand à côté d'une épicerie le petit et l'autre pour aller pour monter alors la route du ***Haveigné*/¹¹* alors ça commence déjà à ce moment *là*/¹²* mais alors du côté pour donc on ***va*** parce qu'il y a beaucoup de ***tournants*** comme ça et alors on ***arrive*/¹³* il y a encore une maison sur le ***coin*** et vous montez un peu plus **haut** et c'est là que ***j'habite*** /¹⁴* moi j'habite par *là*/

J.F.B: c'est un beau coin hein par là?
   F: /oh oui/
J.F.B: c'est c'est la campagne hein?
   F: /parce que heu ce n'est pas vraiment la route du Haveigné hein/la route du Haveigné commence plus loin/heu en montant vers la route du Haveigné il y a un café/donc c'est toujours la route du Haveigné mais un peu plus haut c'est la rue Staline/
J.F.B: oui mais là je ne connais pas bien je vois un petit peu le bas mais

---

J.F.B: je vois où ça se trouve mais
   F: /ben la place c'est juste un petit rond comme ça et alors vous montez à main droite une route et c'est là qu'on va à Stembert/ça oui/moi j'habite entre Banneux et Tancrémont/
J.F.B: j'avais un ami qui habitait là-bas avant
   F: /Banneux c'est sur une grand-place/il y a encore des arbres et un parterre heu où on peut se garer/là il y a toujours des grand-monde là/chaque fois mais ces périodes-ci heu qu'on est en vacances il y a des romanichels hein maintenant à Banneux/
J.F.B: oh oui tiens

3.   F: /¹⁵oui oui/¹⁶* alors on doit faire ***attention*** parce que ils sont forts pour entrer dans les ***maisons*/¹⁷* alors moi je m'***méfie*/¹⁸* chaque fois que je suis souvent enfin rarement mais enfin mon père est ici ***lui*** et il fait son ***tour*** /¹⁹* mais il ne revient que le ***soir*/²⁰* alors souvent le ***jeudi*** nous autres on, se réunit vous savez toutes des /²¹* nous sommes toutes des ***femmes*** et on se réunit en petit nombre pour le goûter et tout ***ça*/²²* alors donc on on s'amuse ***bien*/²³* des fois on joue aux ***cartes*** et des fois ***pas*/²⁴* des fois comme on ***dit***, on passe sa ***flemme*/²⁵* on ***s'assied*** et puis c'est ***tout*/²⁶* oui on doit bien de temps en ***temps*/²⁷* tandis que moi quand il fait des chaleurs comme ***ça*** moi on me voit très rarement à la porte en tous ***cas*/²⁸ oh oui/²⁹ et le chien aussi /³⁰ mon chien/³¹* et ça ne m'étonne ***pas*** parce que les chiens ont toujours trop ***chaud*** quand ils vont à la ***porte*/

J.F.B: les chiens les chats
   F: /les chats je n'sais pas mais les chiens bien/moi j'ai mon petit chien moi/c'est un beau petit chien bien comment bien enrobé comme on dit/il a beaucoup d'poils hein/quand il n'est pas encore à peine à la porte il a tellement chaud qu'on le rentre tout de suite/y a rien à faire/c'est bien simple heu heu/iln'est pas encore à peine rentré il se couche déjà même par terre/il a comme il a un divan que nous en étant

petits quand on était petit on a fait les 400 coups/on a monté sur le divan avec notre pied et tout ça que pour finir le divan il devient en décrapitude là vous savez/il devient en je n'dirai pas en lambeaux mais presque enfin hein/

J.F.B: il a fait son temps

F: /oui c'est ça/alors maintenant c'est l'chien maintenant/c'est la place du chien là/

J.F.B: à quel moment êtes-vous allée là-bas?

F: /ben vers la période qui ont eu leur anniversaire de mariage/donc au mois de septembre/

J.F.B: au mois de septembre et il faisait beau?

F: /oui il faisait beau oui/moi évidemment le plus d'problèmes moi c'est de me lever évidemment hein/à mais enfin ce jour-là ça avait encore été/ça allait encore/

J.F.B: vous êtes restés longtemps à Amsterdam?

F: /ben 3 jours/

J.F.B: trois jours

J.F.B: et la ville c'est bien? je suis jamais allé là-bas

---

4. F: $/^{32*}$c'est si j'peux l'*dire* c'est un peu comme *ici* enfin/^{33*}que vous *voyez* $/^{34*}$même à *Liège* que vous voyez même des des drôles de gens drôl'dement si j'peux l'dire *platement* drôl'dement habillés/^{35*}toute façon ici à Liège c'est comme ça *aussi*/^{36*}je prends *Amsterdam* comme je prends Liège enfin $/^{37*}$c'est une grande *ville*/^{38*}c'est *vrai*/^{39*}mais vous voyez tout l'monde habillé si je peux l'dire tout *platement* aussi habillé comme *l'as de pique* enfin/^{40}vraiment comme ça/^{41}et des coiffures mirobolantes/^{42*}au lieu, d'être coiffés comme tout le *monde* les hommes ont à la/^{43*}comment ça *s'appelle* donc/^{44*}vous ça va *encore*/^{45*}vous n'êtes pas encore comme *ça*/^{46*}enfin excusez-*moi* quand même mais enfin/

J.F.B: non il y a pas de problème

F: /excusez-moi quand même/je veux dire vous savez les coiffures des hommes là maintenant/comment ça s'appelle donc?/

J.F.B: oui un peu pink là

F: /oui voilà c'est ça/

J.F.B: presque comme des iroquois

F: /oui c'est ça/ben moi je considère Amsterdam vraiment comme Liège aussi/au fond on y mange bien/c'est vrai/pour dire aussi tout platement on mange encore mieux à Liège/ah oui/

J.F.B: ça on me l'a déjà dit la Hollande

. . . une fois de temps en temps/et encore très rare/vais savez ça peut être à une fête ou quelque chose comme ça ou une fête de fin d'année/peut-être bien une oui peut-être/on n'a quand même pas l'habitude quand même hein/quand vous ne quand vous ne fumez jamais vous n'avez jamais l'habitude évidemment/

J.F.B: ça c'est un gros avantage

F: /ça c'est normal/vous vous fumez parce que peut-être que vous aimez bien c'goût là/

J.F.B: oh c'est par habitude aussi hein

5. F: /^{47*}c'est ça *oui*/^{48*}mais mon beau-frère il fumait *avant*/^{49*}maintenant il n'fume *plus*/^{50*}mais le pire comme dit ma *soeur*/^{51*}il est *marié*/^{52*}mais il a une de ces *panses* qu'elle dit mais en *riant* maintenant/^{53*}mais évidemment bon quand il *fumait* ça *allait*/^{54*}il prenait la *pipe*/^{55*}un petit coup et on la *reposait*/^{56*}on reprenait la *pipe* et on refumait deux trois petits *coups* comme vous *faites*/^{57*}on la *reposait*/^{58*}oui mais maintenant c'est *pire* parce que maintenant toutes les tous les *chemises* qu'il a vraiment sur son estomac qu'elle dit ma *soeur*/^{59*}et bien oui mais c'est une *pénitence* qu'elle *dit* parce que ma mère est toujours en train de soit de l'élargir sur les *pinces* /^{60*}oui mais c'est un ouvrage *ça*/^{61*}enfin maman le *fait* bon j'vais vous l'*dire* parce que c'est son *beau-fils* enfin/^{62*}donc elle le fait quand même par *plaisir* mais au total/

J.F.B: ce serait mieux de n'pas l'faire évidemment
    F: /ben oui justement/vous savez il fait/évidemment il mesure/je n'sais pas combien que vous vous mesurez quand vous vous mettez debout/mettez-vous un peu debout/vaguement hein moi je dirais 1 mètre 85 comme ça/
J.F.B: non moins 75 allez
    F: /75 ah ça va alors/ça va/ben lui vous il/vous vous êtes mis debout/ben lui il a attendez attendez heu vaguement certainement bien 3 têtes de plus/donc il mesure maintenant 1 mètre 92/donc vous vous rendez compte 1m 92/ils ont fait un lit pour un couple/à combien qu'elle m'a dit ma soeur?/1m 92/ ben je m'demande si c'est pas 2 mètres/
J.F.B: ah ben il faut bien ça
    F: /il m'semble que si/il m'semble que c'est ça/et encore avec une avec une fente là/vous savez ce sont des lits avec une fente au milieu là un peu comme avec des lattes/alors il y a comme une fente entre hein/mais on y

Second speech sample

    F: /c'était vraiment/il fallait vraiment qu'on rie/y a rien à faire/mais le p'tit qu'on a le p'tit chien c'est pas à nous hein/
J.F.B: non c'est un chien trouvé?
    F: /oui c'est un chien trouvé malheureusement encore pendant la période des vacances évidemment hein/
J.F.B: ah c'est souvent hein ça c'est souvent
    F: /mais attention c'est qu'il aime bien d'partir hein/parce sitôt que on n'avait pas à peine ouvert la porte que flupch il s'en va hein/
J.F.B: il s'en va tout seul?
    F: /oh oui/
J.F.B: oui

6. F: /^{63}une fois y avait quelqu'un qui est venu chez nous/^{64}je n'sais pas qui /^{65}c'était pour ma mère justement/^{66}je n'sais comment je fais/^{67}vous savez quand c'est comme ça il commence à aboyer vraiment comme un perdu même sur le facteur qui par exemple a un képi par exemple/^{68}ça il n'supporte pas ça non ça/^{69}je n'sais pas l'vôtre quand vous l'avez mais le mien c'est comme ça/

J.F.B: non le chien que j'avais il n'aimait pas les facteurs non plus

---

J.F.B: oui c'est vrai

F: /ça ne paraît pas/y en a beaucoup y en a beaucoup que j'connais qui m'disent oh t'es bien jeune t'as sûrement oh dans les 20 ans passés/je dis ben merci beaucoup quand même parce que ça fait quand même hein/

J.F.B: mais ils sont passés les 20 ans

---

7. F: /^{70}oui justement/^{71}parce que pour bien vous l'dire honnêtement quand j'ai eu mes trente ans j'ai été faire un voyage comme je vous l'avais dit pas en Rolls Royce comme dirait l'autre/^{72}le voyage qu'on a fait en train je vous ai raconté là/^{73}donc justement pour mon anniversaire/^{74}je connais une une petite une petite fille qui a probablement maintenant dix ans probablement /^{75}c'est bizarre à dire mais j'l'ai encore raconté à mon père tantôt/^{76}elle a son anniversaire tous les quatre ans/^{77}c'est-à-dire que elle est née au mois d'février/^{78}blague à part on dit toujours que le mois d'février il n'a que 28 ou 29 jours/

J.F.B: oui 29 jours tous les 4 ans

J.F.B: tu aimais bien l'école?

F: /boh c'est à voir laquelle/ce serait à celle de Dolhain oui mais celle-là non/c'est bizarre à dire mais/

J.F.B: qu'est-ce qui était bien à Dolhain?

---

8. F: /^{79}ce qu'y avait d'bien c'est-à-dire que c'était une école premièrement c'était une école de soeurs premièrement/^{80}ensuite il n'avait que des filles /^{81}donc au fond là on n'pouvait pas ni s'bagarrer ni rien du tout puisqu'on n'pouvait pas dire oh oui mais c'est celui-là qui m'a donné un coup d'pied et patati des histoires comme ça enfin/^{82}là y n'avait que des filles/^{83}donc comme y a une dans mon année qui faisait des crises de nerfs/^{84}si vous savez c'que c'est/^{85}c'est pas d'la petite bière/

J.F.B: non non certainement pas

. . . vous vous n'êtes ni docteur ni rien du tout/comme je peux voir vous êtes comme je peux dire un peu dans les enregistreurs enfin pour heu pour faire entendre celle qui parle/c'est ça qu'je veux dire/je n'sais pas dire vraiment le mot que c'est/

J.F.B: ce n'est pas que ça mon travail

F: /c'est pas programmeur quand même?/c'est pas ça?/

J.F.B: non je n'y connais rien en mathématiques

F: /non mais c'est pas mathématique puisque/mais la dame où je vais aller tantôt par exemple c'est une dame qui ne fait que de parler vous savez?/

J.F.B: c'est une psychologue

9. F: /^{86}oui voilà/^{87}c'est ça oui une femme psychologue si j'peux dire/^{88}donc au fond moi des trucs comme ça ça va parce que alors je peux m'installer comme maintenant m'asseoir et alors je peux parler/^{89}donc au fond tout ce que j'ai en moi je peux vraiment le le sortir/^{90}j'peux l'dire comme ça/^{91}tandis que si je vais chez un autre médecin si j'peux dire parce que c'est quand même un médecin puisqu'elle est quand même psychologue/

J.F.B: c'est une forme de médecine

J.F.B: est-ce qu'il te vient parfois à l'idée de te dire tiens aujourd'hui il y a ce programme là j'aimerais bien de le voir?

F: /ben des fois/

J.F.B: et c'est quel programme à part le journal?

10. F: /^{92}si c'est un genre de variétés qui me plaît oui des fois qu'je l'regarde/^{93}si c'est même des trucs de variétés/^{94}ma foi si c'est vraiment tout l'temps des trucs en anglais alors je dis ah non laisse tomber/^{95}ferme-le/^{96}moi je ne l'regarde pas/^{97}c'est inutile/^{98}je n'comprends/^{99}je parle peut-être bien l'français/^{100}il m'faut déjà toutes les plumes pour voler/^{101}alors pour entendre ceux qui chantent en anglais c'est complètement inutile de l'ouvrir /^{102}maintenant c'est ce qu'on chante la plupart du temps/

J.F.B: c'est souvent en anglais

F: /vous n'avez pas à peine ouvert la télévision on entend déjà chanter en anglais/alors je m'suis dit c'est complètement inutile enfin hein/voilà on a eu quelquefois l'eurovision là/n'en parlons pas non plus enfin hein/y en a qui chantent en danois d'autres qui chantent en suédois/

Appendix 2 English translation of the speech turns used in the linguistic analysis

Note: At times, the translation may not sound "very English." This is because I have tried to remain as close as possible to the French wording in such a way as to allow the reader to better follow the analysis.

First speech sample

1. F: /^{1}like that directly/^{2*}and my brother he lives on the rocks/^{3*}when you come therefore from the valley between Verviers and Liège like that my brother lives right above in a chalet right on the rocks/^{4}a large a large piece of road like that/^{5*}one must be very cautious there because there is a large turn and then in order to turn one really needs every caution/^{6}because at times it makes encounter/

2. F: /^{7}that is to say that Fraipont/^{8*}I have a girlfriend who lives right on Fraipont Square church square/^{9*}that is fairly simple/^{10*}there is a church right at the bottom and then you go up a little more like that crossing the a large bridge because there is a small one and a large one next to a grocery store the small one and the other one to go to go up then Haveigné Road /[11*] then that begins already at that moment/[12*] but then on the side to therefore one goes because there are many turns like that and then one is arrived/[13*] there is one more house on the corner and you go a little upper and that is there that I live/[14*] me I live over there/

3. F: /[15] yes yes/[16*] then one must be cautious because they are clever at breaking into the houses/[17*] then me I am wary/[18*] each time that I am often that is rarely but in the end my father is here him and he makes his turn/[19*] but he comes back only at night/[20*] then often on Thursdays we get together you know all/[21*] we are all women and one gets together in small number for tea and all that/[22*] then therefore one has a good time/[23*] sometimes one plays cards and sometimes not/[24*] sometimes as they say one just passes the time/[25*] one sits down and then that is all/[26*] yes one must from time to time/[27*] whereas me when it is hot like that me one sees me very rarely outdoors anyway/[28*] oh yes /[29] and also the dog/[30] my dog/[31*] and that does not surprise me because dogs are always too warm when they go outdoors/

4. F: /[32*] that is if I may say it that is a bit like here in the end/[33*] that you see /[34*] even in Liège that you see even funny people in a funny way if I may say it flatly dressed in a funny way/[35*] anyway here in Liège that is like that too/[36*] I take Amsterdam as I take Liège in the end/[37*] that is a big city /[38*] that is true/[39*] but you see everyone dressed if I may say it bluntly also dressed like "l'as de pique"[1] in the end/[40] really like that/[41] and fantastic haircuts /[42*] instead of being hairdressed like everyone men have/[43*] how do you call that again/[44*] you that may go/[45*] you are not yet like that/[46*] then excuse me for the rest but then/

5. F: /[47*] that is it yes/[48*] but my brother-in-law he smoked before/[49*] now he does not smoke anymore/[50*] but the worse as says my sister/[51*] he is married/[52*] but he has one of those bellies that she says but laughing now /[53*] but of course all right when he smoked that could go/[54*] he was taking the pipe/[55*] a little stroke and one was putting it aside/[56*] one was taking the pipe back and one was smoking again two three little strokes like you do /[57*] one was putting it aside/[58*] yes but now that is worse because now all the all the shirts that he really has on his belly that she says my sister /[59*] and well yes but that is a punishment that she says because my mother is always busy either enlarging it on the pinches/[60*] yes but that is quite a work/[61*] then mother does it well I will tell it to you because he is her son-in-law in the end/[62*] thus she does it even for fun but in the whole/

Second speech sample

6. F: /[63] one time there was someone who came by us/[64] I don't know who/[65] that was for my mother actually/[66] I don't know how I do/[67] you know when that is like that he begins to bark really like a lost one even after the mailman who for example has a cap for example/[68] that he cannot stand that not that/[69] I don't know yours when you have it but mine that is like that/

7. F: /[70] yes precisely/[71] because to tell it to you honestly when I reached my thirty years I went to make a trip as I told it to you not with a Rolls Royce as one would say/[72] the trip that we made by train I told you/[73] thus precisely on my birthday/[74] I know a a little a little girl who is probably now ten years old probably/[75] that is odd to say but I told it again to my father a while ago /[76] she has her birthday every four years/[77]that is to say that she was born in the month of February/[78]no kidding one says always that the month of February it only has 28 or 29 days/

8. F: /[79]what was good that is to say that was a school first that was a school of sisters first/[80]then there were only girls/[81]thus in the end there one could not fight or anything as one could not say oh yes but that is this one who kicked me and so on stories like that then/[82]there were only girls/[83]therefore as there is one in my class who had nervous crises/[84]if you know what that is/[85]that is no piece of cake[2]/

9. F: /[86]yes that is/[87]that is so yes a woman psychologist if I may say/[88]thus in the end I things like that that goes because then I can set myself like now sit and then I can talk/[89]thus in the end all that I have in me I can really express it/[90]I can say it like that/[91]whereas if I go see another doctor if I may say because that is a doctor all right as she is a psychologist all right/

10. F: /[92]when that is a kind of varieties that pleases me yes at times that I watch it/[93]when that is things of varieties/[94]my god when that is really all the time things in English then I say oh no drop it/[95]shut it out/[96]I do not watch it/[97]it is useless/[98]I don't understand/[99]I speak perhaps well French/[100]I already need all I have[3]/[101]then to hear those who sing in English that is totally useless to open it/[102]now that is what one sings most of the time/

Notes

1. To be dressed like "l'as de pique" means to be dressed in a funny way. This regional expression literally refers to the ace of spades of playing cards.

2. The actual (conventional) French expression Françoise used literally translates "that is no little beer."

3. What Françoise actually said literally translates "I already need all the feathers to fly." The genuine French expression literally translated, however, is "to need all *one's* feathers to fly" (see Section 5.4.1.2.3).

Appendix 3 List of active and passive sentences

Abbreviations for transitivity features: AP, action-punctual verb; ANP, action-nonpunctual verb; NAP, nonaction-punctual verb; NANP, nonaction-nonpunctual verb; PPR, plausible and plausibly reversible sentence; IPR, implausible but plausibly reversible sentence; PNPR, plausible but not plausibly reversible sentence; INPR, implausible and not plausibly reversible sentence.

Block 2		Kinesis-punctuality	Plausibility
1.	Le garçon frappe la fille (The boy hits the girl)	AP	PPR
2.	Le garçon frappe le divan (The boy hits the sofa)	AP	PNPR
3.	Le divan frappe le garçon (The sofa hits the boy)	AP	IPR
4.	Le divan frappe l'armoire (The sofa hits the cupboard	AP	INPR
5.	La maman soigne le papa (The mother nurses the father)	ANP	PPR
6.	La maman soigne l'oiseau (The mother nurses the bird)	ANP	PNPR
7.	L'oiseau soigne la maman (The bird nurses the mother)	ANP	IPR
8.	L'armoire soigne le divan (The cupboard nurses the sofa)	ANP	INPR
9.	Le monsieur aperçoit la dame (The man sees the lady)	NAP	PPR
10.	Le monsieur aperçoit la boîte (The man sees the box)	NAP	PNPR
11.	La boîte aperçoit le monsieur (The box sees the man)	NAP	IPR
12.	La boîte aperçoit le téléphone (The box sees the telephone)	NAP	INPR
13.	La fille déteste le garçon (The girl hates the boy)	NANP	PPR
14.	La fille déteste le livre (The girl hates the book)	NANP	PNPR
15.	Le livre déteste la fille (The book hates the girl)	NANP	IPR
16.	Le livre déteste le vélo (The book hates the bike)	NANP	INPR
17.	La fille est frappée par le garçon (The girl is hit by the boy)	AP	PPR
18.	Le divan est frappé par le garçon (The sofa is hit by the boy)	AP	PNPR
19.	Le garçon est frappé par le divan (The boy is hit by the sofa)	AP	IPR
20.	L'armoire est frappée par le divan (The cupboard is hit by the sofa)	AP	INPR

Block 2	Kinesis-punctuality	Plausibility
21. Le papa est soigné par la maman (The father is nursed by the mother)	ANP	PPR
22. L'oiseau est soigné par la maman (The bird is nursed by the mother)	ANP	PNPR
23. La maman est soignée par l'oiseau (The mother is nursed by the bird)	ANP	IPR
24. Le divan est soigné par l'armoire (The sofa is nursed by the cupboard)	ANP	INPR
25. La dame est aperçue par le monsieur (The lady is seen by the man)	NAP	PPR
26. La boîte est aperçue par le monsieur (The box is seen by the man)	NAP	PNPR
27. Le monsieur est aperçu par la boîte (The man is seen by the box)	NAP	IPR
28. Le téléphone est aperçu par la boîte (The telephone is seen by the box)	NAP	INPR
29. Le garçon est détesté par la fille (The boy is hated by the girl))	NANP	PPR
30. Le livre est détesté par la fille (The book is hated by the girl)	NANP	PNPR
31. La fille est détestée par le livre (The girl is hated by the book)	NANP	IPR
32. Le vélo est détesté par le livre (The bike is hated by the book)	NANP	INPR

Block 2	Kinesis-punctuality	Plausibility
1. Le garçon mord la fille (The boy bites the girl)	AP	PPR
2. Le garçon mord la pomme (The boy bites the apple)	AP	PNPR
3. La pomme mord le garçon (The apple bites the boy)	AP	IPR
4. La pomme mord la banane (The apple bites the banana)	AP	INPR
5. La maman porte le papa (The mother carries the father)	ANP	PPR
6. La maman porte le divan (The mother carries the sofa)	ANP	PNPR
7. Le divan porte la maman (The sofa carries the mother)	ANP	IPR
8. L'armoire porte le divan (The cupboard carries the sofa)	ANP	INPR
9. La fille oublie le garçon (The girl forgets the boy)	NAP	PPR
10. La fille oublie le livre (The girl forgets the book)	NAP	PNPR

Block 2	Kinesis-punctuality	Plausibility
11. Le livre oublie la fille (The book forgets the girl)	NAP	IPR
12. Le livre oublie le vélo (The book forgets the bike)	NAP	INPR
13. Le monsieur imagine la dame (The man imagines the lady)	NANP	PPR
14. Le monsieur imagine le livre (The man imagines the book)	NANP	PNPR
15. Le livre imagine le monsieur (The book imagines the man)	NANP	IPR
16. La boîte imagine le livre (The box imagines the book)	NANP	INPR
17. La fille est mordue par le garçon (The girl is bitten by the boy)	AP	PPR
18. La pomme est mordue par le garçon (The apple is bitten by the boy)	AP	PNPR
19. Le garçon est mordu par la pomme (The boy is bitten by the apple)	AP	IPR
20. La banane est mordue par la pomme (The banana is bitten by the apple)	AP	INPR
21. Le papa est porté par la maman (The father is carried by the mother)	ANP	PPR
22. Le divan est porté par la maman (The sofa is carried by the mother)	ANP	PNPR
23. La maman est portée par le divan (The mother is carried by the sofa)	ANP	IPR
24. Le divan est porté par l'armoire (The sofa is carried by the cupboard)	ANP	INPR
25. Le garçon est oublié par la fille (The boy is forgotten by the girl)	NAP	PPR
26. Le livre est oublié par la fille (The book is forgotten by the girl)	NAP	PNPR
27. La fille est oubliée par le livre (The girl is forgotten by the book)	NAP	IPR
28. Le vélo est oublié par le livre (The bike is forgotten by the book)	NAP	INPR
29. La dame est imaginée par le monsieur (The lady is imagined by the man)	NANP	PPR
30. Le livre est imaginé par le monsieur (The book is imagined by the man)	NANP	PNPR
31. Le monsieur est imaginé par le livre (The man is imagined by the book)	NANP	IPR
32. Le livre est imaginé par la boîte (The book is imagined by the box)	NANP	INPR

Appendix 4 List of sentences with relative subordinates

Abbreviations for sentence feature types: SS, nominal coreferent subject in the main clause – relative pronoun subject (parallel grammatical functions); SO, nominal coreferent subject – relative pronoun object (nonparallel functions); OO, nominal coreferent object – relative pronoun object (parallel functions); OS, nominal coreferent object – relative pronoun subject (nonparallel functions); PPR, plausible and plausibly reversible clause; PNPR, plausible but not plausibly reversible clause.

1. Qui-relatives, juxtaposed, OS type, PPR.

1. Philippe frappe David qui bouscule Jacques
   (Philippe hits David who hurts Jacques)

2. Catherine regarde Isabelle qui soigne Didier
   (Catherine looks at Isabelle who nurses Didier)

3. Le chien mord Anne qui frappe Nathalie
   (The dog bites Anne who hits Nathalie)

4. Stéphanie gronde le bébé qui pousse Brigitte
   (Stéphanie scolds the baby who pushes Brigitte)

5. Dominique pousse Sophie qui regarde Grégory
   (Dominique pushes Sophie who looks at Grégory)

6. Myriam voit Pierre qui admire Séverine
   (Myriam sees Pierre who admires Séverine)

7. Annie frappe le chat qui regarde l'oiseau
   (Annie hits the cat who looks at the bird)

8. Bernard admire le cheval qui voit le chien
   (Bernard admires the horse who sees the dog)

2. Qui-relatives, juxtaposed, OS type, PNPR.

9. Martin pousse Céline qui tient le chat
   (Martine pushes Céline who holds the cat)

10. Florence voit Cédric qui casse le disque
    (Florence sees Cédric who breaks the record)

11. Aurore attrape le chat qui griffe la souris
    (Aurore catches the cat who scratches the mouse)

12. Eric oublie le hamster qui mord la cage
    (Eric forgets the hamster who bites the cage)

13. Sophie brosse Magali qui brosse le chien
    (Sophie brushes Magali who brushes the dog)

14. Patrick admire Claire qui écoute le disque
    (Patrick admires Claire who listens to the record)

15. Cédric pousse le bébé qui regarde la cage
    (Cédric pushes the baby who looks at the cage)

16. Martine oublie le poussin qui regarde les graines
    (Martine forgets the chick who looks at the seeds)

3. Qui-relatives, embedded, SS type, PPR.

17. Olivier qui frappe Mireille pousse Gaëtan
    (Olivier who hits Mireille pushes Gaëtan)

18. Catherine qui coiffe Alain préfère Jean-Paul
    [Catherine who combs Alain('s hair) prefers Jean-Paul]

19. Claudine qui pousse Henri renverse la brouette
    (Claudine who pushes Henri turns the wheelbarrow over)

20. Christelle qui défend Jean-Pierre oublie la mallette
    (Christelle who defends Jean-Pierre forgets the briefcase)

21. Virginie qui regarde Grégory coiffe Dominique
    [Virginie who looks at Grégory combs Dominique('s hair)]

22. Isabelle qui préfère Adrien écoute Serge
    (Isabelle who prefers Adrien listens to Serge)

23. Benjamin qui apprécie Cathy ouvre la porte
    (Benjamin who appreciates Cathy opens the door)

24. Christine qui attend Gérard regarde la voiture
    (Christine who waits for Gérard looks at the car)

4. Qui-relatives, embedded, SS type, PNPR.

25. Murielle qui frappe le chien éclabousse le chat
    (Murielle who hits the dog splashes the cat)

26. Marc qui soigne le lapin aperçoit la tortue
    (Marc who nurses the rabbit sees the turtle)

27. La maman qui tient le bébé ferme la porte
    (The mummy who holds the baby closes the door)

28. Viviane qui soigne le chien regarde le ballon
    (Viviane who nurses the dog looks at the balloon)

29. Liliane qui admire le chat éclabousse le chien
    (Liliane who admires the cat splashes the dog)

30. Marie qui gronde le poussin regarde le moineau
    (Marie who scolds the chick looks at the sparrow)

31. Paul qui brosse le chat renverse le vase
    (Paul who brushes the cat turns the vase over)

32. Denis qui oublie la mallette regarde la fenêtre
    (Denis who forgets the briefcase looks at the window)

5. Qui-relatives, juxtaposed, OO type, PPR.

33. Philippe frappe David que Jacques bouscule
    (Philippe hits David whom Jacques hurts)

34. Catherine regarde Isabelle que Didier soigne
    (Catherine looks at Isabelle whom Didier nurses)

35. Le chien mord Anne que Nathalie frappe
    (The dog bites Anne whom Nathalie hits)

36. Stéphanie gronde le bébé que Brigitte pousse
    (Stéphanie scolds the baby whom Brigitte pushes)

37. Dominique pousse Sophie que Grégory regarde
    (Dominique pushes Sophie at whom Grégory looks)

38. Myriam voit Pierre que Séverine admire
    (Myriam sees Pierre whom Séverine admires)

39. Annie frappe le chat que l'oiseau regarde
    (Annie hits the cat at whom the bird looks)

40. Bernard admire le cheval que le chien voit
    (Bernard admires the horse whom the dog sees)

6. Que-relatives, juxtaposed, OO type, PNPR.

41. Martin pousse le chat que Céline tient
    (Martin pushes the cat whom Céline holds)

42. Florence voit le disque que Cédric casse
    (Florence sees the record that Cédric breaks)

43. Aurore attrape la souris que le chat griffe
    (Aurore catches the mouse whom the cat scratches)

44. Eric oublie la cage que le hamster mord
    (Eric forgets the cage that the hamster bites)

45. Sophie brosse le chien que Magali admire
    (Sophie brushes the dog whom Magali admires)

46. Patrick admire l'oiseau que Claire soigne
    (Patrick admires the bird whom Claire nurses)

47. Cédric pousse le chat que le bébé brosse
    (Cédric pushes the cat whom the baby brushes)

48. Martine oublie les graines que le poussin regarde
    (Martine forgets the seeds at which the chick looks)

7. Que-relatives, embedded, SO type, PPR.

49. Olivier que Mireille frappe pousse Gaëtan
    (Olivier whom Mireille hits pushes Gaëtan)

50. Catherine que Alain coiffe préfère Jean-Paul
    [Catherine whom Alain combs (whose hair Alain combs) prefers Jean-Paul]

51. Claudine que Henri pousse renverse la brouette
    (Claudine whom Henri pushes turns the wheelbarrow over)

52. Christelle que Jean-Pierre défend oublie la mallette
    (Christelle whom Jean-Pierre defends forgets the briefcase)

53. Virginie que Grégory regarde coiffe Dominique
    [Virginie at whom Grégory looks combs Dominique('s hair)]

54. Isabelle que Adrien préfère écoute Serge
    (Isabelle whom Adrien prefers listens to Serge)

55. Benjamin que Cathy apprécie ouvre la porte
    (Benjamin whom Cathy appreciates opens the door)

56. Christine que Gérard atttend regarde la voiture
    (Christine whom Gérard expects looks at the car)

8. Qui-relatives, embedded, SO type, PNPR

57. Le chien que Muriel coiffe éclabousse le chat
    [The dog whom Murielle combs (whose hair Murielle combs) splashes the cat]

58. Le lapin que Marc soigne aperçoit la tortue
    (The rabbit whom Marc nurses sees the turtle)

59. Le bébé que la maman tient ferme la porte
    (The baby whom the mummy holds closes the door)

60. Le chien que Viviane soigne regarde le ballon
    (The dog whom Viviane nurses looks at the balloon)

61. Le chat que Liliane admire éclabousse le chien
    (The cat whom Liliane admires splashes the dog)

62. Le poussin que Marie défend regarde le moineau
    (The chick whom Marie defends looks at the sparrow)

63. Le chat que Paul brosse renverse le vase
    (The cat whom Paul brushes turns the vase over)

64. L'oiseau que Denis tient regarde la fenêtre
    (The bird whom Denis holds looks at the window)

Appendix 5 List of sentences with causative and temporal subordinates

1. Sentences with parce que (because)

1. Parce que Philippe a frappé le chat, Nathalie pousse Philippe
   (Because Philippe hit the cat, Nathalie pushes Philippe)

2. Parce que le chien a soigné ses petits, Pierre admire le chien
   (Because the dog nursed his young ones, Pierre admires the dog)

3. Parce que le chien a goûté la viande, Johan punit le chien
   (Because the dog tasted the meat, Johan punishes the dog)

4. Parce que Raphaël a écouté l'instituteur, Sandrine félicite Raphaël
   (Because Raphaël listened to the teacher, Sandrine congratulates Raphaël)

5. Nathalie pousse Philippe parce que Philippe a frappé le chat
   (Nathalie pushes Philippe because Philippe hit the cat)

6. Pierre admire le chien parce que le chien a soigné ses petits
   (Pierre admires the dog because the dog nursed his young ones)

7. Johan punit le chien parce que le chien a goûté la viande
   (Johan punishes the dog because the dog tasted the meat)

8. Sandrine félicite Raphaël parce que Raphaël a écouté l'instituteur
   (Sandrine congratulates Raphaël because Raphaël listened to the teacher)

9. Parce que Philippe frappe le chat, Nathalie pousse Philippe
   (Because Philippe hits the cat, Nathalie pushes Philippe)

10. Parce que le chien soigne ses petits, Pierre admire le chien
    (Because the dog nurses his young ones, Pierre admires the dog)

11. Parce que le chien goûte la viande, Johan punit le chien
    (Because the dog tastes the meat, Johan punishes the dog)

12. Parce que Raphaël écoute l'instituteur, Sandrine félicite Raphaël
    (Because Raphaël listens to the teacher, Sandrine congratulates Raphaël)

13. Nathalie pousse Philippe parce que Philippe frappe le chat
    (Nathalie pushes Philippe because Philippe hits the cat)

14. Pierre admire le chien parce que le chien soigne ses petits
    (Pierre admires the dog because the dog nurses his young ones)

15. Johan punit le chien parce que le chien goûte la viande
    (Johan punishes the dog because the dog tastes the meat)

16. Sandrine félicite Raphaël parce que Raphaël écoute l'instituteur
    (Sandrine congratulates Raphaël because Raphaël listens to the teacher)

17. Parce que Philippe a frappé le chat, Nathalie écoute Philippe
    (Because Philippe hit the cat, Nathalie listens to Philippe)

18. Parce que le chien a soigné ses petits, Pierre entend le chien
    (Because the dog nursed his young ones, Pierre hears the dog)

19. Parce que le chien a goûté la viande, Johan entend le chien
    (Because the dog tasted the meat, Johan hears the dog)

20. Parce que Raphaël a écouté l'instituteur, Sandrine voit Raphaël
    (Because Raphaël listened to the teacher, Sandrine sees Raphaël)

21. Nathalie écoute Philippe parce que Philippe a frappé le chat
    (Nathalie listens to Philippe because Philippe hit the cat)

22. Pierre entend le chien parce que le chien a soigné ses petits
    (Pierre hears the dog because the dog nursed his young ones)

23. Johan entend le chien parce que le chien a gouté la viande
    (Johan hears the dog because the dog tasted the meat)

24. Sandrine voit Raphaël parce que Raphaël a écouté l'instituteur
    (Sandrine sees Raphaël because Raphaël listened to the teacher)

25. Parce que Philippe frappe le chat, Nathalie écoute Philippe
    (Because Philippe hits the cat, Nathalie listens to Philippe)

26. Parce que le chien soigne ses petits, Pierre entend le chien
    (Because the dog nurses his young ones, Pierre hears the dog)

27. Parce que le chien goûte la viande, Johan entend le chien
    (Because the dog tastes the meat, Johan hears the dog)

28. Parce que Raphaël écoute l'instituteur, Sandrine voit Raphaël
    (Because Raphaël listens to the teacher, Sandrine sees Raphaël)

29. Nathalie écoute Philippe parce que Philippe frappe le chat
    (Nathalie listens to Philippe because Philippe hits the cat)

30. Pierre entend le chien parce que le chien soigne ses petits
    (Pierre hears the dog because the dog nurses its young ones)

31. Johan entend le chien parce que le chien goûte la viande
    (Johan hears the dog because the dog tastes the meat)

32. Sandrine voit Raphaël parce que Raphaël écoute l'instituteur
    (Sandrine sees Raphaël because Raphaël listens to the teacher)

2. Sentences with quand (when)

33. Quand Philippe a frappé le chat, Nathalie pousse Philippe
    (When Philippe has hit the cat, Nathalie pushes Philippe)

34. Quand le chien a soigné ses petits, Pierre admire le chien
    (When the dog has nursed his young ones, Pierre admires the dog)

35. Quand le chien a goûté la viande, Johan punit le chien
    (When the dog has tasted the meat, Johan punishes the dog)

36. Quand Raphaël a écouté l'instituteur, Sandrine félicite Raphaël
    (When Raphaël has listened to the teacher, Sandrine congratulates Raphaël)

37. Nathalie pousse Philippe quand Philippe a frappé le chat
    (Nathalie pushes Philippe when Philippe has hit the cat)

38. Pierre admire le chien quand le chien a soigné ses petits
    (Pierre admires the dog when the dog has nursed his young ones)

39. Johan punit le chien quand le chien a goûté la viande
    (Johan punishes the dog when the dog has tasted the meat)

40. Sandrine félicite Raphaël quand Raphaël a écouté l'instituteur
    (Sandrine congratulates Raphaël when Raphaël has listened to the teacher)

41. Quand Philippe frappe le chat, Nathalie pousse Philippe
    (When Philippe hits the cat, Nathalie pushes Philippe)

42. Quand le chien soigne ses petits, Pierre admire le chien
    (When the dog nurses its young ones, Pierre admires the dog)

43. Quand le chien goûte la viande, Johan punit le chien
    (When the dog tastes the meat, Johan punishes the dog)

44. Quand Raphaël écoute l'instituteur, Sandrine félicite Raphaël
    (When Raphaël listens to the teacher, Sandrine congratulates Raphaël)

45. Nathalie pousse Philippe quand Philippe frappe le chat
    (Nathalie pushes Philippe when Philippe hits the cat)

46. Pierre admire le chien quand le chien soigne ses petits
    (Pierre admires the dog when the dog nurses his young ones)

47. Johan punit le chien quand le chien goûte la viande
    (Johan punishes the dog when the dog tastes the meat)

48. Sandrine félicite Raphaël quand Raphaël écoute l'instituteur
    (Sandrine congratulates Raphaël when Raphaël listens to the teacher)

49. Quand Philippe a frappé le chat, Nathalie écoute Philippe
    (When Philippe has hit the cat, Nathalie listens to Philippe)

50. Quand le chien a soigné ses petits, Pierre entend le chien
    (When the dog has nursed its young ones, Pierre hears the dog)

51. Quand le chien a goûté la viande, Johan entend le chien
    (When the dog has tasted the meat, Johan hears the dog)

52. Quand Raphaël a écouté l'instituteur, Sandrine voit Raphaël
    (When Raphaël has listened to the teacher, Sandrine sees Raphaël)

53. Nathalie écoute Philippe quand Philippe a frappé le chat
    (Nathalie listens to Philippe when Philippe has hit the cat)

54. Pierre entend le chien quand le chien a soigné ses petits
    (Pierre hears the dog when the dog has nursed its young ones)

55. Johan entend le chien quand le chien a goûté la viande
    (Johan hears the dog when the dog has tasted the meat)

56. Sandrine voit Raphaël quand Raphaël a écouté l'instituteur
    (Sandrine sees Raphaël when Raphaël has listened to the teacher)

57. Quand Philippe frappe le chat, Nathalie écoute Philippe
    (When Philippe hits the cat, Nathalie listens to Philippe)

58. Quand le chien soigne ses petits, Pierre entend le chien
    (When the dog nurses its young ones, Pierre hears the dog)

59. Quand le chien goûte la viande, Johan entend le chien
    (When the dog tastes the meat, Johan hears the dog)

60. Quand Raphaël écoute l'instituteur, Sandrine voit Raphaël
    (When Raphaël listens to the teacher, Sandrine sees Raphaël)

61. Nathalie écoute Philippe quand Philippe frappe le chat
    (Nathalie listens to Philippe when Philippe hits the cat)

62. Pierre entend le chien quand le chien soigne ses petits
    (Pierre hears the dog when the dog nurses its young ones)

63. Johan entend le chien quand le chien goûte la viande
    (Johan hears the dog when the dog tastes the meat)

64. Sandrine voit Raphaël quand Raphaël écoute l'instituteur
    (Sandrine sees Raphaël when Raphaël listens to the teacher)

3. Sentences with *après que (after)*

65. Après que Philippe ait frappé le chat, Nathalie pousse Philippe
    (After Philippe hit the cat, Nathalie pushes Philippe)

66. Après que le chien ait soigné ses petits, Pierre admire le chien
    (After the dog nursed its young ones, Pierre admires the dog)

67. Après que le chien ait goûté la viande, Johan punit le chien
    (After the dog tasted the meat, Johan punishes the dog)

68. Après que Raphaël ait écouté l'instituteur, Sandrine félicite Raphaël
    (After Raphaël listened to the teacher, Sandrine congratulates Raphaël)

69. Nathalie pousse Philippe après que Philippe ait frappé le chat
    (Nathalie pushes Philippe after Philippe hit the cat)

70. Pierre admire le chien après que le chien ait soigné ses petits
    (Pierre admires the dog after the dog nursed its young ones)

71. Johan punit le chien après que le chien ait goûté la viande
    (Johan punishes the dog after the dog tasted the meat)

72. Sandrine félicite Raphaël après que Raphaël ait écouté l'instituteur
    (Sandrine congratulates Raphaël after Raphaël listened to the teacher)

73. Après que Philippe ait frappé le chat, Nathalie écoute Philippe
    (After Philippe hit the cat, Nathalie listens to Philippe)

74. Après que le chien ait soigné ses petits, Pierre entend le chien
    (After the dog nursed its young ones, Pierre hears the dog)

75. Après que le chien ait goûté la viande, Johan entend le chien
    (After the dog tasted the meat, Johan hears the dog)

76. Après que Raphaël ait écouté l'instituteur, Sandrine voit Raphaël
    (After Raphaël listened to the teacher, Sandrine sees Raphaël)

77. Nathalie écoute Philippe après que Philippe ait frappé le chat
    (Nathalie listens to Philippe after Philippe hit the cat)

78. Pierre entend le chien après que le chien ait soigné ses petits
    (Pierre hears the dog after the dog nursed its young ones)

79. Johan entend le chien après que le chien ait goûté la viande
    (Johan hears the dog after the dog tasted the meat)

80. Sandrine voit Raphaël après que Raphaël ait écouté l'instituteur
    (Sandrine sees Raphaël after Raphaël listened to the teacher)

Appendix 6 List of coreferential paragraphs

Notation. In the English translation of the French material (as in preceding sections), I have tried to stick as much as possible to the French word ordering and formal marking. This, at times, yields English sentences or paragraphs that are somewhat clumsy or at least inelegant. My apologies to the English-speaking reader. The third-person anaphoric personal pronouns on which the interpretative requests are borne are italicized in the text.

1. Nonambiguous paragraphs

1. Souvent, après le travail, Catherine invite Pierre à la terrasse du petit café. Vous *le* prendrez à part pour discuter un moment.
   (Often, after work, Catherine invites Pierre to sit outside the little café. You will take *him* into a corner to chat a while.)

2. Demain à l'école, la directrice présentera le nouvel instituteur aux élèves. Vous *le* rencontrerez après la classe.
   (Tomorrow, in school, the headmistress will introduce the new teacher to the pupils. You will meet *him* after class.)

3. En partant au travail, Monsieur Jean dépose sa femme à l'arrêt du bus. A partir de cet endroit, vous *la* suivrez, disons jusqu'à onze heures.
   (En route to work, Mr. Jean drops off his wife at the bus-stop. From this place on, you will follow *her*, let's say till eleven o'clock.)

4. Le docteur examine Madame Dufer demain après-midi. Tout de suite après, vous *la* mettrez au courant de notre plan.
   (The doctor examines Mrs. Dufer tomorrow afternoon. Immediately after, you will let *her* know about our plan)

5. Généralement, le postier attend sa femme vers cinq heures devant la poste. Empêchez-*le* de quitter son travail plus tôt que d'habitude.
   (Most of the time, the mailman waits for his wife around five o'clock in front of the post office. Prevent *him* from leaving his work earlier than usual.)

6. Après-midi, la propriétaire accompagnera le directeur de la banque au commissariat. Vous *la* reconduirez, c'est plus sûr.
   (This afternoon, the owner – feminine person – will accompany the director of the bank – masculine person – to the police station. You will carry *her* home, it's safer.)

7. Le coiffeur de la rue Duchêne coiffe la boulangère le vendredi à midi. Vérifiez qu'*il* nous téléphone de là vers midi comme prévu.
   (The hairdresser of Duchêne street does the baker's – feminine – hair on Fridays at noon. Make sure that *he* phones us around noon as planned.)

8. La patronne du café a averti le serveur de notre plan. *Elle* vous demandera les derniers renseignements quand vous arriverez.
   (The café's owner – feminine – has warned the waiter regarding our plot. *She* will request the latest information from you when you arrive.)

9. Demain, Madame Sulon ira encourager son cousin à la piscine. *Elle* vous remettra ensuite une enveloppe que vous ouvrirez directement.
   (Tomorrow, Mrs. Sulon will go and encourage her cousin at the pool. *She* then will give you an envelope that you will open right away.)

10. Demain, Carlo entraînera Françoise sur le terrain près de la gare. *Elle* est dans le coup et vous fera signe si quelque chose se passe.
    (Tomorrow, Carlo will take Françoise along to the ground nearby the railway station. *She* is with us and will make you a sign if something happens.)

11. Chaque matin, Madame Dubois promène le vieux Jules sur la route du château. *Il* a remarqué quelque chose et vous le montrera demain.
    (Every morning, Mrs. Dubois walks old Jules along the castle road. *He* has noticed something and will show it to you tomorrow.)

12. Tous les vendredis, Jacky rencontre Martine à la Maison des Jeunes. *Elle* connaît bien les gens du village, essayez d'en savoir le plus possible.
    (Every Friday, Jacky meets Martine at the Youth Club. *She* knows the people of the village well; try to learn as much as you can about them.)

2. Ambiguous paragraphs

13. L'institutrice reçoit la mère Pichat demain matin. *Elle* vous apprendra ensuite une chose qui peut nous être utile.
    (The teacher – feminine – entertains mother Pichat tomorrow morning. *She* will then tell you something that may be useful to us.)

14. Le vendredi vers 4 heures, Madame Lerouge retrouve Madame Lilas devant la boulangerie pour leurs courses. *Elle* sera peut-être attaquée, restez avec.
    (On Fridays, around four o'clock, Mrs. Lerouge meets Mrs. Lilas in front of the bakers' shop for doing their shopping together. *She* may be attacked; stay with her.)

15. Après leur partie de ping-pong, Rose quitte Annette vers quatre heures et demie. *Elle* a suivi des cours de tir à la carabine, surveillez bien cette jeune fille.
(Following their table tennis game, Rose leaves Annette around half past four. *She* took rifle shooting lessons; keep a good eye on this girl.)

16. Un mécanicien assistera le garagiste pour vérifier l'état de la camionnette. *Il* devra être protégé jusqu'à l'embarquement des sacs.
(A mechanic will help the garage owner to check the state of the van. *He* must be protected until the loading of the bags.)

17. Demain, le garde de la banque accompagnera le chauffeur en camionnette. Avant de partir, *il* vous demandera les dernières instructions.
(Tomorrow, the security officer of the bank will accompany the driver with a van. Before leaving, *he* will ask you the latest instructions.)

18. Quand le train s'arrêtera sur le quai, le chef de train appellera un transporteur. *Il* ne peut rester seul un instant.
(When the train will stop on the platform, the chief of station will call a porter. *He* may not be left alone one moment.)

19. Le vendredi matin, Madame Stiff emmène sa voisine au supermarché. Vous *la* questionnerez près des cigarettes où il fait tranquille.
(On Friday mornings, Mrs. Stiff takes her neighbor (feminine) to the supermarket. You will question her next to the cigarette department where it is quiet.)

20. Le soir, quand il fait beau, Madame Vertpré rejoint Madame Bolette dans le parc. Vous *la* surveillerez attentivement.
(In the evening, when the weather is fine, Mrs. Vertpré joins Mrs. Bolette in the park. You will watch *her* carefully.)

21. A huit heures, Madame Sophie aide la vieille Jeanne à sortir les poubelles. Appelez-*la* pour parler un peu des gens du quartier.
(At eight o'clock, Mrs. Sophie helps old Jeanne to carry the trash cans out. Call *her* to talk a bit about the people in the neighborhood.)

22. Demain, l'électricien retrouvera le serrurier devant la banque pour contrôler les sécurités. Vous irez *le* trouver pour savoir si tout fonctionne bien.
(Tomorrow, the electrician will join the locksmith in front of the bank to check the safety services. You will go and see *him* to know whether everything is in order.)

23. Chaque jour, à la gare, un employé charge le facteur des colis à distribuer. Prévenez-*le* que demain, c'est la police qui s'en occupera.
(Everyday, at the railway station, an employee supplies the mailman with the mail. Forewarn *him* that tomorrow it is the police who will take care of it.)

24. Le maçon verra le chef de chantier demain. Vous *le* remplacerez avant que les sacs soient arrivés à la banque.
(The bricklayer will see the foreman tomorrow. You will replace *him* before the bags have arrived at the bank.)

Appendix 7 Reading material

1. Logatomes

Liste 1:

1. esp ....
2. stur ....
3. erb ....
4. olp ....
5. spli ....
6. spic ....
7. blist ....

Liste 4:

1. riskapé ....
2. nuronli ....
3. sizado ....
4. faviker ....
5. jifazeu ....
6. koguchi ....
7. dimanko ....
8. moluné ....
9. bimindal ....
10. todoukin ....

Liste 2:

1. ortis ....
2. igzo ....
3. adzi ....
4. obju ....
5. adjo ....
6. crouo ....
7. tsui ....

Liste 5:

1. mandurnalo ....
2. otrudiré ....
3. ibapedu ....
4. esartaldi ....
5. moenulivou ....
6. sinzanchujon ....
7. goutiduran ....
8. akoutebo ....

Liste 3:

1. mouko ....
2. fanvé ....
3. yéroi ....
4. linou ....
5. chanedu ....
6. gontra ....
7. zulseu ....
8. bartin ....
9. lurir ....
10. panbi ....

Liste 6:

1. vafitaruder ....
2. sanzibidélu ....
3. pudounurital ....
4. munignameso ....
5. pulblagoritel ....
6. anslingelitil ....
7. zoltiduseltor ....
8. varduostivar ....

2. Words

pelle ....
buis ....
arbre ....
brouette ....

spectacle ....
espiègle ....
prestidigitateur ....
anticonstitutionnellement ....

3. Sentences

1. Il fait tout noir ....
2. J'ai perdu ma bicyclette ....
3. Maman a mis le parapluie dans le jardin ....
4. Papa a acheté un journal au magasin ....
5. J'aimerais bien m'asseoir dans l'herbe toute fraîche ....

Figure A7–1. List of logatomes and conventional words from Borel-Maisonny (after Rondal, 1979a)

Le printemps.

Le temps est beau, le ciel est bleu, le soleil brille.
Joyeux printemps, bonjour.

Michel et Nicole gambadent dans les prés et les champs.
Déjà la pâquerette montre sa collerette blanche et rose.
La violette, au doux parfum, se cache dans les buissons.
Les petits oiseaux chantent. Tout revit, tout est en fête.
Vive le beau printemps!

Lecture : **La Pâquerette.**

Petite pâquerette, tu souris dans l'herbette.
J'aime ton bouton jaune, ta blanche collerette.
Mais je préfère encore, ta sœur, la violette.

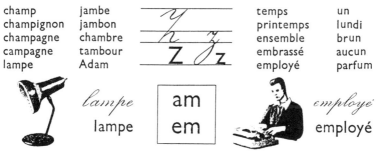

champ	jambe		temps	un
champignon	jambon		printemps	lundi
champagne	chambre		ensemble	brun
campagne	tambour		embrassé	aucun
lampe	Adam		employé	parfum

am
em

lampe

employé

30 - trente

Figure A7–2. Text 1, second-grade level.

47

Le printemps est là.

le printemps vient   les jonquilles nous l'ont dit.
le printemps arrive   les jonquilles ont annoncé
le printemps revient   le printemps.

        regardez quel beau soleil bien chaud.
        regardez quels rayons.
        il se lève très tôt.

———

au printemps le soleil a des rayons chauds.
dans ma mallette j'ai des crayons jaunes.
les bourgeons ont annoncé le printemps.
les jonquilles l'ont fait il y a longtemps.
regardez le printemps, c'est un bel enfant.
il a toutes les couleurs. il porte un panier
plein de fleurs.

il marche en
chantant.
il parle aux
papillons.
il dit aux arbres
de pousser.
il dit aux herbes
de fleurir.
il dit au vent
de se réchauffer.
il dit au soleil
de nous réjouir.

Figure A7–3. Text 2, third-grade level.

Appendix 8 Written text and dictation

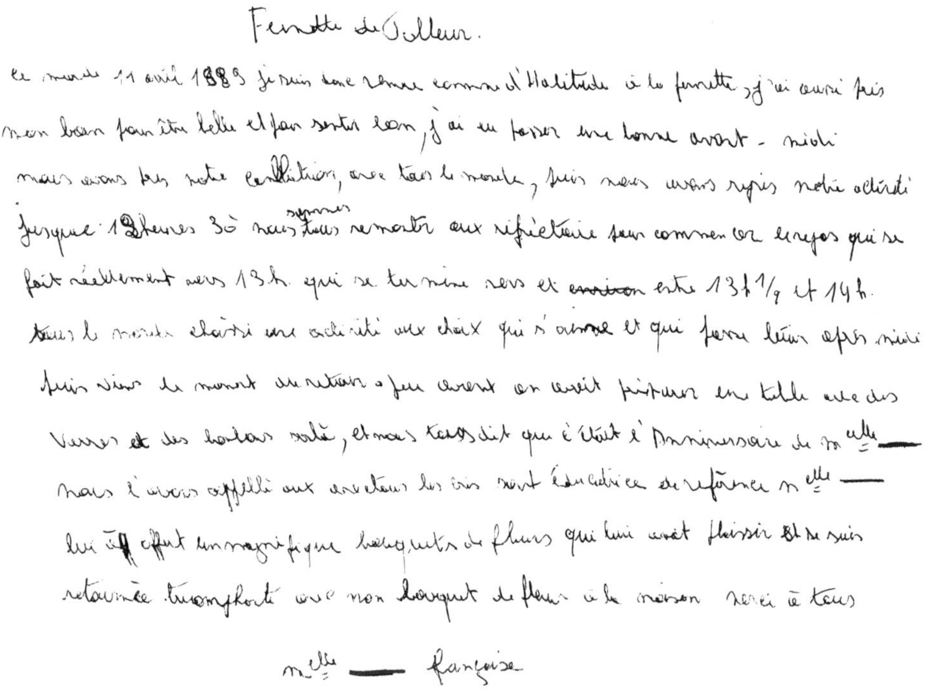

Little farm of Polleur

this monday 11 April 1989 I have thus come as usual to the little farm, I have also taken my bath to be beautiful and to smell good, I have had a good morning we have had our snack, with everybody, then we have resumed our activity until 12:30 hours we have all gone up to the dining room to start the meal that actually takes place around 13 hours which finishes around and 13 H.1/2 and 14 H. everyone chooses an activity freely which one likes and that goes on for the afternoon then comes the time to leave shortly before they had set a table with glasses and crackers there, and we all say that it was the birthday of ms _____ we have called her with all the shouting her educator of reference ms _____ has offered her a magnificent bouquet of flowers that had given her pleasure and I have gone home in a triumph with my bouquet of flowers thanks to all

ms _____ françoise

Figure A8–1. Spontaneous writing and English translation.

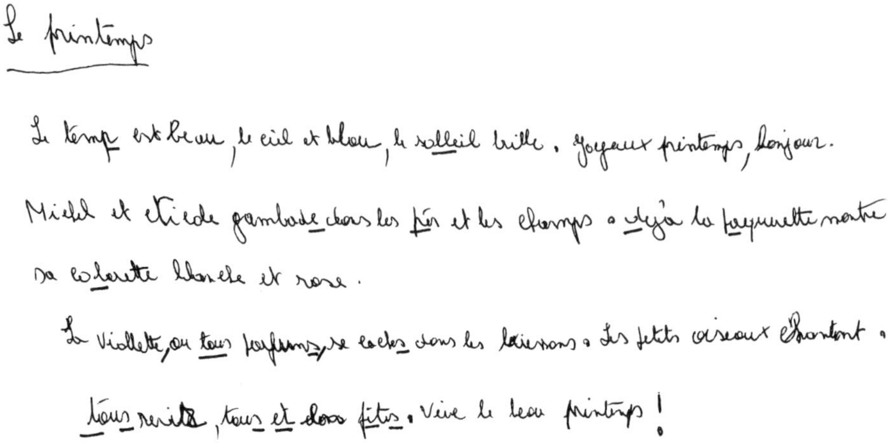

Le printemps

Le temps est beau, le ciel et bleu, le soleil brille. Joyeux printemps, bonjour.

Michel et Étiede gambade dans les prés et les champs a déjà la pâquerette montre sa collerette blanche et rose.

La violette, au tous parfums, se caches dans les buissons a les petits oiseaux chantent a

Tous revient, tous et bons fêtes. Vive le beau printemps !

Figure A8–2. Dictation from Text 1 (Figure A7–2).

Appendix 9 Visuographic testing

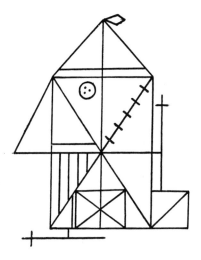

Figure A9–1. Complex figure of Rey (model).

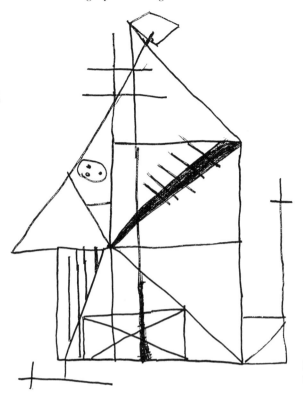

Figure A9–2. Rey's figure as copied by Françoise.

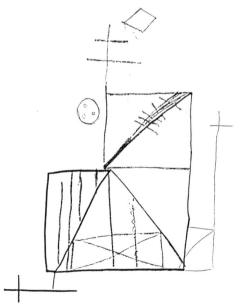

Figure A9–3. Françoise's drawing from memory.

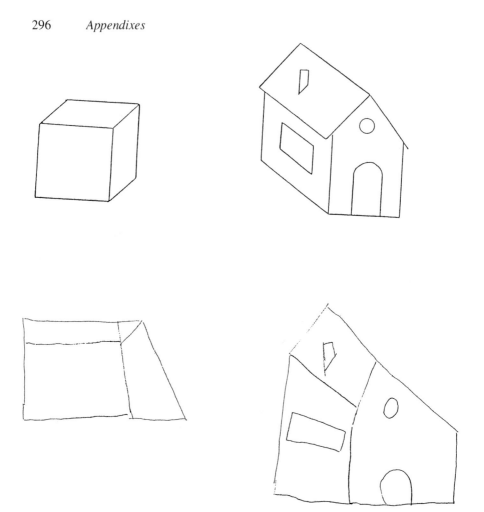

Figure A9–4. Cubes and houses in perspective: model and Françoise's copying.

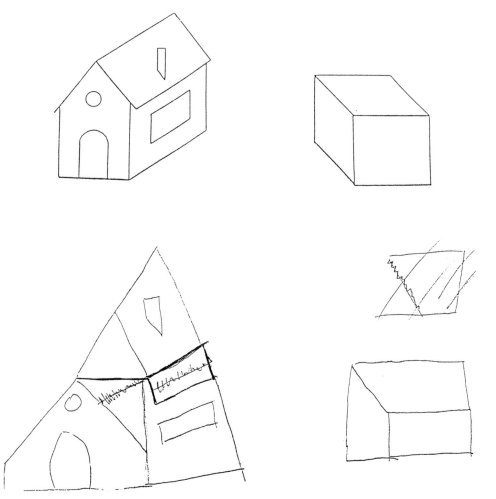

Figure A9–5. Cubes and houses in perspective (different arrangment): model and Françoise's copying.

References

Abbeduto, L., Davies, B., Solesby, S., & Furman, L. (1991). Identifying the referents of spoken messages: Use of context and clarification requests by children with and without mental retardation. *American Journal of Mental Retardation, 95,* 551–562.

Abbeduto, L., & Rosenberg, S. (1980). The communication competence of mildly retarded adults. *Applied Psycholinguistics, 1,* 405–426.

Albert, M., Yamadori, A., Gardner, H., & Howes, D. (1973). Comprehension in alexia. *Brain, 96,* 317–328.

Alegria, J., & Morais, J. (1979). Le développement de l'habilité d'analyse phonétique consciente de la parole et l'apprentissage de la lecture. *Archives de Psychologie, 47,* 251–270.

Alegria, J., Pignot, E., & Morais, J. (1982). Phonetic analysis of speech and memory codes in beginning readers. *Memory and Cognition, 10,* 451–456.

Amy, G. (1983a). L'intervention des facteurs pragmatiques dans la compréhension des phrases relatives chez l'adulte. *L'Année Psychologique, 83,* 423–442.

Amy, G. (1983b). Etude génétique de la compréhension des phrases relatives. In J. P. Bronckart, M. Kail, & G. Noizet (Eds.), *Psycholinguistique de l'enfant. Recherches sur l'acquisition du langage* (pp. 135–154). Paris: Delachaux & Niestlé.

Amy, G., & Vion, M. (1976). Stratégies de traitement des phrases relatives: Quelques considérations d'ordre génétique [Special issue on memory]. *Bulletin de Psychologie, 65,* 295–303.

Anderson, E., & Spain, B. (1977). *The child with spina bifida.* London: Methuen.

Antinucci, F., Duranti, A., & Gebert, L. (1979). Relative clause structure, relative clause perception, and the change from SOV to SVO. *Cognition, 7,* 145–176.

Aram, D., & Healy, J. (1988). Hyperlexia: A review of extraordinary word recognition. In L. Obler & D. Fein (Eds.), *The exceptional brain* (pp. 70–102). New York: Guilford.

Arnaud, A., & Lancelot, C. (1660). *Grammaire générale et raisonnée de Port-Royal.* Paris: Bossange & Masson. (New edition, 1810)

Atkinson, M. (1982). *Explanation in the study of child language development.* Cambridge University Press.

Atkinson, M. (1987). Mechanisms for language acquisition. *First Language, 7,* 3–30.

Atkinson, R., & Shiffrin, R. (1968). Human memory: A proposed system and its control processes. In K. Spence (Ed.), *The psychology of learning and motivation: Advances in research theory* (Vol. 2, pp. 90–197). New York: Academic.

Austin, J. (1962). *How to do things with words.* Oxford: Clarendon Press.

Baddeley, A. (1983). Working memory. *Philosophical Transactions of the Royal Society, London, 302,* 311–324.

Baddeley, A. (1986). *Working memory.* Oxford: Oxford Science Publications.

Baddeley, A. (1990). *Human memory.* Hillsdale, NJ: Erlbaum.

Baddeley, A. (1992, June). Personal communication.

299

Baddeley, A. (in press). Working memory, *Science.*

Baddeley, A., & Hitch, G. (1974). Working memory. In G. Bower (Ed.), *The psychology of learning and motivation* (Vol. 8, pp. 47–90). New York: Academic.

Baddeley, A., & Hitch, G. (1977). Recency reexamined. In S. Dornic (Ed.), *Attention and performance* (Vol. 6, pp. 647–667.). Hillsdale, NJ: Erlbaum.

Baddeley, A., Lewis, V., & Vallar, G. (1984). Exploring the articulatory loop. *Quarterly Journal of Experimental Psychology, 36,* 233–252.

Baddeley, A., Papagno, C., & Vallar, G. (1988). When long-term learning depends on short-term storage. *Journal of Memory and Language, 27,* 586–595.

Baddeley, A., & Wilson, B. (1988). Comprehension and working memory: A single case neuropsychological study. *Journal of Memory and Language, 27,* 479–498.

Balkom, H. van (1991). *The communication of language impaired children.* Amsterdam: Swets & Zeitlinger.

Bandura, A. (1976). *Social learning theory.* Englewood Cliffs, NJ: Prentice-Hall.

Barblan, L., & Chipman, H. H. (1978). Temporal relationships in language: A comparison between normal and language retarded children. In G. Drachman (Ed.), *Salzburger Beitrage zur Linguistik* (pp. 46–65). Salzburg: W. Neugebauer.

Barrett, M., & Diniz, F. (1989). Lexical development in mentally handicapped children. In M. Beveridge, G. Conti-Ramsden, & Y. Leudar (Eds.), *Language and communication in mentally handicapped people* (pp. 3–32). London: Chapman & Hall.

Bartel, N., Bryen, S., & Keehn, S. (1973). Language comprehension in the moderately retarded child. *Exceptional Children, 39,* 375–382.

Bateman, B., & Whetherell, J. (1965). Psycholinguistic aspects of mental retardation. *Mental Retardation, 3,* 8–13.

Bates, E. (1976). *Language and context.* New York: Academic.

Bates, E., Bretherton, I., & Snyder, L. (1988). *From first words to grammar: Individual differences and dissociable mechanisms.* Cambridge University Press.

Bates, E., & MacWhinney, B. (1982). Functionalist approaches to grammar. In E. Wanner & L. Gleitman (Eds.), *Language acquisition: The state of the art* (pp. 173–218). Cambridge University Press.

Bates, E., & MacWhinney, B. (1987). Competition, variation, and language learning. In B. Macwhinney (Ed.), *Mechanisms of language acquisition* (pp. 157–193). Hillsdale, NJ: Erlbaum.

Bauer, R., & Rubens, A. (1985). Agnosia. In K. Heilman & E. Valenstein (Eds.), *Clinical neuropsychology* (pp. 187–241). Oxford University Press.

Baumeister, A. (1967). Problems in comparative studies of mental retardates and normals. *American Journal of Mental Deficiency, 71,* 869–875.

Beauzée, N. (1767). *Grammaire générale, ou exposition raisonnée des éléments nécessaires du langage.* Paris. (Edition revue, 1819)

Bebout, L., Segalowitz, S., & White, G. (1980). Children's comprehension of causal constructions with because and so. *Child Development, 51,* 563–568.

Becker, L., Mito, T., Takashima, S., & Onodera, K. (1991). Growth and development of the brain in Down syndrome. In C. Epstein (Ed.), *The morphogenesis of Down syndrome* (pp. 133–152). New York: Wiley-Liss.

Bedrosian, J. L., & Prutting, C. A. (1978). Communicative performance of mentally retarded adults in four conversational settings. *Journal of Speech and Hearing Research, 21,* 79–95.

Beier, E., Starkweather, J., & Lambert, M. (1969). Vocabulary usage of mentally retarded children. *American Journal of Mental Deficiency, 73,* 927–934.

Beilin, H., & Sack, H. (1975). The passive: Linguistic and psychological theory. In H. Beilin (Ed.), *Studies in the cognitive basis of language development* (pp. 116–138). New York: Academic.

Bellugi, U. (1968). Linguistic mechanisms underlying child speech. In E. Zale (Ed.), *Language and language behavior* (pp. 36–50). New York: Crofts.

Bellugi, U., Marks, S., Bihrle, A., & Sabo, H. (1988). Dissociation between language and cognitive functions in Williams syndrome. In D. Bishop & K. Mogford (Eds.), *Language development in exceptional circumstances* (pp. 177–189). London: Churchill Livingstone.

Belmont, J. (1972). Relations of age and intelligence to short term color memory. *Child Development, 43,* 19–29.

Benda, C. (1949). *Mongolism and cretinism.* New York: Grune & Stratton.

Berg, J. M. (1975). Aetiological aspects of mental subnormality: Pathology factors. In A. M. Clark & A. B. D. Clark (Eds.), *Mental deficiency: The changing outlook* (pp. 27–58). London: Methuen.

Bergès, J., & Lézine, I. (1978). *Test d'Imitation de Gestes.* Paris: Masson.

Berndt, R., & Carramazza, A. (1980). A redefinition of the syndrome of Broca's aphasia. *Applied Psycholinguistics, 1,* 225–278.

Berry, P. (1972). Comprehension of possessive and present countinuous sentences by non-retarded, mildly retarded, and severely retarded children. *American Journal of Mental Deficiency, 76,* 540–544.

Berry, P., Groenweg, G., Gibson, D., & Brown, R. (1984). Mental development of adults with Down's syndrome. *American Journal of Mental Deficiency, 89,* 252–256.

Berry, P., Pountney, C., & Powell, I. (1978). Meal-time communication in moderately and severely retarded adults: An ethological study. *Australian Journal of Mental Retardation, 5,* 105–108.

Bertelson, P., & de Gelder, B. (1991). The emergence of phonological awareness: Comparative approaches. In I. Mattingly & M. Studdert-Kennedy (Eds.), *Modularity and the motor theory of speech perception* (pp. 393–412). Hillsdale, NJ: Erlbaum.

Bertoncini, J. (1991). Initial equipment for speech perception. In G. Piérault le Bonniec & M. Dolitsky (Eds.), *Language bases and discourse bases* (pp. 45–55). Amsterdam: Benjamins.

Bever, T. (1970). The cognitive basis for linguistics structures. In J. Hayes (Ed.), *Cognition and the development of language* (pp. 279–362). New York: Wiley.

Bialystok, E., & Ryan, E. (1985). A metacognitive framework for the development of first and second language skills. In D. Forrest-Pressley, G. MacKinnon, & T. Waller (Eds.), *Metacognition, cognition, and human performance* (Vol.1, pp. 158–197). New York: Academic.

Bichakjian, B. (1989). Language innateness and speech pathology. In J. Wind, E. Pulleyblank, E. de Grolier, & B. Bichakjian (Eds.), *Studies in language origins* (pp. 209–232). Amsterdam: Benjamins.

Bickerton, D. (1981). *Roots of language.* Ann Arbor, MI: Karoma.

Bickerton, D. (1984). The language bioprogram hypothesis. *Behavioral and Brain Sciences, 7,* 173–188.

Bickerton, D. (1986). Beyond Roots: The five-year test. *Journal of Pidgin and Creole Languages, 1,* 225–232.

Bickerton, D. (1988). Creole languages and the bioprogram. In F. Newmeyer (Ed.), *Linguistics: The Cambridge Survey* (Vol. 2, pp. 268–284). Cambridge University Press.

Bickerton, D. (1990). *Language and species.* Chicago: University of Chicago Press.

Bilovsky, D., & Share, J. (1965). The ITPA and Down's syndrome: An exploratory study. *American Journal of Mental Deficiency, 70,* 78–83.

Bishop, D. (1983). Linguistic impairment after left hemidecortication for infantile hemiplegia? A reappraisal. *Quarterly Journal of Experimental Psychology, 35A,* 199–207.

Bishop, D., & Mogford, K. (Eds.). (1988). *Language development in exceptional circumstances.* London: Churchill Livingstone.

Blanchard, I. (1964). Speech pattern and etiology in mental retardation. *American Journal of Mental Deficiency, 68,* 612–617.

Blank, M., Gessner, M., & Esposito, A. (1978). Language without communication: A case study. *Journal of Child Language, 6,* 329–352.

Bloom, A. (1981). *The linguistic shaping of thought.* Hillsdale, NJ: Erlbaum.

Bloom, L., Hood, L., & Lightbown, P. (1974). Imitation in language development: If, when, and why. *Cognitive Psychology, 6,* 380–420.

Bloom, L., Lightbown, P., & Hood, L. (1975). Structure and variation in child language. *Monographs of the Society for Research in Child Development, 40* (Serial No. 160).

Boehm, A. (1969). *Test of Basic Concepts.* New York: The Psychological Corporation.

Boehm, A. (1971). *The Boehm Test of Basic Concepts.* New York: The Psychological Corporation.

Bohannon, J., & Stanowicz, L. (1988). The issue of negative evidence: Adult responses to children's language errors. *Developmental Psychology, 24,* 684–689.

Bolognini, M., Guidollet, B., Plancherel, B., & Bettschart, W. (1988). Mentally retarded adolescents: Evaluation of communication strategies in different settings. *International Journal of Rehabilitation Research, 11,* 369–378.

Borel-Maisonny, S. (1953). *Langage oral et écrit. Epreuves sensorielles et tests de langage.* Neuchâtel: Delachaux & Niestlé.

Borer, H., & Wexler, K. (1987). The maturation of syntax. In T. Roeper & E. Williams (Eds.), *Parameter setting* (pp. 123–172). Boston: Reidel.

Botwinick, J., & Storandt, M. (1974). *Memory related functions and age.* Springfield, IL: Thomas.

Boysson-Bardies, B. de (1991). Target-language influences on prespeech. In G. Piérault le Bonniec & M. Dolitsky (Eds.), *Language bases and discourse bases* (pp. 57–72). Amsterdam: Benjamins.

Boysson-Bardies, B. de, Halle, P., Sagart, L., & Durand, C. (1989). A cross-linguistic investigation of vowel formants in babbling. *Journal of Child Language, 16,* 1–17.

Bradley, L., & Bryant, P. (1983). Categorising sounds and learning to read: A causal connection. *Nature, 301,* 419–421.

Braine, M. (1987). What is learned in acquiring word classes – A step toward an acquisition theory. In B. MacWhinney (Ed.), *Mechanisms of language acquisition* (pp. 65–87). Hillsdale, NJ: Erlbaum.

Brédart, S., & Rondal, J. A. (1982). *L'analyse du langage chez l'enfant. Les activités métalinguistiques.* Brussels: Mardaga.

Bresnan, J. (Ed.). (1982). *The mental representation of grammatical relations.* Cambridge, MA: MIT Press.

Bresson, F. (1991). Phylogeny and ontogeny of languages. In G. Piérault le Bonniec & M. Dolitsky (Eds.), *Language bases and discourse bases* (pp. 11–29). Amsterdam: Benjamins.

Broadley, I., & MacDonald, J. (1993). Teaching short term memory skills to children with Down's syndrome. *Down's Syndrome: Research and Practice,1,* 56–62.

Bronckart, J. P. (1976). *Genèse et organisation des formes verbales chez l'enfant.* Brussels: Dessart & Mardaga.

Bronckart, J. P. (1977). *Théories du langage. Une introduction critique.* Brussels: Mardaga.

Bronfenbrenner, U. (1979). *The ecology of human development: Experiments by nature and design*. Cambridge, MA: Harvard University Press.

Brown, A. (1976). Semantic integration in children's reconstruction of narrative sentences. *Cognitive Psychology, 8,* 247–262.

Brown, I. (1979). Language acquisition: Linguistic structure and rule-governed behavior. In G. Whitehurst & B. Zimmerman (Eds.), *The functions of language and cognition* (pp. 141–173). New York: Academic.

Brown, J. (1958). Some tests of the decay theory of immediate memory. *Quarterly Journal of Experimental Psychology,10,* 12–21.

Brown, R. (1968). *Words and things.* New York: Free Press.

Brown, R. (1973). *A first language.* Cambridge, MA: Harvard University Press.

Brown, R. (1986). *Social psychology: The second edition.* New York: Free Press.

Brown, R., & Berko, J. (1960). Word association and the acquisition of grammar. *Child Development, 31,* 1–14.

Brown, R. & Hanlon, C. (1970). Derivational complexity and order of acquisition in child speech. In J. Hayes (Ed.), *Cognition and the development of language* (pp. 11–53). New York: Wiley.

Bruce, D. (1964). The analysis of word sounds by young children. *British Journal of Educational Psychology, 34,* 158–170.

Bruck, M., & Treiman, R. (1990). Phonological awareness and spelling in normal children and dyslexics: The case of initial consonant clusters. *Journal of Experimental Child Psychology, 50,* 156–178.

Bryden, M. (1982). *Laterality: Functional asymmetry in the intact brain.* New York: Academic.

Bryden, M. (1988). An overview of the dichotic listening procedure and its relation to cerebral organization. In K. Hughdahl (Ed.), *Handbook of dichotic listening: Theory, methods and research* (pp. 1–43). New York: Wiley.

Bryden, M., Munhall, K., & Allard, F. (1983). Attentional biases and the right-ear effect in dichotic listening. *Brain and Language, 18,* 236–248.

Buckhalt, J. A., Rutherford, R. B., & Goldberg, I. (1978). Verbal and non-verbal interaction of mothers with their Down's syndrome and non-retarded infants. *American Journal of Mental Deficiency, 82,* 337–343.

Buckley, S. (1985). Attaining basic educational skills: Reading, writing and number. In D. Lane & B. Stratford (Eds.), *Current approaches to Down's syndrome* (pp. 315–343). London: Holt, Rinehart, & Winston.

Buckley, S., & Bird, G. (1993). Teaching children with Down's syndrome to read. *Down's Syndrome: Research and Practice, 1,* 34–39.

Buddenhagen, R. (1971). *Establishing vocal verbalizations in mute mongoloid children.* Champaign, IL: Research Press.

Buium, N., Rynders, J., & Turnure, J. (1974). *A semantic relation concepts based theory of language acquisition as applied to Down's syndrome children* (unpublished Research Rep. No. 62). University of Minnesota, Minneapolis: Research, Development, and Demonstration Center in Education of Handicapped Children.

Bullock, M., & Gelman, R. (1979). Preschool children's assumptions about causes and effects: Temporal ordering. *Child Development, 50,* 89–96.

Burani, C., Vallar, G., & Bottini, G. (1991). Articulatory coding and phonological judgments on written words and pictures: The role of the phonological output buffer. *European Journal of Cognitive Psychology, 3,* 379–398.

Burt, C. (1937). *The backward child.* London: University Press.

Buschke, H. (1973). Selective reminding for the analysis of memory and learning. *Journal of Verbal Learning and Verbal Behavior, 12,* 543–556.

Buschke, H. (1984). Cued recall in amnesia. *Journal of Clinical Neuropsychology, 16,* 433–440.

Butterworth, B. (1980). Evidence from pauses in speech. In B. Butterworth (Ed.), *Language production* (Vol. 1, pp. 155–176). London: Academic.

Butterworth, B., Campbell, R., & Howard, D. (1986). The uses of short-term memory: A study. *Quarterly Journal of Experimental Psychology, 38A,* 705–738.

Butterworth, B., Shallice, T., & Watson, F. (1990). Short-term retention without short-term memory. In G. Vallar & T. Shallice (Eds.), *Neuropsychological impairments of short-term memory* (pp. 187–213). Cambridge University Press.

Byrd Fazio, B., Johnston, J., & Brandl, L. (1992). Relationship between mental age and the development of vocabulary consisting of labels versus relational terms among mildly mentally handicapped children. Unpublished manuscript, University of British Columbia, Department of Linguistics, Vancouver.

Caltagirone, C., & Nocentini, U. (1990). Cognitive functions in adult Down's syndrome. *International Journal of Neuroscience, 54,* 221–230.

Caplan, D., & Hildebrandt, N. (1988). *Disorders of syntactic comprehension.* Cambridge, MA: MIT Press.

Caplan, D., & Waters, G. (1990). Short-term memory and language comprehension: A critical review of the neuropsychological literature. In G. Vallar & T. Shallice (Eds.), *Neuropsychological impairments of short-term memory* (pp. 337–389). Cambridge University Press.

Caramazza, A., Basili, A., Koller, J., & Berndt, R. (1981). An investigation of repetition and language processing in a case of conduction aphasia. *Brain and Language,14,* 235–271.

Caramazza, A., Grober, E., Garvey, C., & Yates, J. (1977). Comprehension of anaphoric pronouns. *Journal of Verbal Learning and Verbal Behavior, 16,* 601–609.

Caramazza, A, Miceli, G., & Villa, G. (1986). The role of the (output) phonological buffer in reading, writing and repetition. *Cognitive Neuropsychology, 2,* 81–114.

Caravolas, M., & Bruck, M. (1993). The effect of oral and written language input on children's phonological awareness: A cross-linguistic study. *Journal of Experimental Child Psychology, 55,* 1–30.

Cardoso-Martins, C., Mervis, C. B., & Mervis, C. A. (1985). Early vocabulary acquisition by children with Down syndrome. *American Journal of Mental Deficiency, 90,* 177–184.

Carey, S. (1985). *Conceptual change in childhood.* Cambridge, MA: MIT Press.

Caron, J. (1989). *Précis de psycholinguistique.* Paris: Presses Universitaires de France.

Carrow, E. (1968). The development of auditory comprehension of language structure in children. *Journal of Speech and Hearing Research, 38,* 99–111.

Carrow, E. (1973). *Test for Auditory Comprehension of Language* (5th ed.). Austin, TX: Learning Concepts.

Cavalli-Sforza, L. L. (1991). Genes, peoples and languages. *Scientific American,* November, 104–110.

Cesselin, F. (1968). *Comment évaluer le niveau intellectuel? Adaptation Française du Test de Terman-Merrill (1937).* Paris: Colin.

Chafe, W. (1970). *Meaning and the structure of language.* Chicago: University of Chicago Press.

Chaney, C. (1992). Language development, metalinguistic skills, and print awareness in 3-year-old children. *Applied Psycholinguistics, 13,* 485–514.

Chevrie-Muller, C. (1975). *Epreuve pour l'Examen du Langage.* Paris: Editions du Centre de Psychologie Appliquée.

Chi, M. (1976). Short-term memory limitations in children: Capacity or processing deficits? *Memory and Cognition, 4,* 559–572.

Chipman, H. H. (1979, August). *Understanding language retardation: A developmental perspective.* Communication presented at the 5th Conference of the International Association for the Scientific Study of Mental Deficiency (IASSMD), Jerusalem.

Chipman, H. H., & Gérard, J. (1983). Stratégies de traitement de l'anaphore. In J. P. Bronckart, M. Kail, & G. Noizet (Eds.), *Psycholinguistique de l'enfant. Recherche sur l'acquisition du langage* (pp. 123–133). Paris: Delachaux & Niestlé.

Chitham, R., Gibson, J., Loesch, D., & Rundle, A. (1977). A probable case of 8q trisomy. *Journal of Mental Deficiency Research, 21,* 47–54.

Chomsky, N. (1957a). *Syntactic structures.* The Hague: Mouton.

Chomsky, N. (1957b) [Review of B. F. Skinner's "Verbal Behavior"]. *Language, 35,* 26–58.

Chomsky, N. (1965). *Aspects of the theory of syntax.* Cambridge, MA: MIT Press.

Chomsky, N. (1966). *Cartesian linguistics.* New York: Harper & Row.

Chomsky, N. (1968). *Language and mind.* New York: Harcourt, Brace, Jovanovich.

Chomsky, N. (1969). La nature formelle du langage. In N. Chomsky, *La linguistique cartésienne suivi de La nature formelle du langage* (pp. 123–183). Paris: Seuil.

Chomsky, N. (1975a). *Reflections on language.* New York : Random House.

Chomsky, N. (1975b). *The logical structure of linguistic theory.* New York: Plenum (partial edition). (Original work published in 1955)

Chomsky, N. (1979). *Language and responsibility* (Based on conversations with Mitsou Ronat). New York: Pantheon.

Chomsky, N. (1980). *Rules and representations.* New York: Columbia University Press.

Chomsky, N. (1981). *Lectures on government and binding.* Dordrecht: Foris.

Chomsky, N. (1982). *Some concepts and consequences of the theory of government and binding.* Cambridge, MA: MIT Press.

Chomsky, N. (1984). *Modular approaches to the study of mind.* San Diego, CA: San Diego State University Press.

Chomsky, N. (1986a). *Barriers.* Cambridge, MA: MIT Press.

Chomsky, N. (1986b). *Knowledge of language.* New York: Praeger.

Chomsky, N. (1987). On the nature, use and acquisition of language. In N. Chomsky, *Generative grammar: Its basis, development and prospects* (pp. 227–246). Kyoto University of Foreign Studies.

Chomsky, N. (1988). *Language and problems of knowledge: The Managua lectures.* Cambridge, MA: MIT Press.

Cicchetti, D., & Beeghly, M. (Eds.). (1990). *Children with Down syndrome: A developmental perspective.* Cambridge University Press.

Clahsen, H. (1989). The grammatical characterization of developmental dysphasia. *Linguistics, 27,* 897–920.

Clahsen, H., Rothweiler, M., Woest, A., & Marcus, G. (1992). Regular and irregular inflection in the acquisition of German nouns plurals. *Cognition, 45,* 225–255.

Clarke, C., Edwards, J., & Smallpiece, V. (1961). Trisomy 21 normal mosaicism in an intelligent child with some mongoloid characters. *Lancet,* 1028–1030.

Clausen, J. (1968). Behavioral characteristics of Down's syndrome subjects. *American Journal of Mental Deficiency, 73,* 118–126.

Coggins, T. (1979). Relational meaning encoded in two-word utterance of stage 1 Down's syndrome children. *Journal of Speech and Hearing Research, 22,* 166–178.

Coker, P. (1978). Syntactic and semantic factors in the acquisition of *before* and *after. Journal of Child Language, 5,* 261–277.

Comblain, A. (1989). *Compréhension de la voix passive chez l'adulte trisomique 21*. Mémoire de licence (unpublished). Laboratoire de Psycholinguistique, Université de Liège, Liège.

Conrad, R. (1964). Acoustic confusion in immediate memory. *British Journal of Psychology, 55*, 75–84.

Conrad, R. (1971). The chronology of the development of covert speech in children. *Developmental Psychology, 5*, 398–405.

Content, A. (1984). L'analyse phonétique explicite de la parole et l'acquisition de la lecture. *L'Année Psychologique, 84*, 555–572.

Content, A. (1985). Le développement de l'habileté d'analyse phonétique de la parole. *L'Année Psychologique, 85*, 73–99.

Cook, N. (1977, August). *Semantic development in children with Down's syndrome*. Communication presented at the 85th Annual Convention of the American Psychological Association, San Francisco.

Cordemoy, Géraud de. (1666). *Discours physique de la parole*. Paris: Seuil. (New edition, Bibliothèque du Graphe, 1968)

Cossu, G., Rossini, F., & Marshall, J. (1993). When reading is acquired but phonemic awareness is not: A study of literacy in Down's syndrome. *Cognition, 46*, 129–138.

Cowan, N. (1992). Verbal memory span and the timing of spoken recall. *Journal of Memory and Language, 31*, 668–684.

Cowie, V. (1970). *A study of the early development of mongols*. Oxford: Pergamon.

Craig, R., & Tracy, K. (Eds.). (1983). *Conversational coherence: Form, structure, and strategy*. Beverly Hills, CA: Sage.

Craik, F. (1971). Primary memory. *British Medical Bulletin, 27*, 232–236.

Craik, F. (1984). Age differences in remembering. In L. Squire & N. Butters (Eds.), *Neuropsychology of memory* (pp. 3–12). New York: Guilford.

Craik, F., & Byrd, M. (1982). Aging and cognitive deficits: The role of attentional resources. In F. Craik & S. Trehub (Eds.), *Aging and cognitive processes* (pp. 191–211). New York: Plenum.

Craik, F., & Lockhart, R. (1972). Levels of processing: A framework for memory research. *Journal of Verbal Learning and Verbal Behavior, 11*, 671–684.

Craik, F., & Massani, P. (1969). Age and intelligence differences in coding and retrieval of word lists. *British Journal of Psychology, 63*, 315–319.

Crick, F., & Koch, C. (1992). The problem of consciousness. *Scientific American*, September, 153–159.

Crome, L., & Stern, J. (1967). *The pathology of mental retardation*. London: Churchill.

Cromer, R. (1987). The cognition hypothesis revisited. In F. Kessel (Ed.), *The development of language and language researches* (pp. 48–65). Hillsdale, NJ: Erlbaum.

Cromer, R. (1988). Differentiating language and cognition. In R. Schiefelbusch & L. Lloyd (Eds.), *Languages perspectives: Acquisition, retardation and intervention* (pp. 128–156). Austin, TX: Pro-Ed.

Cromer, R. (1991). *Language and thought in normal and handicapped children*. London: Blackwell.

Cromer, R. (1993). A case study of dissociations between language and cognition. In H. Tager-Flusberg (Ed.), *Constraints on language acquisition: Studies of atypical children* (pp. 141–153). Hillsdale, NJ: Erlbaum.

Crowder, R. (1982). The demise of short-term memory. *Acta Psychologica, 50*, 291–323.

Crowder, R., & Morton, J. (1969). Precategorial acoustic storage (PAS). *Perception and Psychophysics, 5*, 365–379.

Crystal, D. (1979). *Working with LARSP*. New York: Elsevier.

Culicover, P., & Wexler, K. (1977). Some syntactic implications of a theory of language learnability. In P. Culicover, T. Wason, & A. Akmajian (Eds.), *Formal syntax* (pp. 105–157). New York: Academic.

Culioli, A. (1968). La formalisation en linguistique. *Cahiers pour l'Analyse, 9,* 106–117.

Cunningham, C. (1979). *Aspects of early development in Down's syndrome infants.* Unpublished doctoral dissertation, University of Manchester, Manchester.

Cunningham, C. (1983). *Early development and its facilitation with infants with Down's syndrome. Final Report, Part 1, to DHSS* (unpublished). London: HMSO.

Cunningham, C. (1990). L'intervention précoce avec les enfants atteint du syndrome de Down. In M. T. Lysens & J. A. Rondal (Eds.), *Actes du Premier Congrès Européen sur le syndrome de Down (Liège, 1987)* (pp. 40–61). Heusy-Verviers: Association de Parents d'Enfants Mongoliens (APEM).

Cunningham, C., & Sloper, P. (1984). The relationship between maternal ratings of first word vocabulary and Reynell language scores. *British Journal of Educational Psychology, 54,* 160–167.

Curtiss, S. (1977). Genie: A psycholinguistic study of modern day "wild child." New York: Academic.

Curtiss, S. (1981). Dissociation between language and cognition. *Journal of Autism and Developmental Disorders, 11,* 15–30.

Curtiss, S. (1982). Developmental dissociations of language and cognition. In L. Obler & L. Menn (Eds.), *Exceptional language and linguistics* (pp. 285–312). New York: Academic.

Curtiss, S. (1988). The special talent of grammar acquisition. In L. Obler & D. Fein (Eds.), *The exceptional brain* (pp. 364–386). New York: Guilford.

Curtiss, S. (1989). Abnormal language acquisition and the modularity of language. In F. Newmeyer (Ed.), *Linguistics: The Cambridge Survey* (Vol. 2, pp. 96–116). Cambridge University Press.

Curtiss, S., Fromkin, V., Krashen, S., Rigler, D., & Rigler, M. (1974). The linguistic development of Genie. *Language, 50,* 528–554.

Curtiss, S., Fromkin, V., & Yamada, J. (1979). How independent is language? On the question of formal parallels between grammar and action. *UCLA Working Papers in Cognitive Linguistics, 1,* 131–157.

Curtiss, S., Kempler, D., & Yamada, J. (1981). The relationship between language and cognition in development. *UCLA Working Papers in Cognitive Linguistics, 3,* 1–59.

Curtiss, S., & Yamada, J. (1981). Selectively intact grammatical development in the retarded child. *UCLA Working Papers in Cognitive Linguistics, 3,* 87–120.

Curtiss, S., & Yamada, J. (1992). *The Curtiss-Yamada Comprehensive Language Evaluation (CYCLE).* Los Angeles: UCLA, Department of Linguistics.

Dale, P. (1977, August). *Syntactic development in Down's syndrome children.* Communication presented at the 85th Annual Convention of the American Psychological Association, San Francisco.

Damasio, H., & Damasio, A. (1989). *Lesion analysis in neuropsychology.* Oxford University Press.

Damasio, A., & Damasio, H. (1992). Brain and language. *Scientific American,* September, 89–95.

Daneman, M. (1991). Working memory as a predictor of verbal fluency. *Journal of Psycholinguistic Research, 20,* 445–464.

Daneman, M., & Green, I. (1986). Individual differences in comprehending and producing words in context. *Journal of Memory and Language, 25,* 1–18.

Das, J. P. (1985). Aspects of digit-span performance: Naming, time and order memory. *American Journal of Mental Deficiency, 91,* 398–405.

Dawkins, R. (1986). *The blind watchmaker.* Harlow, Essex: Longman.

Defleur, P. (1989). *Approche procédurale des altérations conceptuelles sous-jacentes au problème de recouvrement des mots.* Mémoire de licence (unpublished). Laboratoire de Psycholinguistique, Université de Liège, Liège.

Deltour, J. J. (1982). *Test des Relations Topologiques.* Issy-les-Moulineaux: Editions Scientifiques et Psychologiques.

Deltour, J. J., & Hupkens, D. (1980). *Test de Vocabulaire Actif et Passif.* Issy-les-Moulineaux: Editions Scientifiques & Psychologiques.

Demetras, M., Post, K., & Snow, C. (1986). Feedback to first language learners: The role of repetitions and clarification questions. *Journal of Child Language, 13,* 275–292.

De Renzi, E., & Vignolo, L. (1962). The Token Test: A sensitive test to detect receptive disturbances in aphasics. *Brain, 85,* 665–678.

Despert, L. (1968). *Schizophrenia in children.* New York: Brunner.

Devenny, D., Silverman, W., Balgley, H., Well, M., & Sidtis, J. (1990). Specific motor abilities associated with speech fluency in Down's syndrome. *Journal of Mental Deficiency Research, 34,* 437–443.

De Villiers, J., & De Villiers, P. (1973). A cross-sectional study of the acquisition of grammatical morphemes in child speech. *Journal of Psycholinguistic Research, 2,* 267–278.

DeVries, G., Debruin, J., Uylings, H., & Corner, M. (Eds.). (1984). *Progress in Brain Research: Vol. 61, Sex differences in the brain: The relation between structure and function.* New York: Elsevier.

Dewart, H. H. (1979). Language comprehension processes of mentally retarded children. *American Journal of Mental Deficiency, 84,* 117–183.

Deyts, J. P., & Noizet, G. (1973). Etude génétique de la production des subordonnées relatives. *Cahiers de Psychologie Cognitive, 16,* 199–212.

DiSimoni, F. (1978). *The Token Test for Children.* Boston, MA: Teaching Resources.

Dodd, B. (1972). Comparison of babbling patterns in normal and Down's syndrome infants. *Journal of Mental Deficiency, 16,* 35–40.

Dodd, B. (1976). A comparison of the phonological systems of mental age matched normal, severely subnormal and Down's syndrome children. *British Journal of Communicative Disorders, 11,* 27–42.

Dodd, B., & Leahy, J. (1989). Phonological disorders and mental handicap. In M. Beveridge, G. Conti-Ramsden, & Y. Leudar (Eds.), *Language and communication in mentally handicapped people* (pp. 33–56). London: Chapman & Hall.

Dooley, J. (1976). *Language acquisition and Down's syndrome: A study of early semantics and syntax.* Unpublished doctoral dissertation, Harvard University, Cambridge, MA.

Down, J. L. (1887). *On some of the mental affections of childhood and youth.* London: Churchill.

Drachman, D., & Leavitt, J. (1972). Memory impairment in the aged: Storage versus retrieval deficit. *Journal of Experimental Psychology, 93,* 302–308.

Druks, J., & Marshall, J. (1991). Agrammatism: An analysis and critique, with new evidence from four Hebrew-speaking aphasic patients. *Cognitive Neuropsychology, 8,* 415–433.

Dubois, D. (1982). *Normes de production d'exemplaires appartenant à 22 catégories sémantiques à partir d'une consigne classique et d'une consigne d'imagerie.* Unpublished manuscript, Laboratoire de Psychologie, Université de Paris VIII, Paris.

Dubois, J., & Dubois-Charlier, F. (1970). *Eléments de linguistique française.* Paris: Larousse.

Duchan, J. F., & Erickson, J. G. (1976). Normal and nonretarded children's understanding of semantic relations in different verbal contexts. *Journal of Speech and Hearing Research, 19,* 767–776.

Dunn, L., & Dunn, L. (1965). *Peabody Picture Vocabulary Test.* Circle Pines, MN: American Guidance Service.

Dunn, L., & Dunn, L. (1982). *British Picture Vocabulary Scale.* Windsor, England: Nelson.

Edwards, D. (1973). Sensory-motor intelligence and semantic relations in early child grammar. *Cognition, 2,* 395–424.

Ehri, L., & Galanis, A. (1980). Teaching children to comprehend propositions conjoined by *before* and *after. Journal of Experimental Child Psychology, 30,* 308–324.

Eisele, J. (1991). Selective deficits in language comprehension following early left and right hemisphere damage. In I. Pavao Martins, A. Castro-Caldas, H. Van Dongen, & A. Van Hout (Eds.), *Acquired aphasia in children* (pp. 225–238). Boston: Kluwer.

Elliott, D., Edwards, J. M., Weeks, D., Lindley, S., & Carnahan, H. (1987). Cerebral specialization in young adults with Down syndrome. *American Journal on Mental Retardation, 91,* 480–485.

Elliott, D., Weeks, D., & Elliott, C. (1987). Cerebral specialization in individuals with Down syndrome. *American Journal on Mental Retardation, 92,* 263–271.

Ellis, A. (1980). Errors in speech production and short-term memory: The effects of phonemic similarity and syllable position. *Journal of Verbal Learning and Verbal Behavior, 19,* 624–634.

Ellis, N. (1963). The stimulus trace and behavioral inadequacy. In N. Ellis (Ed.), *Handbook of mental deficiency* (pp. 134–158). New York: McGraw-Hill.

Ellis, N. (1978). Do the mentally retarded have memory deficits? *Intelligence, 2,* 41–45.

Ellis, N., & Hennelly, R. (1980). A bilingual word length effect: Implication for intelligence testing and the relative case of mental calculation in Welsh and English. *British Journal of Psychology, 71,* 43–52.

Elman, J. (1990a). Representation and structure in connectionist models. In G. Altman (Ed.), *Cognitive models of speech processing* (pp. 345–382). Cambridge, MA: MIT Press.

Elman, J. (1990b). Finding structure in time. *Cognitive Science, 14,* 179–211.

Emerson, H. (1979). Children's comprehension of *because* in reversible and non-reversible sentences. *Journal of Child Language, 6,* 279–300.

Entwistle, D. (1966). Form class and children's word association. *Journal of Verbal Learning and Verbal Behavior, 5,* 558–565.

Entwistle, D., Forsyth, D., & Muuss, R. (1964). The syntagmatic-paradigmatic shift in children's word associations. *Journal of Verbal Learning and Verbal Behavior, 3,* 19–29.

Epstein, C. (1986). Trisomy 21 and the nervous system: From causes to cure. In C. Epstein (Ed.), *The neurobiology of Down syndrome* (pp. 1–15). New York: Raven.

Epstein, C. (1987). The consequences of altered gene dosage in trisomy 21. In S. Pueschel, C. Tingey, J. Rynders, A. Crocker, & D. Crutcher (Eds.), *New perspectives on Down syndrome* (pp. 69–80). Baltimore: Brookes.

Epstein, C. (1991). Aneuploidy and morphogenesis. In C. Epstein (Ed.), *The morphogenesis of Down syndrome* (pp. 1–18). New York: Wiley-Liss.

Erhlich, S. (1972). *La capacité d'appréhension verbale.* Paris: Presses Universitaires de France.

Erwin, S. (1961). Changes with age in the verbal determinants of word association. *American Journal of Psychology, 74,* 361–372.

Esperet, E. (1984). Processus de production, genèse et rôle du schéma narratif dans la conduite du récit. In M. Moscato & G. Pieraut-Le Bonniec (Eds.), *Le langage, construction et actualisation* (pp. 179–196). Rouen: Presses Universitaires de Rouen.

Esquirol, J. (1838). *Des maladies mentales considérées sous les rapports médical, hygiénique, et médico-légal* (2 Vols.). Paris: Baillière.

Evans, D., & Hampson, M. (1968). The language of mongols. *British Journal of Disorders of Communication, 3,* 171–181.

Evenhuis, H., van Zanten, G., Brocaar, M., & Roerdinkholder, W. (1992). Hearing loss in middle-age persons with Down syndrome. *American Journal on Mental Retardation, 97,* 47–56.

Facon, B., & Bollengier, T. (1991). *Contribution à l'étude des effets de la dissociation entre efficience et expérience sur le profil psychologique des retardés mentaux.* Mémoire de D.E.A. (unpublished). Département de Psychologie Cognitive, Université de Lille, Lille.

Fay, W. (1993). Infantile autism. In D. Bishop & K. Mogford (Ed.), *Language development in exceptional circumstances* (pp. 190–202). Hove, UK: Erlbaum.

Fay, W., & Schuler, A. (1980). *Emerging language in autistic children.* London: Arnold.

Fernald, G., & Keller, H. (1936). On certain language disabilities, their nature and treatment. *Mental Measurement Monographs,* No. 11.

Flavell, J. (1977). *Cognitive development.* Englewood Cliffs, NJ: Prentice-Hall.

Ferreiro, E. (1971). *Les relations temporelles dans le langage de l'enfant.* Genève: Droz.

Ferreiro, E., Othenin Girard, C., Chipman, H., & Sinclair, H. (1976). How do the children handle relative clauses? A study in comparative developmental psycholinguistics. *Archives de Psychologie, 44,* 229–266.

Ferreiro, E., & Sinclair, H. (1971). Temporal relationships in language. *International Journal of Psychology, 6,* 39–47.

Ferri, R., Bergonzi, P., Colognola, R., Musumeci, S., Sanfillippo, S., Tomassetti, P., Viglianesi, A., & Gigli, G. (1986). Brainstem auditory evoked potentials in subjects with mental retardation and different kariotypes. In V. Gallai (Ed.), *Maturation of CNS and evoked potentials* (pp. 369–392). Amsterdam: Excerpts Medica.

Feuerbach, A. von (1832). *Example of a crime on intellectual life of a man.* Iena: Ausbach.

Fillmore, C. (1967). The case for case. In E. Bach & R. Harms (Eds.), *Universals in linguistics theory* (pp. 1–88). New York: Holt, Rinehart, & Winston.

Finer, D., & Roeper, T. (1989). From cognition to thematic roles. In R. Matthews & W. Demopoulos (Eds.), *Learnability and linguistic theory* (pp. 177–210). Boston: Kluwer.

Fishler, K., & Koch, R. (1991). Mental development in Down's syndrome mosaicism. *American Journal of Mental Retardation, 96,* 345–351.

Fishler, K., Share, J., & Koch, R. (1964). Adaptation of Gesell developmental scales for evaluation of development in children with Down's syndrome. *American Journal of Mental Deficiencies, 68,* 642–646.

Flavell, J. (1963). *The developmental psychology of Jean Piaget.* New York: Van Nostrand.

Flavell, J. (1977). *Cognitive development.* Englewood Cliffs, NJ: Prentice-Hall.

Flavell, J., Beach, D., & Chinsky, J. (1966). Spontaneous verbal rehearsal in a memory task as function of age. *Child Development, 37,* 283–299.

Fodor, J. (1983). *The modularity of mind.* Cambridge, MA: MIT Press.

Fodor, J. (1985). Introduction. In Précis of the modularity of mind. *Behavioral and Brain Sciences, 8,* 1–5.

Fodor, J. (1987). Modules, frames, fridgeons, sleeping days, and the music of the spheres. In J. Garfield (Ed.), *Modularity in knowledge representation and natural-language understanding* (pp. 25–36). Cambridge, MA: MIT Press.

Fodor, J. (1991). Panel discussion: Modularity of speech and language. In I. Mattingly & M. Studdert-Kennedy (Eds.), *Modularity and the motor theory of speech perception* (pp. 359–373). Hillsdale, NJ: Erlbaum.

Fodor, J. Dean (1989). Learning the periphery. In R. Matthews & W. Demopoulos (Eds.), *Learnability and linguistic theory* (pp. 129–154). Boston: Kluwer.

Fox, B., & Routh, D. (1975). Analyzing spoken language into words, syllables, and phonemes: A developmental study. *Journal of Psycholinguistic Research, 4,* 331–342.

Fox, B., & Routh, D. (1980). Phonemic analysis and severe reading disability in children. *Journal of Psycholinguistic Research, 9,* 115–120.

Fowler, A. (1988). Determinants of rate of language growth in children with Down syndrome. In L. Nadel (Ed.), *The psychobiology of Down syndrome* (pp. 217–245). Cambridge, MA: MIT Press.

Fowler, A. (1990). Language abilities in children with Down syndrome: Evidence for a specific syntactic delay. In D. Cicchetti & M. Beeghly (Eds.), *Children with Down syndrome: A developmental perspective* (pp. 302–328). Cambridge University Press.

Francis, H. (1972). Toward an explanation of the syntagmatic-paradigmatic shift. *Child Development, 43,* 949–958.

François, F. (1987). Morphologie, syntaxe, et discours. In J. A. Rondal & J. P. Thibaut (Eds.), *Problèmes de psycholinguistique* (pp. 175–247). Brussels: Mardaga.

Frith, U., & Frith, C. (1974). Specific motor disabilities in Down's syndrome. *Journal of Child Psychology and Psychiatry, 15,* 293–301.

Frome Loeb, D., & Leonard, L. (1988). Specific language impairment and parameter theory. *Clinical Linguistics and Phonetics, 2,* 317–327.

Fulton, R., & Lloyd, L. (1968). Hearing impairment in a population of children with Down's syndrome. *American Journal of Mental Deficiency, 73,* 298–302.

Furth, H. (1969). *Piaget and knowledge.* Englewood Cliffs, NJ: Prentice-Hall.

Gaiffe, F., Maille, E., Breuil, E., Jahan, S., Wagner, L., & Marijon, M. (1936). *Grammaire Larousse du XXè siècle.* Paris: Larousse.

Galifret-Granjon, N. (1979). *L'évolution des praxies idéomotrices.* Unpublished doctoral thesis, Université de Paris X, Paris.

Gall, F. J. (1809). *Recherches sur le système nerveux en général et sur celui du cerveau en particulier.* Paris: Baillière.

Gall, F. J., & Spurzheim, G. (1810). *Anatomie et physiologie du système nerveux.* Paris: Baillière.

Ganis, G., & Chater, N. (1991). Can double dissociation uncover the modularity of cognitive processes? *Proceedings of the 13th Annual Meeting of the Cognitive Science Society.* Chicago: Cognitive Science Society.

Gardner, H. (1983). *Frames of mind: The theory of the multiple intelligences.* New York: Basic.

Gardner, H. (1985). The centrality of modules. In Précis of the modularity of mind. *Behavioral and Brain Sciences, 8,* 12–14.

Garfield, J. (Ed.). (1987a). *Modularity in knowledge representation and natural-language understanding.* Cambridge, MA: MIT Press.

Garfield, J. (1987b). Introduction: Carving the mind at its joints. In J. Garfield (Ed.), *Modularity in knowledge representation and natural-language understanding* (pp. 1–13). Cambridge, MA: MIT Press.

Garvey, C., & Caramazza, A. (1974). Implicit causality in verbs. *Linguistic Inquiry, 5,* 459–464.

Garvey, C., Caramazza, A., & Yates, J. (1975). Factors influencing assignments of pronoun antecedents. *Cognition, 3,* 227–243.

Gathercole, S., & Baddeley, A. (1989). Development of vocabulary in children and short-term phonological memory. *Journal of Memory and Language, 28,* 200–213.

Gathercole, S., & Baddeley, A. (1990a). The role of phonological memory in vocabulary acquisition: A study of young children learning new names. *British Journal of Psychology, 81,* 439–454.

Gathercole, S., & Baddeley, A. (1990b). Phonological memory deficits in language disordered children: Is there a causal connection? *Journal of Memory and Language, 29,* 336–360.

Genesee, F., Hamers, J., Lambert, W., Mononen, L., Seitz, M., & Starck, R. (1978). Language processing in bilinguals. *Brain and Language, 5,* 1–12.

Gérard, C. L. (1991). *L'enfant dysphasique.* Paris: Editions Universitaires.

Geschwind, N., & Galaburda, A. (Eds.). (1984). *Cerebral dominance: The biological foundations.* Cambridge, MA: Harvard University Press.

Geschwind, N., & Galaburda, A (1985). Cerebral lateralization. *Archives of Neurology, 42,* 428–459.

Gibson, D. (1981). *Down's syndrome: The psychology of mongolism.* Cambridge University Press.

Gigli, G., Ferri, R., Musumeci, S., Tomassetti, P., & Bergonzi, P. (1984). Brainstem auditory evoked responses in children with Down syndrome. In J. M. Berg (Ed.), *Perspectives and progress in mental retardation* (Vol. 2, pp. 277–286). London: International Association for the Scientific Study of Mental Deficiency.

Gil, D. (1987). On the scope of grammatical theory. In S. Modgil & C. Modgil (Eds.), *Noam Chomsky, consensus and controversy* (pp. 119–141). New York: Famer.

Gilham, B. (1979). *The first words language programme: A basic language programme for mentally handicapped children.* London: Allen & Unwin.

Gilon, S. (1988). *Mémoire et trisomie 21.* Mémoire de licence (unpublished). Laboratoire de Psycholinguistique, Université de Liège, Liège.

Glenn, S., & Cunningham, C. (1982). Recognition for the familiar words of nursery rhymes by handicapped and non-handicapped infants. *Journal of Child Psychology and Psychiatry, 23,* 319–327.

Gleitman, L., & Gleitman, H. (1970). *Phrase and paraphrase: Some innovative uses of language.* New York: Norton.

Gleitman, L., Gleitman, H., & Shipley, E. (1972). The emergence of the child as a grammarian. *Cognition, 1,* 137–164.

Glovsky, L. (1970). A comparison of mentally retarded children on the ITPA. *Training School Bulletin, 67,* 4–14.

Goddard, H. (1916). *Feeblemindedness: Its causes and consequences.* New York: Macmillan.

Goldfield, B., & Snow, C. (1985). Individual differences in language acquisition. In J. Berko Gleason (Ed.), *The development of language* (pp. 307–330). Columbus, OH: Merrill.

Goldman-Eisler, F. (1968). *Psycholinguistics: Experiments in spontaneous speech.* New York: Academic.

Goldman-Eisler, F. (1972). Pauses, clauses, sentences. *Language and Speech, 15,* 103–113.

Gombert, J. E. (1990). *Le développement métalinguistique.* Paris: Presses Universitaires de France.

Goodluck, H., & Tavakolian, S. (1982). Competence and processing in children's grammar of relative clauses. *Cognition, 11,* 1–27.

Gopnik, M. (1987, July). *Language before stage six.* Communication presented at the 4th International Congress for the Study of Child Language, Lund, Sweden.

Gopnik, M. (1990). Feature-blind grammar and dysphasia. *Nature, 344,* 715.

Gopnik, M. (1992). A model module [Review of Yamada, J. (1990). *Laura: A case for the modularity of language*]. *Cognitive Neuropsychology, 9,* 253–258.

Gopnik, M., & Crago, M. (1991). Familial aggregation of a developmental language disorder. *Cognition, 39,* 1–50.

Gordon, W., & Panagos, J. (1976). Developmental transformational capacity of children with Down's syndrome. *Perceptual and Motor Skills, 43,* 967–973.

Goswami, U., & Bryant, P. (1990). *Phonological skills and learning to read.* Hillsdale, NJ: Erlbaum.

Gottardo, A., & Rubin, H. (1991). Language analysis skills of children with mental retardation. *Mental Retardation, 29,* 269–274.

Gottsleben, R. (1955). The incidence of stuttering in a group of mongoloids. *Training School Bulletin, 51,* 209–218.

Gougenheim, G., Rivenc, P., Michéa, R., & Sauvageot, A. (1964). *L'élaboration du français fondamental.* Paris: Didier.

Gould, S. (1987, October). *The limits of adaptation: Is language a spandrel of the human brain?* Communication presented at the Cognitive Science Seminar, Center for Cognitive Science, MIT, Cambridge, MA.

Gould, S., & Eldredge, N. (1977). Punctuated equilibria: The "tempo" and "mode" of evolution reconsidered. *Paleobiology, 3,* 115–151.

Graham, N. (1968). Short-term memory and syntactic structure in educationally subnormal children. *Language and Speech, 11,* 209–219.

Grammaire Larousse du 20e. siècle. (1936). *Traité complet de la langue française.* Paris: Librairie Larousse.

Grégoire, M. N. (1980). *Aspects lexicaux et morpho-syntaxiques du développement du langage.* Mémoire de licence (unpublished). Laboratoire de Psycholinguistique, Université de Liège, Liège.

Grice, H. (1975). Logic and conversation. In P. Cole & J. L. Morgan (Eds.), *Syntax and semantics: Vol. 3. Speech acts* (pp. 89–126). New York: Academic.

Grimshaw, J. (1990). *Argument structure.* Cambridge, MA: MIT Press.

Grober, E., Beardsley, W., & Caramazza, A. (1978). Parallel function strategy in pronoun assignement. *Cognition, 6,* 117–133.

Grodzinsky, Y. (1984). The syntactic characterization of agrammatism. *Cognition, 16,* 99–120.

Grodzinsky, Y. (1986). Language deficits and the theory of syntax. *Brain and Language, 27,* 135–159.

Grodzinsky, Y. (1990). *Theoretical perspectives on language deficits.* Cambridge, MA: MIT Press.

Gropen, J., Pinker, S., Hollander, M., & Goldberg, R. (1991). Affectedness and direct objects: The role of lexical semantics in the acquisition of verb argument structure. *Cognition, 41,* 153–195.

Grossman, H. (Ed.). (1983). *Classification in mental retardation.* Washington, DC: American Association on Mental Deficiency.

Guillaume, P. (1925). *L'imitation chez l'enfant.* Paris: Alcan.

Gunn, P. (1985). Speech and language. In D. Lane & B. Stradford (Eds.), *Current approaches to Down's syndrome* (pp. 260–281). London: Cassell.

Gunnar, M., & Maratsos, M. (Eds.). (1992). *Modularity and constraints in language and cognition: The Minnesota Symposia on Child Psychology* (Vol. 25) Hillsdale, NJ: Erlbaum.

Guralnick, M., & Bennett, F. (Eds.). (1987). *The effectiveness of early intervention for at-risk and handicapped children.* New York: Academic.

Guralnick, M., & Bricker, D. (1987). The effectiveness of early intervention for children with cognitive and general developmental delays. In M. Guralnick & F. Bennet (Eds.), *The effectiveness of early intervention for at-risk and handicapped children* (pp. 115–173). New York: Academic.

Gutmann, A., & Rondal, J. A. (1979). Verbal operants in mother's speech to nonretarded and Down's syndrome children matched for linguistic level. *American Journal of Mental Deficiency, 83,* 446–452.

Hadenius, A., Hagberg, B., Hyttnas-Bensch, K., & Sjogren, I. (1962). The natural prognosis of infantile hydrocephalus. *Acta Paediatrica, 51*, 117–118.

Hagège, C. (1985). *L'homme de parole. Contribution linguistique aux sciences humaines.* Paris: Fayard.

Hakes, D. (1980). *The development of metalinguistic abilities in children.* New York: Springer-Verlag.

Hakes, D., Evans, J., & Brannon, L. (1976). Understanding sentences with relatives clauses. *Memory and Cognition, 4*, 283–290.

Hall, R. (1966). *Pidgin and creole languages.* New York: Cornell University Press.

Halliday, M. (1985). *An introduction to functional grammar.* London: Arnold.

Hamerton, J., Giannelli, F., & Polani, P. (1965). Cytogenetics of Down's syndrome (mongolism) I. Data on consecutive series of patients referred for genetic counselling and diagnosis. *Cytogenetics, 4*, 171–185.

Harnois, G. (1927). *Les théories du langage en France de 1660 à 1821.* Paris: Les Belles Lettres.

Harris, A., & Gibson, D. (1986, May). *Asymmetries in language processing and syndrome specificity in the mentally handicapped.* Communication presented at the Annual Meeting of the Canadian Psychological Association, Toronto.

Harris, J. (1983). What does mean length of utterance mean? Evidence from a comparative study of normal and Down's syndrome children. *British Journal of Disorders of Communication, 18*, 153–169.

Harris, M., & Davies, M. (1987). Learning and triggering. *First Language, 7*, 31–39.

Hartley, X. (1981). Lateralisation of speech stimuli in young Down's syndrome children. *Cortex, 17*, 241–248.

Hartley, X. (1982). Receptive language processing of Down's syndrome children. *Journal of Mental Deficiency Research, 26*, 263–269.

Hartley, X. (1985). Receptive language processing and ear advantage of Down's syndrome children. *Journal of Mental Deficiency Research, 29*, 197–205.

Hatch, E. (1971). The young child's comprehension of time connectives. *Child Development, 42*, 2111–2113.

Hatcher, A. (1944a). Il me prend le bras vs. Il prend mon bras. *Romanic Review, 35*, 156–164.

Hatcher, A. (1944b). Il tend les mains vs. Il tend ses mains. *Studies in Philology, 41*, 457–481.

Hauser-Cram, P. (1989). The efficiency of early intervention. *Ab Initio, 1*(2), 1–2.

Hayhurst, H. (1967). Some errors of young children in producing passive sentences. *Journal of Verbal Learning and Verbal Behavior, 6*, 634–639.

Hawkins, P. (1971). The syntactic location of hesitation pauses. *Language and Speech, 14*, 277–288.

Haxby, J. (1992). Longitudinal study of neuropsychological function in older adults with Down syndrome. In L. Nadel & C. Epstein (Eds.), *Alzheimer disease and Down syndrome. (Progress in biological research,* Vol. 379, pp. 150–164). New York: Wiley-Liss.

Head, H., & Holmes, G. (1911). Troubles sensoriels dus à des lésions cérébrales. In J. Corraze (Ed.), *Schéma corporel et images du corps* (original texts translated) (pp. 48–74). Toulouse: Privat.

Hecaen, H., & Albert, M. (1978). *Human neuropsychology.* New York: Wiley.

Hecaen, H., & Anglelergues, R. (1965). *Pathologie du langage.* Paris: Larousse.

Hermelin, B., & O'Connor, N. (1986). Idiot-savant calendrical calculators: Rules and regularities. *Psychological Medicine, 16*, 885–893.

Hermelin, B., & O'Connor, N. (1990a). Factors and primes: A specific numerical ability. *Psychological Medicine, 20*, 163–169.

Hermelin, B., & O'Connor, N. (1990b). Art and accuracy: The drawing ability of idiot-savants. *Journal of Psychology and Psychiatry, 31,* 217–228.

Hermelin, B., O'Connor, N., & Lee, S. (1987). Musical inventiveness of five idiot-savants. *Psychological Medicine, 17,* 685–694.

Hermelin, B., O'Connor, N., Lee, S., & Treffert, D. (1989). Intelligence and musical improvisation. *Psychological Medicine, 19,* 447–457.

Hickok, G. (1992). *Agrammatic comprehension and the trace deletion hypothesis.* Occasional Paper No. 45 (unpublished). Cambridge, MA: MIT, Center for Cognitive Science.

Hirsh-Pasek, K., Treiman, R., & Schneiderman, M. (1984). Brown & Hanlon revisited: Mothers' sensitivity to ungrammatical forms. *Journal of Child Language, 11,* 81–88.

Hiscock, M., & Decter, M. (1988). Dichotic listening in children. In K. Hughdahl (Ed.), *Handbook of dichotic listening: Theory, methods and research* (pp. 431–473). New York: Wiley.

Hiscock, M., & Kinsbourne, M. (1980). Asymmetries of selective listening and attention switching in children. *Developmental Psychology, 86,* 667–674.

Hitch, G. (1990). Developmental fractionation of working memory. In G. Vallar & T. Shallice (Eds.), *Neuropsychological impairments of short-term memory* (pp. 221–246). Cambridge University Press.

Hochberg, J., & Pinker, S. (1985). *Syntax-semantics correspondences in parental speech.* Unpublished manuscript, MIT, Department of Brain and Cognitive Sciences, Cambridge, MA.

Hodapp, R., & Zigler, E. (1990). Applying the developmental perspective to individuals with Down syndrome. In D. Cicchetti & M. Beeghly (Eds.), *Children with Down syndrome: A developmental perspective* (pp. 1–28). Cambridge University Press.

Hogrefe, C. (1962). *Test D2. Göttingen: Verlag für Psychologie.* (French adaptation, R. Brickenhamp, Brussels, Editest, 1966)

Holmes, V. (1988). Hesitations and sentence planning. *Language and Cognitive Processes, 3,* 323–361.

Hoosain, R., & Salili, F. (1988). Language differences, working memory, and mathematical ability. In M. Gruneberg, P. Morris, & R. Sykes (Eds.), *Practical aspects of memory: Current research and issues* (Vol. 2, pp. 512–517). New York: Wiley.

Hopper, P., & Thompson, S. (1980). Transitivity in grammar and discourse. *Language, 56,* 251–299.

Howe, M., & Rabinowitz, F. (1989). On the uninterpretability of a dual task performance. *Journal of Experimental Child Psychology, 47,* 32–38.

Hulme, C., & Mackenzie, S. (1992). *Working memory and severe learning difficulties.* Hove, UK: Erlbaum.

Hulme, C., & Muir, C. (1985). Developmental changes in speech rate and memory span: A causal relationship? *British Journal of Developmental Psychology, 3,* 175–181.

Hulme, C., Thomson, N., Muir, C., & Lawrence, A. (1984). Speech rate and the development of short-term memory span. *Journal of Experimental Child Psychology, 38,* 241–253.

Humboldt, W. von. (1836). *Uber die Verschiedenheit des Menschlichen Sprachbaues.* Bonn: Dümmlers Verlag. (Facsimile, 1960)

Hupet, M., & Costermans, J. (1976). Un passif pour quoi faire? *La Linguistique, 12,* 3–26.

Hupet, M., & Le Bouedec, B. (1975). Definitiveness and voice in the interpretation of active and passive sentences. *Quarterly Journal of Experimental Psychology, 27,* 323–330.

Hurford, J. (1991). The evolution of critical period for language acquisition. *Cognition, 40,* 159–201.

Hurst, J., Baraitser, M., Anger, E., Graham, F., & Norell, S. (1990). An extended family with a dominantly inherited speech disorder. *Developmental Medicine and Child Neurology, 32,* 352–355.

Huteau, M. (1987). *Style cognitif et personnalité. La dependance – indépendance à l'égard du champ.* Lille: Presses Universitaires de Lille.

Hyams, N. (1986). *Language acquisition and the theory of parameters.* Boston: Reidel.

Hyams, N. (1987). The theory of parameters and syntactic development. In T. Roeper & E. Williams (Eds.), *Parameter setting* (pp. 1–22). Boston: Reidel.

Ingram, D. (1976). *Phonological disability in children.* London: Arnold.

Inhelder, B. (1969). *Le diagnostic du raisonnement chez les débiles mentaux.* Neuchêtel: Delachaux & Niestlé.

Inhelder, B. (1976). *The sensori-motor origins of knowledge.* In B. Inhelder & H. Chipman (Eds.), *Piaget and his school: A reader in developmental psychology* (pp. 150–165). New York: Springer-Verlag.

Inhelder, B. (1979). Langage et connaissance dans le cadre constructiviste. In M. Piattelli-Palmarini (Ed.), *Théorie du langage. Théories de l'apprentissage. Le débat entre Jean Piaget et Noam Chomsky* (pp. 200–207). Paris: Seuil.

Irigaray, L. (1973). *Le langage des déments.* The Hague: Mouton.

Jarbinet, A. (1991). *Passation de l'UDN 80 auprès de 34 sujets trisomiques 21 adultes.* Unpublished report in progress, Laboratoire de Psycholinguistique, Université de Liège, Liège.

Jarvis, C. (1980). *A comparison of the phonologies of young adults Down's syndrome and non-Down's syndrome subjects resident in an institution.* Unpublished bachelor's thesis, University of Newcastle, Newcastle.

Johnson, J., & Newport, E. (1989). Critical period effects in second language learning: The influence of maturational stage on the acquisition of English as a second language. *Cognitive Psychology, 21,* 60–99.

Johnson, J., & Newport, E. (1991). Critical period effects on universal properties of language: The status of subjacency in the acquisition of a second language. *Cognition, 39,* 215–258.

Johnston, J. (1988). Specific language disorders in the child. In N. Lass, L. McReynolds, J. Northern, & D. Yoder (Eds.), *Handbook of speech pathology and audiology* (pp. 268–298). Philadelphia: Decker.

Kaens, A. M. (1988). *Le role de l'imagerie mentale dans la compréhension des phrases déclaratives chez l'enfant.* Mémoire de Licence (unpublished). Laboratoire de Psycholinguistique, Université de Liège, Liège.

Kahn, J. (1975). Relationship of Piaget's sensorimotor period to language acquisition of profoundly retarded children. *American Journal of Mental Deficiency, 79,* 640–643.

Kahn, J. (1993). Niveau de développement sensori-moteur et compréhension du langage signé par des enfants retardés menteaux sévères et profonds. *Revue Francophone de la Déficience Intellectuelle, 4,* 49–56.

Kail, M. (1976). Stratégies de compréhension des pronoms personnels chez le jeune enfant. *Enfance, 4–5, 447–466.*

Kail, M. (1983). La coréférence des pronoms: Pertinence de la stratégie des fonctions parallèles. In J. P. Bronckart, M. Kail, & G. Noizet (Eds.), *Psycholinguistique de l'enfant. Recherches sur l'acquisition du langage* (pp. 107–122). Paris: Delachaux & Niestlé.

Kail, M., & Leveillé, M. (1977). Compréhension de la coréférence des pronoms personnels chez l'enfant et chez l'adulte. *L'Année Psychologique, 77,* 79–94.

Kail, R. (1984). *The development of memory in children.* New York: Freeman.

Kail, R. (1992). General slowing of information-processing by persons with mental retardation. *American Journal on Mental Retardation, 97,* 333–341.

Kamhi, A., & Masterson, J. (1989). Language and cognition in mentally handicapped people: Last rites for the difference-delay controversy. In M. Beveridge, G. Conti-Ramsden, & I.

Leudar (Eds.), *Language and communication in mentally handicapped people* (pp. 83–111). London: Chapman & Hall.

Kaneko, M. (1989). Variability of speech durations in mentally retarded children. *Journal of Human Development, 25*, 44–56.

Kanizsa, G. (1979). *Organization in vision.* New York: Praeger.

Kanner, L. (1943). Autistic disturbances of affective contact. *Nervous Child, 2*, 217–250.

Karmiloff-Smith, A. (1979). *A functional approach to child language.* Cambridge University Press.

Kaye, J. (1989). *Phonology: A cognitive view.* Hillsdale, NJ: Erlbaum.

Ke, C. (1992). Dichotic listening with Chinese and English tasks. *Journal of Psycholinguistic Research, 21*, 463–471.

Kean, M. L. (1989). Brain structures and linguistic capacity. In F. Newmeyer (Ed.), *Linguistics: The Cambridge survey* (Vol. 2, pp. 74–75.). Cambridge University Press.

Keil, F. (1989). *Concepts, kinds, and cognitive development.* Cambridge, MA: MIT Press.

Keilman, P., & Moran, L. (1967). Association structures of mental retardates. *Multivariate Behavioral Research, 2*, 35–45.

Keiser, H., Montague, J., Wold, D., Maune, S., & Pattison, D. (1981). Hearing loss of Down's syndrome adults. *American Journal of Mental Deficiency, 85*, 467–472.

Kemper, T. (1988). Neuropathology of Down syndrome. In L. Nadel (Ed.), *The psychobiology of Down syndrome* (pp. 269–289). Cambridge, MA: MIT Press.

Kempler, D. (1984). *Syntactic and symbolic abilities in Alzheimer's disease.* Unpublished doctoral dissertation, Department of Linguistics, UCLA, Los Angeles.

Kempler D., Curtiss, S., & Jackson, C. (1987). Syntactic preservation in Alzheimer's disease. *Journal of Speech and Hearing Research, 30*, 343–350.

Kernan, K. (1990). Comprehension of syntactically indicated sequence by Down's syndrome and other mentally retarded adults. *Journal of Mental Deficiency Research, 34*, 169–178.

Kettler, Laurent, and Thireau. (1964). *Echelle KLT.* Issy-Les-Moulineaux: Editions Scientifiques & Psychologiques. [Authors' initials not given.]

Khomsi, A. (1985). *Epreuve de compréhension O52.* Nantes: Presses Universitaires de Nantes.

Kimberling, W. (1983). Linkage analysis of communication disorders. In C. Ludlow & L. Cooper (Eds.), *Genetic aspects of speech and language disorders* (pp. 151–156). New York: Academic.

Kimura, D. (1992). Sex differences in the brain. *Scientific American*, September, 119–125.

Kinsbourne, M., & Hicks, R. (1978). Functional cerebral space: A model for overflow, transfer, and interference effects in human performance. In J. Requin (Ed.), *Attention and performance* (Vol. 7, pp. 345–362). New York: Academic.

Kinsbourne, M., & Hiscock, M. (1983). Asymmetries of dual task performance. In J. Hellige (Ed.), *Cerebral hemisphere asymmetry: Method, theory, and application* (pp. 255–334). New York: Praeger.

Klapp, S., Grein, D., & Marshburn, E. (1981). Buffer storage of programmed articulation and articulatory loop: Two names for the same mechanism or two distinct components of short-term memory? In J. Long & A. Baddeley (Eds.), *Attention and performance* (pp. 114–129). Hillsdale, NJ: Erlbaum.

Klee, T., & Fitzgerald, M. (1985). The relation between grammatical development and mean length of utterances in morphemes. *Journal of Child Language, 12*, 251–269.

Klima, E., & Bellugi, U. (1979). *The signs of language.* Cambridge, MA: Harvard University Press.

Koenig, O., Wetzel, C., & Caramazza, A. (1992). Evidence for different types of lexical representations in the cerebral hemispheres. *Cognitive Neuropsychology, 9,* 33–45.

Kohlberg, L. (1968). Early education: A cognitive-developmental view. *Child Development, 39,* 1013–1062.

Kosslyn, S. (1980). *Image and mind.* Cambridge, MA: Harvard University Press.

Kraus, B., Clark, A., & Oka, S. (1968). Mental retardation and abnormalities of the dentition. *American Journal of Mental Deficiency, 72,* 905–917

Kriauciunas, R. (1968). The relationship of age and retention interval activity in short term memory. *Journal of Gerontology, 23,* 169–173.

Kuhn, D., & Phelps, H. (1976). The development of children's comprehension of causal direction. *Child Development, 47,* 248–251.

Lackner, J. (1968). A developmental study of language behavior in retarded children. *Neuropsychologia, 6,* 301–320.

Lafontaine, A. (1988). *La mémoire de travail. Construction d'une batterie pour l'évaluation de sa composante verbale.* Mémoire de Licence (unpublished). Liège: Université de Liège, Laboratoire de Psycholinguistique.

Laine, M., Niemi, P., Niemi, J., & Koivuselkä-Sallinen, P. (1990). Semantic errors in a deep dyslexic. *Brain and Language, 37,* 73–89.

Lake, D., & Bryden, M. (1976). Handedness and sex differences in hemispheric asymmetry. *Brain and Language, 3,* 266–282.

Lakoff, R. (1987). *Women, fire and dangerous things: What categories tell us about the nature of thought.* Chicago: University of Chicago Press.

Lambert, J.-L., & Rondal, J. A. (1980). *Le mongolisme.* Brussels: Mardaga.

Landau, B., & Gleitman, L. (1985). *Language and experience: Evidence from the blind child.* Cambridge, MA: Harvard University Press.

Langacker, R. (1987). *Foundations of cognitive grammar.* Stanford, CA: Stanford University Press.

Lasnik, H. (1989). On certain substitutes for negative data. In R. Matthews & W. Demopoulos (Eds.), *Learnability and linguistic theory* (pp. 89–105). Boston: Kluwer.

Layton, T., & Sharifi, H. (1979). Meaning and structure of Down's syndrome and nonretarded children spontaneous speech. *American Journal of Mental Deficiency, 83,* 139–445.

Leahy, M., & Kallen, J. (Eds.). (1993). *Interdisciplinary perspectives in speech and language pathology.* Selected papers from the 1992 Trinity College Anniversary Conference. Dublin: School of Clinical Speech and Language Studies, Trinity College.

Leblanc, R., & Page, J. (1989). Autisme infantile précoce. In J. A. Rondal & X. Seron (Eds.), *Troubles du langage. Diagnostic et rééducation* (pp. 299–324). Brussels: Mardaga.

Lebrun, Y., & Van Borsel, J. (1991). Final sound repetitions. *Journal of Fluency Disorders, 15,* 107–113.

Lebrun, Y., Van Endert, C., & Szliwowski, H. (1988). Trilingual hyperlexia. In L. Obler & D. Fein (Eds.), *The exceptional brain* (pp. 253–264). New York: Guilford.

Lee, L. (1969). *The Northwestern Syntax Screeening Test.* Evanston, IL: Illinois University Press.

Lee, L. (1975). *Developmental sentence analysis.* Boston: Northwestern University Press.

Leibniz, G. W. (1765). *Nouveaux essais sur l'entendement humain.* Paris: Alcan. (New trans. 1927)

Leifer, J., & Lewis, M. (1984). Acquisition of conversational response skills by young Down syndrome and nonretarded young children. *American Journal of Mental Deficiency, 88,* 610–618.

Legé, Y., & Dague, P. (1974). *Test de Vocabulaire en Images.* Paris: Editions du Centre de Psychologie Appliquée.

Lejeune, J., Turpin, R., & Gautier, M. (1959). Le mongolisme, premier exemple d'abérration autosomique humaine. *L'Année Génétique*, *2*, 41–49.

Lenneberg, E. (1967). *Biological foundations of language*. New York: Wiley.

Lenneberg, E., Nichols, I., & Rosenberger, E. (1964). Primitive stages of development in mongolism. In D. McRioch & A. Weinstein (Eds.), *Disorders of communication* (pp. 119–137). Baltimore: Williams & Wilkins.

Leonard, L. (1985). Unusual and subtle phonological behavior in the speech of phonologically disordered children. *Journal of Speech and Hearing Disorders, 50*, 4–13.

Leonard, L. (1989). Language learnability and specific language impairment in children. *Applied Psycholinguistics, 10*, 179–202.

Leonard, L. (1992). The use of morphology by children with specific language impairment: Evidence from three languages. In R. Chapman (Ed.), *Processes in language acquisition and disorders* (pp. 40–67). Chicago: Mosby-Yearbook.

Leonard, L., Bortolini, U., Caselli, M., McGregor, K., & Sabbadini, L. (1992). *Morphological deficits in children with specific language impairment: The status of features in the underlying grammar*. Unpublished manuscript, Department of Linguistics, Purdue University, West Lafayette, IN.

Leonard, L., Bortolini, U., Caselli, M., & Sabbadini, L. (1992). *The use of articles by Italian-speaking children with specific language impairment*. Unpublished manuscript, Department of Linguistics, Purdue University, West Lafayette, IN.

Leonard, L., & Brown, B. (1984). The nature and boundaries of phonological categories: A case study of an unusual phonologic pattern in a language-impaired child. *Journal of Speech and Hearing Disorders, 49*, 419–428.

Leonard, L., Sabbadini, L., Volterra, V., & Leonard, J. (1988). Some influences on the grammar of English- and Italian-speaking children with specific language impairment. *Applied Psycholinguistics, 9*, 39–57.

Leonard, L., Schwartz, R., Swanson, L., & Frome Loeb, D. (1987). Some conditions that promote unusual phonological behaviour in children. *Clinical Linguistics and Phonetics, 1*, 23–34.

Levelt, W. (1989). *Speaking: From intention to articulation*. Cambridge, MA: MIT Press.

Levelt, W. (1992). Accessing words in speech production: Stages, processes and representations. *Cognition, 42*, 1–22.

Levinson, S. (1983). *Pragmatics*. Cambridge University Press.

Levy, Y., Amir, N., & Shalev, R. (1992). Linguistic development of a child with a congenital localised L.H. lesion. *Cognitive Neuropsychology, 9*, 1–32.

Liberman, A., & Mattingly, I. (1985). The motor theory of speech perception revised. *Cognition, 21*, 1–36.

Liberman, A., & Mattingly, I. (1989). A specialization for speech perception. *Science, 243*, 489–494.

Liberman, I., Shankweiler, D., Liberman, A., Fowler, C., & Fisher, W. (1977). Phonetic segmentation and recoding in the beginning reader. In A. Reber & D. Scarborough (Eds.), *Toward a psychology of reading* (pp. 48–63). Hillsdale, NJ: Erlbaum.

Lieberman, P. (1984). *The biology and evolution of language*. Cambridge, MA: Harvard University Press.

Lieury, A., Iff, M., & Duris, P. (1976). *Normes d'associations verbales*. Unpublished manuscript. Laboratoire de Psychologie Expérimentale, Université de Paris V, Paris.

Lightfoot, D. (1989). The child's trigger experience: Degree-0 learnability. *Behavioral and Brain Sciences, 12*, 321–375.

Linebarger, M., Schwartz, M., & Saffran, E. (1983a). Syntactic processing in agrammatism: A reply to Zurif and Grodzinsky. *Cognition, 15*, 215–225.

Linebarger, M., Schwartz, M., & Saffran, E. (1983b). Sensitivity to grammatical structure in so-called agrammatic aphasia. *Cognition, 13*, 361–392.

Locke, J. (1983). *Phonological acquisition and change.* New York: Academic.

Locke, J., & Pearson, D. (1990). Linguistic significance of babbling: Evidence from a tracheostomized infant. *Journal of Child Language, 17*, 1–16.

Lombardi, L., & Potter, M. (1992). The regeneration of syntax in short-term memory. *Journal of Memory and Language, 31,* 713–733.

Lord, C. (1985). Language comprehension and cognitive disorder in autism. In L. Siegel & F. Morrison (Eds.), *Cognitive development in atypical children* (pp. 67–82). New York: Springer-Verlag.

Lot, I. (1986). The neurology of Down syndrome. In C. Epstein (Ed.), *The neurobiology of Down syndrome* (pp. 17–27). New York: Raven.

Lozar, B., Wepman, J., & Hass, W. (1972). Lexical use of mentally retarded and non-retarded children. *American Journal of Mental Deficiency, 76*, 534–539.

Luria, A. R. (1958). Le rôle du langage dans la formation des processus psychiques. *La Raison, 22*, 3–26.

Luria, A. R. (1961). *The role of speech in the regulation of normal and abnormal behaviour.* London: Pergamon.

Luria, A. R. (1978). *Les fonctions corticales supérieures de l'homme.* Paris: Presses Universitaires de France.

Lust, B. (Ed.). (1986). *Studies in the acquisition of anaphora* (Vols. 1–2). Boston: Reidel.

Lyle, J. (1960). The effect of an institution environment upon the verbal development of imbecile children: II, Speech and language. *Journal of Mental Deficiency Research, 4,* 1–13.

Lyle, J. (1961). Comparison of the language of normal and imbecile children. *Journal of Mental Deficiency Research, 5*, 40–50.

Lyons, J. (1977). *Semantics* (Vols. 1–2). Cambridge University Press.

MacGillivray, R. (1968). Congenital cataract and mongolism. *American Journal of Mental Deficiency, 72*, 631–633.

Macken, M., & Ferguson, C. (1983). Cognitive aspects of phonological development: Model, evidence, and issues. In K. Nelson (Ed.), *Children's language* (Vol. 4, pp. 255–282). Hillsdale, NJ: Erlbaum.

Mackenzie, S., & Hulme, C. (1987). Memory span development in Down's syndrome, severely subnormal and normal subjects. *Cognitive Neuropsychology, 4*, 303–319.

Maclay, H., & Osgood, C. (1959). Hesitation phenomena in spontaneous English speech. *Word, 15*, 19–44.

MacNeilage, P., Rootes, T., & Chase, R. (1967). Speech production and perception in a patient with severe impairment of somesthetic perception and motor control. *Journal of Speech and Hearing Research, 10*, 449–468.

MacWhinney, B. (1987). The competition model. In B. MacWhinney (Ed.), *Mechanisms of language acquisition* (pp. 249–308). Hillsdale, NJ: Erlbaum.

Mahoney, G., Glover, A., & Finger, I. (1981). Relationship between language and sensorimotor development of Down syndrome and nonretarded children. *American Journal of Mental Deficiency, 86,* 21–27.

Mandler, J. (1978). A code in the node: The use of the story schema in retrieval discourse processes. *Discourse Processes, 1*, 14–35.

Manzini, M. (1983). On control and control theory. *Linguistic Inquiry, 14,* 421–446.

Maranto, C., Decuir, A., & Humphrey, T. (1984). A comparison of digit span scores, rhythm span scores, and diagnostic factors of mentally retarded persons. *Music Therapy, 4,* 84–90.

Maratsos, M. (1976). *The use of definite and indefinite reference in young children: An experimental study in semantic acquisition.* Cambridge University Press.

Maratsos, M. (1982). The child's construction of grammatical categories. In E. Wanner & L. Gleitman (Eds.), *Language acquisition: The state of the art* (pp. 240–266). Cambridge University Press.

Maratsos, M., & Chalkley, M. (1981). The internal language of children's syntax: The ontogenesis and representation of syntactic categories. In K. Nelson (Ed.), *Children's language* (Vol. 2, pp. 127–214). New York: Gardner.

Maratsos, M., Fox, D., Becker, J., & Chalkley, M. (1985). Semantic restrictions on children's passives. *Cognition, 19*, 167–191.

Marcell, M., & Armstrong, V. (1982). Auditory and visual sequential memory of Down syndrome and nonretarded children. *American Journal of Mental Deficiency, 87*, 86–95.

Marcell, M., & Weeks, S. (1988). Short-term memory difficulties and Down's syndrome. *Journal of Mental Deficiency Research, 32*, 153–162.

Marcus, G. (1993). Negative evidence in language acquisition. *Cognition, 46*, 53–85.

Marcus, G., Pinker, S., Ullman, M., Hollander, M., Rosen, T., & Xu, F. (1992). Overregularization in language acquisition. *Monographs of the Society for Research in Child Development, 57*(4, Serial No. 228).

Marinosson, G. (1974). Performance profiles of matched normal, educationally subnormal and severely subnormal children on the revised ITPA. *Journal of Child Psychology and Psychiatry, 15*, 139–148.

Marsh, G., Friedman, M., Welch, V., & Desberg, P. (1980). A cognitive-developmental approach to reading acquisition. In G. Mackinnon & J. Waller (Eds.), *Reading research: Advances in theory and practice* (Vol. 3, pp. 221–254). New York: Academic.

Marshall, J. (1984). Multiple perspectives on modularity. *Cognition, 17*, 209–242.

Marshall, J. (1987). Language learning, language acquisition, or language growth? In S. Modgil & C. Modgil (Eds.), *Noam Chomsky, consensus and controversy* (pp. 41–49). New York: Falmer.

Marshall, J. (1990). Foreword to J. Yamada, *Laura: A case for the modularity of language* (pp. vii–xi). Cambridge, MA: MIT Press.

Marslen-Wilson, W. (1989). Access and integration: Projecting sound onto meaning. In W. Marslen-Wilson (Ed.), *Lexical representation and process* (pp. 3–24). Cambridge, MA: MIT Press.

Marslen-Wilson, W. (1990). Activation, competition, and frequency in lexical access. In G. Altmann (Ed.), *Cognitive models of speech processing* (pp. 148–172). Cambridge, MA: MIT Press.

Marslen-Wilson, W., Brown, C., & Komisarjersky Tyler, L. (1988). Lexical representations in spoken language comprehension. *Language and Cognitive Processes, 3*, 1–16.

Marslen-Wilson, W., & Komisarjersky Tyler, L. (1987). Against modularity. In J. Garfield (Ed.), *Modularity in knowledge representation and natural-language understanding* (pp. 37–62). Cambridge, MA: MIT Press.

Marslen-Wilson, W., & Tyler, L. (1980). The temporal structure of spoken language understanding. *Cognition, 8*, 1–71.

Martin, R., & Feher, E. (1990). The consequences of reduced memory span for the comprehension of syntactic versus semantic information. *Brain and Language, 38*, 1–20.

Martin, R., Wetzel, W., Blossom-Stack, C., & Feher, E. (1989). Syntactic loss versus processing deficit: An assessment of two theories of agrammatism and syntactic comprehension deficits. *Cognition, 32*, 157–191.

Martin, R., Yaffee, L., & Shelton, J. (1992). *Phonological and semantic codes in short-term memory and sentence processing*. Unpublished manuscript. Department of Psychology, Rice University, Houston, TX.

Masur, E. (1989). Individual and dyadic patterns of imitation: Cognitive and social aspects. In G. Speidel & K. Nelson (Eds.), *The many faces of imitation in language learning* (pp. 53–71). New York: Springer.

Mattingly, I., & Studdert-Kennedy, M. (Eds.). (1991). *Modularity and the motor theory of speech perception*. Hillsdale, NJ: Erlbaum.

Mauner, G., Fromkin, V., & Cornell, T. (1993). *Comprehension and acceptability judgments in agrammatism: Disruptions in the syntax of referential dependency*. Unpublished manuscript, Department of Linguistics, UCLA, Los Angeles.

McCarthy, J. M. (1965). *Patterns of psycholinguistic development of mongoloid and non-mongoloid severely retarded children*. Unpublished doctoral dissertation, University of Illinois, Chicago.

McCawley, J. (1968). The role of semantics in grammar. In E. Bach & R. Harms (Eds.), *Universals in linguistics theory* (pp. 125–169). New York: Holt, Rinehart, & Winston.

McCoy, E., & Enns, L. (1986). Current status of neurotransmitter abnormalities in Down syndrome. In C. Epstein (Ed.), *The neurobiology of Down syndrome* (pp. 73–87). New York: Raven.

McGuigan, F. (1966). *Thinking: Studies of covert language processes*. New York: Appelton-Century-Crofts.

McIntire, M., & Dutch, J. (1964). Mongolism and generalized hypotonia. *American Journal of Mental Deficiency, 68*, 669–670.

McNeil, D. (1966). A study of word association. *Journal of Verbal Learning and Verbal Behavior, 5*, 548–557.

McShane, J. (1990). *Cognitive development*. London: Blackwell.

McTear, M., & Conti-Ramsden, G. (1992). *Pragmatic disability in children*. London: Whurr.

Mehler, J., & Dupoux, E. (1990). *Naître humain*. Paris: Jacob.

Mein, R. (1961). A study of the oral vocabularies of severaly subnormal patients: II, Grammatical analysis of speech samples. *Journal of Mental Deficiency Research, 5*, 52–59.

Mein, R., & O'Connor, N. (1960). A study of the vocabularies of severely subnormal patients. *Journal of Mental Deficiency Research, 4*, 130–143.

Meline, T. (1986). Referential communication skills of learning disabled/language impaired children. *Applied Psycholinguistics, 7*, 129–140.

Menn, L. (1983). Development of articulatory, phonetic, and phonological capabilities. In B. Butterworth (Ed.), *Language production* (Vol. 2, pp. 3–50). New York: Academic.

Menyuk, P., & Quill, K. (1985). Semantic problems in autistic children. In E. Schopler & G. Mesibov (Eds.), *Communication problems in autism* (pp. 127–145). New York: Plenum.

Mervis, C. B. (1988). Early lexical development: Theory and application. In L. Nadel (Ed.), *The psychobiology of Down syndrome* (pp. 101–143). Cambridge, MA: MIT Press.

Mervis, C. B. (1990). Early conceptual development of children with Down syndrome. In D. Cicchetti & M. Beeghly (Eds.), *Children with Down syndrome: A developmental perspective* (pp. 252–301). Cambridge University Press.

Mesulam, M. (1982). Slowly progressive aphasia without generalized dementia. *Annals of Neurology, 11*, 592–598.

Mesulam, M. (1987). Primary progressive aphasia: Differentiation from Alzheimer disease. *Annals of Neurology, 22*, 533–534.

Meyerson, M., & Frank, R. (1987). Language, speech and hearing in Williams syndrome: Intervention approaches and research needs. *Developmental Medicine and Child Neurology, 88*, 536–545.

Miceli, G., Mazzucchi, A., Menn, L., & Goodglass, H. (1983). Contrasting cases of Italian agrammatic aphasia without comprehension disorder. *Brain and Language, 2*, 420–433.

Michaelis, C. (1977). *The language of a Down's syndrome child* (Doctoral dissertation, University of Utah 1977). *Dissertation Abstracts International, 37*, 9.

Millberg, W., & Blumstein, S. (1981). Lexical decisions and aphasia: Evidence for semantic processing. *Brain and Language, 14*, 371–385.

Millberg, W., Blumstein, S., & Dworetzky, B. (1987). Processing of lexical ambiguities in aphasia. *Brain and Language, 31*, 138–150.

Miller, G. A. (1956). The magical number seven, plus or minus two: Some limits on our capacity for processing information. *Psychological Review, 63*, 81–97.

Miller, G. A., & Selfridge, J. (1950). Verbal context and the recall of meaningful material. *American Journal of Psychology, 63*, 176–185.

Miller, J. (1981). *Assessing language production in children: Experimental procedures.* Baltimore: University Park Press.

Miller, J. (1987). Language and communication characteristics of children with Down syndrome. In S. Pueschel, C. Tingey, J. Rynders, A. Crocker, & D. Crutcher (Eds.), *New perspectives on Down syndrome* (pp. 233–262). Baltimore: Brookes.

Miller, J. (1988). The developmental asynchrony of language developement in children with Down syndrome. In L. Nadel (Ed.), *The psychobiology of Down syndrome* (pp. 167–198). Cambridge, MA: MIT Press.

Miller, J., & Chapman, R. (1981). The relation between age and mean length of utterances in morphemes. *Journal of Speech and Hearing Research, 24*, 154–161.

Miller, J., Chapman, R., & Mackenzie, H. (1981). Individual differences in the language acquisition of mentally retarded children. *Proceedings of the Second Wisconsin Symposium on Research in Child Language Disorders, 2*, 130–147.

Mills, A. (1993). Visual handicap. In D. Bishop & K. Mogford (Eds.), *Language development in exceptional circumstances* (pp. 150–164). Hove, UK: Erlbaum.

Mittler, P. (1970). The use of morphological rules by four years old children: An item analysis of the Auditory-Vocal Automatic Test of the ITPA. *British Journal of Disorders of Communication, 5*, 99–109.

Mittler, P. (1972). Language development and mental handicaps. In M. Rutter & J. Martin (Eds.), *The child with delayed speech* (pp. 136–146). Philadelphia: Lippincott.

Moerk, E. (1983). *The mother of Eve⁻ as a first language teacher.* Norwood, NJ: Ablex.

Moerk, E. (1989a). The LAD was a lady and the tasks were ill-defined. *Developmental Review, 9*, 21–57.

Moerk, E. (1989b, October). *Personal communication.*

Moerk, E. (1991). Positive evidence for negative evidence. *First Language, 11*, 219–251.

Moerk, E. (1992). *First language taught and learned.* Baltimore: Brookes.

Mogford, K. (1993). Language development in twins. In D. Bishop & K. Mogford (Eds.), *Language development in exceptional circumstances* (pp. 110–131). Hove, UK: Erlbaum.

Monseur, M. (1988). *Approche psycholinguistique de la compréhension et de la coréférence pronominale dans le cas de phrases subordonnées relatives chez des enfants âgés de 5 ans, 7 ans, et 9 ans.* Mémoire de Licence (unpublished). Laboratoire de Psycholinguistique, Université de Liège, Liège.

Montague, J., & Hollien, H. (1973). Perceived voice quality disorders in Down's syndrome children. *Journal of Communication Disorders, 6*, 76–87.

Montague, J., & Hollien, H. (1974). Perceived voice quality disorders in Down's syndrome. *Training School Bulletin, 71*, 80–89.

Moor, L. (1967). Le niveau intellectuel dans la trisomie 21. *Annales Médico-Psychologiques, 2*, 808–809.

Morais, J. (1987a). Phonetic awareness and reading acquisition. *Psychological Research, 49,* 147–152.

Morais, J. (1987b). Segmental analysis of speech and its relation to reading ability. *Annals of Dyslexia, 37,* 126–141.

Morais, J., Alegria, J., & Content, A. (1987). The relationship between segmental analysis and alphabetic literacy: An interactive view. *Cahiers de Psychologie Cognitive, 7,* 415–438.

Morais, J., Cary, L., Alegria, J., & Bertelson, P. (1979). Does awareness of speech as a sequence of phones arise spontaneously? *Cognition, 7,* 323–331.

Morgan, J., & Newport, E. (1981). The role of constituent structure in the induction of an artificial language. *Journal of Verbal Learning and Verbal Behavior, 20,* 67–85.

Morton, J. (1970). A functional model of memory. In D. Norman (Ed.), *Models of human memory* (pp. 203–254). New York: Academic.

Morton, J. (1979). Facilitation in word recognition: Experiments causing change in the logogen model. In P. Kolers, M. Wrolstead, & H. Bouma (Eds.), *Processing of visible language* (Vol. 1, pp. 66–89). New York: Plenum.

Moscovitch, M., & Umilta, C. (1990). Modularity and neuropsychology: Modules and central processes in attention and memory. In M. Schwartz (Ed.), *Modular deficits in Alzheimer-type dementia* (pp. 1–59). Cambridge, MA: MIT Press.

Moss, M., Albert, M., Butters, N., & Payne, M. (1986). Differential patterns of memory loss among patients with Alzheimer's disease, Huntington's disease, and alcoholic Korsakoff's syndrome. *Archives Neurologiques, 43,* 121–157.

Mueller, M., & Weaver, S. (1964). Psycholinguistic abilities of institutionalized and non-institutionalized trainable mental retardates. *American Journal of Mental Deficiency, 68,* 775–783.

Muysken, P. (1988). Are Creoles a special type of language? In F. Newmeyer (Ed.), *Linguistics: The Cambridge survey* (Vol. 2, pp. 285–301). Cambridge University Press.

Nadel, L. (1986). Down syndrome in neurobiological perspective. In C. Epstein (Ed.), *The neurobiology of Down syndrome* (pp. 239–251). New York: Raven.

Nelson, K. (1973). Structure and strategy in learning to talk. *Monographs of the Society for Research in Child Development, 38*(Serial No. 143).

Newport, E. (1990). Maturational constraints on language learning. *Cognitive Science, 14,* 11–28.

Newport, E. (1992). Contrasting conceptions of the critical period for language. In S. Carey & R. Gelman (Eds.), *The epignesis of mind: Essays on biology and cognition* (pp. 111–130). Hillsdale, NJ: Erlbaum.

Newport, E., Gleitman, L., & Gleitman, H. (1977). "Mother, I'd rather do it myself": Some effects and noneffects of maternal speech style. In C. Snow & C. Ferguson (Eds.), *Talking to children* (pp. 109–150). Cambridge University Press.

Nicolson, R. (1981). The relationship between memory span and processing speed. In M. Friedman, J. P. Das, & N. O'Connor (Eds.), *Intelligence and learning* (pp. 179–184). New York: Plenum.

Noizet, G., & Pichevin, C. (1966). Organisation paradigmatique et organisation syntagmatique du discours: Une approche comparative. *L'Année Psychologique, 66,* 91–110.

Norman, D. (1970). *Models of human memory.* New York: Academic.

Obler, L., & Fein, D. (Eds.). (1988). *The exceptional brain: Neuropsychology of talent and special abilities.* New York: Guilford.

O'Connell, D., Kowal, S., & Kaltenbacher, E. (1990). Turn-taking: A critical analysis of the research tradition. *Journal of Psycholinguistic Research, 19,* 345–373.

O'Connor, N. (1989). The performance of the "idiot-savant": Implicit and explicit. *British Journal of Disorders of Communication, 24,* 1–10.

O'Connor, N., & Hermelin, B. (1959). Some effects of word learning in imbeciles. *Language and Speech, 2,* 63–71.

O'Connor, N., & Hermelin, B. (1963). *Speech and thought in severe subnormality.* London: Macmillan.

O'Connor, N., & Hermelin, B. (1984). Idiot savant calendrical calculators: Maths or memory? *Psychological Medicine, 14,* 801–806.

O'Connor, N., & Hermelin, B. (1987a). Visual memory and motor programmes: Their use by idiot-savant artists and controls. *British Journal of Psychology, 78,* 307–323.

O'Connor, N., & Hermelin, B. (1987b). Visual and graphic abilities of the idiot-savant artists. *Psychological Medicine, 17,* 79–90.

O'Connor, N., & Hermelin, B. (1988). Low intelligence and special abilities. *Journal of Child Psychology and Psychiatry, 29,* 391–396.

O'Connor, N., & Hermelin, B. (1989). The memory structure of autistic idiot-savant mnemonists. *British Journal of Psychology, 80,* 97–111.

O'Connor, N., & Hermelin, B. (1990). The recognition failure and graphic success of idiot-savant artists. *Journal of Child Psychology and Psychiatry, 31,* 203–215.

O'Connor, N., & Hermelin, B. (1991). A specific linguistic ability. *American Journal on Mental Retardation, 95,* 673–680.

Oetting, J., & Rice, M. (1991). Influence of the social context on pragmatic skills of adults with mental retardation. *American Journal of Mental Retardation, 95,* 435–443.

O'Grady, W. (1987). *Principles of grammar and learning.* Chicago: University of Chicago Press.

O'Keefe, J., & Nadel, L. (1978). *The hippocampus as a cognitive map.* Oxford University Press.

Oldfield, R. (1971). The assessment and analysis of handedness: The Edinburgh Inventory. *Neuropsychologia, 9,* 97–113.

Oliver, C., & Holland, A. (1986). Down's syndrome and Alzheimer's disease: A review. *Psychological Medicine, 16,* 307–322.

Olson, D., & Bialystok, E. (1983). *Spatial cognition: The structure and development of mental representations of spatial relations.* Hillsdale, NJ: Erlbaum.

Oster, J. (1953). *Mongolism.* Copenhagen: Danish Science Press.

Owens, R. (1989). Cognition and language in the mentally retarded population. In M. Beveridge, G. Conti-Ramsden, & I. Leudar (Eds.), *Language and communication in mentally handicapped people* (pp. 112–142). London: Chapman & Hall.

Owings, N., & McManus, M. (1980). An analysis of communication functions in the speech of a deinstitutionalized adult mentally retarded client. *Mental Retardation, 309,* 314.

Paivio, A. (1986). *Mental representations: A dual-coding approach.* New York: Oxford University Press.

Paivio, A. (1971). *Imagery and verbal process.* New York: Holt, Rinehart, & Winston.

Papania, N. (1954). A qualitative analysis of the vocabulary responses of institutionalized mentally retarded children. *Journal of Clinical Psychology, 10,* 361–365.

Paraskevopoulos, J., & Kirk, S. (1969). *The development and psychometric characteristics of the Revised Test of Psycholinguistic Abilities.* Urbana: University of Illinois Press.

Patterson, D. (1987). The causes of Down syndrome. *Scientific American, 257,* 42–48.

Payne, J. (1968). *S. L. Rubinstein and the philosophical foundation of Soviet psychology.* New York: Humanities Press.

Penner, S. (1987). Parental responses to grammatical and ungrammatical child utterances. *Child Development, 58,* 376–384.

Penney, C. (1975). Modality effects in short-term verbal memory. *Psychological Bulletin, 82,* 68–84.

Perron-Borelli, M., & Misés, R. (1974). *Epreuves différentielles d'efficience intellectuelle.* Issy-les-Moulineaux: Editions Scientifiques et Psychologiques.

Peters, A. (1983). *The units of language acquisition.* Cambridge University Press.

Peterson, L., & Peterson, M. (1959). Short-term retention of individual verbal items. *Journal of Experimental Psychology, 58,* 193–198.

Petitto, A. (1987). On the autonomy of language and gesture: Evidence from the acquisition of personal pronouns in American sign language. *Cognition, 27,* 1–50.

Petitto, A. (1992). Modularity and constraints in early lexical acquisition: Evidence from children's early language and gesture. In M. Gunnar & M. Maratsos (Eds.), *Modularity and constraints in language and cognition* (pp. 25–58). Hillsdale, NJ: Erlbaum.

Piaget, J. (1923). *Le langage et la pensée chez l'enfant.* Neuchâtel: Delachaux & Niestlé.

Piaget, J. (1925). De quelques formes primitives de causalité chez l'enfant. *L'Année Psychologique, 26,* 31–71.

Piaget, J. (1928). *Le jugement et le raisonnement chez l'enfant.* Neuchâtel: Delachaux & Niestlé.

Piaget, J. (1930). *The child's conception of physical causality.* London: Kegan Paul.

Piaget, J. (1936). *La naissance de l'intelligence chez l'enfant.* Neuchâtel: Delachaux & Niestlé.

Piaget, J. (1937). *La construction du réel chez l'enfant.* Neuchâtel: Delachaux & Niestlé.

Piaget, J. (1945). *La formation du symbole chez l'enfant.* Neuchâtel: Delachaux & Niestlé.

Piaget, J. (1946). *Le développement de la notion du temps chez l'enfant.* Paris: Presses Universitaires de France.

Piaget, J. (1955). The development of time concepts in the child. In P. Hoch & J. Zubin (Eds.), *Psychopathology of childhood* (pp. 34–44). New York: Grune & Stratton.

Piaget, J. (1963). Le langage et les opérations intellectuelles. In *Problèmes de psycholinguistique* (Proceedings of the Symposium of the Association de Psychologie Scientifique de Langue Française, Neuchâtel, 1962; pp. 51–61). Paris: Presses Universitaires de France.

Piaget, J. (1968). *Le structuralisme.* Paris: Presses Universitaires de France.

Piaget, J. (1970). Piaget's theory. In P. Mussen (Ed.), *Manual of child psychology* (Vol. 2, pp. 703–792). New York: Wiley.

Piaget, J. (1976). Piaget's theory. In B. Inhelder & H. Chipman (Eds.), *Piaget and his school: A reader in developmental psychology* (pp. 11–23). New York: Springer-Verlag.

Piaget, J. (1979a). Schèmes d'action et apprentissage du langage. In M. Piattelli-Palmarini (Ed.), *Théorie du langage. Théories de l'apprentissage. Le débat entre Jean Piaget et Noam Chomsky* (pp. 247–251). Paris: Seuil.

Piaget, J. (1979b). La psychogenèse des connaissances et sa signification épistémologique. In M. Piattelli-Palmarini (Ed.), *Théorie du langage. Théories de l'apprentissage. Le débat entre Jean Piaget et Noam Chomsky* (pp. 53–64). Paris: Seuil.

Piaget, J., & Inhelder, B. (1969). *The psychology of the child.* London: Routledge & Kegan Paul.

Piattelli-Palmarini, M. (Ed.). (1979). *Théories du langage. Théories de l'apprentissage. Le débat entre Jean Piaget et Noam Chomsky.* Paris: Seuil.

Piattelli-Palmarini, M. (Ed.). (1980). *Language and learning: The debate between Jean Piaget and Noam Chomsky.* Cambridge, MA: Harvard University Press.

Piattelli-Palmarini, M. (1989). Evolution, selection, and cognition. From "learning" to parameter setting in biology and the study of language. *Cognition, 31,* 1–44.

Pichevin, L., & Noizet, G. (1968). Etude génétique de la structure linguistique de l'association verbale. *L'Année Psychologique, 68,* 391–408.

Pinker, S. (1984). *Language learnability and language development.* Cambridge, MA: Harvard University Press.

Pinker, S. (1985). Language learnability and children's language: A multi-faceted approach. In K. Nelson (Ed.), *Children's language* (Vol. 5, pp. 399–442.). Hillsdale, NJ: Erlbaum.

Pinker, S. (1987). The bootstrapping problem in language acquisition. In B. MacWhinney (Ed.), *Mechanisms of language acquisition* (pp. 399–441). Hillsdale, NJ: Erlbaum.

Pinker, S. (1989a). *Learnability and cognition: The acquisition of argument structure.* Cambridge, MA: MIT Press.

Pinker, S. (1989b). Markedness and language development. In R. Matthews & W. Demopoulos (Eds.), *Learnability and linguistic theory* (pp. 107–127). Boston: Kluwer.

Pinker, S. (1991). Rules of language. *Science, 253,* 530–535.

Pinker, S. (1993). Interview with J. A. Rondal. *International Journal of Psychology, 28,* 459–480.

Pinker, S., & Bloom, P. (1990). Natural language and natural selection. *Behavioral and Brain Sciences, 13,* 707–727.

Pinker, S., Lebeaux, D., & Frost, L. (1987). Productivity and constraints in the acquisition of the passive. *Cognition, 26,* 195–267.

Pinker, S., & Prince, A. (1988). On language and connectionism: Analysis of a parallel distributed processing model of language acquisition. *Cognition, 28,* 73–193.

Pinker, S., & Prince, A. (1991). Regular and irregular morphology and the psychological status of rules of grammar. In L. Sutton, C. Johnson, & R. Shields (Eds.), *Proceedings of the 17th Annual Meeting of the Berkeley Linguistics Society* (February 15–18, 1991; pp. 230–251).

Piolat, A. (1983). Localisation syntaxique des pauses et planification du discours. *L'Année Psychologique, 83,* 377–394.

Pipe, M. E. (1983). Dichotic-listening performance following auditory discrimination training in Down's syndrome and developmentally retarded children. *Cortex, 19,* 481–491.

Plomin, R., & Thompson, L. (1993). Genetics and high cognitive ability. In R. Bock & K. Ackrill (Eds.), *The origins and development of high ability* (pp. 67–79). New York: Wiley.

Poizner, H., Klima, E., & Bellugi, U. (1987). *What the hands reveal about the brain.* Cambridge, MA: MIT Press.

Poppelreuter, S. (1985). *Test des Figures Enchevêtrées.* Brussels: Editest.

Prasada, S., & Pinker, S. (1993). Generalisation of regular and irregular morphological patterns. *Language and Cognitive Processes, 8,* 1–56.

Preus, A. (1972). Stuttering in Down's syndrome. *Scandinavian Journal of Educational Research, 16,* 89–100.

Price, P. (1989). Language intervention and mother-child interaction. In M. Beveridge, G. Conti-Ramsden, & I. Leudar (Eds.), *Language and communication in mentally handicapped people* (pp. 185–217). London: Chapman & Hall.

Pueschel, S. (1988). Visual and auditory processing in children with Down syndrome. In L. Nadel (Ed.), *The psychobiology of Down syndrome* (pp. 199–216). Cambridge, MA: MIT Press.

Putnam, H. (1984). Models and modules. *Cognition, 17,* 253–264.

Quinlan, P. (1991). *Connectionism and psychology.* New York: Harvester Wheatsheaf.

Ramer, A. (1976). The function of imitation in child language. *Journal of Speech and Hearing Research, 19,* 700–717.

Raven, J. (1981). *Progressive Matrices* (Adaptation française de A. Schutzenberger & D. Mavre). Issy-les-Moulineaux: Editions Scientifiques & Psychologiques.

Reinhart, C. (1976). *The cerebral lateralization of speech process in Down's syndrome and normal individuals.* Unpublished master's thesis, University of Saskatchewan, Saskatoon.

Rempel, E. (1974, May). *Psycholinguistic abilities of Down's syndrome children.* Communication presented at the 98th Annual Meeting of the American Association on Mental Deficiency, Toronto.

Reuchlin, M., & Bacher, F. (1989). *Les différences individuelles dans le développement cognitif de l'enfant.* Paris: Presses Universitaires de France.

Rey, A. (1964). *L'examen clinique en psychologie.* Paris: Presses Universitaires de France.

Rey, A. (1966). *Connaissance de l'individu par les tests.* Brussels: Dessart.

Rey, A. (1967). *Les troubles de la mémoire et leur examen psychométrique.* Brussels: Dessart.

Richards, B. (1969). Mosaic mongolism. *Journal of Mental Deficiency Research, 13,* 66–83.

Rigrodsky, S., Prunty, F., & Glovsky, G. (1961). A study of the incidence, types and associated etiologies of hearing loss in an institutionalized mentally retarded population. *Training School Bulletin, 58,* 30–44.

Rizzi, L. (1985). Two notes on the linguistic interpretation of Broca's aphasia. In M. Kean (Ed.), *Agrammatism* (pp. 153–164). Orlando, FL: Academic.

Roeper, T. (1987a). The acquisition of implicit arguments and the distinction between theory, processes, and mechanism. In B. MacWhinney (Ed.), *Mechanisms of language acquisition* (pp. 309–343). Hillsdale, NJ: Erlbaum.

Roeper, T. (1987b). The modularity of meaning in language acquisition. In S. Modgil & C. Modgil (Eds.), *Noam Chomsky, consensus and controversy* (pp. 157–172). New York: Falmer.

Roeper, T., & Williams, E. (Eds.). (1987). *Parameter setting.* Boston: Reidel.

Rondal, J. A. (1975a). Développement du langage et retard mental: Une revue critique de la littérature en langue anglaise. *L'Année Psychologique, 75,* 513–547.

Rondal, J. A. (1975b). Aspects du développement cognitif envisagés selon les écoles genevoise et moscovite: Aperçu, réflexions critiques et implications générales pour une axiologie de la première éducation. *Scientia Paedagogica Experimentalis, 12,* 216–230.

Rondal, J. A. (1976). Investigation of the regulatory power of the impulsive and the meaningful aspects of speech. *Genetic Psychology Monographs, 94,* 3–33.

Rondal, J. A. (1977a). Développement du langage et retard mental: Une revue des études ayant utilisé l'Illinois Test of Psycholinguistic Abilities. *Psychologica Belgica, 17,* 24–34.

Rondal, J. A. (1977b). *L'emploi de l'adjectif possessif et de l'article devant le nom des parties du corps dans l'expression de la possession intrinsèque en français: Etude synchronique et diachronique, et référence comparative à d'autres langues.* Unpublished manuscript. Laboratoire de Psychologie Expérimentale, Université de Liège, Liège.

Rondal, J. A. (1977c). L'emploi de l'adjectif possessif et de l'article devant le nom des parties du corps dans l'expression de la possession intrinsèque en Français: Une étude génétique. *Psychologica Belgica, 17,* 165–181.

Rondal, J. A. (1978a). Developmental sentence scoring procedure and the delay-difference question in language development of Down's syndrome children. *Mental Retardation, 16,* 169–171.

Rondal, J. A. (1978b). Maternal speech to normal and Down's syndrome children matched for mean length of utterance. In E. Meyers (Ed.), *Quality of life in severely and profoundly mentally retarded people: Research foundations for improvement* (pp. 193–265). Washington, DC: American Association on Mental Deficiency, Monograph Series No. 3.

Rondal, J. A. (1978c). Patterns of correlations for various language measures in mother-child interactions for normal and Down's syndrome children. *Language and Speech, 21,* 242–252.

Rondal, J. A. (1979a). *Votre enfant apprend à parler.* Brussels: Mardaga.

Rondal, J. A. (1979b). "Maman est au courant": Une étude des connaissances maternelles quant aux aspects formels du langage du jeune enfant. *Enfance, 2,* 95–105.

Rondal, J. A. (1980a). Verbal imitation by Down syndrome and nonretarded children. *American Journal of Mental Deficiency, 85*, 318–321.

Rondal, J. A. (1980b). Une note sur la théorie cognitive-motivationnelle d'Edward Zigler en matière de retard mental culturel-familial. *Psychologica Belgica, 20*, 61–82.

Rondal, J. A. (1980c). Fathers' and mothers' speech in early language development. *Journal of Child Language, 7*, 353–369.

Rondal, J. A. (1983). Quel rôle peut jouer l'imitation verbale dans l'acquisition du langage par l'enfant? *Rééducation Orthophonique, 21*, 393–407.

Rondal, J. A. (1984). Linguistic development in mental retardation. In J. Dobbing, A. D. B. Clarke, J. Corbett, J. Hog, & R. Robinson (Eds.), *Scientific studies in mental retardation* (pp. 323–345). London: Royal Society of Medicine and Macmillan.

Rondal, J. A. (1985a). *Langage et communication chez les handicapés mentaux.* Brussels: Mardaga.

Rondal, J. A. (1985b). *Adult-child interaction and the process of language acquisition.* New York: Praeger.

Rondal, J. A. (1986). Développement linguistique. In J. A. Rondal & M. Hurtig (Eds.), *Manuel de psychologie de l'enfant* (Vol. 2, pp. 455–491). Brussels: Mardaga.

Rondal, J. A. (1987). Language development and mental retardation. In W. Yule & M. Rutter (Eds.), *Language development and disorders* (pp. 248–261). Oxford: Blackwell.

Rondal, J. A. (1988a). Down's syndrome. In D. Bishop & K. Mogford (Eds.), *Language development in exceptional circumstances* (pp. 165–176) London: Churchill Livingstone; rpt., Hove, Sussex: Erlbaum, 1993.

Rondal, J. A. (1988b). Language development in Down's syndrome: A life-span perspective. *International Journal of Behavioural Development, 11*, 21–36.

Rondal, J. A. (1988c). Indications positives et négatives dans l'acquisition des aspects grammaticaux de la langue maternelle. *European Bulletin of Cognitive Psychology, 8*, 383–398.

Rondal, J. A. (1993a). Exceptional language development in mental retardation: Theoretical implications. In M. Leahy & J. Kallen (Eds.), *Interdisciplinary perspectives in speech and language pathology.* Selected papers from the 1992 Trinity College Anniversary Conference (pp. 43–53). Dublin: School of Clinical Speech and Language Studies, Trinity College.

Rondal, J. A. (1993b). Exceptional cases of language development in mental retardation: The relative autonomy of language as a cognitive system. In H. Tager-Flusberg (Ed.), *Constraints on language acquisition: Studies of atypical children* (pp. 155–174). Hillsdale, NJ: Erlbaum.

Rondal, J. A. (in press). Especificidad sistemica del lenguaje en el sindrome de Down. In J. Perera (Ed.), *Especifidad del sindrome de Down* (pp. 70–102). Madrid: Salvat.

Rondal, J. A., Bachelet, J. F., & Perée, F. (1986). Analyse du langage et des interactions verbales adulte-enfant. *Bulletin d'Audiophonologie, 5–6*, 507–535.

Rondal, J. A., & Brédart, S. (1985). Langage oral: Aspects développementaux. In J. A. Rondal & X. Seron (Eds.), *Troubles du langage: Diagnostic et rééducation* (pp. 21–61). Brussels: Mardaga.

Rondal, J. A., & Cession, A. (1990). Input evidence regarding the semantic bootstrapping hypothesis. *Journal of Child Language, 17*, 711–717.

Rondal, J. A., Cession, A., & Vincent, E. (1988). *Compréhension des phrases déclaratives selon la voix et l'actionalité du verbe chez un groupe d'adultes trisomique 21.* Unpublished manuscript. Laboratoire de Psycholinguistique, University of Liège, Liège.

Rondal, J. A., & Defays, D. (1978). Reliability of mean length of utterance as a function of sample size in early language development. *Journal of Genetic Psychology, 133*, 305–306.

Rondal, J. A., Ghiotto, M., Brédart, S., & Bachelet, J. F. (1987). Age-relation, reliability, and grammatical validity of measures of utterance-length. *Journal of Child Language, 14,* 433–446.

Rondal, J. A., Ghiotto, M., Brédart, S., & Bachelet, J. F. (1988). Mean length of utterance of children with Down syndrome. *American Journal on Mental Retardation, 93,* 64–66.

Rondal, J. A., Henrot, F., & Charlier, M. (1986). *Le langage des signes.* Brussels: Mardaga.

Rondal, J. A., & Lambert, J. L. (1983). The speech of mentally retarded adults in a dyadic communication situation: Some formal and informative aspects. *Psychologica Belgica, 23,* 49–56.

Rondal, J. A., Lambert, J. L., & Chipman, H. (1981). *Psycholinguistique et handicap mental.* Brussels: Mardaga.

Rondal, J. A., Lambert, J. L., & Sohier, C. (1980a). Analyses des troubles articulatoires chez les enfants arriérés mentaux mongoliens et non-mongoliens. *Bulletin d'Audiophonologie, 10,* 13–20.

Rondal, J. A., Lambert, J. L., & Sohier, C. (1980b). L'imitation verbale et non verbale chez l'enfant retardé mental mongolien et non mongolien. *Enfance, 3,* 107–122.

Rondal, J. A., Lambert, J. L., & Sohier, C. (1981). Elicited verbal and non-verbal imitation in Down's syndrome and other mentally retarded children: A replication and an extension of Berry. *Language and Speech, 24,* 245–254.

Rondal, J. A., Leyen, N., Brédart, S., & Perée, F. (1984). Coréférence et stratégies des fonctions parallèles dans le cas des pronoms anaphoriques ambigus. *Cahiers de Psychologie Cognitive, 4,* 151–170.

Rondal, J. A., & Seron, X. (Eds.). (1989). *Troubles du langage. Diagnostic et rééducation.* Brussels: Mardaga.

Rondal, J. A., & Thibaut, J. P. (1990). *Decision time in adult sentence interpretation: Transitivity effects.* Unpublished manuscript. Laboratoire de Psycholinguistique, University of Liège, Liège.

Rondal, J. A., & Thibaut, J. P. (1992). Facteurs de transitivité sémantique dans la compréhension des énoncés déclaratifs chez l'enfant. *Glossa, 29,* 26–34.

Rondal, J. A., Thibaut, J. P., & Cession, A. (1990). Transitivity effects on children's sentence comprehension. *European Bulletin of Cognitive Psychology, 10,* 385–400.

Rosch, E. (1975). Cognitive representation of semantic categories. *Journal of Experimental Psychology: General, 104,* 192–233.

Rosch, E. (1978). Principles of categorization. In E. Rosch & B. Lloyd (Eds.), *Cognition and categorization* (pp. 27–48). Hillsdale, NJ: Erlbaum.

Rosch, E., & Mervis, C. B. (1975). Family resemblance studies in the internal structure of categories. *Cognitive Psychology, 7,* 573–605.

Rosch, E., Simpson, C., & Miller, R. (1976). Structural bases of typicality effects. *Journal of Experimental Psychology: Human Perception and Performance, 2,* 491–502.

Rosenbaum, B., & Sonne, H. (1986). *The language of psychosis.* New York: New York University Press.

Rosenberg, S. (1982). The language of the mentally retarded: Development, processes, intervention. In S. Rosenberg (Ed.), *Handbook of applied psycholinguistics: Major thrusts of research and theory* (pp. 329–393). Hillsdale, NJ: Erlbaum.

Rosenberg, S., & Abbeduto, L. (1986). *Indicators of linguistic competence in the peer group conversational behavior of mildly retarded adults.* Unpublished manuscript, University of Illinois, Chicago.

Rosin, M., Swift, E., & Bless, D. (1987, May). *Communication profiles of people with Down syndrome.* Communication presented at the annual convention of the American Speech and Hearing Association (ASHA), New Orleans.

Rosin, M., Swift, E., Bless, D., & Vetter, D. (1988). Communication profiles of adolescents with Down syndrome. *Journal of Childhood Communication Disorders, 12,* 49–64.

Rosner, J., & Simon, D. (1971). The auditory analysis test: An initial report. *Journal of Learning Disabilities, 4,* 384–392.

Ross, M., Galaburda, A., & Kemper, T. (1984). Down's Syndrome: Is there a decreased population of neurons? *Neurology, 34,* 909–916.

Ross, T. (1961). The mental growth of mongoloid defectives. *American Journal of Mental Deficiency, 66,* 736–738.

Rouveret, A. (1987). *Noam Chomsky, La nouvelle syntaxe. Présentation et commentaire.* Paris: Seuil.

Rumelhart, D., & McClelland, J. (1986). On learning the past tenses of English verbs. In D. Rumelhart & J. McClelland (Eds.), *Parallel distributed processing: Explorations in the microstructure of cognition* (Vol. 1, pp. 216–271). Cambridge, MA: MIT Press.

Rumelhart, D., & McClelland, J. (1987). Learning of the past tenses of English verbs: Implicit rules or parallel distributed processing. In B. MacWhinney (Ed.), *Mechanisms of language acquisition* (pp. 195–248). Hillsdale, NJ: Erlbaum,

Russel, J. (1987). Three kinds of question about modularity. In S. Modgil & C. Modgil (Eds.), *Noam Chomsky, consensus and controversy* (pp. 223–232). New York: Falmer.

Ryan, J. (1975). Mental subnormality and language development. In E. Lenneberg (Ed.), *Foundations of language development: A multidisciplinary approach* (Vol. 2, pp. 269–277). New York: Wiley.

Ryan, J. (1977). The silence of stupidity. In J. Morton & J. Marshall (Eds.), *Psycholinguistics: Developmental and pathological* (pp. 101–124). Ithaca, NY: Cornell University Press.

Ryan, E., & Ledger, G. (1979). Grammaticality judgments, sentence repetitions, and sentence corrections of children learning to read. *International Journal of Psycholinguistics, 6,* 23–40.

Sachs, J. (1967). Recognition memory for syntactic and semantic aspects of connected discourse. *Perception and Psychophysics, 2,* 437–442.

Sack, H., Schegloff, E., & Jefferson, G. (1974). A simplest systematics for the organization of turn-taking in conversation. *Language, 50,* 696–735.

Saffran, E. (1982). Neuropsychological approaches to the study of language. *British Journal of Psychology, 73,* 317–337.

Saffran, E., & Marin, O. (1975). Immediate memory for word lists and sentences in a patient with deficient auditory-verbal short-term memory. *Brain and Language, 2,* 420–433.

Saffran, E., & Martin, N. (1990). Neuropsychological evidence for involvement in short-term memory. In G. Vallar & T. Shallice (Eds.), *Neuropsychological impairments of short-term memory* (pp. 101–124). Cambridge University Press.

Salkie, R. (1987). Core grammar and periphery. In S. Modgil & C. Modgil (Eds.), *Noam Chomsky, consensus and controversy* (pp. 109–117). New York: Falmer.

Santucci, H., & Galifret-Granjon, N. (1960). *Test Bender-Gestalt* (adaptation H.H.R.). Brussels: Editest.

Sapir, E. (1921). *Language.* New York: Harcourt, Brace, & Jovanovich.

Schellenberg, G., Kamino, K., Bryant, E., Moore, D., & Bird, T. (1992). Genetic heterogeneity, Down syndrome, and Alzheimer disease. In L. Nadel & C. Epstein (Eds.), *Progress in biological research: Down syndrome and Alzheimer disease* (Vol. 379, pp. 215–226). New York: Wiley-Liss.

Scherer, N., & Owings, N. (1984). Learning to be contingent: Retarded children's responses to their mothers' requests. *Language and Speech, 27,* 255–267.

Schlanger, B. B., & Gottsleben, R. (1957). Analysis of speech defects among the institutionalized mentally retarded. *Journal of Speech and Hearing Disorders, 22,* 98–103.

Schneider, W., & Pressley, M. (1989). *Memory development between 2 and 20*. New York: Springer-Verlag.

Scholnick, E. (1983). Why are new trends in conceptual representation a challenge to Piaget's theory? In E. Scholnick (Ed.), *New trends in conceptual representation* (pp. 41–70). Hillsdale, NJ: Erlbaum.

Schwartz, M., & Chawluck, J. (1990). Deterioration of language in progressive aphasia: A case study. In M. Schwartz (Ed.), *Modular deficits in Alzheimer-type dementia* (pp. 207–244). Cambridge, MA: MIT Press.

Schwartz, M., Linebarger, M., Saffran, E., & Pate, D. (1987). Syntactic transparency and sentence interpretation in aphasia. *Language and Cognitive Processes, 2*, 85–113.

Schwartz, M., Marin, O., & Saffran, E. (1979). Dissociations of language function in dementia: A case study. *Brain and Language, 7*, 277–306.

Schwartz, M., Saffran, E., & Marin, O. (1980). Fractionating the reading process in dementia: Evidence for word-specific print-to-sound associations. In M. Coltheart, K. Patterson, & J. Marshall (Eds.), *Deep dyslexia* (pp. 259–270). London: Routledge & Kegan Paul.

Schwartz, M., & Schwartz, B. (1984). In defence of organology. *Cognitive Neuropsychology, 1*, 25–42.

Seagoe, M. (1965). Verbal development in a mongoloid. *Exceptional Children, 6*, 229–275.

Searle, J. (1979). *Expression and meaning: Studies in the theory of speech acts*. Cambridge University Press.

Seitz, S., Goulding, P., & Conrad, R. (1969). The effect of maturation on word associations of the mentally retarded. *Multivariate Behavioral Research, 4*, 79–88.

Seitz, S., & Stewart, C. (1975). Imitations and expansions: Some developmental aspects of mother-child communications. *Developmental Psychology, 11*, 763–768.

Semmel, M., Barritt, L., Bennett, S., & Perfetti, C. (1968). A grammatical analysis of word associations of educable mentally retarded and normal children. *American Journal of Mental Deficiency, 72*, 567–576.

Semmel, M., & Dolley, D. (1970). Comprehension and imitation of sentences by Down's syndrome children as a function of transformational complexity. *American Journal of Mental Deficiency, 75*, 739–745.

Sersen, E., Astrup, E., Floistad, I., & Wortis, J. (1970). Motor conditioned reflexes and word association in retarded children. *American Journal of Mental Deficiency, 74*, 495–501.

Seyfort, B., & Spreen, O. (1979). Two-plated tapping performance by Down's syndrome and non–Down's syndrome retardates. *Journal of Child Psychology and Psychiatry, 20*, 351–355.

Shallice, T. (1984). More functionally isolable subsystems but fewer modules. *Cognition, 17*, 243–252.

Shallice, T. (1987). Impairments of semantic processing: Multiple dissociations. In M. Coltheart, J. Job, & G. Sartori (Eds.), *The cognitive neuropsychology of language* (pp. 94–146). Hillsdale, NJ: Erlbaum.

Shallice, T. (1988). *From neuropsychology to mental structure*. Cambridge University Press.

Shallice, T., & Vallar, G. (1990). The impairment of auditory verbal short-term storage. In G. Vallar & T. Shallice (Eds.), *Neuropsychological impairments of short-term memory* (pp. 11–53). Cambridge University Press.

Shallice, T., & Warrington, E. (1970). Independent functioning of verbal memory stores: A neuropsychology study. *Quarterly Journal of Experimental Psychology, 22*, 261–273.

Shankweiler, D., Crain, S., Garrell, P., & Tuller, B. (1989). Reception of language in Broca's aphasia. *Language and Cognitive Processes, 4*, 1–33.

Shapiro, T., Roberts, A., & Fish, B. (1970). Imitation and echoing. *Journal of the American Academy of Child Psychiatry, 9*, 421–439.

Share, J. (1975). Developmental progress in Down's syndrome. In R. Koch & F. de la Cruz (Eds.), *Down's syndrome (mongolism): Research, prevention and management* (pp. 78–86). New York: Brunner-Mazel.

Sheldon, A. (1977). On strategies for processing relative clauses: A comparison of children and adults. *Journal of Psycholinguistic Research, 6,* 305–318.

Shelton, J., Martin, R., & Yaffee, L. (1992). Investigating a verbal short-term memory deficit and its consequences for language processing. In D. Margolin (Ed.), *Cognitive neuropsychology in clinical practice* (pp. 131–167). Cambridge University Press.

Shriberg, L., & Widder, C. (1990). Speech and prosody characteristics of adults with mental retardation. *Journal of Speech and Hearing Research, 33,* 627–653.

Siegel, G. (1963). Verbal behavior of retarded children assembled with pre-instructed adults. *Journal of Speech and Hearing Disorders Monograph, 10,* 47–53.

Siegel, G., & Harkins, J. (1963). Verbal behavior of adults in two conditions with institutionalized retarded children. *Journal of Speech and Hearing Disorders Monograph, 10,* 39–46.

Silverstein, A., Legutki, G., Friedman, S., & Takayama, D. (1982). Performance of Down syndrome individuals on the Stanford-Binet Intelligence Scale. *American Journal of Mental Deficiency, 86,* 548–551.

Simon, H. (1974). How big is a chunk? *Science, 183,* 482–488.

Sinclair, H. (1970). The transition from sensory-motor behaviour to symbolic activity. *Interchange, 1,* 119–126.

Sinclair, H. (1971). Sensorimotor action patterns as a condition for the acquisition of syntax. In R. Huxley & E. Ingram (Eds.), *Language acquisition: Models and methods* (pp. 121–135). New York: Academic.

Sinclair, H. (1973). Language acquisition and cognitive development. In T. Moore (Ed.), *Cognitive development and the acquisition of language* (pp. 9–25). New York: Academic.

Sinclair, H. (1975). Language and cognition in subnormals: A Piagetian view. In N. O'Connor (Ed.), *Language, cognitive deficits, and retardation* (pp. 147–158). London: Butterworths.

Sinclair, H., & Ferreiro, E. (1970). Etude génétique de la compréhension, production et répétition des phrases au mode passif. *Archives de Psychologie, 40,* 1–42.

Sinclair, A., Sinclair, H., & de Marcellus, O. (1971). Young children's comprehension and production of passive sentences. *Archives de Psychologie, 39,* 1–22.

Skinner, B. F. (1957). *Verbal behavior.* Englewood Cliffs, NJ: Prentice-Hall.

Skuse, D. (1993). Extreme deprivation in early childhood. In D. Bishop & K. Mogford (Eds.), *Language development in exceptional circumstances* (pp. 29–46). Hove, UK: Erlbaum.

Slobin, D. (1966). Grammatical transformations and sentence comprehension in childhood and adulthood. *Journal of Verbal Learning and Verbal Behavior, 5,* 219–227.

Slobin, D. (1973). Cognitive prerequisites for the development of grammar. In C. Ferguson & D. Slobin (Eds.), *Studies of child language development* (pp. 607–619). New York: Holt, Rinehart, & Winston.

Slobin, D. (1977). Language change in childhood and in history. In J. Macnamara (Ed.), *Language learning and thought* (pp. 185–214). New York: Academic.

Slobin, D. (1978). A case study of early linguistic awareness. In A. Sinclair, R. Jarvella, & W. Levelt (Eds.), *The child conception of language* (pp. 45–54). New York: Springer-Verlag.

Slobin, D. (Ed.). (1985). *The cross-linguistic study of language acquisition* (Vol. 1). Hillsdale, NJ: Erlbaum.

Slobin, D., & Welsh, L. (1973). Elicited imitation as a research tool in developmental psycholinguistics. In C. Ferguson & D. Slobin (Eds.), *Studies in child language development* (pp. 485–496). New York: Holt, Rinehart, & Winston.

Sloboda, J., Hermelin, B., & O'Connor, N. (1985). An exceptional music memory. *Music Perception, 3,* 155–170.

Smirni, P., Villardita, C., & Zappalia, G. (1983). Influence of different paths on spatial memory performance in block-tapping test. *Journal of Clinical Neuropsychology, 5*, 355–359.

Smith, B. (1977, August). *Phonological development in Down's syndrome children*. Communication presented at the 85th Annual Convention of the American Psychological Association, San Francisco.

Smith, B., & Oller, K. (1981). A comparative study of pre-meaningful vocalizations produced by normally developing and Down's syndrome infants. *Journal of Speech and Hearing Disorders, 46*, 46–51.

Smith, L., & Von Tetzchner, S. (1986). Communicative, sensorimotor and language skills of young children with Down syndrome. *American Journal of Mental Deficiency, 91*, 57–66.

Snow, C. (1977). The development of conversation between mothers and babies. *Journal of Child Language, 4*, 1–22.

Snow, C. (1989). Imitativeness: A trait or a skill? In G. Speidel & K. Nelson (Eds.), *The many faces of imitation in language learning* (pp. 73–90). New York: Springer.

Snow, C. (1990). The development of definitional skill. *Journal of Child Language, 17*, 697–710.

Snyder-McLean, L., & McLean, J. (1987). Effectiveness of early intervention for children with language and communication disorders. In M. Guralnick & F. Bennett (Eds.), *The effectiveness of early intervention for at-risk and handicapped children* (pp. 97–128). New York: Academic.

Sokolov, A. N. (1967). Speech-motor afferentation and the problem of brain mechanisms of thought. *Voprosy Psikhologii, 13*, 41–54.

Sokolov, A. N. (1971). Internal speech and thought. *International Journal of Psychology, 6*, 79–92.

Sokolov, A. N. (1972). *Inner speech and thought*. New York: Plenum.

Solan, L. (1983). *Pronominal reference: Child language and the theory of grammar*. Boston: Reidel.

Sommers, R. K., & Starkey, K. L. (1977). Dichotic verbal processing in Down's syndrome children having qualitatively different speech and language skills. *American Journal of Mental Deficiency, 82*, 44–53.

Speidel, G., & Nelson, K. (Eds.). (1989). *The many faces of language learning*. New York: Springer.

Sperber, D., & Wilson, D. (1986). *Relevance: Communication and cognition*. Oxford: Blackwell.

Spitz, H. (1973). The channel capacity of educable mental retardates. In D. Routh (Ed.), *The experimental psychology of mental retardation* (pp. 133–156). Chicago: Aldine.

Spitzer, R., Rabinowitch, J., & Wybar, K. (1961). A study of the abnormalities of the skull, teeth and lenses in mongolism. *Canadian Medical Association Journal, 84*, 567–572.

Squire, L. (1992). Memory and the hippocampus: A synthesis from findings with rats, monkeys, and humans. *Psychological Review, 99*, 195–231.

Staats, A. (1968). *Language, learning and cognition*. New York: Holt, Rinehart, & Winston.

Staats, A. (1971a). Linguistic-mentalistic theory versus an explanatory S-R learning theory of language development. In D. Slobin (Ed.), *The ontogenesis of grammar: A theoretical symposium* (pp. 103–150). New York: Academic.

Staats, A. (1971b). *Child learning, intelligence and personality*. New York: Harper & Row.

Staats, A. (1975). *Social behaviorism*. Homewood, IL: Dorsey.

Staats, A. (1976). Social behaviorism and neo-psycholinguistics. *Die Neueren Sprachen, 2*, 127–141.

Stassart, J. (1991, July). *Personal communication.*

Sternberg, R. (1985). Controlled versus automatic processing. *Behavioral and Brain Sciences, 8*, 32–33.

Stoel-Gammon, C. (1980). Phonological analysis of four Down's syndrome children. *Applied Psycholinguistics, 1*, 31–48.

Stoel-Gammon, C. (1981). Speech development of infants and children with Down's syndrome. In J. Darby (Ed.), *Speech evaluation in medicine* (pp. 341–360). New York: Grune & Stratton.

Stokoe, W. (1972). *The study of sign language.* Silver Spring, MD: National Association of the Deaf.

Strazzula, M. (1953). Speech problems of the mongoloid child. *Quarterly Review of Pediatrics, 8*, 268–272.

Studdert-Kennedy, M. (1992). Leap of faith: A review of language and species. *Applied Psycholinguistics, 13*, 515–527.

Sudhalter, V., & Braine, M. (1985). How does passive develop? A comparison of actional and experiential verbs. *Journal of Child Language, 12*, 455–470.

Sudhalter, V., Cohen, I., Silverman, W., & Wolf-Schein, E. (1990). Conversational analyses of males with fragile X, Down syndrome, and autism: Comparison of the emergence of deviant language. *American Journal on Mental Retardation, 94*, 431–441.

Swinney, D. (1979). Lexical access during sentence comprehension: (Re)consideration of context effects. *Journal of Verbal Learning and Verbal Behavior, 18*, 645–659.

Swisher, L., & Pinsker, E. (1971). The language characteristics of hyperverbal, hydrocephalic children. *Developmental Medicine and Child Neurology, 13*, 746–755.

Tager-Flusberg, H. (1981). On the nature of linguistic functioning in early infantile autism. *Journal of Autism and Developmental Disorders, 11*, 45–56.

Tager-Flusberg, H. (1985). Psycholinguistic approaches to language and communication in autism. In E. Shopler & G. Mesibov (Eds.), *Communication problems in autism* (pp. 69–87). New York: Plenum.

Tager-Flusberg, H. (Ed.). (1993). *Constraints on language acquisition: Studies of atypical children.* Hillsdale, NJ: Erlbaum.

Tallal, P., Ross, R., & Curtiss, S. (1989). Familial aggregation in specific language impairment. *Journal of Speech and Hearing Disorders, 54*, 167–173.

Talland, G. A. (1965). Three estimates of the word span and their stability over the adult years. *Quarterly Journal of Experimental Psychology, 17*, 301–307.

Tannock, R., Kershner, J., & Oliver, J. (1984). Do individuals with Down's syndrome possess right hemisphere language dominance? *Cortex, 20*, 221–231.

Tew, B. (1979). The "cocktail party syndrome" in children with hydrocephalus and spina bifida. *British Journal of Disorders of Communication, 14*, 89–101.

Thase, M. (1988). The relationship between Down syndrome and Alzheimer's disease. In L. Nadel (Ed.), *The psychobiology of Down syndrome* (pp. 345–368). Cambridge, MA: MIT Press.

Thibaut, J. P., Rondal, J. A., & Kaens, A. M. (in press). Actionality and mental imagery in children's comprehension of declaratives. *Journal of Child Language.*

Tissot, R., Mounin, G., & Lhermitte, F. (1973). *L'agrammatisme.* Brussels: Dessart.

Tomblin, B. (1989). Familial concentration of developmental language impairment. *Journal of Speech and Hearing Disorders, 54*, 287–285.

Tourette, G. (1991). *Langage et styles cognitifs.* Unpublished doctoral dissertation, Université de Paris V, Paris.

Treiman, R. (1985). Onsets and rimes as units of spoken syllables: Evidence from children. *Journal of Experimental Child Psychology, 39*, 161–181.

Treiman, R., & Baron, J. (1981). Segmental analysis ability: Development and relation to reading ability. In G. Mackinnon & T. Waller (Eds.), *Reading research: Advances in theory and practice* (Vol. 3, pp. 159–168). New York: Academic.

Trosborg, A. (1981). Children's comprehension of *before* and *after* reinvestigated. *Journal of Child Language, 9*, 381–402.

Tyler, L., & Marslen-Wilson, W. (1977). The on-line effects of semantic context on syntactic processing. *Journal of Verbal Learning and Verbal Behavior, 16*, 683–692.

Uzgiris, I., & Hunt, J. McV. (1975). *Assessment in infancy.* Urbana: University of Illinois Press.

Vallar, G., & Baddeley, A. (1984a). Fractionation of working memory: Neuropsychological evidence for a phonological short-term store. *Journal of Verbal Learning and Verbal Behavior, 23*, 151–161.

Vallar, G., & Baddeley, A. (1984b). Phonological short-term store, phonological processing and sentence comprehension: A neuropsychological case study. *Cognitive Neuropsychology, 1*, 121–141.

Vallar, G., & Baddeley, A. (1987). Phonological short-term store and sentence processing. *Cognitive Neuropsychology, 4*, 417–438.

Vallar, G., & Baddeley, A. (1989). Developmental disorders of verbal short-term memory and their relation to sentence comprehension. *Cognitive Neuropsychology, 6*, 465–473

Vallar, G., & Cappa, S. (1987). Articulation and verbal short-term memory: Evidence from anarthria. *Cognitive Neuropsychology, 4*, 55–78.

Vallar, G., Papagno, C., & Baddeley, A. (1991). Long-term recency effects and phonological short-term memory: A neuropsychological case study. *Cortex, 27*, 323–326.

Vallar, G., & Shallice, T. (Eds.). (1990). *Neuropsychological impairments of short-term memory.* Cambridge University Press.

Van Borsel, J. (1988). An analysis of the speech of five Down's syndrome adolescents. *Journal of Communication Disorders, 21*, 409–422.

Van Borsel, J. (1991, August). *Personal communication.*

Van Borsel, J. (1993). *De articulatie bij adolescenten en volwassenen met het syndroom van Down.* Unpublished doctoral dissertation, Vrije Universiteit Brussels, Brussels.

Van der Linden, M. (1989). *Les troubles de la mémoire.* Brussels: Mardaga.

Van der Linden, M., & Brédart, S. (1993). *Age-related differences in updating working memory.* Manuscript submitted for publication.

Van der Linden, M., Coyette, F., & Seron, X. (1992). Selective impairment of the "central executive" component of working memory: A single case study. *Cognitive Neuropsychology, 9*, 301–326.

Van Hout, A. (1991). Characteristics of language in acquired aphasia in children. In I. Pavao Martins, A. Castro-Caldas, H. Van Dongen, & A. Van Hout (Eds.), *Acquired aphasia in children* (pp. 117–124). Boston: Kluwer.

Van Hout, A., & Seron, X. (1983). *L'aphasie de l'enfant.* Brussels: Mardaga.

Varnhagen, C., Das, J. P., & Varnhagen, S. (1987). Auditory and visual memory span: Cognitive processing by TMR individuals with Down's syndrome or other etiologies. *American Journal of Mental Deficiency, 91*, 398–405.

Veit, S. W., Allen, G. J., & Chinsky, J. M. (1976). Interpersonal interactions between institutionalized retarded children and their attendants. *American Journal of Mental Deficiency, 80*, 535–542.

Vihman, M. (1991). Ontogeny of phonetic gestures: Speech production. In I. Mattingly & M. Studdert-Kennedy (Eds.), *Modularity and the motor theory of speech perception* (pp. 69–84). Hillsdale, NJ: Erlbaum.

Von Armin, G., & Engel, P. (1964). Mental retardation related to hypercalcemia. *Developmental Medicine and Child Neurology*, *6*, 366–377.

Vygotsky, L. S. (1962). *Thought and language*. Cambridge, MA: MIT Press. (First publication in Russian, 1929)

Wardell, D., & Royce, J. (1978). Towards a multifactor theory of styles and their relationship to cognition and affect. *Journal of Personality*, *46*, 474–505.

Waters, G., Caplan, D., & Hildebrandt, N. (1991). On the structure of verbal short-term memory and its functional role in sentence comprehension: Evidence from neuropsychology. *Cognitive Neuropsychology*, *8*, 81–442.

Wechsler, D. (1957). *Wechsler Intelligence Scale for Children – WISC – (French Version)*. Paris: Centre de Psychologie Appliquée.

Wechsler, D. (1968). *Wechsler Adult Intelligence Scale – WAIS – (French Version)*. Paris: Centre de Psychologie Appliquée.

Wechsler, D. (1972). *Wechsler Preschool and Primary Scale of Intelligence – WIPPSI – (French Version)*. Paris: Centre de Psychologie Appliquée.

Wechsler, D. (1974). *Echelle clinique (French Version)*. Paris: Centre de Psychologie Appliquée.

Weil-Halpern, F., & Chevrie-Muller, C. (1974). *Evaluation des Aptitudes Syntaxiques chez l'Enfant*. Issy-Les Moulineaux: Editions Scientifiques et Psychologiques.

Weinberg, B., & Zlatin, M. (1970). Speaking fundamental frequency characteristics of five- and six-year-old children with mongolism. *Journal of Speech and Hearing Research, 13*, 418–425.

Wepman, J., & Morency, A. (1973). *Auditory Memory Span Test*. Chicago: Language Research Associates.

Werker, J. (1991). The ontogeny of speech perception. In I. Mattingly & M. Studdert-Kennedy (Eds.), *Modularity and the motor theory of speech perception* (pp. 91–109). Hillsdale, NJ: Erlbaum.

Wexler, K. (1982). A principled theory for language acquisition. In E. Wanner & L. Gleitman (Eds.), *Language acquisition: The state of the art* (pp. 288–315). Baltimore: University Park Press.

Wexler, K., & Culicover, P. (1980). *Formal principles of language acquisition*. Cambridge, MA: MIT Press.

Wheldall, K. (1976). Receptive language in the mentally handicapped. In P. Berry (Ed.), *Language and communication in the mentally handicapped* (pp. 36–55). Baltimore: University Park Press.

Whitaker, H. (1976). A case of isolation of the language function. In H. Whitaker & W. A. Whitaker (Eds.), *Studies in neurolinguistics* (Vol. 2, pp. 145–173). New York: Academic.

Whorf, B. (1956). Science and linguistics. In J. B. Carroll (Ed.), *Language, thought and reality: Selected writings of Benjamin Lee Whorf* (pp. 207–219). Cambridge, MA: MIT Press.

Wimmer, H., Landerl, K., Linortner, K., & Hummer, P. (1991). The relationship of phonemic awareness to reading acquisition: More consequence than precondition but still important. *Cognition, 40*, 219–249.

Winograd, T. (1983). *Language as a cognitive process: Vol. 1. Syntax*. Reading, MA: Addison-Wesley.

Wishart, J., & Duffy, L. (1990). Instability of performance on cognitive tests in infants and young children with Down's syndrome. *British Journal of Educational Psychology, 60,* 10–22.

Wisniewski, K., Dalton, A., Crapper-McLachlan, D., Wen, G., & Wisniewski, H. (1985). Alzheimer's disease in Down's syndrome: Clinicopathological studies. *Neurology, 35,* 957–961.

Wisniewski, K., Laure-Kamionowska, M., Connell, F., & Wen, G. (1986). Neuronal density and synaptogenesis in the postnatal stage of brain maturation in Down syndrome. In C. Epstein (Ed.), *The neurobiology of Down syndrome* (pp. 29–44). New York: Raven.

Witelson, S. (1977). Early hemisphere specialization and interhemisphere plasticity. In S. Segalowitz & F. Gruber (Eds.), *Language development and neurological theory* (pp. 182–197). New York: Academic.

Wolf-Schein, E., Sudhalter, V., Cohen, I., Fisch, G., Hanson, D., Pfadt, A., Hagerman, R., Jenkins, E., & Brown, W. (1987). Speech-Language and the fragile X syndrome: Initial findings. *Journal of the American Speech and Hearing Association, 29,* 35–38.

Woods, B. (1991). The ontogenesis of hemispheric specialization: Insights from acquired aphasia of childhood. In I. Pavao Martins, A. Castro-Caldas, H. Van Dongen, & A. Van Hout (Eds.), *Acquired aphasia in children* (pp. 73–81). Boston: Kluwer.

Wozniak, R. (1972). Dialectism and structuralism: The philosophical foundations of Soviet psychology and Piagetian cognitive developmental theory. In K. Riegel (Ed.), *Issues in developmental and historical structuralism* (pp. 56–118). Basel: Karger.

Wykes, T. (1981). Inference and children's comprehension of pronouns. *Journal of Experimental Child Psychology, 32,* 264–278.

Yamada, J. (1981). Evidence for the independence of language and cognition: A case study of a "hyperlinguistic" adolescent. *UCLA Working Papers in Cognitive Linguistics, 3,* 121–160.

Yamada, J. (1983). *The independence of language: A case study.* Unpublished doctoral dissertation, UCLA, Los Angeles.

Yamada, J. (1990). *Laura: A case for the modularity of language.* Cambridge, MA: MIT Press.

Yoder, D., & Miller, J. (1972). What we may know and what we can do: Input towards a system. In J. McLean, D. Yoder, & R. Schiefelbusch (Eds.), *Language intervention with the retarded: Developing strategies* (pp. 89–107). Baltimore: University Park Press.

Youssef, V. (1988). The language bioprogram hypothesis revisited. *Journal of Child Language, 15,* 451–458.

Yu, B., Zhang, W., Jing, R., Peng, R., Zhang, G., & Simon, H. (1985). STM capacity for Chinese and English language materials. *Memory and Cognition, 13,* 202–207.

Zeaman, D., & House, B. (1962). Mongoloid MA is proportional to logCA. *Child Development, 33,* 481–488.

Zekulin-Hartley, X. (1978). *Hemispheric asymmetries in Down's syndrome children.* Unpublished doctoral dissertation, University of Toronto, Toronto.

Zekulin-Hartley, X. (1981). Hemsipheric asymmetries in Down's syndrome children. *Canadian Journal of Behavioral Sciences, 13,* 210–217.

Zekulin-Hartley, X. (1982). Selective attention to dichotic input in retarded children. *Cortex, 18,* 311–316.

Zhang, G., & Simon, H. (1985). STM capacity for Chinese words and idioms: Chunking and acoustical loop hypothesis. *Memory and Cognition, 13,* 193–201.

Zhurova, L. (1973). The development of analysis of words into their sounds by preschool children. In C. Ferguson & D. Slobin (Eds.), *Studies of child language development* (pp. 141–154). New York: Holt, Rinehart, & Winston.

Zigler, E. (1966). Mental retardation: Current issues and approaches. In M. Hoffman & L. Hoffman (Eds.), *Review of child development research* (Vol. 2, pp. 107–168). New York: Russel Sage.

Zisk, P., & Bialer, I. (1967). Speech and language problems in mongolism: A review of the literature. *Journal of Speech and Hearing Disorders, 32*, 228–241.

Zurif, E., & Grodzinsky, Y. (1983). Grammatical sensitivity in agrammatism: A reply to Linebarger et al. *Cognition, 15*, 207–213.

Index

Lozar, B., 33
Luria, A., 51
Lust, B., 166
Lyle, J., 7, 32
Lyons, J., 149

MacDonald, J., 242
MacGillivray, R., 4
Macken, M., 260
Mackenzie, H., 17
Mackenzie, S., 16, 33, 232, 235, 239, 240, 241, 242, 252
Maclay, H., 248
MacNamara, J., 256
MacNeilage, P., 222
MacWhinney, B., 19, 56, 57, 58, 223, 264
Mahoney, G., 15, 214
Maille, E., 73
Mandler, J., 239
Manzini, M., 67
Maranto, C., 239
Maratsos, M., 11, 56, 58, 69, 157, 165, 256, 257
Marcell, M., 15, 207, 208, 240, 241
Marcellus, O. de, 54
Marcus, G., 218, 265, 305
Marijon, M., 73
Marin, O., 220, 245, 259
Marinosson, G., 239
Marks, S., 25
Marsh, G., 173
Marshall, J., 44, 55, 63, 64, 65, 68, 172
Marshburn, E., 249
Marslen-Wilson, W., 222, 225
Martin, N., 235, 261
Martin, R., 63, 238, 261
Massani, P., 246
Masterson, J., 43
Masur, E., 214
Mattingly, I., 221, 222, 226, 229
maturational hypothesis in language development, 63
Maune, S., 4
Mauner, G., 224, 259
Mazzucchi, A., 223
McClelland, J., 264
McCoy, E., 262
McGregor, K., 44, 260
McGuigan, F., 233
McIntire, M., 4
McLean, J., 211, 212
McManus, M., 12
McNeil, D., 196
McShane, J., 238
McTear, M., 46, 47
mean length of utterance, 8–9, 40–2, 47, 74–6
Mehler, J., 54, 230
Mein, R., 7, 33, 35

Meline, T., 47
Menn, L., 6, 223, 260
Menyuk, P., 46
Mervis, C. A., 7, 34
Mervis, C. B., 3, 7, 34, 197, 304
Mesulam, M., 223
metalinguistic ability, 168–76
metasyntactic ability, 174–5
methodological dualism, 59
Meyerson, M., 26
Miceli, G., 223, 249, 304
Michaelis, C., 6
Michéa, R., 152
Millberg, W., 224
Miller, G. A., 234, 246
Miller, J., 3, 17, 19, 33, 40, 42
Miller, R., 197
Mills, A., 20
Misés, R., 153, 188
Mito, T., 262
Mittler, P., 35, 42
modality effect, 207–8
modularity of language, 63–5, 68, 220–6
modularity of mind, 64–6, 68–9
Moerk, E., 214, 215, 216, 217, 219
Mogford, K., 19, 20, 302
Mononen, L., 18
Monseur, M., 160, 161, 162
Montague, J., 4, 317
Moor, L., 5, 210
Moore, D., 72
Morais, J., 172, 299
Moran, L., 196
Morency, A., 242
Morgan, J., 256
morphosyntactic capacity, 8–12, 155–68
Morton, J., 261, 262
mosaicism, 13–14
Moscovitch, M., 220, 221, 223, 224, 225, 231
Moss, M., 206
Mounin, G., 223
Mueller, M., 34
Muir, C., 235, 236
multiple intelligence, 65–6
Munhall, K., 181
Musumeci, S., 4
Muuss, R., 196
Muysken, P., 215

Nadel, L., 262, 263
negative information, 216–18
Nelson, K., 21, 214
Newport, E., 63, 215, 256, 264, 316
Nichols, I., 8, 35
Nicolson, R., 236
Niemi, J., 220
Niemi, P., 220